D1130488

DATE DUE

MAR – 5 1996			
FEB – 7 1997			
MAY 1 5 2001			

DEMCO 38-297

Lives and Letters in American Parapsychology

Lives and Letters
in American Parapsychology
A Biographical History, 1850–1987

by
Arthur S. Berger

McFarland & Company, Inc., Publishers
Jefferson, North Carolina, and London

Library of Congress Cataloguing-in-Publication Data

Berger, Arthur S., 1920–
  Lives and letters in American parapsychology.

  Includes references.
  Includes index.
  1. Psychical research—United States—Biography.
  2. Psychical research—United States—History.
  I. Title.
  BF1026.B46 1988   133.8'092'2 [B]   88-42537

ISBN 0-89950-345-4 (lib. bdg.; 50# acid-free natural paper)

Printed in the United States of America.

McFarland & Company, Inc., Publishers
  Box 611, Jefferson, North Carolina 28640

Table of Contents

Acknowledgments

First and foremost, I wish to thank Gertrude R. Schmeidler for her numerous valuable suggestions which have helped greatly to improve portions of this book.

I also want to thank a number of colleagues and friends who helped in other ways in the preparation of this book. Gertrude Schmeidler and Montague Ullman were kind enough to write the sections of this book which relate to their work and personal histories. The 27 colleagues whose miniature portraits I wrote helped by furnishing me with information relating to their careers and interests. My thanks as well go to R.A. McConnell, William E. Cox and D. Scott Rogo for helpful observations of Laura A. Dale, J. Gaither Pratt and Walter F. Prince. I want especially to single out Jule Eisenbud for my particular appreciation for the information he supplied about Laura Dale and for his comments on the section dealing with her. Laura F. Knipe and Dorothy Wenberg were also most helpful by sharing with me some of their recollections of her. I am also grateful to Lois B. Murphy for corresponding with me about her husband, Gardner Murphy.

Historians could do little without the cooperation of archivists and libraries. I wish to thank James G. Matlock, the American Society for Psychical Research, Houghton Library and Harvard University, and the Diocesan Library of the Episcopal Diocese of Massachusetts, for sending me, or allowing me access to, useful information.

I have left for the last my wife, Joyce Berger. For her patient support and labors in editing this book, a truckful of dictionaries would not provide enough words to convey my gratitude.

Acknowledgment is made to the following for the use of quotations in the text:

The New York Times for excerpts from: the article "Dr. Prince Resigns Over Margery Row" in the issue of March 6, 1925; the article "This Week in Science: Telepathy and Clairvoyance" by Waldemar Kaempffert in the issue of May 20, 1934; the article "Some Research in Telepathy" by Livingstone Welch in the issue of December 15, 1935. Copyright © 1925, 1934, 1935 by the New York Times Company. Reprinted by permission.

Jule Eisenbud, William E. Cox, D. Scott Rogo, Lois B. Murphy, Rex G.

Stanford, Gertrude R. Schmeidler, and Jan Ehrenwald for permission to quote extracts from their letters to me.

Jule Eisenbud, D. Scott Rogo and William E. Cox for permission to quote from letters to them from Laura A. Dale.

Montague Ullman for permission to quote from an interview he conducted with Gardner Murphy.

The Houghton Library, Harvard University, for specified extracts from the Richard Hodgson and William James manuscripts. Reprinted by permission of the Houghton Library.

The Journal of Parapsychology for permission to reprint from Gardner Murphy, "Notes for a Parapsychological Autobiography," *Journal of Parapsychology,* 1957, **21,** 165–178; Gertrude R. Schmeidler, "Gardner Murphy and His Thinking: A Retrospect and a Prospect," *Journal of Parapsychology,* 1979, **43,** 86–89.

The Society for Psychical Research and Jonn Beloff for permission to reprint from the following articles in the *Proceedings of the Society for Psychical Research* or the *Journal of the Society for Psychical Research:*

Richard Hodgson, "Account of Personal Investigations in India and Discussion of the Authorship of the 'Koot Hoomi' Letters," PSPR, 1885, **3,** 207–380; "A Record of Observations of Certain Phenomena of Trance," PSPR, 1892, **8,** 1–167; "A Further Record of Observations of Certain Phenomena of Trance," PSPR, 1898, **13,** 284–582;

William James, "Report on Mrs. Piper's Hodgson-Control," PSPR, 1909, **23,** 2–121;

William McDougall, "Presidential Address," PSPR, 1920, **31,** 105–123; "Professor William McDougall," JSPR, 1938, **30,** 294;

Gardner Murphy, "Psychical Research and Personality," PSPR, 1949, **49,** 1–15; "Psychology and Psychical Research," PSPR, 1953, **50,** 26–49;

Walter Franklin Prince, "Presidential Address," PSPR, 1930, **39,** 247–304;

J.B. Rhine, "Experiment in Extra-Sensory Perception," JSPR, 1938, **30,** 257–258.

The American Society for Psychical Research for permission to reprint material from the following articles by Arthur S. Berger in the *Journal of the American Society for Psychical Research:*

"The Early History of the American Society for Psychical Research: Origins to 1907," JASPR, 1985, **79,** 39–60;

"Problems of the ASPR Under J.H. Hyslop," JASPR, 1985, **79,** 205–219.

The American Society for Psychical Research for permission to reprint material from the following articles by other authors in the *Journal* or the *Proceedings* of the ASPR:

Sir William F. Barrett, "In Memory of Dr. Hyslop," JASPR, 1920, **14,** 440–444;

Weston D. Bayley, "Entrance Upon Psychical Research and Characteristics," JASPR, 1920, **14,** 433–440;

J. Malcolm Bird, "The Margery Mediumship," PASPR, 1926–1927, 20–21, 1–491;

William H. Button, "President's Report to the Voting Members of the ASPR," January 3, 1939, American Society for Psychical Research Archives;

Laura A. Dale, "Dr. John F. Thomas (In Memoriam)," JASPR, 1941, **35**, 1–8; "Henri Bergson, Realist, 1859–1941," JASPR, 1941, **35**, 57–69; "A Letter from A. Conan Doyle," JASPR, 1923, **17**, 265–266;

Lucy Edmunds correspondence with J.H. Hyslop in 1907, American Society for Psychical Research Archives, various excerpts;

Frederick Edwards, "Sir Arthur Conan Doyle," JASPR, 1923, **17**, 271–272; "Leakage," JASPR, 1923, **17**, 267;

Jan Ehrenwald, "Gentle Guide," JASPR, 1983, **77**, 281–282;

E.W. Friend correspondence with J.H. Hyslop in 1915, American Society for Psychical Research Archives, an excerpt;

H.N. Gardiner, "Reminiscences," JASPR, 1920, **14**, 469–473;

J.T. Hackett correspondence with J.H. Hyslop in 1917, American Society for Psychical Research Archives, various excerpts;

Richard Hodgson correspondence with J.T. Hackett 1877–1905, various excerpts; and correspondence with J.H. Hyslop, W.D. Bayley, C.J. Capron in 1910, various excerpts; American Society for Psychical Research Archives;

George H. Hyslop, "James H. Hyslop: His Contribution to Psychical Research," JASPR, 1950, **44**, 129–137;

James H. Hyslop, "Autobiography" dated March 6, 1904, American Society for Psychical Research Archives, various excerpts; correspondence with W.D. Bayley in 1906, 1908, 1909, 1911, American Society for Psychical Research Archives, various excerpts; "A Record of Experiments," PSPR, 1912, **6**, 1–976;

S. David Kahn, "Ave Atque Vale: Gardner Murphy," JASPR, 1980, **74**, 37–52;

William McDougall, "The Need for Psychical Research," JASPR, 1923, **17**, 4–14; "Mr. Dingwall's Study of 'Margery'," JASPR, 1925, **19**, 122–134; "Further Observations on the 'Margery' Case," JASPR, 1925, **19**, 297–309;

Gardner Murphy, "Difficulties Confronting the Survival Hypothesis," JASPR, 1945, **39**, 67–94; "Field Theory and Survival," JASPR, 1945, **39**, 181–209; "The Importance of Spontaneous Cases," JASPR, 1953, **47**, 89–103; "Plan for Research on Spontaneous Cases," JASPR, 1955, **49**, 85–95; "Presidential Remarks by Gardner Murphy," JASPR, 1962, **56**, 275–288; "George H. Hyslop and the American Society for Psychical Research," JASPR, 1966, **60**, 3–5;

William R. Newbold, "An Estimate," JASPR, 1920, **14**, 493–494;

Karlis Osis, "The American Society for Psychical Research 1941–1985: A Personal View," JASPR, 1985, **79**, 501–529;

G. Pagenstecher, "A Notable Psychometric Test," JASPR, 1920, **14**, 386–417;

Ralph B. Perry, "William James and Psychical Research," JASPR, 1935, **29**, 275–288;

Theodate Pope correspondence with W. Peyton in 1915, American Society for Psychical Research Archives, an excerpt;

J.G. Pratt, "William McDougall and Present-Day Psychical Research," JASPR, 1970, 385–403; "Some Notes for the Future Einstein for Parapsychology," JASPR, 1974, **68**, 133–155; "Gardner Murphy: Teacher, Mentor, Co-Worker, Friend," JASPR, 1980, **74**, 65–77;

Walter F. Prince, "The Doris Case of Multiple Personality," PASPR, 1915, **9**, 1–627; "James Hervey Hyslop. Biographical Sketch and Impressions," JASPR, 1920, **14**, 425–432; "Psychometric Experiments with Señora Maria Reyes de Z.," PASPR, 1921, **15**, 189–314; "A Survey of American Slate Writing Mediumship," PASPR, 1921, **15**, 315–592; "Is the Possession of 'Psychical' Faculty Pathological?" JASPR, 1923, **17**, 473–480;

J.B. Rhine, "My Partner, Gardner Murphy," JASPR, 1980, **74**, 62–65;

Gertrude R. Schmeidler, "Gardner Murphy: A Short Biography," JASPR, 1980, **74**, 1–14; "Memories of Laura Dale," JASPR, 1983, **77**, 273–276;

Rex G. Stanford, "A Tribute to Laura Dale," JASPR, 1983, **77**, 284–286;

Ian Stevenson, "Some Implications of Parapsychological Research on Survival After Death," PASPR, 1969, **28**, 18–35; "Gaither Pratt—An Appreciation," JASPR, 1980, **74**, 277–288;

Gertrude O. Tubby, "Testimony of a Co-Worker," JASPR, 1920, **14**, 481–485; "My Relation to James H. Hyslop as His Secretary," JASPR, 1956, **50**, 137–142;

Montague Ullman, "Letter to a Late Friend—Gardner Murphy," JASPR, 1980, **74**, 14–26; "A Tribute to Laura Dale," JASPR, 1982, **76**, 251–255.

Arthur S. Berger

Introduction

A woman drops a cup she had been drying and exclaims: "My God, he's hurt." At that very moment, her husband is struck by a car as he is crossing a road miles from his home. Another woman has a dream, heralding the death of a friend. A man wakes in the middle of the night and sees an apparition by his bedside. A gambler at a "craps" table shakes a pair of dice and by his will makes a 4 come up on one die and a 3 on the other. A medium displays knowledge during a seance she could never have gotten through the use of her eyes, ears or wits.

Such phenomena, whether "damned facts," as Charles Fort would have described them, or "paranormal," as the philosopher C.D. Broad defined them[1] or, following Thouless and Wiesner, merely designated "psi,"[2] have been reported throughout history. From a number of standpoints, they merit close scrutiny.

If the reports of such phenomena are totally false, if the events reported never took place, the fact that they have been reported by and have been accepted by individuals of sound mind and good moral character would be intriguing from the viewpoint of the psychology of human testimony, hallucination and credibility.

On the other hand, if these reports have been confirmed, they would have diverse and far-reaching implications and that so many highly intelligent and well-educated persons continue to deny such occurrences would then be equally intriguing from the viewpoint of the psychology of human bias and incredulity.[3] If the reports of such events are true, they would be exceedingly interesting from a philosophical perspective, for they raise the ancient question of the relationship between mind and brain.

Dualism long ago was toppled in favor of a materialist view that mind is a function of processes of the brain and totally dependent on it. But the occurrence of paranormal events that seem to resist and baffle physical explanations might point to the existence of a nonphysical mental component interacting with yet autonomous of the brain and which, at certain times, has the ability to influence physical objects or become aware of other minds whose physical bodies may be either living or dead. Such events, if they in fact occur, would collide with materialism and the impact would restore mind-body dualism to the attention of thinkers. From the standpoint of religion, the ability of one

1

mind to be conscious of or to affect another despite the distance between them and without the use of the senses, would also be of great interest. It suggests the very thing which characterizes the life of religion: an unseen order beyond the visible world of space and time. As the late Professor H.H. Price said: "We must conclude, I think, that there is no room for telepathy in a Materialistic universe."[4]

In whose hands does it rest to examine paranormal phenomena? Not in the hands of orthodox scientists who place these phenomena in what William James called "the unclassified residuum," a kind of dust-cloud of exceptional occurrences that floats about the accredited and orderly facts of established science and which it is easier to ignore than to examine. "The ideal of every science," he wrote in a powerful essay, "is that of a closed and completed system of truth.... Phenomena unclassifiable within the system are therefore paradoxical absurdities, and must be held untrue."[5]

It is fortunate that some critical minds, able to perceive the potential significance of the "unclassified residuum," have been willing to attend to it. These minds belong to those who work in the borderlands of science just beyond its established systems of truth, frontier scientists known as para-psychologists or, in earlier days and still in England, as psychical researchers. Here I shall use the more modern and American term "parapsychology." The floating cloud of bizarre occurrences which menaces established science belongs to parapsychologists and forms the subject matter for their inquiries whether in the laboratory or in life experiences.

In one sense the year 1985 marked the hundredth anniversary of para-psychology in America. In 1885 the American Society for Psychical Research was founded, by William James among others. One of the two reasons for writing this book was to provide the first handbook of historically prominent facts of these one hundred and two years.

It is possible to make a good case for the proposition that the historical roots of parapsychology have no beginning—that they spread wide and without limit and can be traced back to antiquity. For in every place and time, the subject matter of parapsychology has existed. The belief in the paranormal can be seen in the ancient world of the Near East. Biblical literature is filled with instances of extrasensory perception, psychokinesis, unorthodox healing, mental and physical mediumship and out-of-the-body experiences. Four centuries before Christ, Plato's *Phaedo* exhibits a concern among some Greeks with the soul's immortality and reincarnation. About A.D. 270 Plotinus, the leading figure in the school of Neo-Platonism, also expressed a theory of spirit survival.

Paranormal phenomena occurred also in the practices of savage races, in the visions of Swedenborg and in the trances induced by the followers of Mesmer in France, Germany and Great Britain.

But the history of American parapsychology is not this history, not the general story of paranormal events and experiences in the daily lives of people, ancient or modern, and not that of philosophical arguments *à la* Plato or of mystical visions. Its real history is the history of scientific investigation into these events and experiences, and this special kind of history, in turn, as Emerson urged, is the product of the lives and exertions of commanding figures who made invaluable contributions to this investigation.

The second and principal fact which led to the writing of this book was a certain mysterious gap. There are many books on parapsychology. Several large public and university libraries in Great Britain and the United States have impressive collections of them as well as relevant periodicals. Special libraries in organizations such as the English and American societies for psychical research and the Parapsychology Foundation have similar collections. But there is one book that has never appeared in these collections, one that, against the background of the historical periods in which they lived, presents the life stories and work of the predominant figures of American parapsychology who shaped the events and represent the growth and development of the field.

These figures are unfamiliar because parapsychology, the field to which they devoted their lives, remains largely *terra incognita*. This book proposes to make better known for all who wish to explore this field the life stories and accomplishments of all the figures who came or continue to come to the forefront during more than a century of research into paranormal phenomena. Although the book will present a chronology of the main historical events, these individuals are the center of attention because people are more interesting than dry facts, and their life stories will better reveal the high points of the periods in which they flourished.

The last century or more of parapsychology has been divided into five historical periods: Independence Gained and Lost, Out of the Ashes, the Blue-Eyed Woman and Storms and Reorientation are the historical periods; in order to make this book up to date, a fifth period, Harassment and Contemporary Parapsychology, has been included, along with Chapter 6, Brief Portraits of Contemporary Psychologists.

Facts are presented chronologically and the narration is impersonal and orderly. An introductory commentary is given for each period and following this are full-length portraits developed from published sources or, in some cases, also from unpublished letters and archival material. These portraits reveal the lives, characteristics and work of the six dominating personalities who flourished during these periods: an Australian as colorful as he was brilliant, a university professor, a Methodist and Episcopal clergyman, one British and one American psychologist and a botanist. Details of a seventh personality, a farmer and pigeon fancier, who also lived and worked in the fourth period will be provided to a lesser extent.

The fifth period will furnish an account of the significant events of the 1980s. It presents cameos of two outstanding women—one also with a doctorate in botany, the other a deeply respected editor and dog show judge—who died in the period. Also presented are two self-portraits by senior figures, an emeritus professor of psychology and a psychiatrist and psychoanalyst, both former presidents of the American Society for Psychical Research, who con-

tinue to leave ineradicable marks on the history of American parapsychology
and who have kindly supplied their own career histories with special emphasis
on parapsychology.

Following the fifth period is Chapter 6, which contains brief portraits of
a number of individuals presently making major contributions to the field.

All these portraits, self-portraits and cameos will allow the reader to experience a deeper, closer and more personal knowledge of the people who
shaped parapsychology in the United States in the past more than one hundred
years.

I have used the following abbreviations: ASPR for the American Society
for Psychical Research, SPR for the Society for Psychical Research in England,
and BSPR for the Boston Society for Psychic Research; JASPR for the *Journal of
the American Society for Psychical Research*, PASPR for the *Proceedings of the
American Society for Psychical Research*, JSPR for the *Journal of the Society for
Psychical Research*, and PSPR for the *Proceedings of the Society for Psychical
Research*.

1
Independence Gained and Lost
(1851–1905)

Commentary

Just as every American political and legal institution — county, borough, popular election, common law, jury trial, rights of assembly and petition — came to these shores from the mother country, so did parapsychology. It is one of the ironies of the history of American parapsychology, in fact, that the impetus for serious collective research into paranormal phenomena should not have come from the United States.

The Spiritualist movement began one night in 1848 in a farmhouse near Rochester, New York. Young Kate Fox had clapped her hands a number of times and told "Mr. Splitfoot" to do as she did. Whereupon an equal number of raps were heard. When the older child, Margaretta Fox, commanded the source of the rappings to count to four, it did. Many Americans, including such distinguished figures as Harriet Beecher Stowe, author of *Uncle Tom's Cabin*, and Horace Greeley, editor of the *New York Tribune,* were attracted to Spiritualism. Its physical and mental phenomena and its glowing assertions about another world drew believers estimated to range from two to eleven million.[1] Its phenomena were so impressive and its claims so great that, in 1854, 13,000 people signed a petition asking Congress to establish a scientific commission to examine the phenomena.[2]

Although Spiritualism was as native to America as its national emblem, the majestic bald eagle, and its phenomena certainly demanded close scrutiny, the movement could not stimulate sufficient scholarly or scientific interest for a proper examination. Nor could the strange stories of ghosts or hauntings, telepathy or precognitive dreams, make scholars and scientists less aloof. And neither could the phenomenon of animal magnetism, now called hypnotism, whose techniques had been used by a Viennese doctor, Franz Mesmer, and which had aroused the attention of thinking people on the Continent. It seemed that scholarly and scientific people in nineteenth century America, like many of those in America in the twentieth, were determined to keep their doors and windows tightly closed to prevent the odor of puzzling and disturbing experiences from creeping into their sanctuaries.

5

But in the land of the Industrial Revolution where Victoria reigned as queen, Spiritualism invaded from America and became king. As in America, it ruled over the masses and for the same reasons. Since Spiritualism is not the same for everyone, both the English working people and the middle class hailed it either as a new religion alien to an abandoned Christianity or as adding to Christianity proof of a spirit world and a future life. But, in contrast to America, the phenomena of Spiritualism, along with other paranormal phenomena and Mesmer's discovery, also caught the eyes and ears of the intelligentsia beset by philosophical speculations, religious doubts and an insatiable curiosity about levitating tables and ghostly agencies. The forerunners of American parapsychology were about to evolve.

Chronological Narrative

1851

In Cambridge, a "Ghost Society" was formed by Edward White Benson, a future archbishop of Canterbury, to investigate paranormal phenomena. The chief importance of the Society lay in its having as one of its members Professor Henry Sidgwick, a lecturer in moral science at Cambridge University.

1869

A Committee was authorized by the London Dialectical Society to investigate the phenomena of Spiritualism.

In the same year, Frederic W.H. Myers, who had been a student of Sidgwick in 1860, took a "star-light walk" with him. Given some hope by Sidgwick that phenomena like ghosts and spirits might lead to some knowledge concerning an unseen reality, Myers resolved to pursue the quest for these phenomena with Sidgwick.[3] Without their close friendship, an organization for the collective investigation of paranormal phenomena would not have come into being[4] and the way would not have been prepared for the eventual birth of American parapsychology.

1878

Richard Hodgson, a young Australian, matriculated at the University of Cambridge as a student at St. John's College. There he came into contact with Henry Sidgwick whose admiring student he was.

1882

Nor would the English Society for Psychical Research have been formed in this year if it had not been for Sir William Barrett, a professor of physics at the Royal College of Science in Dublin. After the British Association refused to publish a paper he had presented to it describing an experiment in telepathy he had conducted,[5] Barrett realized that the hour had struck for removing the investigation of paranormal phenomena from the hands of individuals and placing it in those of a scientific society. It was his energy and initiative that generated interest in such a society and stimulated the key people who were to be its founders: Sidgwick, Myers and Edmund Gurney, another of Sidgwick's students.

Although they had all been interested in investigating paranormal phenomena and had done so in previous years, they had become discouraged because of disappointing results.[6] Barrett's zeal renewed their interest. Following a conference, with Barrett as the Chairman, convened in London on January 6 to take up the founding of a society, the Society for Psychical Research (SPR) was actually founded on February 20 with Henry Sidgwick as its president and Barrett one of its vice-presidents.[7] Myers and Gurney were appointed to its Council. In Sidgwick's Presidential Address, he emphasized that the dispute concerning the reality of the phenomena which the SPR had been established to investigate was nothing less than a scandal. The aim of the English society, he said, was to make a systematic effort to remove this scandal by investigating the facts "without any foregone conclusion as to their nature."[8]

The first members of the SPR included painters such as Frederick Leighton, poets such as Alfred Tennyson, writers such as John Ruskin, Lewis Carroll and John A. Symonds. A British prime minister — William Gladstone — was also included in the membership rolls, as were two interested Americans, William James and Mark Twain. Also among the earliest members were two more of Sidgwick's students — Arthur Balfour, who would become prime minister, and a promising young man named Richard Hodgson.

1884

Hodgson was appointed by the new SPR to conduct one of its first major investigations. Sent to India, he was to look into the phenomena supposed to be occurring in connection with the Theosophical Society and Madame Blavatsky, who claimed paranormal powers.

In 1884, also, Barrett visited the United States where, as energetically and convincingly as he had in London, he spoke at meetings of scholars in Boston and Philadelphia of the need for a society to investigate paranormal phenomena.

Among the scholars listening to Barrett was William James who, six years later, would publish his famous *Principles of Psychology*.

Besides teaching a course in physiological psychology at Harvard University, James gravitated toward the study of the paranormal both as a psychologist hoping to discover new aspects of human personality and as a philosopher concerned with the place of the human being in the cosmos.

As a result of Barrett's American tour, a committee of nine, including James, was established with full powers to weigh and dispose of the question of forming a society like the SPR. Several meetings were held in October and November, a constitution agreed upon and invitations sent out to scientific people to join the contemplated society.

1885

The formal organization of "the American Society for Psychical Research" (ASPR) was completed on January 8, 1885. It was formed as an independent organization with purposes similar to those of the SPR. The Council of the ASPR stated that it felt "that the evidence published by the English Society is of a nature not to be ignored by scientific men ... [and] that the duty can no longer be postponed of systematically repeating observations similar to those made in England, with a view to confirming them if true, to definitely pointing out the sources of error in them if false."[9]

It is interesting to notice that neither the ASPR's name nor this first formal statement issued by it provides any justification for the idea fixed both in lay thought and that of scientific orthodoxy that American parapsychology is just another and fancy name for Spiritualism. There is nothing in the name of the ASPR to suggest a creed and there is no suggestion in its initial document of any intention to provide evidence of a spirit world or of spirit communications.

Although James, undeniably a leading force behind the formation of the ASPR, was a Harvard man, its slate of officers did not constitute any exclusive Harvard club. The president of the newly born group was Simon Newcomb, head of the astronomy department at Johns Hopkins University. Three vice-presidents, Professor Edward C. Pickering, Dr. Henry Bowditch and Dr. Charles S. Minot, all came from Harvard, but two—Professor G. Stanley Hall, president of Clark University, and Professor George S. Fullerton of the University of Pennsylvania—did not.

Along with the birth of the ASPR, another development of great importance occurred in 1885. In the autumn, James discovered Mrs. Leonora E. Piper,[10] a Boston housewife of limited education. She was to become the trance-medium most investigated by the English and American societies over the next thirty years.

1886

These positive developments were followed almost immediately by disso-
nant ones. While, in 1882, Sidgwick of the SPR had called on the English to
make a fair and open-minded investigation of the facts, Newcomb in his
Presidential Address to the Americans discouraged the investigation of
telepathy. Thought, he said, was a bodily function and incapable of transfer
over any distance. How is it, Newcomb asked, that with ample opportunities
of observation and experiment over the centuries "no living person knows any
more about the conditions of transference today than men did a thousand years
ago?"[11] He placed the investigation of telepathy on the same level with looking
for a different kind of gold: It would be a waste of time.

There were other important contrasts. The English confessed that they
would feel ten times more interest in proving the action of intelligences other
than those of living people than in proving the paranormal communication of
living human minds.[12] But the Americans felt ten times less interest in such
proof. One observer wrote: "What? an orthodox college professor acknowledge
the credentials of a spirit and still retain his job? A physician hobnob with the
ghosts and keep hold of even the ghost of a practice? Lor' bless us, what are
we coming to?"[13]

A further difference ran even deeper. The SPR was made up of a group
of enthusiastic and extraordinary people, many of whom, like Sidgwick, Myers
and Gurney, were wealthy enough to allow them to take the time to engage
in the work of their organization. Excluding James, people of such caliber and
disposition did not exist in the American group.

Not that the Americans did not try to make progress. The ASPR pursued
several lines of inquiry: telepathy or thought-transference;[14] hypnosis;[15]
mediumship;[16] Reichenbach's phenomena which included the supposed existence of flames coming from the poles of magnets;[17] apparitions and haunted
houses.[18]

But there were too many ominous cracks in the structure of the Society.
While the ASPR tried to make progress, not very much was made. Some experiments were completed but what was done consisted mainly of preliminary
reports and preparations for research. Membership declined. The gloomy
situation led James on October 4, 1886, to write to a friend: "I mailed you
t'other day Part II of the *Proceedings* of the American Society for Psychical
Research, a rather sorry 'exhibit' from the 'President's' address down. There is
no one in the Society who can give any time to it, and I suspect it will die by
the new year."[19]

1887

The ASPR was indeed in a sickly condition and fast approaching the last
stages. Radical and immediate surgery had to be performed. The Americans

looked to the mother country for the "scalpel" needed to save their organization. They perceived it in the mind of Richard Hodgson who was invited to come from England to become the secretary of the ASPR.

1888–1889

James had prophesied that the ASPR would die by 1887. It managed to survive only because Hodgson accepted the invitation and managed it. But, in December 1889, the organization was forced to abandon its independence and to ask to be converted into a branch of the London Society. The causes of its lost independence, which not even Hodgson could root out, are not hard to discover. It died partly because it achieved little except for the Piper mediumship and support fell away from it. It died partly because its workers lacked the animus of the English workers. It died "partly of fright when some of its illustrious members began to realize that after all there might be real spooks in Spiritualism; and heavens! it would not do for such as they to really find 'em out without the logical necessity of conceding to them official recognition."[20]

There was also the poverty of the ASPR. There was not enough money to prepare complete stenographic records of sittings with Mrs. Piper. A time of economic depression in the United States had affected adversely the funds of the ASPR. It could not continue without financial assistance. Sidgwick and Myers had to send money from England to subsidize it and sometimes to pay Hodgson's salary.[21] The SPR also advanced funds to it,[22] which probably caused some resentment and friction in England because the American group had some wealthy members who might have supported it if they had chosen to do so.[23]

Hodgson continued as secretary of the American branch.

1892

Hodgson conducted lengthy studies of Mrs. Piper on the basis of which he wrote two monumental reports. These, together with reports on her by James and James Hervey Hyslop, were the only notable achievement of American parapsychology during the period identified in the present work as "Independence Gained and Lost." Hodgson's first report appeared in 1892.

1897

James' powerful criticism of orthodox science for ignoring "the unclassified residuum" of paranormal phenomena appeared.[24]

1898

Hodgson's second Piper report was published to affirm that her medium-ship had produced striking evidence of survival after death.

1901

The *New York Herald* sought to discredit Mrs. Piper by headlining an interview with her as a "Confession."

1905

The ASPR suffered a great loss in December with the "ultra-sudden" death of Richard Hodgson.

James has been the subject of many biographies. Scant attention has been paid, however, to Hodgson who, like James, marked out the early path along which American parapsychology moved. It is upon him that we now focus.

Richard Hodgson: A Portrait

It was foul and cold in Boston two days before Christmas, 1905, but a few people, braving the Saturday rain, made their way to the Tavern Club. Some were members of the Club, some members of the Union Boat Club, others were simply friends of the dead man.

His coffin lay in the hall of the Tavern Club covered with a purple pall, wreaths of ivy, a spray of violets and a few white roses. Behind the coffin, flowers were piled high on a bench.

A clergyman conducted a funeral service in the crowded, candle-lit hall. When he finished, the assemblage sang "Integer Vitae." After all outsiders had left, the members of the Tavern Club came close to the coffin and sang the Club song. "[T]he singing of the Club song at this time was indescribable. . . . I believe nothing we could have done would have given Dick Hodgson more pleasure than this last act here at the Tavern Club."[25]

In England, decorous obituary notices were published in the PSPR.[26] William James who, in 1885, had asked, "By the way, who is Mr. Richard Hodgson?"[27], saluted him after his death as "a man among men anywhere."[28]

Who was this Hodgson whose friends came to mourn on a wet day in Boston and who were so moved by his death? Why did he make such a vivid impression on James? When and how did the doors of parapsychology open to him and what important contributions did he make in this field?

Richard Hodgson

To answer these questions I have gone to the archives of the Houghton Library at Harvard, which yielded some interesting letters to and from Hodgson, and to the archives of the ASPR, where I discovered the voluminous letters Hodgson sent to his close childhood friend James T. Hackett in Australia. None of these letters has previously been published.

Early Life

The son of a Yorkshireman, Richard Hodgson was born on September 24, 1855, in West Melbourne, Australia. He received his early schooling in the central common schools of Melbourne and later attended the University of Melbourne, where he received a B.A. degree in 1874, an LL.B. in 1875, an M.A. in 1876 and an LL.D. in 1878. The manly sports attracted him so that, before the boxing season in Australia, he would be "off to swing my dumbbells a little, as a preparation for . . . some fellow's head. . . ."[29] The law was quite another matter. When forced to study for his law exams, he felt "as dry as a very dry bone"[30] as "the horrid Law loomed up" to smother his other impulses.[31] One of these was poetic. Poetry, which he wrote and read at social meetings in Melbourne, thrilled him. Philosophy drew him as well, in particular that of Herbert Spencer, whom Hodgson declared to be "the greatest thinker the world has ever seen."[32] By the time he was 23, Hodgson had abandoned law and sailed for England to matriculate at the University of Cambridge as a student at St. John's College. One of his chief reasons for choosing St. John's was that Wordsworth, whom he also admired, was a Johnian.[33]

In 1881, Hodgson qualified for a degree and took honors after reading for the Moral Science Tripos. Then he attended the university at Jena, Germany, where, besides an opportunity to "smoke and jaw and also [drink] a little 'lager-bier'" with German students,[34] he studied philosophy, ethics, psychology and zoology. After six months, he returned to England in 1882 to lecture on Robert Browning and Spencerian philosophy in the north of the country as part of the University Scheme of Extension Lectures.

Physical and Intellectual Qualities

"Outwardly," wrote William James's son, Henry James, Jr., "Hodgson didn't look in the least like a student or scholar. He was muscular, very light on his feet, had a very sharp eye which seemed to be noticing everything, and a serene, untroubled countenance."[35] A Boston friend said: "He was picturesque, with his great booming voice, hearty laugh, white beard and ruddy cheeks"[36] as the photograph of Hodgson taken in 1900[37] confirms.

He rarely complained of his health. His strong feelings of vitality never ceased. When he reached Cambridge, one of his first acts was to join "a place where there are fencing, clubs and dumbbells."[38] When he got to Boston, his skill as a handball player ranked him as one of the best players at the Union Boat Club.[39] He played on the squash court of the Tavern Club there and was an ardent fan at college boat races and football games.[40]

His mannerisms were distinguished by what James called "great animal spirits."[41] Hodgson liked to argue, enjoyed repartee, gesticulated a lot. He did not talk in terms of petty details. He enjoyed describing his experiences with the broad sweeps of an artist—this was "splendid" or that was "glorious."[42]

Through these animal spirits, those who knew and worked with him perceived a man, in Eleanor Sidgwick's words, "of great power of observation and acute inference,"[43] a person whom William James was able to compare favorably to the Sidgwicks who possessed the most skeptical, critical and brilliant minds in England.[44]

At the same time, there is a good deal of evidence that Hodgson was a colorful character. In Cambridge, it was customary to wear a black evening suit. Hodgson shocked the very proper English by wearing an indecorous brown.[45] His nonconformity almost cost him the degree for which he had qualified at Cambridge in 1881 because the ceremony involved kneeling to the vice-chancellor. It was with difficulty that his friends convinced him to do so. He was likewise unconventional at the staid Tavern Club. His companions there raised their eyebrows in horror when Hodgson came into their sacred precincts with a pesky pet parrot who would snap angrily at any person other than Hodgson who tried to pick it up.[46]

In religious matters, and in harmony with his independent character, he was a nonconformist.[47] But he was no atheist. As he wrote in 1900 to Cynthia Capron: "Scientific investigation consists in finding out how God does things."[48]

A letter in the Harvard archives to James tells of a remarkable experience Hodgson had in September 1884 when he was in bed in his rooms at Cambridge:

> I felt my left forearm seized by a hand. . . . I jerked myself to a sitting posture ready to strike out with my right. I felt nothing, saw nothing, heard nothing unusual ... I reached out for the matchbox on the table and struck a match . . . [I] could find no trace of any person.[49]

This experience produced in him a sensation he described as

> keener than the most poignant pain, but it seems to be much deeper in me, and has all the quality of Joy. . . . While it lasts, there is a sure knowledge of the close and brooding presence of a Mighty Person, and after it has gone, the memory of it persists as the one perception of Reality. Everything else may be a dream, but not that.[50]

Strangely, no one was allowed to enter Hodgson's lodgings in Boston perhaps because, according to Hereward Carrington:

> During those years Dr. Hodgson believed that he himself constantly received direct communications from 'Imperator', 'Rector' and the regular band in charge of Mrs. Piper on the other side. . . . For this reason, he allowed no one to enter the room, in case they should upset the 'conditions' or in some way disturb the 'magnetic atmosphere'.[51]

It was in this same "magnetic atmosphere" that he was awakened one night in 1892 by what he said in a letter to James was a "horrible sensation" which lasted about 15 minutes.[52] It was an experience in which he was conscious of the presence of a friend who, unknown to Hodgson, had died four hours earlier. It was only one of several similar episodes in Boston and

Cambridge. These presences, he told James, were intensely more real than any ordinary perception.[53]

Outside his rooms, however, Hodgson "was the most sociable of beings."[54] One friend recalled, "I don't remember his ever saying a sharp or unkind word to anyone. In fact, he was one of the most truly good men I have ever known."[55]

The Opposite Sex

Hodgson insisted on respect for women. "It is a very serious thing for men to talk lightly about women, and coarsely. I cannot help despising a man who does so. Nothing is so sickening...."[56]

When it came to social sex, he was a Puritan living in the Victorian age. He condemned prostitution with the fervor of a fanatical preacher. "Cambridge is a fearfully immoral place," Hodgson complained to Hackett. "There is a saying that there are only four (4) virtuous women in Cambridge and those are the stone monuments on the House of Justice.... To 30,000 (Thirty Thousand) inhabitants, including University men, there are 600 (six hundred) prostitutes known to the police!! Isn't it awful? ... 'Oh, it is pitiful'. God help them."[57]

Although a defender of the female of the species, especially English womanhood,[58] references in his letters to his personal relationships with women are virtually nonexistent. There is a vague suggestion in the literature[59] that he might have had a love affair with his cousin whose name he suppressed and to whom he referred merely as "Q" during his sittings with Mrs. Piper. Hodgson, however, pointedly remarked that "No ring has ever passed between the lady and myself."[60] "Q" died in Australia in 1879 while Hodgson was in England.[61]

Hodgson never married. In 1887, he wrote to Jimmy Hackett, "I have no regret that I haven't married, because there is no one living for me to have the regret about."[62] But in later years a somewhat different tone can be detected: "Being still a bachelor and likely to remain so though I wish it were otherwise."[63]

Pier thought that Hodgson did not marry in later years because he "believed that his power to receive spirit messages depended on his freeing himself as completely as possible from all fleshly desires and pleasure."[64]

Development of Interest in Parapsychology

It is impossible to say when Hodgson's interest in the phenomena of Spiritualism began. It was already present in Australia although tempered with an obvious skepticism. In this tongue-in-cheek letter to Hackett, Hodgson said: "I have in the last few days read A.R. Wallace on Spiritualism.... I

have ... been transformed into an ardent Spiritist and jig around the study table nightly, capering in many modes and producing marvellous phenomena, such as noises, loud sounds, strange air-wave concussions and so forth...."[65]
We know that Henry Sidgwick, as a member of the Cambridge "Ghost Society," was himself interested in the investigation of paranormal phenomena. During his studentship at Cambridge, Hodgson was Sidgwick's admiring pupil: "I am attending Sidgwick of Trinity on Ancient Ethics.... He is an able man and recognized as such, — stutters tremendously so that it is absolutely painful to listen to him."[66] Sidgwick made it a practice of working with his pupils individually. Friendship and mutual respect between him and Hodgson grew to the extent that Sidgwick offered to subsidize the financially strapped Hodgson to enable him to atend the university at Jena[67] and offered to send to the publication *Mind* Hodgson's paper on Spencer's philosophy.[68] Their relationship of teacher and bright promising pupil was a lasting one.[69] It is more than probable that Sidgwick contributed considerably to the further sprouting at Cambridge of Hodgson's budding interest in Spiritualism and the phenomena related to it. So, in 1879 he wrote Hackett from Cambridge: "re Spiritualism. I don't deny there is some truth in the phenomena."[70]
By May 1879, he had become active in an undergraduate society established to investigate paranormal phenomena.[71] He was in Jena, Germany, when the SPR was formed in 1882, but the name "Hodgson, Richard, B.A., St. John's College, Cambridge" appears on the membership list published in the first PSPR.[72]

The High-Priestess of Theosophy

During the summer months of 1884, Countess Helena Petrovna de Blavatsky, Colonel Olcott and some members of the group they had established in 1875 as the Theosophical Society were in Cambridge. Mme. Blavatsky left a deep enough mark on Sidgwick to lead him to form a Committee of the SPR to look into the phenomena connected with her Theosophical Society. The Committee, which consisted of Edmund Gurney, Frederic W.H. Myers, Frank Podmore, Eleanor and Henry Sidgwick — and Richard Hodgson — heard evidence from Colonel Olcott and others concerning a mysterious brotherhood of adepts or mahatmas in Tibet who were drawn to the Theosophical Society which was then located in India. They had the power to project themselves as apparitions called "astral forms." A mahatma who made several such appearances was Koot Hoomi. The Committee was favorably impressed.
But no definite judgment could be made until someone trusted by the SPR was able to live in India for some time and observe for himself what was going on. That someone was Hodgson, the young scholar Sidgwick knew and respected. Even Colonel Olcott had heard of Hodgson. As Hodgson told Jimmy: "Olcott ... was round in my rooms in the morning and had lunch, talking re the views of the Hindu Adepts!"[73]

Hodgson's visit to India had two purposes. In September and October 1884, letters had been published in the Madras *Christian College Magazine* that were supposed to have been written by Madame Blavatsky to Monsieur and Madame Coulomb, who had been trusted associates of the Theosophical Society before their ouster by the Society. These letters, dismissed by Madame Blavatsky as forgeries, involved her in a conspiracy to produce fraudulent phenomena. One letter to Madame Coulomb in 1883, for instance, requested her to send to Madame Blavatsky a false telegram which was supposed to be a letter transported by a mahatma. The object was to make an impression on someone ready to turn over to Madame Blavatsky 10,000 rupees if a mahatma gave some sign. One of Hodgson's purposes was to ascertain the genuineness of the letters of which he obtained several. He sent them to England for inspection by handwriting experts, two of whom arrived separately at the conclusion that the letters had indeed been written by Madame Blavatsky. The letters not only implicated her in the fraudulent preparation and transportation of Mahatma letters; they also made it appear that the mahatma Koot Hoomi was an invention and that "astral forms" were provided by disguised living agents of Theosophy's high-priestess.

Being convinced that Madame Blavatsky's hand wielded the pen that wrote the Blavatsky-Coulomb letters and that she also was the author of the mahatma documents, in particular the Koot Hoomi series of letters, Hodgson nevertheless realized that some confirmation was needed that the phenomena connected with the Society were spurious. The testimony of the witnesses before the SPR Committee had to be examined. Hodgson inspected the headquarters of the Theosophical Society in Madras and the former headquarters in Bombay where a great number of the phenomena were supposed to have taken place. He also visited Adyar where the Society maintained an Occult Room which had contained a shrine where letters from the mahatma were supposed to have been received. Although the shrine had been removed, Hodgson found sliding and hinged panels which could have facilitated trickery by Madame Blavatsky and her confederates in the production of letters.

Hodgson summed up his conclusion:

> In short, my lengthy examinations of the numerous array of witnesses to the phenomena showed that they were, as a body, excessively credulous, excessively deficient in the powers of common observation, — and too many of them prone to supplement that deficiency by culpable exaggeration. . . . I finally had no doubt whatever that the phenomena connected with the Theosophical Society were part of a huge fraudulent system worked by Madame Blavatsky with the assistance of the Coulombs and several other confederates, and that not a single genuine phenomenon could be found among them all.[74]

The news of "dear old father's death" which "was very sudden . . . bowled [him] over like a shot,"[75] but it did not delay his report. The Hodgson investigation allowed the SPR Committee to make a final report, whose author was Eleanor Sidgwick, and which Professor Broad described as "easily the most

dramatic and entertaining bit of work that the Society has ever published."[76]
The Committee reached a unanimous conclusion: "[I]t would be a waste of
time to prolong the investigation"[77] of the Theosophical Society and its
phenomena. Concerning the Lady herself, the Committee said: "For our own
part, we regard her neither as the mouthpiece of hidden seers, nor as a mere
vulgar adventuress; we think that she has achieved a title to permanent remem-
brance as one of the most accomplished, ingenious, and interesting imposters
in history."[78]

Not unexpectedly, a loud cry of protest went up from the Theosophists.
Annie Besant attacked Hodgson's Report in 1891 in an article which appeared
in *Time* magazine. A.P. Sinnett, who resigned from the SPR, also attacked
Hodgson on the ground that he never gave Madame Blavatsky any chance to
explain matters. But in a paper, "The Defence of the Theosophists,"[79] Hodgson met every criticism so effectively that the Theosophists were virtually
muted by it at the time.

Today this affair of the past may seem insignificant to many of us. But it
continues to be of great significance to members of the Theosophical Society
whose founder Hodgson labelled the operator of "a huge fraudulent system"
and who was branded an "imposter" in consequence of his report. When, in a
recent paper,[80] I mentioned, as a matter of historical fact, Hodgson's report on
Madame Blavatsky, Theosophists reacted sharply as they did in Hodgson's day.

Not all who have questioned Hodgson's report are members of the
Theosophical Society. The SPR itself has produced two of his sharpest critics.
One was the late Robert H. Thouless, British psychologist and past SPR president, who challenged Hodgson's explanation of the motives of Madame
Blavatsky and her Theosophical Society. Hodgson thought that his report
would not be complete unless he essayed some answer to the question of why
Madame Blavatsky should have labored for ten years to create a giant system
based on fraud and trickery. Russian espionage activity in the 1880's, in comparison to the KGB's counterintelligence system operating in the 1980's, was
puny and pathetic. Yet even then, Russia had sent its *agents provocateurs*
around the world.

Hodgson came to believe that the Madame and her organization were
politically motivated and that she was a Russian spy whose mission was to fo-
ment dissatisfaction in India against British rule. Thouless said that this charge
was unfounded and showed Hodgson's hostility toward Madame Blavatsky. He
believed that Hodgson had decided the truth of the matter very early in the
investigation and had then presented evidence in a way that supported this
truth.[81]

An examination of Hodgson's report, however, shows that, from his point
of view, the charge had adequate grounds. Madame Blavatsky had been under
surveillance by the Indian Government as a possible Russian agent. From conversations with her and from some passages in letters she wrote to a Hindu and
to the Coulombs, he had reached the conclusion that the object of this
daughter of a colonel in the Russian Horse Artillery was to further the interests

of the Czar.[82] Thouless's observation that Hodgson twisted the evidence from the start in order to crucify Madame Blavatsky seems unwarranted. Hodgson himself maintained that he had not only gone to India as an impartial investigator but that he was even pro–Theosophy. "Indeed," he said, "whatever prepossessions I may have had were distinctly in favor of Occultism and Madame Blavatsky—a fact which . . . is well known to several leading Theosophists."[83]

In 1986 another SPR member made the most determined attack against the Hodgson report since the days of Annie Besant and Sinnett. In his paper entitled "J'Accuse" (after Emile Zola's open letter published in a French newspaper to denounce the General Staff of the French Army in the Dreyfus case), Vernon Harrison, an expert on forged writings, rejected Hodgson's conclusions that both the Blavatsky-Coulomb letters and the Koot Hoomi letters were the handiwork of Madame Blavatsky. She had always sworn by the Master she served that she was not the author of these documents and now this line of defense was urged on her behalf by Harrison. He argued that the possible motives for forging the Blavatsky-Coulomb letters should be taken into account. Madame Blavatsky's motive was not clear but that of the Coulombs who had been dismissed by the Society was: revenge and the desire to bring down the Madame. Harrison also was critical of the report of Hodgson's handwriting expert for its omissions (such as not stating which Blavatsky-Coulomb letters had been examined by him) and was critical also of Hodgson's methods of analyzing small letters in the Koot Hoomi documents and his statements in regard to them.

Altogether Hodgson's was a "thoroughly bad report" made in order to implicate Madame Blavatsky in forgery and fraud. If only Madame Blavatsky had been allowed by Hodgson to defend herself, Harrison argued, Hodgson would not have been able to "bamboozle" the SPR into condemning her on the basis of his report which the SPR Committee and Council rubber-stamped but never examined critically. A similar charge was also made by the British writer and historian Brian Inglis, who claimed that Hodgson "conned" Sidgwick.[84]

Although Harrison is not a Theosophist, he seems assured of veneration by Theosophists because, with his arguments and analyses, he has done much to restore the image of their founder and to give impetus to the Back-to-Blavatsky movement. But will these arguments justify a repudiation of the Hodgson report by the SPR Council and an apology to the Theosophists for having left for 100 years an ugly smear on their founder's name? Such an event seems highly unlikely on the basis of the Harrison critique.

In the first place, in legal contemplation, if Madame Blavatsky in fact forged the Blavatsky-Coulomb letters, her motive is unimportant. But if motive were of consequence, her 1883 letter to Madame Coulomb to defraud 10,000 rupees out of a potential donor would seem relevant. Second, it was not only Hodgson and the two English handwriting experts, Richard Sims of the British Museum and F.G. Netherclift, who thought the letters genuine. There were other independent opinions that Madame Blavatsky was their author.

Before the letters were published in the Madras *Christian College Magazine,* its publishers were convinced on the basis of their evidence that the letters were genuine. Also, it is hard to perceive the value of an expert opinion expressed by someone even with Harrison's credentials when it is impossible now to compare the genuine handwriting of Madame Blavatsky with the original Blavatsky-Coulomb letters which disappeared long ago.

The Koot Hoomi letters are another matter: They are available for examination in the British Museum. Harrison's opinion is that there is no clear evidence that Madame Blavatsky wrote them. But the expert Netherclift (after holding first that she was not their author) finally concluded that the Koot Hoomi letters were undoubtedly written by Madame Blavatsky. Any disavowal of Hodgson's report would not seem justified on the basis of conflicting expert opinions. Nor would it be if, aside from the handwriting question, there is taken into account the content, style, errors in punctuation or spelling, which the Koot Hoomi letters and those of the Madame have in common and which point to her as the writer of both.

Whether Hodgson was right or wrong, did or did not "bamboozle" or "con" even the brightest minds in the SPR such as Myers and the two Sidgwicks, William James was impressed by Hodgson's work. Better said, James was delighted: "I am glad of [Hodgson's] demolition of that jade, Blavatsky."[85] Madame Blavatsky was finished as far as the history of parapsychology was concerned.

These investigations, however, had brought Hodgson into contact with conjuring tricks and puzzles. And it was this early interest that led him to detect tricks and frauds whenever he could.

Slate-Writing

After completing his report on Theosophy and its high-priestess, Hodgson, while resuming the lecturing career which his trip to India had interrupted, was also taken up with the evidence for slate-writing. In due course, Hodgson informed Hackett: "I have no doubt the slate-writing is all conjuring."[86] When he compared the accounts of people who had witnessed the feats of Indian jugglers with what actually had taken place, he saw how even intelligent witnesses who do not know the jugglers' methods can be deceived. The accounts of witnesses to the physical phenomena which were produced by Eglinton, the great slate-writing medium, too, he thought might be misdescriptions of the phenomena by people who were not aware of the *modus operandi* of the medium. Yet Spiritualists claimed that this testimony was sufficient to establish the genuineness of the phenomena Eglinton had produced.

The only course open to Hodgson was to find someone who, with conjuring tricks, could duplicate the Eglinton phenomena. That someone was S.J. Davey, a young man who had had seances with Eglinton and had begun to practice with slate-writing himself. Soon Davey was performing for his friends and discovered that he was able to deceive them. He noticed that the statements they made about the conditions producing the writing were as wrong as his own reports had been about Eglinton.

Hodgson and Davey set about in 1886 to conduct a systematic investigation. Davey would hold a series of sittings in which sitters, many of whom were SPR members, would agree to complete an account in writing of what they had observed. The purpose of the investigation, first, was to demonstrate by means of the seances how wrong witnesses' observations and statements would be about the conditions producing the phenomena, and, second, to demonstrate that there was essentially no difference between Davey's seances and Eglinton's, that is, between seances governed by conjuring tricks and those which were claimed to be genuine. These purposes were accomplished. The witnesses had overlooked the devices Davey used so that their accounts were altogether imperfect. They were prime examples of malobservation and lapses of memory.

Hodgson's paper[87] showed that testimony concerning slate-writing was totally unreliable in that "it is demonstrably fallible in precisely those particular points where it must be shown infallible before the phenomena can be accepted as supernormal."[88] Hodgson's paper on this important subject has been lauded as a "textbook" for the investigation of physical phenomena[89] and as "among the 'classic' papers in [the] Proceedings" of the SPR.[90] James added to the praise of Hodgson's labor: "This Davey-Hodgson contribution is probably the most damaging document concerning eye-witnesses' evidence that has ever been produced."[91]

The ASPR: A New Chapter

Hodgson's excursion to India had temporarily interrupted his appointment as Cambridge lecturer. In 1887, the interruption became permanent. In one respect, the finish of Madame Blavatsky as a result of Hodgson's investigation of her and of the Theosophical movement she founded closed one chapter in the history of parapsychology in England. In another respect, the Countess opened a chapter for American parapsychology.

In 1887, as Hodgson explained to Hackett, "[t]he ASPR wasn't getting along, the men couldn't give time, etc."[91] In short, the ASPR was dying and needed new blood. R. Pearsall Smith, a member of the ASPR Council, was as deeply impressed as James by Hodgson's powerful report on the phenomena connected with Theosophy. In Hodgson's letter to Hackett, he said that Smith "was 'taken' with my exposure of Mad. B. and anxious to get me for the American Society."[93] Proposed by Smith, Hodgson was offered the secretaryship of the ASPR in the hope of giving it an infusion of new life. At first, Hodgson was reluctant to leave England and his friends. So, he wrote, he "refused, as I had made a temporary arrangement in England, — but finally accepted [the offer], as Sidgwick and the others thought it was advisable."[94] Hodgson left England on April 8, 1887, and arrived in New York on April 15. From there he went on to Boston where, almost immediately on his arrival, he found what was to be his second home, the "Tavern Club," next door to his lodgings.

He set to work in his new post. Jimmy Hackett was told that Hodgson was charged with every detail, financial, petty and otherwise: dictating and signing letters; conferring with ASPR members; going out to investigate reports and to interview witnesses; attending meetings of the Council and committees; collecting dues; preparing proofs and reading and publishing material. He wrote in 1888: "I practically 'boss' this Society of 400 members."[95] In another letter, he said: "I am sacrificing myself on the shrine of P.R. [psychical research] but I am stimulating considerably the work of P.R. here."[96]

Indeed, the work of the ASPR which had proceeded at the pace of the proverbial snail, now accelerated. The *Proceedings* it issued in 1889 showed a "moderate progress" made in the investigation of mediumistic phenomena[97] and experiments in telepathy.[98] There were other interesting contributions such as Minot's report[99] on diagram tests in which postcards had been distributed with the request that ten diagrams be drawn on the card without the participant's receiving suggestions from other people. Over five hundred cards were received with circles, squares, triangles, crosses, diamonds, faces, etc. The similarity of the visual images led to the conclusion that "even in trifles we differ but little.... [W]e are in mental matters all pure communists."[100]

An article about Hodgson and the ASPR appeared in an unidentified American paper:

> Dr. Hodgson in [sic] as [sic] Englishman, about thirty-seven (32) [sic] years old, a graduate of Cambridge University, a profoundly learned scholar and a level headed man of much common sense. He is an enthusiast, and is devoted heart and soul to the work of the A.S.P.R. He certainly doesn't look like a man who hobnobs with ghosts and is on speaking terms with spirits. In his clerical work, which includes a vast correspondence, he is aided by a good robust-looking apparition. She is also young and quite pretty.[101]

With Hodgson at the helm, it was smoother sailing for the ASPR. As James put it: "Mr. Hodgson had to be imported from Europe before any tangible progress was made."[102] The original offer from the ASPR had been for one year. But Hodgson was still at his post in 1888, and in 1889 he wrote Jimmy: "Nothing new here except that I shall probably stay another year at least, if not longer."[103] Again in 1890 when the ASPR had become a branch of the SPR he wrote that he was likely to remain for at least another year.[104]

After about ten years in America, Hodgson's residence there ended in 1897. He returned to England bringing with him from America "a batch of nearly 500 type-copied cases" of paranormal experiences. In his new capacity as editor of the JSPR and PSPR, he issued a plea for more and fresher documentary cases.[105] In 1898 his name appears as an SPR Council member.[106]

Suddenly, however, Hodgson returned to Boston in 1898 to resume his work. He resigned his editorship of the JSPR and PSPR and was succeeded by Alice Johnson of Newnham College in Cambridge.[107] Hodgson's letters to Hackett from England had already indicated the clear wish to return to Boston. But, in all the letters available to us in the Harvard and ASPR archives, Hodgson's free and flowing pen never confided to Hackett any reason for wishing to do so. Mrs. Sidgwick believed that Hodgson left England because "the attraction of America and of the work in America was too strong."[108] Even so, England was still close to his heart. A letter from Lucy Edmunds, who was Hodgson's assistant in Boston for many years, tells us that Hodgson "talked of going to England the last three summers of his life but did not go" because of "the trouble he was having with Miss Johnson and Mrs. Myers. Otherwise he would have gone."[109] What "trouble" Hodgson had with the new editor of the JSPR and PSPR and with Eveleen Myers was not described. Whatever it was, it could have caused his failure to return to England. The episode is puzzling and has a definite air of mystery about it which I will attempt to clear up when we deal with Hodgson's role in the birthing of Myers' posthumous book, *Human Personality and Its Survival of Bodily Death.*

Mrs. Piper

About two weeks after Hodgson's first coming to Boston in 1887, his career took a turn that was to result in one of the great achievements of American parapsychology. William James had discovered Mrs. Leonora E. Piper of Boston, a trance medium who impressed him with her honesty and persuaded him that she was possessed of some unexplained power.[110] Sittings with her were to be among the tasks Hodgson was to perform as the new ASPR secretary.

He wrote to Hackett his observations of Mrs. Piper and his current view of her mediumship:

> Her state is perhaps akin to selfenduced [sic] hypnotic trance, with the assumption of a personality entirely different from her normal working one, — and purporting to be that of a deceased French physician. She believes this herself, in my opinion. But the Spiritualistic theory is probably erroneous, partly at least if not entirely. And it is long work finding out the capacities and limitations of this freak-personality, whatever it is, with its varying phases, and supernormal "faculty."[111]

Beginning with his first sitting, the medium displayed with him, as she had with James, extraordinary and intimate knowledge about his dead friends and relatives. When he brought 50 strangers for sittings with her, she displayed the same extraordinary powers. But Hodgson, fresh from his exposure of that "jade," Madame Blavatsky, and his demonstration of the valuelessness of human testimony regarding slate-writing and physical phenomena in general, was not satisfied. Hodgson employed detectives to "shadow" and watch Mr. and Mrs. Piper. Her correspondence was opened. But there was not the slightest indication of anything that might cast suspicion on the medium. Hodgson concluded that she had come by her information paranormally. The question was whether the explanation might be telepathy from the living or the dead.

An example of the precautions Hodgson took can be appreciated by considering the arrangements he made for her sittings with Professor Hyslop. Arrangements were made while Mrs. Piper was in a state of trance rather than in her normal waking state. No clue whatever of Hyslop's identity was given to the medium. The arrangement was made using a pseudonym such as "four times friend." Hyslop would arrive at Mrs. Piper's home in a closed coach. Before entering he donned a mask which covered his entire face and which he wore as he entered the house and sat with the medium. Hodgson introduced him to Mrs. Piper as "Mr. Smith," the name Hodgson used also to introduce all strange sitters to her. Sitters like Hyslop were instructed to say nothing so that voice, in addition to face, was concealed. Like Hyslop, sitters merely bowed when introduced to the medium. During the sitting they never spoke in a normal tone. Moreover, during the sittings Mrs. Piper was never touched by a sitter so as to avoid any muscular suggestion. Nor were clues given by questions asked in order that facts obtained might not be suggested by questions. Finally, the sitters stood behind the medium so that she could not see them or their movements.[112]

Hodgson also took notes of all sittings with Mrs. Piper or had a secretary do so in order that a record would be compiled.

After over 50 sittings with Mrs. Piper, Hodgson's report in 1892 held to the hypothesis that Mrs. Piper's secondary personality had made itself out to be a "spirit." The report read:

> Putting aside all the facts which can be explained by direct thought-transference from the sitter, and considering simply the information given which was not known to the sitter and which purports to come from "deceased" persons, but which was known to, and afterwards verified by, distant living persons, — is there sufficient ground for concluding that Phinuit is in direct communication with "deceased" persons, and that he is a "deceased" person himself as he alleges? I think that the evidence here presented, together with that previously published, is very far from sufficient to establish any such conclusion. . . .[113]

The foregoing was based on sittings held through 1891. Starting in 1892, Hodgson held more sittings with Mrs. Piper to try to obtain more information, and, in an addendum to his report added in May 1892, he noted that evidence of a stronger nature had been received.[114]

By the time Hodgson's second Report was finished and published in 1898, circumstances had changed and so had the quality of Mrs. Piper's evidence. A series of communications came through her that Hodgson believed were strongly suggestive of survival. These were of "Madame Elisa Mannors,"[115] the "Kalua" case,[116] and that of "Louis R."[117] A young lawyer whom Hodgson knew called "G.P." or George Pelham (George Pellew) died accidentally in 1892, and, about a month later, "G.P." allegedly began a series of communications through Mrs. Piper. Of all the communications purporting to come through her from "deceased" persons, "G.P."'s were, in Hodgson's language, "the longest and most remarkable."[118] One of "G.P."'s remarkable demonstrations was the true recognition of 30 of 150 strangers who had sittings with Mrs. Piper after his death with not one case of false recognition. In addition, said Hodgson,

> the continual manifestation of this personality, — so different from Phinuit or other communicators, — with its own reservoir of memories, with its swift appreciation of any reference to friends of G.P., with its "give and take" in little incidental conversations with myself, has helped largely in producing a conviction of the actual presence of the G.P. personality. . . .[119]

A factor that Hodgson considered significant in the change that took place was Mrs. Piper's development of a new channel of communication. During her trance state, Phinuit, the personality who claimed to be a French doctor, had control of her voice. But with the advent of "G.P.," the medium began to write automatically, and a channel was opened for communicators other than Phinuit.

Hodgson, no longer skeptical about the medium, was now persuaded that the evidence obtained through her supported the survival hypothesis. In a section of his second report entitled "Indications that the 'Spirit' Hypothesis Is True," Hodgson made these important statements:

> [A]t the present time I cannot profess to have any doubt but that the chief "communicators," to whom I have referred in the foregoing pages, are veritably the personalities that they claim to be, that they have survived the change we call death, and that they have directly communicated with us whom we call living, through Mrs. Piper's entranced organism.[120]

Hodgson also believed that the phenomena produced by Mrs. Piper's mediumship which had convinced him had convinced others also. "Nearly all the chief workers in P.R. are satisfied that the Spiritistic exp. must be applied to the Piper case, all I think except Podmore, e j Lodge, Barrett and Mrs. Sidgwick think that discarnate spirits are concerned."[121] Hodgson also ventured the opinion that "[James] has always maintained both publicly and privately, and before I came to this country at all, that Mrs. P's manifestations were genuine. I think he does believe that 'spirits' are concerned, but he has never publicly said so, so far as I know."[122]

The amount of devotion and time Hodgson gave to his studies of Mrs. Piper and the extent of his contribution to American parapsychology are evident from the number of sittings he had with her. An examination of the PSPRs shows that 53 sittings were held with Mrs. Piper in the period 1887–1891,[123] 13 sittings from 1892–1893 to try for more information concerning "G.P.,"[124] 11 other sittings from 1891–1893,[125] 19 sittings from 1893–1895,[126] and 12 sittings from 1892–1893.[127] After Hodgson's return to America from his second trip to England, he conducted 65 more sittings with Mrs. Piper over a five and one half year period from 1899 to within one month of his death. These sittings were published in a paper by Mrs. H. de G. Verrall (Mrs. Salter).[128] In addition to attending sittings personally, he arranged them for others.

The sittings not only exhausted Mrs. Piper; it is a curious fact that they also affected Hodgson. In spite of his being athletic and of powerful build, he found working with her not merely time-consuming but, as William James recalled, "excessively fatiguing."[129]

Because of the enervating character of the work with Mrs. Piper, Hodgson felt it necessary to adopt a purely business tone with the medium, entering, starting the trance and leaving when it was over, with as few unnecessary words as possible. "Great *brusquerie* was among the excellent R.H.'s potentialities"[130] which "led to a state of feeling on [Mrs. Piper's] part of which a *New York Herald* reporter once took advantage to exploit publicly"[131] in an article published on October 20, 1901, headlined "Confession," which said that Mrs. Piper was not willing to be investigated further. She was quoted as saying: "I do not believe that spirits of the dead have spoken through me when I have been in the trance state. . . . It may be that they have, but I do not affirm it."

The *Herald* article did not alter the evidential value of Mrs. Piper's phenomena. Her opinion favoring the telepathic hypothesis over the spiritistic one was not of any more significance than her opinion favoring the spiritistic hypothesis over the telepathic one would have been. The single achievement of the article was that it probably improved Hodgson's relationship with Mrs. Piper because, after the *Herald* incident, "R.H. was remonstrated with, and was more considerate afterwards."[132]

Richard Hodgson devoted so many years to Mrs. Piper that there were those, including James, who grew impatient with him. Yet prior to Hodgson's "obsessive" researches with Mrs. Piper, James had made vain attempts to stimulate interest in her. As Hodgson wrote to Hyslop: "I may remind you that some years ago Prof. James took special pains to try and get various scientific men to have sittings with Mrs. Piper [such as] Prof. Royce and Prof. Münsterberg . . . also . . . the Seybert Commission. . . . They refused to do so."[133] But in consequence of Hodgson's work with her, the result was very different:

"I have had I think hundreds of applicants for sittings during the past year. . . . I know of persons who are willing to journey half round the world for the purpose of having sittings."[134]

The interest created by Hodgson in Mrs. Piper released a stream of scientific and scholarly papers focused on her. These were published by Myers,[135] Lodge[136] and Leaf[137] and dealt with 83 sittings she had given them when brought to England on the basis of information furnished by Hodgson and James. Frank Podmore discussed her trance phenomena in 1898. Andrew Lang wrote about her in 1900. Piddington studied her in 1908. Hyslop dealt with Mrs. Piper in 1901, and, in separate reports, James and Lodge wrote about her in 1909.[138] Mrs. Sidgwick, Mrs. A.W. Verrall and Piddington analyzed her in 1910. In other papers, Mrs. Sidgwick weighed Mrs. Piper's trance phenomena both in 1900 and in 1915 and advanced conclusions which disagreed with Hodgson's.

The Double Consciousness and Other Cases

The case of the Watseka Wonder[139] is familiar to students of parapsychology as a case of "possession" by the spirit of a dead person. Lurancy Vennum, about 14 years of age, who lived in Watseka, Illinois, apparently was controlled by the personality of Mary Roff who had died when Lurancy was only fifteen months old. The possession lasted fourteen weeks. Hodgson went to Watseka in April 1890 to cross-examine the main witnesses in the case. In his view, the only alternative interpretation of the case, besides the spiritist one, was that it was a case of alternate personality with paranormal powers. After his cross-examination, however, Hodgson wrote: "My personal opinion is that the 'Watseka Wonder' case belongs in the main manifestations to the spiritistic category."[140]

But other cases belong in the category of multiple personality. Hodgson provided us with one which has become a classic case of this kind. He called it "A Case of Double Consciousness." Ansel Bourne, an itinerant preacher, disappeared from his home in Rhode Island in 1887. He arrived in Pennsylvania where he operated a store for two months and became A.J. Brown. James, who accompanied Hodgson when sittings were held with the hypnotized Bourne, described the case in his *Principles of Psychology*.[142] He said that Bourne's skull "covers two distinct personalities."[143]

Besides reporting on his own experiments and investigations, Hodgson reported to the SPR cases from America into which he made inquiries and which became important in the annals of parapsychology. The Conley case is one example. There a dead farmer apparently appeared to reveal that a roll of bills, of which no living person knew anything, had been sewed inside his shirt.[144] Another example of Hodgson's contributions along this line is the Wiltsie case in which occurred what today would be called a near-death experience accompanied by an out-of-the-body experience.[145]

The Palladino and Thompson Phenomena

Hodgson's management of the ASPR and his obsession with Mrs. Piper did not prevent him from roaring like a bull into the tidy china shops savants had constructed on the Continent and in England and from shattering their suppositions about two mediums.

Eusapia Palladino, the physical medium from Naples, had enjoyed a complete triumph on the Continent. Scientists and scholars were persuaded by the genuineness of the phenomena created in her presence. Articles appeared in the *Annales des Sciences Psychiques* in 1893 giving accounts of phenomena consisting of levitations, movements of furniture, raps and hands appearing in the dark[146] which allegedly had been produced by the medium in experiments in Milan conducted by a committee composed of savants.[147] The medium's fame spread to England so that when Professor Charles Richet of France invited Sir Oliver Lodge and F.W.H. Myers of the SPR and Professor J. Ochorowicz of Warsaw to his Mediterranean island in 1894 for some experiments with the gifted Italian peasant woman, they accepted eagerly. A month later, Lodge and Henry and Eleanor Sidgwick returned for more sittings with Eusapia at Richet's chateau near Toulon. As a result of the sittings, the originally skeptical Lodge said: "I have now definitely to state my conviction that certain phenomena of this class may, under certain conditions, have a real and objective existence."[148]

This was the setting into which Hodgson made his entry. In a powerful paper,[149] he examined the conditions of the experiments reported by Lodge and found the report inadequate. He then analyzed in some detail the lack of precautions which shocked James. Years later, he wrote Hodgson:

> All I can then say is that if Richet & the rest had that woman in their house all that time *without* [searching her clothing], and then came to conclusions, there is no fool's name too hard to be applied to them. It fills one with pain & disgust, the whole episode. It makes one realize also *your* invaluable presence.[150]

Of course Myers,[151] Lodge,[152] Richet[153] and Ochorowicz[154] were forced to respond to these sharp criticisms. But Hodgson remained firm and went to England to join with Myers, Alice Johnson and the Sidgwicks in further experiments with the medium which were held in Cambridge in 1895. In the course of these sittings, Hodgson was able to detect that Eusapia was able to maneuver one of her hands to create phenomena. When Henry Sidgwick realized this fact, he recorded:

> [W]e — that is, Mr. and Mrs. Myers, Miss Johnson, Mrs. Sidgwick, and myself, as well as Dr. Hodgson, — unanimously adopted the conclusion that nothing but trickery had been at work in the Cambridge series of experiments.[155]

Hodgson was attacked then and continues to be attacked now on the ground that he and not the medium was responsible for the trickery. This point of view was presented by Inglis who, in saying that Hodgson "conned" Sidgwick not only over Madame Blavatsky but also over the medium Palladino, argued that everyone knew that Eusapia Palladino would cheat if she could. By allowing her to do so, Hodgson was the guilty party.[156] Manfred Cassirer likewise charges Hodgson with complicity in the medium's fraud because, during a seance, he released one of her hands to allow her to do as she pleased.[157] The curious contention made by these critics not only would exonerate criminals who had entered a house and stripped it of all its contents because the owner had left the door unlocked, it would also convict the owner as an accomplice in the crime. Hodgson did not instigate or induce the medium's fraud. It seems an extreme position to take to blame him for giving her the opportunity to manuever her hands in order to determine her *modus operandi*. If we see the situation through the eyes of Eleanor Sidgwick who was at the sittings and held Hodgson blameless, this was "the only scientific procedure" to follow.[158]

As far as the SPR was concerned, "Falsus in uno, falsus in omnibus, once a cheat, always a cheat, such has been the motto of the English psychical researchers in dealing with mediums."[159] Critics, however, thought the verdict was unjust. French investigators further said that, even if Eusapia had cheated at Cambridge, fraud did not account for the genuine phenomena which appeared in her presence when fraud was not possible. And some years later, Myers became convinced once more that genuine phenomena were taking place in her presence.[160] So Hodgson who had had the first word in the Palladino affair did not necessarily have the last.

In about 1896 Rosalie (Mrs. Edmund) Thompson, the daughter of a prosperous London merchant, discovered that she was possessed of paranormal powers. She saw spirits, writing on walls, pictures in crystal balls, and spoke in trances to deliver communications from spirits.

She gave sittings for prominent members of the SPR such as Mrs. A.W. Verrall, Alice Johnson and Myers. Myers was completely persuaded that he had "good reason for ascribing many of these messages to definite surviving personalities, known while on earth to friends of mine whose presence with Mrs. Thompson has evoked the messages, or to myself."[161]

Then in 1900 Hodgson read over a large number of the records of her phenomena. He noted that her earlier physical phenomena had not been performed under very stringent conditions and that her later trance phenomena resembled Mrs. Piper's early phenomena.[162] He then had six sittings with Mrs. Thompson in July and August, 1900, during which he and a Mrs. Barker were present. Following these sittings, he reported that none of the statements the medium had made about him and his friends and relatives suggested any supernormal power at all. The statements relative to Mrs. Barker suggested the conclusion "either that some supernormal power was manifested, or that Mrs. Thompson, or her trance-personality, had obtained information surreptitiously."[163] But did she do so in her normal state or when she had been taken over by a secondary personality? Hodgson did not hesitate to state: "There may be some who will adopt this latter view. For myself, I saw no reason to suppose, in the whole course of my six sittings, that Mrs. Thompson was at any time in any 'trance' state of any sort whatever."[164] He never said expressly that the medium was fraudulent but the implication was clear enough.

Since Myers, Lodge and Mrs. Verrall, among others, had affirmed the genuineness of Mrs. Thompson's phenomena, Hodgson's unfavorable report drew fire. Soon after Myers died in 1901, however, Mrs. Thompson decided to cease her mediumship. Was it his death or Hodgson's negative report, or perhaps both, that influenced her?

Myers' Classic

Although Hodgson wrote lengthy papers for the SPR *Proceedings,* carried on much correspondence as secretary of the ASPR and dreamed of writing a novel, he never wrote one book. But his hand can be seen in one of the great pieces of literature in parapsychology. When Myers died in January 1901, he left unfinished two volumes of a work entitled *Human Personality and Its Survival of Bodily Death.* In 1896, he had arranged that, in case of his premature death, the book on which he was working would be completed by Hodgson. He also had given to Alice Johnson the responsibility of organizing the appendices and seeing to the printing of the book.

It is here that an attempt may be made to unravel the mystery of Hodgson's "trouble" with Mrs. Myers and Alice Johnson that may have been behind his failure to return to England from Boston. It is known that Myers had been infatuated with Annie Marshall and, deeply stricken when she drowned herself, received some solace from impressive postmortem communications through the trance medium Mrs. Thompson which he believed to come from his love. He wrote about the sittings and intended to include them in his *Human Personality.* Following his death, however, Eveleen Myers found out about his affair with Annie Marshall, and, although it had taken place several years prior to her marriage to Myers, was so enraged and jealous by her discovery that she did away with all records of the sittings and opposed the inclusion of any passages about them in Myers' work. We may speculate that Hodgson's "trouble" with her and Alice Johnson arose out of discord among them concerning the exclusion from the book of all references to the sittings.

There were signs of other disagreements between Hodgson and Alice Johnson. But in spite of them and the possible discord to which we have just alluded, the editorial work necessary to complete the book — without any mention of Annie Marshall or Mrs. Thompson — and to enable it to see the light of day after Myers died was performed. In this Hodgson surely had some share although an Editorial Note in the book, to which the names of Hodgson and Alice Johnson are appended, acknowledges that she did the greater part of the work.[165]

The Magnificent Opportunity

That Hodgson should have been designated by Myers to complete his book is not surprising. The two thought alike; both were persuaded that empirical evidence of the survival of death had been supplied. In Hodgson's case, the persuasion produced an inner tranquility which, in 1903, James could not fail to observe. In his letter to Theodore Flournoy, he said: "Hodgson left us this morning after a visit of 10 days. It is a pleasure to see a man in such an absolute state of moral & physical health. His very face shows the firmness of a soul in equilibrium — another proof of the strength which a belief in future life may give one!"[166]

Both Myers and Hodgson faced the prospect of death alike. When Myers was dying and in pain, he recited his own poetry as he welcomed death.[167] Even when in robust health, Hodgson had faced the thought of death with a similar eager spirit. On a cold clear night two weeks before he died, he was walking across the Boston Common with a friend. Hodgson looked up into the starry sky. "Sometimes," he said to Arthur Stanwood Pier, "I can hardly wait to get over there."[168] Another acquaintance of Hodgson spoke of his "sincere readiness, almost eagerness"[169] to die.

For Hodgson, death presented a magnificent opportunity to strengthen the evidence of survival after death. "I am sure," he told Pier, "that [after death] I can establish the truth beyond a possibility of doubt."[170] James recalled that Hodgson said very often that, if Mrs. Piper were still living when he died, "he would control her better than she had ever yet been controlled in her trances because he was so thoroughly familiar with the difficulties and conditions on this side."[171]

Hodgson could not have been thinking of death, survival evidence and postmortem communications on December 20, 1905. Some months before, he had written to Hackett that he was "first rate physically."[172] Only two weeks prior to his death, he told Pier: "I suppose I'm good for twenty more years at least."[173] On the afternoon of his death, his spirit was high and his great booming voice was heard in the Tavern Club. Hodgson left for the Union Boat Club still fit and powerful as ever. Then, as he was playing handball on the squash court, he dropped dead. His death was described by James as "ultrasudden."[174] The immediate cause of death recited in Hodgson's death certificate was "acute heart failure."

His body was returned to the Tavern Club which he had left a few hours before. Three days later the funeral service that so moved the members of the Club took place there.

Hodgson was cremated and his ashes placed in Forest Hills Cemetery near Boston.

In Retrospect

Hodgson's apparent conversion to the spiritistic hypothesis appeared in the latter portion of his second report on Mrs. Piper. Whether he would have changed his view must remain a matter of speculation. Hodgson's sudden death intervened before he could complete another report on the trance phenomena of Mrs. Piper. When his second Piper report was prepared, Hodgson was fully aware that others did not agree with his spiritistic conclusions. It was Hodgson's intention to prepare and publish a "Part II" in which "I shall deal with various objections that may be raised to the views which I have here expressed."[175] After Mrs. Sidgwick prepared her critical report on

Mrs. Piper in which she disagreed with Hodgson's conclusions,[176] he wrote to Hyslop:

> I have also read through Mrs. Sidgwick's article last night. There is absolutely nothing whatever new to myself, and probably nothing new to you as regards the difficulties in the way. I can easily dispose of it and in fact should have dealt with all these objections had I been able to write my full report a couple of years ago.[177]

But Hodgson's opportunity to answer never came to the regret of Mrs. Sidgwick who said that "it is only by free discussion that we can hope to arrive at sound conclusions."[178]

In addition, seven months before Hodgson's death he had written to Hackett: "Fresh evidence accumulating from Mrs. Piper's trance."[179] But it is impossible to know what this fresh evidence was. The records of her trances were not only incomplete but some were in Hodgson's cipher.[180] The dry records of the sittings in themselves are not very impressive. "All his work unfinished," lamented James. "No one can ever learn those records as he knew them.... Too bad, too bad!"[181]

But Hodgson did leave American parapsychology two priceless bequests which must stand as enduring memorials to him. Mrs. Piper was one of the classical contributions to it. His laborious and devoted years of research with her made her both the center of many scholarly and scientific papers and the greatest automatist of her time, from whom the richest survival evidence was obtained. This evidence persuaded Myers.[182] Moreover, the Piper sittings conducted by Hodgson supplied survival evidence of a type in which a deceased communicator seemed so life-like that it was difficult even for the most carping critic to reject it on the ground that telepathy from the living was an entirely adequate explanation for it. It forced Mrs. Sidgwick, one of the foremost critics of survival evidence, to acknowledge that the "G.P." and other cases that came through Mrs. Piper when Hodgson worked with her composed "a good deal of the best evidence of this kind."[183] Indeed, Mrs. Sidgwick became "a firm believer both in survival and in the reality of communication between the living and the dead."[184]

Hodgson's second gift was to provide parapsychologists with a powerful example they can hold up always to critics who charge that the phenomena studied by parapsychologists have made their minds soft and deprived them of all critical faculties. Hodgson did more than anyone else to unmask conscious or unconscious deception and to expose malobservation. He was a parapsychologist who, as James had noted, had "uncommon keenness in detecting error."[185] Whether Richard Hodgson, who firmly believed that empirical evidence of survival and communication after death had been produced in his lifetime, added to this evidence after his own death is arguable. James, who evaluated Hodgson's purported communications through Mrs. Piper was not sure whether it was Hodgson communicating or a "spirit counterfeit."[186] On the other hand, Frank Podmore, one of the most skeptical parapsychologists who ever lived, was of the opinion that, "Of the communicators of the last few years, none has produced so vivid an impression of a living personality behind the veil as Richard Hodgson himself."[187]

If survival is the reality Hodgson was convinced it is, then we can hope with James that the vital and fearless Hodgson may "still be *energizing* somewhere—it's not a case for *requiescat.*"[188]

2
Out of the Ashes (1906–1920)

Commentary

The impact of Hodgson's death on American parapsychology and the
ASPR was crushing. He had run the American branch of the SPR alone. The
organization was totally unprepared. Said James:

> Richard Hodgson had always seemed and felt so robust that the
> possibility of his death had been thought of by no one, and no provi-
> sion against it had been made. . .although Prof. Hyslop and I were
> vice-presidents, we had no minute acquaintance with details at the
> office, where Miss Lucy Edmunds, the assistant secretary, was now left
> in charge alone.[1]

Many problems arose immediately. What of the future of the valued Mrs.
Piper? Should the mass of records of sittings which Hodgson had collected be
dispatched to the SPR in London, or should they be left with the Americans?
Then there was the problem of finding a competent successor to manage the
ASPR. So great was this problem that it caused many in England to consider
discontinuing the American branch. The same thought occurred to many
Americans, among them James who suspected "that our American Branch of
the S.P.R. will have to dissolve this year, for lack of a competent secretary.
Hodgson was our only worker."[2]

Chronological Narrative

1906

The disposition of the Piper records became a fiery issue between London
and Boston which James, then ill in California, diplomatically described as "a
state of strain."[3] The English believed that the records were rightfully theirs
and wanted them. From a legal point of view, they were probably entirely correct. They were the parent society and Hodgson, the secretary of the American
branch, had been their officer. But the Americans still resisted. Even if the
English were entitled to the records, some wanted to know what would be done
with them? Other Americans who had been sitters objected vigorously that the

removal of the records of their sittings would deprive them of what they regarded as private property, and they claimed that the records could not be published without their consent.

The problem that confronted the English and Americans, however, was far graver than the controversy over the Piper material, heated as it was. The fundamental problem was whether or not to dissolve the American branch. The most formidable objection to dissolution was that it might sound the death-knell for collective research into the paranormal in America.

In order to confer with the representatives of the American branch the SPR dispatched J.G. Piddington to Boston in May 1906.[4] As a result of their negotiations and deliberations, a document dated May 16 was drawn up and signed by Piddington on behalf of the SPR and by James, James Hervey Hyslop and George B. Dorr, as vice-presidents of the American branch, and duly issued. "After full and anxious consideration," it stated, "it has been decided to dissolve the American Branch of the Society for Psychical Research...."[5]

Besides the issue of dissolution, that generated by the Piper material and which had caused tempers to flare seemed to be settled. It was agreed in writing that the records would be delivered to London for study "under guarantee of suitable privacy"[6] and that the records "were to be published at the earliest available moment."[7] New arrangements would be made for Mrs. Piper. All other records were to be given to the man of the hour.

1907–1920

That man was Hyslop. The English had surrendered their branch in America only because they were satisfied that dissolution would not mean the death of organized parapsychology in America. On the contrary, because of the careful preparation Hyslop had made, dissolution only meant change and renovation. Unlike the sacred phoenix whose life span has been said to extend over thousands of years, that of the American organization lasted only 21 years, from 1885 to 1906. But like that fabulous bird which dies in its nest in flames to be transformed into another, the ASPR came forth in new form in 1907. For over a decade and until Hyslop's death in 1920, its fortunes rode on his shoulders as he personally managed it and helped plot the next course of American parapsychology.

James Hervey Hyslop: A Portrait

On August 18, 1854, near the forests of Xenia, Ohio, where Robert Hyslop worked his farm, his wife gave birth to "two halves of one august event." But one of Martha Hyslop's twins died a month after birth. It was the

female twin. Had the male, James Hervey Hyslop, perished instead, the flag
of parapsychology in America, which fell when Hodgson died, might not have
been picked up by anyone else, and the course of American parapsychology
would have been altered. But Hyslop lived. His early background, however,
seemed to fit him only for tending cows and religious zealotry. His mature
years were ones of academic frustrations and broken health. Yet how he
became fifty-odd years later parapsychology's standard-bearer is one of the
most interesting life-stories in the last century of American parapsychology.

Farmer and Dreamer

In his *Autobiography*, Hyslop looked back to his childhood and the monotony of home life,[8] the routine existence of a farm boy who took care of the
cows and horses, chopped and carried wood and tended the crops and worked
the plow. It was a life he hated. He was, he boasted, like his father whom he
admired, a person with "an intellectual and reflective temperament [who] had
the natural disposition of a dreamer and this took my mind into anything but
money-making."[9] He escaped into books. The dreamer remembered that,
when he was very young, he used to impress people with "the precocity of my
reading and my power to pronounce proper names."[10]

Religious Orthodoxy

But the first half of this dreaming farm boy's life was not dominated by
books. It was entirely overshadowed by religious orthodoxy and beset by
religious perplexity so vexing that it was to culminate in a broken heart.

Hyslop's father, born in 1821 near Xenia, was a member of a very conservative sect of Associate Presbyterians which refused, in 1858, to join the United
Presbyterian Church. The little sect saw its practices and doctrines threatened
by a rising liberalism in religious beliefs, particularly the singing of hymns and
the use of instrumental music in religious services.[11] Although his wife and
daughters joined the United Presbyterian Church as did his best friends, and
all pleaded with Robert Hyslop to follow them, he would not. Such a man was
he — intransigent in religious matters and fiercely loyal to the vows he had
made when he was admitted to his church.

Hyslop remembered, when he was four or five years old, sitting in the old
straight-backed seats in the church his father attended and once becoming so
frightened at the Theological Seminary of Xenia by the loud shouting and wild
gesticulations of a preacher that his parents laughed at him.[12]

Another incident etched in his memory occurred in 1861 when he was
allowed to accompany his father on a business trip to Champaign, Illinois.
After getting off the train, the pair began to walk across the prairie to see people who owed Robert Hyslop money. In the dusk, they stumbled into a swamp.

James H. Hyslop

Wet to the knees and carried out of the swamp by his father, the seven year old Hyslop was badly frightened at the prospect of staying out all night on the prairie. He told his father that, if they went in the direction where some dogs were barking and could stay overnight at some house, he would "stay at this house even if the people were Catholics." He had "a morbid antipathy to the Roman Catholics"[13] produced by reading and seeing the pictures in the bitter book by the English writer John Foxe, whose *History of the Acts and Monuments of the Church, 1563,* popularly known as *Book of Martyrs,* assailed the Inquisition in Spain. When it turned out that the house to which the barking dogs had led the pair was occupied by the very debtors for whom Robert

Hyslop was searching, Hyslop recalled that he went "to sleep from relief that I was not lost or in the house of Catholics."[14]

On Sunday, or the Sabbath, as Robert Hyslop insisted his family call it, rigid religious orthodoxy was king. No games could be played, no singing or whistling was permitted, no secular books could be read, not even a piece of fruit could be plucked from a tree. Only the stock on the farm could be fed; otherwise it was a day on which work or pleasure in any form simply ceased to exist, a day described by Hyslop as "the most serious of our lives."[15]

On the Sabbath there were two church sermons from 10 a.m. to 3 p.m. And when the Hyslop family was not in church, the rest of Sunday was taken up with reading or instruction in religious material. The first task of the children every Sunday was to memorize a part of a psalm or to read from the Bible, followed by reading other religious matter, such as Foxe's *Book of Martyrs*. The Shorter Catechism which would be recited every Sunday evening as the family group gathered around the fireplace also had to be memorized.[16]

Effects of Religious Training

Did the farm boy rebel against this complete religious domination of his life? Actually, "the rest from manual work on the farm made it much more pleasant than it would be for a city family."[17] His strict religious training also produced other effects on him, one dark and terribly destructive. His brother, Charles, and his sister, Annie, both died 12 days apart in 1865 of scarlet fever.[18] Hyslop was not only affected for a long time by this "abrupt snatching away of innocent lives"[19] but also by the fear engendered by the religious training he had received of "the consequences of a life and death unprepared for salvation."[20] Their deaths were described as "a warning to my life."[21]

Death became a "frightful thing" to young Hyslop.[22] When his mother and Aunt Nannie told him that, if he did not walk erect and throw back his shoulders — he was somewhat stoop-shouldered — he would die of consumption, "the effect on my mind was terrible."[23] He became deathly afraid of death from consumption which he knew to be a killer disease, and, for two years, he suffered from the worst form of hypochondria. His ever-watchful morbid eye kept looking for the slightest sign of the dread disease. It did not fail to come. When he found himself spitting up blood from time to time, he was certain that he had consumption and "was frightened by it beyond all measure."[24] After brooding over this horrible discovery for a year during which he continued to spit blood, he found out he was bleeding from the gums. His fear dissipated but not the permanent mark it left on him:

> These two years of fear and fright affected my cheerfulness so that I became unable to smile or laugh ... [W]ith ... the impressive influence of these two years of abnormal, almost insane fear of death, I was so organically affected that a serious half melancholy disposition is characteristic of me ever since.[25]

Education

Although his father was almost tyrannical about his son's religious education, Robert Hyslop had no interest in what other material the boy read at home. The weekly newspapers, and books such as *Aesop's Fables* and *Jack, the Giant Killer*, were provided but, recalled Hyslop, "no urgent attention was paid to any good secular books by my father during the whole of my childhood."[26] What books Hyslop was able to obtain "by present or accident,"[27] he read easily and eagerly, yet, when it came time to begin his education in the public schools, he refused to go and had to be punished before he would consent if, as he said, "consent could be the name for my obedience under duress."[28] For some years he attended school in his district where he studied the three R's, geography, grammar and some history, an education he described as "very poor."[29]

The death of Hyslop's mother in 1869 left a vacuum in the house which was filled by his father's sister Nannie coming to keep house and care for the children. A year later, Hyslop entered high school where "my education really began . . . and I lived in a new world with as much enthusiasm as a traveller."[30] But throughout his travels, he never lost interest in religious matters. On the contrary, the new world he discovered "still further stimulated my interest in the great questions"[31] which religious teachings had raised.

Hyslop retained in high school the religious convictions passed down to him by his father. The school day opened each morning with religious services which included the singing of hymns and instrumental music which Robert Hyslop's church violently opposed. His son refused to take part in the worship because it conflicted with the teachings of his father's church. Hyslop also reported to his father the shocking conduct of a Presbyterian minister who came to the school to join in the hymnal and musical service. It caused "quite a stir"[32] when Robert Hyslop accused the clergyman of breaking his vows. This incident not only gave his father great satisfaction; it also "made my father very proud of me"[33] and allowed him to hope that "I would study for the ministry."[34]

Spurred by this hope, Robert Hyslop, after considering but rejecting the University of Michigan at Ann Arbor as not sufficiently religious for his son, sent Hyslop in 1874 to West Geneva College in Northwood, Ohio, run by the Reformed Presbyterian Church. The purpose of this institution "was to give an education that would preserve the young man's religious convictions, and everything was gauged to sustain this result."[35]

The young man in question, however, found the intellectual atmosphere there, especially the narrowness of views on all questions, unsuitable to him and, after two years, he left. His father's reaction? Instead of a thundering rage, the silence of death. Now that Hyslop was twenty-one, his father conceded to him complete freedom of choice.

Hyslop chose Wooster University in Ohio. Robert Hyslop probably would not have objected to this institution anyway since it was controlled by

Presbyterians and seemed secure enough in religious matters. He could not have suspected that "the greater intellectual spirit" there would operate to create in his son a growing "tide of scepticism."[36] Terrible doubts began to take form in Hyslop's mind—yet he could not bring himself to express them to his father. "My desire to avoid a conflict with [my father] kept me in observances which I wished to abandon[.] I always saw the beauty and purity of his character, even when I differed from him so widely, so clearly that I would not offend it."[37]

But, when Hyslop's doubts turned him away from the ministry, he could not avoid disappointing his father. By the time Hyslop had been graduated from Wooster in 1877, philosophy fascinated him. He chose to become a teacher instead of a minister and was saving his money for a further education abroad.[38]

After graduation, he taught in a county district school but found it so unpleasant "that I became melancholy over it."[39] He tried in vain for a position in high schools and in other counties in Ohio, in Dayton and Springfield. Inquiries of his old professors at Wooster brought him nothing. It was only when his father intervened by writing to the president of a little college controlled by the Presbyterian Church that a position was offered to Hyslop at McCorkle College not far from Concord, Ohio.[40] He accepted the offer out of desperation although "its theological narrowness was so out of sympathy with [his] broader general views"[41] about which he still said nothing to his unsuspecting father. At this tiny college of five students, whose number soared to thirteen by the end of the term, there were two instructors, the President and Hyslop, which allowed Hyslop, in an obvious attempt to brighten the disappointment of the place with some humor, to call himself "the vice-president."[42] It is not hard to imagine his delight in giving up this office five months later when, "as lightning out of a clear sky,"[43] he received an offer from "Lake Forres" [sic] University. Even though this, too, was a Presbyterian institution, Hyslop immediately accepted a position at the Academy there.

The atmosphere he found there was so congenial that, after three years, he was made principal of the Academy. But one day he was summoned before the Board of Trustees and criticized because of his strict policy of weeding out of the Academy students who were mainly boys who had been expelled from other institutions. Hyslop resigned.

Behind his resignation something was troubling him far more deeply: his religious perplexities. They had become too much for him.

His plan now was to go abroad to "settle my convictions."[45] With Edinburgh University in Scotland as his destination in the fall of the year, he went to England that summer to travel. But travel did not settle his convictions. They were settled by a Greek New Testament which he purchased

> to study the life of Christ in the original. I purposely refrained from reading sceptical books, as I knew I would be accused of being influenced in the adoption of my convictions. I was determined to settle my religious beliefs in the most careful manner, and in this reading I did

decide them finally in a most dramatic way. . . . I shall never forget the final moment when this decision came. I do not remember the exact date or month, but it was in the middle of the London summer. The crisis had been approaching for days with increasing melancholy on my part as I saw the inevitable outcome and the consequences to me and the loss of all my friends and their sympathy. I had been reading the New Testament on some miracle and I saw the impossibility of rationally believing it and if not this, then nothing unless a special reason could be given for it. I got up to walk the floor in reflection on the situation and summing up the whole consequences to myself and the necessity of having the matter decided I finally got the courage to exclaim: "Well, I cannot believe it. I shall give up and take the consequences. I shall surrender every position in life and all my friends, rather than give up my conscience in this matter. I will take whatever consequences come."

Immediately on this decision I felt a most intense sense of relief and soon began crying. I walked the floor crying like a child and perspiring like a horse for an hour and a half, but with a sense of relief that I cannot describe.[45]

The decision not only made the foggy streets of London brighter for him; it made him into "simply one mass of boiling enthusiasm" in which his old fear of death dissolved.[46] But it did not mean a dissolution of his interest in religion or the beginning of atheism. His new convictions meant no more than that he would do all his previous reading again from a fresh rationalistic point of view and would see "the life and teaching of Christ in a new light."[47]

A step now could be taken that he could not bring himself to take before. "As soon as I had formed my conclusion I sat down and wrote it to my father."[48] His father "felt the apostasy very keenly."[49] "The information," Hyslop wrote, "nearly broke my father's heart."[50] For many years, the older Hyslop could not reconcile himself to what seemed to him his son's betrayal of religious truths and teachings. "[H]is letters to me," Hyslop recalled sadly, "showed none of the former paternal affection and interest except as they were colored by pity and sorrow. He felt that I was lost."[51] Robert Hyslop's heart only began to mend a little when he began to realize that his son still retained his same moral values in spite of having given up his religious creed.

Tags and Teaching

Now Hyslop changed his plans. Instead of Edinburgh, he decided to go to Leipzig University in Germany. He spent seventeen months there during which he attended Wundt's lectures on philosophy. He learned German well enough to pass an oral examination and began to write his Ph.D. thesis. There he met Mary F. Hall, a Philadelphian who was studying music in Leipzig. Although later she became his wife, it does not seem to have been a passionate or even interesting courtship as Hyslop seemed anxious to point out: "[T]here

were no excitingly romantic incidents in my love affairs. We both took a cool
and rational view of our situation and calmly abided the issue of events. . . ."[52]

Except for the woman he was to marry, Leipzig seemed to him a waste of
time. He was then 26. He wanted to study philosophy, not write a thesis. So
he elected to abandon the degree and to give his entire time to burying himself
in philosophy and to preparing himself for its teaching. But, "On my return
to the United States without a degree it counted for nothing to have studied
in Germany unless you had taken a degree."[53] It was a bitter discovery that the
institutions to which he applied placed no value on actual preparation for one's
work in teaching but high value on a degree gotten by wasting time. "I had
no tag and tags were the supreme test of merit and qualifications."[54]

No barometer rose and fell more than his fortunes at this stage of his life.
In 1884, he managed to obtain a temporary position teaching Latin and the
history of philosophy at Lake Forest University. Afterwards, he was forced to
return to Xenia and to his old life at the farm while he continued to apply to
universities for positions. In 1886, he became an assistant in psychology and
ethics to his friend, Professor H. Norman Gardiner at Smith College in North-
hampton, Massachusetts. After seven months, he left at the suggestion of Professor G. Stanley Hall of the Department of Psychology of Johns Hopkins
University, who persuaded him to apply for a fellowship there. Hyslop obtained it and, in 1887, took his Ph.D. there.

Still no teaching positions could be found. At one time, a vacancy at Columbia University seemed assured but when he arrived in New York to fill it,
"I found to my surprise that, in fact, there was no vacancy. The man who was
supposed to have given up the place had made arrangements to control it, and
I was out again."[55] Back he went to Johns Hopkins to write and study for a year
at the end of which, with no positions having opened up for him, it seemed
that he was doomed not to accomplish his goal.

He abandoned teaching and took a job with the Associated Press in New
York where he edited telegrams. It was not an overly demanding job so that
he was able to spend his time writing papers, one of which was published in
Mind under the title "Wundt's Theory of Psychic Synthesis." These papers
brought him to the attention of the academic community, and, particularly, of
Professor Nicholas Murray Butler of Columbia University through whom Hyslop
received the opportunity of giving some free lectures. In 1888, Hyslop left the
Associated Press to take up an offer of a position at Bucknell University where
he taught philosophy. The following year, when a philosophy professor resigned
at Columbia, Hyslop was at last appointed to fill the vacancy. Before three years
had passed, he became a full professor of ethics and logic at Columbia.

Openness to Parapsychology

In 1886, when Hyslop was at Smith College, his eyes fell upon a letter
published in *The Nation* entitled "Telepathy Again." It gave an account of a
young boy who saw an apparition of his father twenty miles distant who, with

his team, was plunging at the time over a bank and into a stream. Suspecting some illusion of memory concerning the facts, Hyslop asked the writer of the letter a series of questions. The responses suggested that the phenomenon might be genuine.

His mind was now open to the possibility of paranormal phenomena. But, except for talking about the subject with Professor Gardiner, Hyslop went no further with the subject. When he arrived at Johns Hopkins, he remembered that "I came into contact with the Proceedings of [the English Society for Psychical Research] and would have become interested in the work, had it not been tabooed by Prof. G. Stanley Hall."[56]

Hyslop believed that the existence of paranormal phenomena might make a radical change in thought, "But the facts were so discredited by those whose instructions I had to take that I would not trust my own judgment and so neglected the questions altogether."[57] As a result of this neglect, although the ASPR had been established in 1885, Hyslop admitted "I knew nothing at this time of what [the ASPR] was doing."[58]

Soon after Hyslop started at Columbia some friends, with the cooperation of Richard Hodgson, the ASPR secretary, set about to organize a society in New York City to which interested people would be invited. Hyslop was one of those invited to hear Hodgson read a summary of the Ansel Bourne case. After he had finished, some "cranks" present began to speak in favor of Spiritualism. At this point, Hyslop recorded, "the scientific men put on their hats and left the meeting."[59] Hyslop was in sympathy with this reaction.

"There was absolutely nothing in the paper that either suggested or favored such an interpretation. . . . No rational scientist would have thought of spirits as a conclusion of the case."[60] But Hyslop was not among those who put on their hats and left. "I resolved as soon as I heard the paper to be a member of the Society, as I determined to sympathize with that kind of scientific work. . . . For the first time, I fully appreciated what the Society was doing."[61]

A further meeting was held to organize the group in New York. Hyslop became its president. Although the meetings that were held were not very successful, Hyslop did obtain a set of *Proceedings*. The more he read them, the more he became impressed with the seriousness and importance of the investigations conducted into paranormal phenomena.

He was impressed sufficiently to meet Mrs. Piper in 1892 in New York and to have a brief sitting with her.[62] He did not see her again until 1898 when, after Hodgson had made necessary arrangements, he held many more sittings with her which were to culminate in a report Hyslop published three years later in the English *Proceedings*.[63]

In 1898 also, he published a letter on "The Consciousness of Dying" in the *Journal* of the SPR,[64] and, in 1899, was elected by the SPR as one of its vice-presidents.[65] Although as late as March 1899, his name does not appear on the list of members and associates of the ASPR, by early 1900 he had not only become an associate member but was also interested in becoming an officer.

Did he need to become a full member for this purpose? As ASPR secretary, Hodgson assured him it was not necessary.[66]

Resignation from Columbia

Within three days of an attack of spinal meningitis, Mary Hyslop died. Her death came to Hyslop as a "terrible shock" which brought him "only a shattered home and responsibilities that were hard to bear"[67] and forced him to be both father and mother to three children. His health broke down. Since it was his sabbatical year, he had planned to rest for a year and then go back to Columbia. But he developed a persistent cough, he could not eat and his weight dropped to 108 pounds. It was discovered that he had the tuberculosis he had feared as a child and he was sent to a sanatorium at Saranac Lake. In his correspondence with his friend, Theodore Flournoy, the Swiss psychologist, William James wrote on December 26, 1901, "that the microbes of tuberculosis found [Hyslop] an easy prey. He is now in the country taking an open air cure in an almost arctic cold and leading otherwise the life of a vegetable.... He is a very manly fellow, who has had a very hard life, and I am afraid that this is the end of him for worldly purposes."[68] But, at the end of eight months, to everyone's astonishment, Hyslop, apparently recovered and weighing 158 pounds, left the sanatorium. He returned to Columbia in 1902 only to resign six weeks later.

Modern parapsychologists are painfully aware that their frontier science creeps forward mere millimeters instead of kilometers in its attempts to invade the universities as a course of study. University opposition to the subject still persists as a result of hostile skepticism. Hyslop's is the first recorded case in which parapsychology encountered academic hostility. The issue is whether this hostility forced his resignation.

The archival material provides some basis for thinking that it did. In June 1899, at conferences held in Cambridge, Hyslop discussed his sittings with Mrs. Piper and the report he was making. Despite his denials both to newspaper reporters and to Science and The Psychological Review,[69] the newspapers quoted him as saying that he proposed "scientifically [to] demonstrate the immortality of the soul." Was Hyslop quoted correctly? In the same month that he discussed his sittings with Mrs. Piper at the Cambridge meetings, Hyslop's article "Immortality and Psychical Research" appeared in The New World. After an account of the Piper sittings and the medium's trance-communications, Hyslop wrote: "For myself, then, I am reduced to a choice between telepathy and the spiritistic theory to explain the phenomena, and, for the present at least, I prefer the spiritistic view, or, perhaps more respectably stated, the claim that the immortality of the soul has come within the sphere of legitimate scientific belief."[70] That this was probably the language he used at the Cambridge meeting and how wide of the mark the newspapers had been are borne out by Hodgson's comment in one of his letters to Bayley: "Poor

Hyslop has been misrepresented to an extraordinary extent in the newspapers."[71] The press accounts were read so avidly and accepted so readily by the administration and faculty at Columbia, however, that we can hear Hodgson's hearty laugh behind the letter he wrote to Hyslop in March 1900:

> It is really an awful joke that some of the persons connected with the Columbia University should have swallowed the newspaper stories about you and your remarks, etc. It will give you a splendid opportunity for comments on the unscientific credulity in which various persons are wallowing. I think you ought to get up a society for the proper education of those poor unfortunates, whose gospel is according to the newspapers. Your letters to *Science* and the *Psychological Review* don't seem to have had much effect.[72]

But it was not entirely a laughing matter as we note from this letter from Hodgson:

> As to the general situation as regards your position at the university, I do not see possibly how any steps can be taken against you. It would be pretty absurd for the authorities of the college to make any move on the ground of newspaper reports about what you said at the meetings. . . . Be sure and take everything coolly. . . . I wonder if the authorities of the college would turn out any professor who dared to assert that he believed that nearly nineteen hundred years ago a man rose from the dead?[73]

Did Columbia turn out Hyslop who asserted in his Piper report that he believed that the Piper phenomena made it rationally possible to believe that there had been communication from the dead? We know that suddenly Hyslop's courses in psychology and ethics were taken away from him and replaced by metaphysics and epistemology. The reason may not have been only the "swallowing" of newspaper accounts; from what Hyslop wrote in his *Autobiography*, there is an indication that the university authorities could have been made very uncomfortable because Hyslop would not hold his tongue in his university lectures. "My work in [ethics and psychology] continued until my free discussion of subjects in 'psychical research' disturbed the equanimity of the president and the head of the philosophic department."[74] Also, in 1900, in bitterness, he told Professor William Romaine Newbold that, as a result of his stand on parapsychology, he had been made "an outcast from his profession and excluded . . . from every chair of philosophy in the country."[75]

Evidently, this kind of angry declaration reached the ears of Butler, then president of Columbia, and prompted a sharp denial:

> The statement that your personal beliefs as to psychic research or your interest in that subject had anything to do with your resignation from the teaching staff of Columbia in 1902 is a grotesque absurdity. The facts are that your health was at that time seriously impaired. . . . It was for that reason, and in order to restore your health by leading an outdoor life, that you withdrew, of your own accord, from the Department of Philosophy here with the goodwill of everybody.[76]

Could this outstanding educator and future candidate for the American vice-presidency have written a self-serving letter to cover up Columbia's pressure on Hyslop to resign? Every indication is that Butler's letter accurately presents the real cause of Hyslop's resignation. Professor Newbold's statement about Columbia's position with regard to Hyslop's stand on parapsychology is relevant: "President Butler was unconvinced and, so far as I am aware, uninterested, but he assured Professor Hyslop the University would interfere in no way with his academic freedom."[77] More important is the fact that, in his *Autobiography*, Hyslop, himself, seemingly inconsistent with his statement to Newbold and his earlier remark in the same *Autobiography*, blamed his resignation entirely on his health. After he had resumed his duties at Columbia, he wrote, "I lost eighteen pounds in six weeks and found my cough arising again. I resolved to resign at once and did so."[78]

The American Institute for Scientific Research

He considered first mining gold in Vermont. It was an appealing prospect because it seemed "a safe business and it offered me the desired outdoor life."[79] But instead, Hyslop concentrated his attention on parapsychology. He recognized the impoverished state of the ASPR and the need for trying to gain financial support for its work. It struck Hyslop that the study of two fields should be undertaken: psychopathology and parapsychology. In December 1900, he published an article which he hoped would produce an endowment of one million dollars, but it met only indifference on the part of the scientific community and the general public.[80]

He turned to the Carnegie Institute for money but he did so without the influential support of James. "As regards the Carnegie Institute I am declining to back Hyslop's application because it is an absolute moral impossibility that they should give any money; and it is poor policy; in an unpopular cause, to make it a nuisance as well as a victim."[81] James's analysis was correct: Hyslop's appeal for funds to the Carnegie Institute was unsuccessful as well.

He now started to think in terms of the formation of an independent organization which would not compete with the SPR's American branch but which would ultimately merge with it if sufficient funds could be raised. His scheme received wide support. James wrote Hyslop that he thought the scheme a wise plan.[82] From Europe came a lengthy endorsement from the eminent Pierre Janet.[83] Camille Flammarion wrote a letter of support,[84] and Charles Richet and Max Dessoir praised the idea[85] as did prestigious Americans such as Columbia's Butler.[86] The publisher, Isaac K. Funk, also allied himself with Hyslop. "In a small book which I purpose to write...urging a deeper interest on the part of the public in psychic research," he wrote to Hyslop, "I want to give some of the strongest reasons I can think of for a comprehensive support of your Institute idea. I think I can turn over to you some hundreds of members."[87]

When Hyslop discussed his plan with Hodgson in 1904, the two con-curred. "[H]ad Hodgson lived," said Bayley, "he undoubtedly would have entered into. . .[Hyslop's scheme] with all of his energy."[88]

Later that year, Hyslop took the first active steps to implement his idea by organizing the American Institute for Scientific Research and by going out to try to find funds for it. Even though James had not supported his request to the Carnegie Institute, Hyslop went back to him for help. "I have had a visit fm. poor Hyslop today," he wrote to Flournoy from Cambridge on October 11, 1904. "He deludes himself with the belief that he can raise a large fund of money to endow psychical research with, and is trying to do so."[89] But Hyslop did not think himself deluded at all. Numerous private meetings were held with interested persons in 1904. In 1905 larger meetings were held in the sumptuous Waldorf-Astoria Hotel as word of Hyslop's plan spread and interest in it increased. In consequence, a fund of $25,000 was accumulated and the Institute was in readiness; Hyslop's plan was about to be fulfilled.

With Hodgson's unexpected death, Hyslop's entire scheme was severely threatened. Everything came to a standstill pending the determination of the fate of the American branch of the SPR and the resolution of what was to be done with the Piper records.

Hyslop did all in his power to frustrate London's claim to these records. In a letter to his friend Dr. Weston D. Bayley he confided his plan:

> It has occurred to me to get the option of publishing such records from all sitters I can in order to checkmate the English move. Will you give me that option on your records? I do not ask for the right, but only the option at present that we may present a formidable front to any vandalism they may want to commit. . . . Don't waste time in the matter. I know two other parties who have had almost hundreds of sittings and if we can secure this option we can negotiate with the English on equal terms.[90]

Hyslop also proposed to send a circular letter to all members of the American branch to let them know of the intention of the London group with respect to the Piper material and to give them an opportunity to lodge a protest. Hyslop himself could not do so openly. "I shall not take any active part in this, but remain outside," he said. "As I am a candidate for the temporary Secretaryship I cannot act in the matter."[91] He hoped to secure the appointment as Hodgson's successor in order to retain the Piper records and to carry out a drive to increase membership in, and obtain an endowment for, the American branch. But he was not sanguine about his chances of getting the appointment. As he wrote in another letter to Bayley: "I was a candidate for Secretary and I learned that the English Council will have nothing to do with me. They think me indiscreet, and if progressive and constructive work is indiscretion I plead guilty and proud of it."[92]

When, in 1906, the English representative came to meet with his opposite numbers in the American branch, he found one of them to be that "indiscreet" man with whom the English wanted nothing to do. The feeling was mutual. "My reasons for not encouraging a meeting at present are these," he wrote

Bayley. "First the Englsish [sic] Council is not amenable to reason to anything American. They have contempt for all Americans and will stick sternly for the legal aspects of the matter. Then Associates have no votes and this only strengthens the power which the Council will use."[93] But, since a meeting was necessary, he was ready. "I am fighting for the Institute," declared Hyslop, and he gave the SPR a

> choice between two policies. Either cooperation along the old lines or the abandonment of this country. . . . I shall never touch psychics again if they do not come to terms. I shall return all the money I have gotten and abandon psychics forever. I cannot do it alone, and if others will not cooperate I shall neither cooperate nor go it alone. . . .
>
> What I must first do is to get them to decide to abandon the Branch, if they won't let me organize it for a large membership and more funds. When they have thus committed themselves we can take more active measures. . . . It is not the Branch that we want to save, but the work and the English policy will neither save the Branch nor the work. With them out of the way we can get money, and I am confident that I can get the money.[94]

In the end, Hyslop got the English to abandon their American branch. It was dissolved. The English had surrendered it, however, only because they were satisfied that dissolution would not mean the end of organized parapsychology in this country.

Hyslop was not so successful with the Piper records. He had hoped to retain them in America in order to publish them. Instead, under an agreement worked out during the negotiations between Piddington and the representatives of the American branch, the records were to be delivered to London to be published, the privacy of the sitters being protected. Thus, the issue generated by the Piper material which had caused tempers to flare was thought by some, such as Bayley, to have been "amicably disposed of."[95]

With the dissolution of the American branch and with "nineteen heavy cases" of records, Hyslop went forward with the American Institute for Scientific Research which he had organized into sections for the investigation of two fields. Its Section "A" was to deal with psychopathology or abnormal psychology. Its Section "B" was to be concerned with what Hyslop called "supernormal psychology" or parapsychology. Section "A" never really got off the ground. But Section "B" became the new and reorganized ASPR.[96] One of the Institute's aims was to organize and endow investigations into telepathy, clairvoyance, mediumship, and kinetic phenomena,[97] this work to be carried on by Section "B."

Hyslop was to be its secretary with the work being done at his residence.[98] He once wrote his son, "My work is missionary, not mercenary."[99] With no more interest in money-making now than when he was a dreamer on the farm back in Xenia, he declined to accept any remuneration for his full-time work in order that all money might be applied to the work of the ASPR. He was able to sustain himself on a small income with some returns from his lectures and writings.[100] It was not until 1916 that the ASPR had enough money in its coffers to pay him a small salary.[101]

Office Records

But the new ASPR was launched on a "sea of troubles" against which Hyslop, like Hamlet, had to take arms. Hodgson's death had caught James, Hyslop and everyone associated with the SPR branch in America entirely by surprise. No one, except Lucy Edmunds, the assistant secretary of the branch, was familiar with its records and she had left the office. "I shall need some rest from this thing for a time," she wrote Hyslop, "there has been so much unpleasantness and injustice in various ways."[102] Perhaps she had in mind the bitterness that existed between the English SPR and the American branch over the Piper records and the strained relations between the English and Hyslop.

Hyslop was overwhelmed by the crates of records that had been turned over to him—overwhelmed and puzzled. What were these records? Were any missing? Among those he received were clippings of various kinds. When he wrote to the former secretary about them, Lucy Edmunds described for him the office practice she and Hodgson had followed. Newspaper clippings which had seemed worthy of note were placed in an alphabetical file. If replies to letters of inquiry showed that a case was promising, it was filed in a case file. If found to be without foundation, it was filed "set-off." Cuttings not worth writing about were placed in scrapbooks. Lucy Edmunds assured Hyslop: "You have now got them all."[103]

New Materials

But the cuttings were a meager source of material and placed the ASPR in a predicament. With the transmission to England of the important Piper records which Hodgson had accumulated, and the departure of Mrs. Piper to England where she was to remain for at least a year to be studied by the SPR, the ASPR was in desperate need of new material and new subjects for investigations and experiments. It was necessary, Hyslop wrote: "to begin the work of collection anew in this country. . . . [I]t may require several years work to arrive at that point of interest which the collection of Dr. Hodgson had established."[104]

Financial Needs

The Institute envisaged by Hyslop involved extensive as well as expensive investigations. It had another need which Hyslop voiced:

The time has gone by when we should rely upon the sporadic and voluntary contribution of individuals for the sole evidence of the super-normal and some effort should be made in earnest to place the investigations upon the same substantial basis as is enjoyed by other phenomena. It has been made all the more imperative by the dissolution of the American Branch, which never had funds enough to do its work rightly. I wish in the inauguration of this new movement to keep its financial needs as prominent as the importance of its work....[105]

Membership fees were essential but were criticized at once as a radical change from what the English had done. Hyslop told Bayley:

I understand the criticism which may be made of our fees. I knew it would be made when it started, but the following facts make the difference. 1. The English Society has a sufficient endowment to pay for an office and expenses. 2. Men of means and leisure do the work and make no charges. 3. The same men provide additional funds for the publications when needed. We are not supplied with any of these advantages.... We must have these fees or stop, and it makes no difference to me whether it goes on or stops. I shall go to the woods when I stop.[106]

Although a preliminary fund of $25,000 had been obtained for the work of the American Institute for Scientific Research, the new ASPR needed $10,000 annually for its investigations. Hyslop perceived that, besides membership fees, an endowment fund was necessary if the ASPR's work was to continue. In 1907 he campaigned for a permanent endowment fund and devised a scheme of types of membership whose contributions would establish it.[107] Seven years later, the financial situation was still grave. Membership fees were not enough to cover expenses. They fell short of the cost of the ASPR's publications and there was no money for investigations. The small general fund which had had to be tapped to make up for the deficit in membership dues was exhausted. Hyslop was compelled to tell the membership:

[W]e must now emphasize the necessity of an endowment fund adequate to meet the situation, or conclude that the people in this country are not willing to support the work as it is carried on. It must cease unless it is endowed.... We cannot think of undertaking this task until we obtain an adequate endowment, one that will enable us also to obtain proper assistants in the work, trained scientific minds with experience in abnormal psychology, who will have patience enough to undertake a large task. It is useless to try such work without endowment.[108]

Gertrude O. Tubby

One of the "proper assistants" Hyslop needed was a good secretary who would take careful stenographic notes of mediumistic sittings and do office work. Gertrude Ogden Tubby, who had heard Hyslop lecture in 1906 and had her interest in parapsychology aroused, undertook these duties in 1907. She remained loyally at his side for the next thirteen years.

Reorganization

In another letter to Dr. Bayley, Hyslop said: "I am busy with the preliminary steps for reorganization. I shall send out circulars immediately...."[109] But to whom were the circulars to be sent? A good mailing list was needed in addition to the ASPR's comparatively small number of members. Hyslop approached the publisher Isaac Funk with an offer to purchase the subscription lists of the popular *Literary Digest.* Funk replied: "You know not what you ask when you ask for the use of the subscription lists.... Not long ago we refused $7500 for that identical privilege. I presume our Executive Committee would refuse an offer of $10,000...."[110] Although there is no reason to believe that *The Literary Digest* mailing list was purchased, the ASPR membership did increase after Hyslop became the ASPR's manager. On June 20, 1906, the ASPR had only 170 members.[111] By the end of November 1907, it had 677.[112]

But many more were needed. One way of increasing membership was lecture tours whose results, however, were disappointing: "The increase of membership has not been what it ought to have been, judging from the kind of interest manifested in the lectures."[113] A second way was described by Hyslop in another letter to Bayley:

> I want especially to consider ways and means of cooperating with local bodies interested in psychic research all over this country. We can not only increase our members in this way, but prevent the scattering of experiments and work generally. We must concentrate the work.[114]

He developed this idea more fully in a subsequent issue of JASPR:

> In thus encouraging [the formation of local societies] we do not mean that it is advisable to have a number of wholly independent bodies working alone, but groups of members of the central body organized for more serious interest and assistance in the general aims of the Institute.... Each independent group should have as much freedom of action as possible.... [T]he main reason for general co-operation is the necessity of combining the results of investigation in a way to give them the collective force of which they may be capable and the largest possible scientific interest and form. Phenomena of this kind have too long been allowed to perish or to lose their value simply because they have not received the imprimatur of scientific bodies....[115]

Board of Trustees

Another requisite was an impressive Board of Trustees for the Institute. As Funk wrote Hyslop, "[N]o man with a reputation for science would risk it in a movement of this kind unless there is a strong board behind it."[116] The Board Hyslop succeeded in putting together consisted of Dr. James J. Putnam, Dr. Minot J. Savage and Dr. R. Heber Newton. A professor from a large university, however, wondered "why, after twenty odd years in this country, no men better known for psychology and scientific work . . . can be found for your Board."[117]

Within a short time, Putnam and Savage resigned, the former for reasons not disclosed, the latter because of ill health. Newton tendered his resignation because of what Hyslop called a "prejudice against clergymen on such a Board,"[118] but later withdrew his resignation.[119] Hyslop extended invitations to several people he thought suitable as Board members. The kinds of responses he received can be gathered from his bitter letter to Bayley: "Baldwin declines . . . I have not heard from Sanford of Clarke and Lindley of Indiana. They are too cowardly to try."[120] But surely, Hyslop thought, George B. Dorr, a former vice-president of the American Branch of the SPR and one of the administrators of Hodgson's estate, would accept. Dorr replied to Hyslop's invitation: "I dread at the moment undertaking any fresh responsibility. . . . I do not like to go upon Committees without taking an active part in their work . . . and that I could not do at present."[121] Although couched in diplomatic language, it was yet another refusal. And where was William James who had been a staunch supporter and a leader of the ASPR for two decades? Of all people in America, he should have been on the Board but he was not.

Hyslop encountered difficulty in finding people willing to go on the Institute's Board primarily because of two factors. Not many people fully understood the purpose of its Board of Trustees. Hyslop therefore explained that the Board was to be

> constituted of men having a national reputation so far as that is possible that it may be the custodian and disburser of the funds contributed to the investigations and practical work of its Sections. . . . The Institute is modelled after the Carnegie Institute in Washington. . . . The Board of the American Institute will simply stand for the importance and respectability of the work and will be responsible for the care of its endowments.[122]

But no such formal explication could remove what was probably the real reason in the way of getting the people Hyslop wanted on the Board. It was his manner. As Funk told him: "If you will pardon me for saying it, it seems to me that you do not try hard enough to conciliate opposition. On the other hand, you antagonize and very largely so by not being considerate of the experiences of other people who feel that they also are able to investigate. . . ."[123] Funk was not alone in his criticism of Hyslop. James died in 1910 without ever having taken a seat on the Board of Trustees and without ever having cooperated with Hyslop in his Institute or new ASPR. Why? Because, while James admired Hyslop's methods of investigation, his admiration went no further. He once confided to Flourney that "[Hyslop] has all the heroic qualities of human nature and none of the indispensable ones"; and to Hodgson he wrote, "[Hyslop] has no more notion of policy than a street terrier . . . Hyslop is too crude and hot."[124]

Relations with the SPR

Apparently there were some who regarded the Institute and Section "B," now cut loose from the SPR, as a rival of the SPR. Hyslop was at pains to remove this misconception, too. Rivalry in the field of psychical research would be unfortunate if not fatal. He made it plain that:

It will be the policy of the American Society to encourage all who are able to remain members of the English Society while they are asked to join the new American Society. Both Societies have the same object and merely occupy different fields in which it is more convenient to do the work independently than in union. There is to be no competition in their organization and investigations. All that are interested and have the means should support both of them, as it is financial assistance that is most needed for conducting their work rightly. With this understanding there need be nothing but goodwill and a co-operative spirit in carrying on the investigations for which they exist.[125]

Objects of the ASPR

There were other misconceptions, both among the public and ASPR members, about its objects. Some members were angered or left the Society because material was not presented in the *Journal* as propaganda for the spiritistic creed, while others fumed whenever material was presented which even suggested a spiritistic hypothesis. The issue of a life after death was unavoidable "and many people, in their interest and impatience, want that matter settled, in great haste."[126] Hyslop found it necessary to call attention to these misunderstandings of the nature of the new Society. In one of the most important writings bearing on the work of the ASPR, he said:

[I]t is easy to forget that the object of the Society is not to prove any preconceived theory of things. It may find itself forced to accept a theory, but it does not predetermine a view which it will seek to prove. . . .
[T]he object of the Society is not to prove any special theory of phenomena whatever. It is a body for the collection of facts in various fields of the unusual. . . .[127]

He summarized the features which made up the objects of the ASPR as the collection and presentation of unusual human experiences, the subordination of explanations and conclusions to the presentation of facts and the publication of all the details of records.[128] Primarily, the aim was to collect facts, not defend

hypotheses which can come only after the facts are observed. The task required
the greatest patience:

> It required physical science two hundred and fifty years simply to
> prepare for the last fifty years' work, and physical science has infinitely
> larger advantages than psychic research ever had or can be expected to
> have until a differently endowed human race has been evolved.
> Astronomy had to take time to prove the existence of meteors and
> physics was slow to admit the travelling ball of electricity. Psychic
> research may be far longer establishing the simplest of its claims or
> possibilities. Haste is not possible.[129]

Proceedings and Journals

It was important to Hyslop that the work done by the ASPR should be
made known to the public. Its publications, the *Proceedings* and the *Journal*,
were to accomplish this end. The *Proceedings*, to be published annually, were
to consist of detailed records and scientific discussions. The *Journal* was
thought of as a less pretentious organ which would supply readers with general
articles, cases, book reviews, correspondence and editorial matters.[130] The
editorials served as platforms not only for explaining the needs and objects of
the ASPR and for discussing questions raised by correspondence; they also
allowed Hyslop to defend against critics. The policy of the *Journal*, Hyslop
said, was "to show no mercy to men who do not adhere to the strict truth in
the treatment of the subject."[131]

Relations with the Academic World

The publications of the ASPR were beset by a clear absence of articles written by academic people. Hyslop was sharply aware of this deficiency as well as
distressed by it:

> [T]he academic world takes no interest in psychic research, or if it has
> any interest in any quarters is not disposed to take part in it when not
> a part of the college task. Most of the representatives in the colleges do
> not take any interest in the subject at all, unless a casual one. Few see
> the real importance of the work and in spite of many efforts to induce
> co-operation on their part we have not succeeded in getting a single
> man in the universities and colleges to signify any co-operative interest
> in the subject. Until the orthodox bodies of the world awaken to the
> importance of the work it will have to be done in the present manner
> or not be done at all.[132]

Although an academic himself, Hyslop had a low opinion of academics:
"All university men are shy," he said. "I never saw such born cowards in my
life as they are."[133]

On the other hand, some members of the academic world were able to overcome their shyness to take a great deal of interest in the ASPR and psychical research although not the kind for which Hyslop had hoped. They regarded psychical research as a subversive element. As its champion, Hyslop had to defend it against professors of psychology like Joseph Jastrow of the University of Wisconsin[134] and Hugo Muensterberg of Harvard University.[135] In his defense against the latter, he said that Muensterberg's attack was "the kind of evasion, prevarication and misrepresentation which this subject has to meet at the hands of persons who cannot keep company with the best men in Europe and America."[136] The ASPR *Journal* did not remain silent, either, when Amy Tanner of Clark University published her *Studies in Spiritism* as a repudiation of that creed.[137] An introduction written by G. Stanley Hall, president of Clark University and once a vice-president of the old ASPR, was appended to the book. In his introduction, Hall expressed the hope that the book would "mark a turn of the tide" against the spiritism he despised—a reminder of the spectre of the "anti-spiritual bias" that had haunted the ASPR when it was first established. But when Hyslop had finished with his crushing criticisms of Tanner's book, it was left a rubble of factual errors, untruths and omissions.[138]

Internal Problems

As though struggles with critics outside the ASPR were not enough, it was troubled also by internecine conflicts. One involved Eusapia Palladino, the Italian physical medium who had excited great interest in Europe and had been investigated by Lodge, Richet and Myers[139] and again at Cambridge by Sidgwick, Alice Johnson, Myers and Hodgson.[140] (Chapter 1 chronicles Hodgson's role in the decision made by the English Society to drop her as a fraud.)

Hereward Carrington had become a member of the ASPR Council in 1907.[141] He was also an assistant to Hyslop and continued in that capacity until 1908, during which time he established his reputation as an ASPR investigator. His official connection with the ASPR ceased[142] because the perennial lack of funds made it necessary to dispense with his services.[143] The first part of his book *The Physical Phenomena of Spiritualism*[144] was a ruthless exposure of fraudulent mediums. In 1908, Carrington investigated the phenomena at Lily Dale, New York, one of the leading Spiritualist camps in America. His investigation brought to light the fraudulent, sometimes farcical, nature of the phenomena.[145] It was not surprising, therefore, that he should have played a prominent part in the case of Eusapia Palladino.

Despite the English Society's verdict, however, interest in her continued on the Continent and, after further experiments with her, it appeared that she might possess paranormal faculties after all. The SPR therefore decided to reopen its investigation of her. The Committee it appointed included Hereward Carrington. During the autumn of 1908, Carrington persuaded the

medium to hold sittings with the SPR Committee at the Hotel Victoria in
Naples. At the conclusion of the sittings, the Committee issued a report which
appeared in the English *Proceedings*[146] in which Carrington recorded his "absolute conviction of the reality of at least some of the phenomena. . . . [T]he
results witnessed by us were not due to fraud or trickery on the part of
Eusapia."[147] He reaffirmed in the ASPR *Journal* that "[s]ome of the
phenomena. . . [I] regard as absolutely and finally proved. The phenomena of
levitations of the table, raps, and the movement of physical objects without
contact, are . . . established beyond all doubt. . . ."[148]

Carrington was ready to bring the medium to America for experiments
and asked Hyslop for ASPR funds for this purpose. Hyslop refused and Carrington sought and obtained money from other sources.[149] He brought Eusapia
Palladino to America where experiments with her were conducted by Professor
Jastrow and others during 1909 and 1910.[150] Although Hyslop had refused
funds for the medium's trip, he did supply a stenographer to make records of
the experiments. But when newspaper and magazine reporters questioned
Hyslop, he said that he thought the mode of approaching and investigating
the Palladino case was wrong. His conservative attitude was interpreted as
"jealousy" and, after he was accused of being "a dog in the manger" in the
case,[151] Hyslop withdrew. Once again, just as among members of the SPR and
savants in Europe, the case of Eusapia Palladino and Hyslop's part in it aroused
sharp emotions in the ASPR. "[T]he effect of the Palladino affair," wrote
Hyslop, "was a loss of 300 members at one stroke, and we have not more than
recovered that number since that time."[152] The "Palladino affair" also created
an open disagreement between Hyslop and Carrington over the methods of investigation and the medium herself which spilled over into the *Journal.* Hyslop
stated:

> If the men who essayed to investigate her in this country had first tried
> to determine whether she was a hysteric or not they would have saved
> all the foolish discussion that has centered about her phenomena. It
> would have offered a scientific alternative between fraud and miracle
> for investigating it and the problem taken out of the hands of
> mountebanks for its solution.[153]

Carrington was irritated. "You seem to be under the impression," he told
Hyslop, " — quite common but quite erroneous — that Eusapia Palladino was
completely 'exposed' in this country, and her phenomena shown to be nothing
but tricks. Nothing could be further from the truth."[154] Hyslop responded: "I
have not been under any impression whatever that Eusapia Palladino was completely exposed in this country or any other. I have not believed that there was
any 'exposure' whatever except of the people who investigated her."[155] But this
did not mean that the phenomena were genuine. It meant only that the investigation was poorly conducted. Hyslop maintained that the medium was an
hysteric and should have been investigated as such.[156]

Carrington retorted that it made no difference whether or not the
medium was an hysteric. The fundamental question was whether she possessed

paranormal powers and could move objects without contact.[157] Hyslop could not agree:

> The real question for a really scientific man is not whether telekinesis is true or not, but what are the exact facts and all the facts when any such claim is made. . . . The truly scientific man does not want to prove or disprove anything, but to ascertain the facts and what they mean will be determined later.[158]

Hyslop had another internal fight on his hands. For more than a decade, he personally investigated, chose and edited all the material published in the *Journal* and *Proceedings*. He managed the ASPR single-handedly. Gertrude Tubby wrote of these years: "The weight of a most lonely and unshared responsibility was upon Dr. Hyslop."[159] His management led to the development of an opposition faction which campaigned against him and tried to oust him from control over the affairs of the ASPR. "One member of this opposition group," wrote George H. Hyslop, "had given generously to the endowment of the Society and apparently assumed that the power of the purse strings entitled the donor to a dominating voice in the scientific program of the organization."[160]

As a member of the Board of Trustees as well as a donor, Theodate Pope objected vigorously that "the practical work of the Society in almost every aspect has rested with the Secretary and Treasurer. Not only was investigation, research, publication, and correspondence in his hands, but likewise the administration of funds and their disbursement. . . . [T]he main activities of the Society are concentrated in one person. . . ."[161] And Edwin W. Friend, who had been appointed by Hyslop in 1914 as his assistant, objected that parapsychology "is no longer a province to be mastered by one individual."[162] Their opposition faded away and they were forced to resign, however, when the Board of Trustees supported Hyslop.

Hyslop's Publications in Parapsychology

Hyslop had done considerable writing in connection with his interests in logic, ethics and philosophy. He considered his "more pretentious works"[163]: "Elements of Logic" (1892), "The Ethics of Hume" (1893), "Democracy" (1899), "Logic and Argument" (1899) and "Syllabus of Psychology" (1899). His articles on these and related subjects were published in several organs including the *Andover Review, The Yale and New Englander*, the *Forum, The Unitarian Review, Mind* and *The Philosophical Review*.

The fact that Newbold remarked in 1920 that Hyslop could be seen "in recent years sitting unnoticed at the meeting of the American Philosophical Association"[164] suggests that not only had his stand on parapsychology made him an "outcast" but also that his publications had not carved out for him a very high niche in philosophy.

But Hyslop produced very valuable material in parapsychology. There were his six books: *Science and a Future Life* (1905), *Borderland of Psychical Research* (1906), *Enigmas of Psychical Research* (1906), *Psychical Research and* the Resurrection (1908), *Life After Death: Problems of a Future Life and Its Nature* (1918), and *Contact with the Other World* (1919). He also generated experimental reports so bulky and so rich in thoroughness and detail and data that nothing like them has been seen since in American parapsychology. These reports are "his greatest monument; and no marble shaft could be more imperishable."[165]

His first major experimental account of personal sittings he had had with Mrs. Piper was published in 1901 in the English *Proceedings.*[166] The issue as he saw it in this report was whether spiritism or telepathy exclusively from living people was the more rational explanation for the Piper phenomena, in particular, messages allegedly received from his deceased relatives. He concluded his lengthy account by saying that these messages forced him to "give my adhesion to the theory that there is a future life and persistence of personal identity . . . [and] to tolerate the spiritistic theory as rationally possible and respectable, as against stretching telepathy and its adjuncts into infinity and omniscience."[167]

Hyslop's other reports include his investigations of the medium Mrs. Smead (Mrs. Willis M. Cleaveland);[168] the case of Frederic L. Thompson[169] followed by observations on the mediumistic records in the Thompson case;[170] the paranormal ability to diagnose disease;[171] sittings with mediums such as Mrs. Keeler and Miss W.;[172] a further report on sittings with Mrs. Piper after Hodgson's death;[173] a psychological study of Anna Burton in whose presence physical phenomena occurred.[174] Of these, the Thompson case, in which a goldsmith who was not an artist was overcome with an impulse to paint and recreated the style of a deceased painter, Robert Swain Gifford, may be the most interesting. While some of the mediumistic sittings in the case did not provide evidence of any direct communications from the dead Gifford, the case suggests possession of a living subject by a dead person. The case also is a good illustration of Hyslop's method of "cross-references"—his use of different mediums to determine whether there was any similarity among communications.

After William James died, Hyslop embarked on a series of mediumistic experiments with Mrs. Smead and Mrs. Chenoweth (Mrs. Minnie R. Soule) to attempt communications with James, Carroll D. Wright and others.[175] These experiments were followed in 1913 by an essay by Hyslop on the subconscious[176] which dealt with the application of psychology to the psychological issues raised by mediumship and is considered a "special contribution."[177] More reports were written by Hyslop as the years went by: the study of an automatist whose singing voice seemed influenced by a discarnate entity;[178] an investigation of a trumpet medium;[179] another into spirit photography;[180] a report on an automatist's unverified statements.[181] In 1917, as a result of the work he did in the Thompson case, Hyslop made a massive analysis of the Doris Fischer case of multiple personality.[182] In 1919 Hyslop analyzed a case of mediumship in order to present his theory of the "pictographic process," a term he invented to describe a process by which purported deceased communicators elicit sensory images in the minds of mediums which correspond to, but do not necessarily represent, reality.[183] In addition to this major contribution to parapsychology, there are his sittings with Mrs. Chenoweth, published posthumously in 1923, in which purported communications from the mother of Doris Fischer were received. In Prince's words, "[T]here has probably never been printed a more evidential group of communications."[184]

Hyslop's Support of the Survival Hypothesis

Hyslop's books and reports should have accorded him more of a hearing and gained him, the ASPR and parapsychology more respect than he and they received. A chief reason for his failure, and it is the same today as it was in Hyslop's day, is that many people of science and academic pursuits have always found it difficult to understand why some ostensibly intelligent and sane people, from lawyers to psychiatrists to professors of ethics and logic, should be interested in survival after death. This subject is ignored or ridiculed by scientists and academicians, to a large extent because their minds are chained to a materialism which asserts that consciousness is a function of the physical organism and perishes with it. This assumption made Hyslop's frequent assertions, such as "[p]ersonally I regard the fact of survival after death as scientifically proved"[185] appear the product of, if not his religious training or terrible childhood fear of death, a "will to believe" which dulled his critical faculties. Even critics inside parapsychology attacked such statements as loose expressions resulting from loose thinking. So did L.P. Jacks, philosopher and once president of the SPR, say: "The statement of Professor Hyslop that survival has been proved by evidence is one I never read without regret."[186] Hyslop's support of the survival hypothesis has also been attacked more frankly as almost "unbalanced."[187] It not only fettered his efforts to organize a Board of Trustees — "I have tried several people and did not succeed. They will not associate with a spiritistic secretary. There's the rub"[188] — it was a cause of some of the hostility shown toward the ASPR and parapsychology. "Academic and scientific support," he wrote, "probably on account of the avowed spiritistic sympathies of [the ASPR's] secretary, has been weak."[189]

It is legitimate to criticize the "will to believe" but it is also important to remember that the "will to disbelieve" also can impair critical judgment. In any case, a more impartial study of Hyslop may show that he did not come by his sympathies for spiritism because of any "will to believe." Professor Gardiner made this clear: "It is quite a mistake to suppose that [Hyslop] started out to 'demonstrate spiritualism.'"[190] Professor Newbold added in 1920: "When I first knew him, nearly thirty years ago, he was an agnostic as regards the life after death."[191]

In fact, in 1892, when Hyslop first read Hodgson's report on Mrs. Piper, his agnosticism developed into skepticism. He saw clearly the spiritistic suggestions in the report. But, he said, "I could not accept the spiritistic theory, and for want of a more intelligent view of the phenomena accepted the telepathic hypothesis as the possible explanation of it."[192] In a few years, Hyslop was to read over and over again another report by Hodgson on Mrs. Piper in which G.P. had appeared as a communicator and Hodgson had argued for a spiritistic interpretation of the case.[193] Each time he read it, "the spiritistic theory grew in strength. I saw no answer to it."[194] But still he wanted to do some experiments on his own. And as a result of sittings with Mrs. Piper during which Robert Hyslop appeared as the chief communicator, he issued his 1901 report on her trance communications in which he expressed his belief in the theory of a future life.

Hyslop's work with Mrs. Piper and other mediums made him reject the telepathic hypothesis as an explanation for mediumistic information unknown to the sitters, experimenters or other living persons yet susceptible of identification through means given in the communication. He once told his friend Miles Dawson that such results could be explained away only by extending telepathy to preposterous limits. "Such," he said, "would make telepathy a greater marvel than spirit communication."[195] The telepathy theory, he believed, was not legitimate because it went far beyond the experimental evidence for telepathy. Yet, even after he was convinced of the spiritistic theory, Bayley tells us, Hyslop did not swerve from scientific caution in his writings and presentations and was always open to intelligent criticism.[196]

Hyslop was impatient with the skeptical Helmholzes and Faradays in science who stand aloof from the phenomena of parapsychology which might suggest the persistence of consciousness after death or who scoff at them on *a priori* grounds:

> [S]cience, content, without thorough inquiry, to confine its investigations to the physical world in which it has acheived so much, will not open its eyes to anomalies in the realm of mind and nature, and so degenerates into a dogmatism exactly like that of theology.[197]

He had an answer for those who laugh at attempts to investigate survival scientifically: "Such attempts, if the facts prove it or appear to prove it, will only react on the man who sneers, and result only in the forfeiture of his influence on the community."[198]

There is no doubt that another of the significant effects of his father's strict religious orthodoxy was that Hyslop "had imbibed an interest in a future life from the strenuous teaching which I had on this subject."[199] But he also saw in the belief in a future life some very important ethical considerations. One of these considerations is that all actions and ethics pertain to the realization of some end in the future, not in the past or present. Nature would not implant this idea in human beings and then make life meaningless by cutting it short at the grave.[200] The function of the belief in a future life is to assure us that nature allows us a future in which ends can be fulfilled[201] and to show us that nature values human personality above all else and does not snuff it out when the physical organism is dissolved.[202]

He rejected materialism which "can never reproduce anything but a succession of individuals with transient mental states. Sensation and copies of sensation in memory and imagination are all it can secure and these only for a short time. The individual personality is snuffed out of existence."[203]

The question for Hyslop was: Does anything besides the physical body exist which might survive the destruction of the organism? A future life had meaning for him only if personal consciousness and memory survived. This scientific question could not be resolved by appeals to ethical considerations or the consolations of a belief in survival. Hyslop used mediumistic experiments to answer the question by obtaining intelligent messages relating to the identity of deceased persons, messages unknown to the persons through whom they came.

Other Criticisms and Defenses

The annoyance of the English SPR with Hyslop was not his preoccupation with survival but that their "indiscreet" vice-president had fought hard against them in 1906 and used every device to prevent the records of Hodgson's 173 sittings with Mrs. Piper from falling into London's hands. In retrospect, Hyslop's resistance seems justified regardless of whether the English were legally entitled to the records. And although 80 years have passed, the matter of the Hodgson-Piper material still may be more than of just passing interest to us.

For it has turned out that the agreement to publish the records which was made at the time of the dissolution of the American branch of the SPR, in Bayley's words, "was culpably ignored in London."[204] Only one case from all the records has been published by the English SPR since the delivery of the records. In 1910, the sittings with Mrs. Piper in which communications purported to come from Bennie Junot who died at the age of 17 were published.[205] The remainder of the Hodgson-Piper material, however, has never seen the light of day.

In fairness to the English, the publication of lengthy records of all the sittings with Mrs. Piper would have been expensive. The SPR Council once refused to publish one of Hyslop's records because of expense[206] so that Hyslop paid over $1,000 for its printing.[207] Whether the English were right or wrong, nevertheless a possible treasure of survival material provided by a devoted investigator and an extraordinary medium still lies under the dust of time in the SPR's files. It may not be too late for a researcher of the future to rescue from neglect potentially rich survival evidence from the "Golden Age" of mediumship. As Stevenson has observed, "evidence that was once strong does not become weaker with the passing of time in the minds of discriminating persons

62 Out of the Ashes

who are well aware that not all periods in history are equally suited to the bringing forth of certain types of evidence."[208]

The charges made against Hyslop by Pope and Friend when they resigned from the ASPR in 1915 have been reechoed recently by the historian R. Laurence Moore: Hyslop ran the ASPR "like a dictator."[209] It was a one-man rule and Hyslop was no angel. James thought him crude. Funk told Hyslop bluntly: "[Y]ou antagonize."[210] Hyslop's conduct in the Palladino case seems to have been costly to the ASPR.

Hyslop's writings were criticized not only for their inadequacies[211] but for his convoluted style. James's letters in 1901 and 1902 are full of complaints about it. To Hodgson he remarked: "I think Hyslop's discussions and methods admirable in all but literary style," and in his correspondence with Flournoy, he said: "[Hyslop's] report is intolerably ill written and I have not been able to read the whole of it."[212] Sir Oliver Lodge deplored the fact that Hyslop did not have "the gift of expressing himself in clear and simple English. Throughout his voluminous writings the sentences are frequently involved, and sometimes so curiously constructed that it is difficult to disentangle their meaning."[213] Sir William Barrett lamented similarly: "Hyslop would have gained a wider and more respectful hearing had he cultivated a better and more restrained style of writing, and been less dogmatic and combative in the expression of his opinions."[214]

If Hyslop's publications were themselves a psychic phenomenon which deterred others from reading them, it was, Gardiner thought, because Hyslop "cared little about style; what he cared greatly about was thoroughness"[215] and, indeed, the cases reported in his bulky reports were described down to the minutest detail so that the facts could be studied. He felt "that the American public did not like brevity, but wanted full measure and overflowing in the discussion of any subject."[216]

Perhaps Hyslop was combative and dogmatic because of his strict moral character, which also made him intolerant of skeptics who were not truthful or sincere. He was also straitlaced. Once he had an encounter with Theodate Pope who sent someone from her lawyer's office to Hyslop's home to inspect the ASPR's books of account. Hyslop refused to admit the man. Then he came back to the library where the books were kept. His face was white with anger and, in a loud voice, he uttered his choicest epithet: "Sugar Beets! Inspect the books—makes me so mad, Sugar beets!"[217] "Sugar beets" was the best Hyslop could do under trying circumstances.

To describe Hyslop as a "dictator" seems unduly harsh in view of the support given him by the ASPR Board of Trustees and in the light of the opinions of those who were close to him at the time. A Christian clergyman called Hyslop "a secular saint."[218] Gertrude O. Tubby, his secretary, said of Hyslop:

> Mankind he loved.... To have worked under his direction and train-
> ing ... is a privilege as rare as it is desirable. Moral, intellectual and
> spiritual integrity, scientific understanding and patience,

philosophical and religious poise, an appreciation of art . . . these are characteristics of James Hervey Hyslop. . . .[219]

Walter F. Prince, who had been appointed by Hyslop in 1917 as ASPR research officer, was another co-worker. He described Hyslop as

the most delightful man to work with. . . . We often disagreed and debated, but with the utmost good feeling. . . . [Hyslop] was always just. . . . Dr. Hyslop knew what rank he occupied in the field of psychical research, but he knew it without elation. Few men who have accomplished anything have been so devoid of vanity. . . .[220]

Finally from his son: "[Father] believed that each man has his work in the world to perform. He chose his task, and to its completion gave all that he had. His race was well run."[221]

Hyslop was the first American academician to give all his time to parapsychology. He demonstrated his devotion to this field by refusing to accept any salary from the ASPR, and his energy and industry, as evidenced by his voluminous reports, cannot be doubted. Barrett wrote of Hyslop: "No man could long stand this drain on his mental and physical energies, and Hyslop literally sacrificed his life in the cause of psychical research."[222]

In 1920, Hyslop suffered a stroke. His recovery from it was only partial. On June 17 in New Jersey, his death brought his management of the ASPR to an end.

In assessing Hyslop's contribution to parapsychology in America, we cannot fail to realize that, without him, collective parapsychological research in America probably would have ceased with the dissolution of the ASPR in 1906. In 1927, when the ASPR acquired title to a house at 15 Lexington Avenue in New York City to use as its headquarters, it was decided to honor Hyslop by designating the place "Hyslop House." In reality, American parapsychology is "Hyslop House" because it was he who saved it from collapse and laid the foundations for its continuance.

Sometimes Hyslop's achievements are not clearly recognized. One critic wrote: "Given his original aims, Hyslop accomplished relatively little as head of the ASPR."[223] In history, different interpretations of facts are inevitable. But this interpretation of Hyslop's aims and accomplishments is a hasty error of judgment. Hyslop's aim was to organize and endow parapsychology to be carried out in America by the new ASPR. He achieved this aim (1) by becoming its founder and secretary; (2) by becoming, next to James, the foremost American leader in the field; (3) by obtaining through lectures and articles an endowment of about $185,000 for the prosecution of the ASPR's work; (4) by assuring, as administrator of the ASPR, its stability, direction and growth; (5) by presenting, as editor, the fruits of its work in the ASPR's *Journal* and *Proceedings;* (6) by the gathering of facts as the ASPR's chief investigator; and (7) as the author of voluminous and detailed records and other writings which never abandoned scientific caution. In the words of his son, Hyslop "had done his best to carry a message to the world. . . ."[224]

According to his loyal assistant, Gertrude Tubby, death did not end Hyslop's efforts to deliver his message. Five hours after he died and for some years later, she recorded communications from him, including his sign, through American and European mediums to whom she went incognito. As she wrote: "Surviving mortality, he could do no other than 'keep everlastingly at it,' as he has always said."[225]

3
The Blue-Eyed Woman (1921–1938)

Commentary

With the passing of Hyslop, the bell tolled again for parapsychology. Although Hyslop's death did not result in the dissolution of the one organization in America investigating the paranormal, as Hodgson's had, it caused a time of turbulence in the organization and the alienation from it of important figures. It was an era of a parapsychological diaspora. It was the era of a psychologist from England who "dabbled" in parapsychology and of a Methodist and Episcopal minister led from his church into abnormal psychology and parapsychology by a visitor. It was also the era of the first laboratory in which investigators could work on psi experiments. But primarily it was the period of a blue-eyed woman "thought to have been a saint by some and a whore by others"[1] to whom can be linked the eventual appearance of parapsychology in an academic setting and the transformation in America of psychical research, a qualitative investigation, into parapsychology, a quantitative one.

Chronological Narrative

1921

William McDougall, a British psychologist who became a professor at Harvard University, was elected to the presidency of the American Institute for Scientific Research. A Board of Trustees was also elected to care for the affairs of the Institute and ASPR. They included Hyslop's son, Dr. George H. Hyslop, John I.D. Bristol, Lawson Purdy and others.

McDougall accepted the presidency, however, only on condition that the highest standards of evidence be maintained. He insisted that a scientific council consisting of qualified people be appointed to furnish advice and criticism. Such an Advisory Council was appointed and included some eminent names: Joseph Jastrow, professor of psychology at the University of Wisconsin; Waldemar Kaempffert, former editor of the *Scientific American;* William

65

R. Newbold, professor of philosophy at the University of Pennsylvania; Dr. Morton Prince, professor emeritus of nervous diseases at Tufts College; Elwood Worcester, scholar and rector of Emmanuel Church in Boston; John Coover, professor of psychology at Stanford University, who, in 1917, had reported the results of telepathy tests; and Leonard T. Troland, a psychology instructor at Harvard, who, about 1915–1916, had conducted experiments in telepathy.[2]

Walter Franklin Prince, a clergyman and director of psychotherapeutics at St. Mark's Church in New York City, had been appointed research officer by Hyslop in 1917. It was he who discovered and conducted a prolonged study and treatment of "Doris," a case of multiple personality published by the ASPR in 1915 and 1916. Prince now became research director and editor of the ASPR publications. Soon after this appointment, Prince went first to Mexico to investigate a case of psychometry with considerable evidential value and then on to Copenhagen as the American representative at the First International Congress on Psychical Research.

Gertrude Tubby continued in her post as secretary. Eric J. Dingwall arrived from Cambridge, England, to become director of the Department of Physical Phenomena.

By the end of 1921, the name, too, had been changed. "Institute" was dropped and the name "American Society for Psychical Research, Inc." adopted.

1922

Gardner Murphy, a lecturer in psychology at Columbia who had collaborated with Troland in his telepathy experiments, received support from a fund established at Harvard in the name of Richard Hodgson. Since the fund did not provide enough income, the ASPR subsidized a portion of Murphy's research.[3]

In May, McDougall addressed an audience in Boston in his capacity as ASPR president to stimulate interest in parapsychology and to assail groups indifferent to it including Spiritualists.

The Scientific American, after publishing a number of articles on research in parapsychology, made an interesting offer in its December issue. It would award a prize of $2500 to anyone who, under conditions satisfactory to judges, could produce a spirit photograph and another $2500 for the production of any other kind of visible psychic manifestation. Mental phenomena were not included in the contest.

1923

The Reverend Frederick Edwards was elected president of the ASPR in place of McDougall who became a member of the Board of Trustees. Prince was also replaced by Edwards as editor of the ASPR publications. The ASPR now adopted a more populist policy for its work.

A *Scientific American* committee of judges was appointed. Its five members included, besides McDougall, Prince and Carrington, Professor Daniel F. Comstock, a physicist recently of the Massachusetts Institute of Technology; and the great debunker of mediums, the magician Harry Houdini. J. Malcolm Bird, an associate editor of *Scientific American,* was the committee's secretary. The function of committee members was to judge, his to deal with matters of procedure.

By the appointment of this committee, the ASPR, although not as an official body, was drawn into the picture that was beginning to form because McDougall and Prince, two of the principal figures associated with it, were committee members. The ASPR under Hyslop had had its imbroglios before, such as the Palladino case and Hyslop's management of it. But the ingredients now started to come together for a far more heated one.

The little world of parapsychology and the larger one around it were startled by a thunderclap not heard since the days of D.D. Home and Eusapia Palladino. It came in the person of a physical medium at whose home at 10 Lime Street in Boston and in whose presence strange lights were seen, objects moved, the unequally weighted pans of a scale balanced, an electric bell-box rang. Among the more impressive of the seance phenomena were ectoplasm coming from the right ear of the medium and spreading over her head and teleplasmic hands emerging from her vagina while connected to her body by something like an umbilical cord. As if that were not enough, the medium offered something even more amazing: fingerprints left by her deceased brother "Walter" whose spirit voice carried on lively and witty conversations with sitters and who would endure any description of him they wished to invent except one: "You may call me anything but 'It'!"[4]

The person responsible for these extraordinary occurrences was Mina Crandon, wife of a Boston physician, Le Roi Goddard Crandon. Her mediumship apparently began in June 1923, when six people sat with her around a table which began to tilt and levitate.[5] Blue-eyed, brown-haired, charming, gay, disposed to giggle and very attractive to men, she became known as "Margery."

1924

The second phase of the Margery mediumship started after Bird visited the Crandons in Boston, was caught, as all men were, in the spell cast by Margery and asked her to try for the *Scientific American* prize. She was duly investigated by the *Scientific American* committee who held sittings with her. The impressed Bird published an article about "The 'Margery' Mediumship" (to protect the anonymity of the Crandons), and the newspapers of the day began to tout her powers to the public.

But the committee's verdict, although divided, was adverse to her preten-
sions, McDougall and Prince being among those who were unconvinced.
McDougall believed that there were normal explanations for the phenomena
while Prince's view was that all sittings showed that the phenomena were produced by normal means or by trickery. Prince dismissed the great public attention Margery was receiving as due first to her charm which made men more
emotional than rational and, second, to the preference of the masses for the
sensational as opposed to the drily logical.[6] At the end of 1924, Margery and
her husband invited Dingwall, now research officer of the English SPR, to come
from England to resolve the controversy.

1925

The SPR asked Dingwall to accept the Crandons' invitation. After sittings
with her, during which McDougall and Worcester were present, Dingwall
stated: "I cannot at present affirm my belief in the authenticity of [the]
phenomena."[7]

The Margery mediumship then passed into a new phase when, in April,
the *Scientific American* decided not to award her the $2500 prize and closed
her case, and when, in June, Hudson Hoagland, a graduate student at Harvard, who wanted to use the results for a Ph.D. thesis, and four instructors,
subjected Margery to another investigation in the Harvard department of
psychology.

All at once Bird, who was convinced of Margery's powers and her enthusiastic defender, was made, with Prince, co–research director of the ASPR. Bird's
selection and appointment removed the cover from a feud coming to a boil in
the ASPR between Prince and his supporters and those who opposed him as "too
skeptical," a feud that had already been ignited by the new administration's
policy of popularizing parapsychology and a resultant sharp departure from
the high standards of evidence set by Hyslop to which Prince had adhered.

Amid reports that he had been forced to resign, Prince left the ASPR. Also
disenchanted, Elwood Worcester and Gardner Murphy found it impossible to
remain in the ASPR. In May 1925, with the support of a similarly disenchanted
McDougall, Worcester formed the Boston Society for Psychic Research.
McDougall and Murphy became members of its Council. Prince was the new
organization's research officer and editor and issued the first of many high
quality *Proceedings* and *Bulletins* to be written and edited by him in subsequent years.

With Bird now in control of research, the ASPR took its first step officially
to examine the Margery mediumship. Seances were conducted in 1925 with a
major emphasis on psychokinetic phenomena. Bird's view was that the
phenomena were all valid although he felt that the official seances added
nothing to the pre-existing proof of validity.[8]

In 1925, also, the first series of lectures on the subject of parapsychology to be given in any American university was held by Clark University. Those presenting their views were divided into four groups: convinced of the multiplicity of paranormal phenomena; convinced of their rarity; unconvinced; and antagonistic to claims that paranormal phenomena occur at all. Virtually every familiar voice was scheduled to be heard at the symposium: Sir Oliver Lodge, Sir Arthur Conan Doyle and Dr. Crandon defending his wife in the first group; McDougall, Prince, Hans Driesch of Leipzig and F.C.S. Schiller of Oxford in the second; Gardner Murphy and John E. Coover in the third; and Joseph Jastrow and Houdini in the last. But Houdini died before the date of the lectures, and views from his book *A Magician Among the Spirits* were presented instead. McDougall's paper dealt with the admission of parapsychology into universities as a subject of study. Prince's address included a review of the Margery case to offset what Crandon claimed was "typical of all the best mediumships in history."[9]

In November, the *Atlantic Monthly* carried a report by Hoagland to the effect that the Harvard investigations of Margery had produced no paranormal phenomena and that trickery was behind what had appeared. The ASPR dismissed this investigation as inconclusive as Bird went on record with an emphatic favorable judgment on Margery.[10]

1926

As research officer of the Boston Society, Prince investigated the case of Patience Worth, whose alleged spirit writings had been acclaimed literary genius.

John I.D. Bristol now replaced Edwards as ASPR president. Dr. Crandon and others, including Mark W. Richardson, who were members of a group fiercely loyal to Margery, continued to defend her against a growing body of skeptical investigators.[11] Throughout this year, articles favorable to her mediumship made their way into the ASPR *Journal* as the ASPR steadfastly maintained what Prince called its "heroic defense of Margery."[12]

1927

Prince took an important step in the study of spontaneous cases by gathering the psychic experiences of people he called "noted witnesses."

McDougall left Harvard to become head of the Psychology Department at Duke University in Durham, North Carolina. He brought with him an interest in parapsychology. In September, he was joined by Joseph Banks Rhine and Louisa E. Rhine, his wife, who were also interested in parapsychology and who were evaluating mediumistic records collected by John F. Thomas. Their collaboration led soon to experiments with telepathy and clairvoyance as possible sources of mediumistic information.

1928

In January 1928, JASPR was now published in a different form. Its new title was *Psychic Research*, in keeping with the populist policy, the thought being that this title would appeal to the general reader and imply the presentation of matter of interest to the laity rather than to the academic mind alone.[13]

1929

There appeared in *Psychic Research* a report on a series of remarkable sittings by an amateur circle. As the table around which the sitters sat responded to the letters of the alphabet, various communications were received from what are today labelled "drop-in" communicators and which could not be explained satisfactorily as telepathy from the living.[14] It was the first of a series of reports carried in subsequent numbers of ASPR publications under the title "Le Livre des Revenants" and which provided an important contribution to survival evidence.[15]

1930-1931

In 1930, the same year in which his *Enchanted Boundary* was published, Prince was elected president of the English Society for Psychical Research, the only American up to that time, besides William James, to hold that post.

Meanwhile, a change of editorship took place within the ASPR. Frederick Bligh Bond, a British architect, author and editor of *Psychic Science*, a journal published by the College of Psychic Science in London, relieved Bird of this office. Bird remained briefly as research officer and then resigned.

The first suggestion that something was amiss occurred in November 1930, when *Psychic Research* reported that Bird was not able to give an advertised address because of an "indisposition." The real reason was that in May Bird sent the ASPR Board of Trustees a lengthy report in which he said that "the Margery phenomena are not 100 percent supernormal," that he had detected the use of fraudulent techniques and, on one occasion, had even been asked to produce fraudulent phenomena himself.[16] The ASPR Board was shocked at this blasphemy against their idol Margery, and the heretic Bird was made to disappear. A volume of PASPR on which he had been working to present the Margery mediumship was altered and completed by others.

George H. Hyslop, who had remained on the ASPR Board of Trustees, had enough of the "policy of too liberal democracy" which allowed local groups to conduct haphazard mediumistic seances without controls or without recording occurrences at sittings. It was all "silly and unscientific and can easily result in embarrassment and awkwardness to the Society."[17] Bird's departure was followed by Hyslop's resignation from the Board of Trustees.

Meanwhile, Duke became the first American university to allow parapsychology a foothold. Rhine began ESP experiments there and, with a colleague, Dr. Karl E. Zener, devised new kinds of cards called "Zener cards" and later "ESP cards" to be used in ESP tests. These cards proved to be a practical method of testing and came to be adopted as standard everywhere that ESP was tested.

1932

In the spring of 1932, extraordinary experiments conducted at Duke strengthened the resolve to continue the research. In one series of experiments with J. Gaither Pratt, one of Rhine's assistants, the odds against the results being the products of chance were 1 in a billion.[18]

The ASPR publication, *Psychic Research,* now reverted to its original name, *Journal of the American Society for Psychical Research,* although its format remained the same. In June 1932, Bristol died and was succeeded as president by William H. Button, a lawyer who had practiced law in Vermont and New York. His was to be a fateful presidency during which the ASPR was to be involved in one mortifying episode and two great upheavals.

The first had its roots in Bristol's presidency. In 1931, a certain E.E. Dudley had been engaged by the ASPR to prepare material for a volume of the *Proceedings* on Margery which included fingerprints allegedly made by "Walter." Dudley wrote to Button that he questioned their genuineness because the right and left thumbprints attributed to "Walter" actually were those of a living person, "Mr. X" — in fact, Dr. Frederick Caldwell, Margery's dentist who had been one of the sitters at her seances.

The ASPR refused to publish Dudley's findings, deeming them to be unwarranted, and went on with its own investigation of the prints in order to refute him.[19] Some of this investigation was done in a curious way since it involved asking "Walter" his opinion of the prints. The ASPR stated in all seriousness that "Walter" "immediately ridiculed the idea that his prints were identical" with Dr. Caldwell's.[20]

Not to be denied, Dudley had his views published by the very willing Prince in the publication put out by the Boston Society in which he stated that before production of the "Walter" prints, Margery had obtained from her dentist, given the pseudonym "Kerwin," wax impressions of his thumbs, which he delivered to her with extra pieces of wax. Dudley went on to say that he had obtained prints from "Kerwin" which upon comparison proved to be identical to "Walter's." The Boston group published the Dudley material with a preface stating that it was doing so because otherwise this evidence would be suppressed.

The ASPR angrily denied the charge of suppression and said that the Boston publication carefully did not inform its readers that the whole matter was still under investigation by the ASPR. Prince, as BSPR editor, was branded a "pseudo-scientist" who should recall the moral law "Thou shalt not bear false witness against thy neighbor."[21] The SPR in London until then had stood aloof

72 The Blue-Eyed Woman

from the Margery case. In 1927, it had said: "Our desire is to have as little as possible to do either in *Proceedings* or in the *Journal* with the whole Margery question";[22] but this was too much and the English could not restrain themselves any longer. Commenting on this angry reply by the ASPR, the SPR *Journal* called it "inadequate and discourteous."[23]

1933

At Duke University, as the first experiments in precognition were being conducted there, John F. Thomas received the first Ph.D. from an American university for a thesis on a parapsychological subject.

1934

There came off the presses in March a monograph by J.B. Rhine with the peculiar title, *Extra-Sensory Perception,* to denote the author's idea of perception without the use of the senses and to provide a convenient description of telepathy and clairvoyance. The monograph contained a full account of card-guessing experiments that had been carried on at Duke, and simple, standard procedures for statistically analyzing the results. In effect, this book presented new research to confirm old truths that had been told and retold about the power of the mind to acquire information without sensory functions. In the next five years it was to create both public excitement and academic indignation.

The introduction to the monograph was written by Walter Franklin Prince, research officer of the BSPR and one of the figures most prominent in the history of parapsychology to date. It was his last piece of writing. He died on August 7. Although he had been one of its leading lights, the ASPR managed to ignore his death. Prince had chosen Rhine to succeed him as BSPR research officer. But Rhine's commitment to Duke was so great that he could not devote himself fully to the office. He accepted it only as "honorary" research officer.

With Prince's death, the BSPR lost its voice as an effective group and struggled on for a few years more until it disappeared in a merger with the ASPR. Meanwhile, it continued with Worcester as its president, John F. Thomas as vice president, and Lydia Allison as Council member and secretary. Soon, its Research Committee would include René Warcollier, the French experimenter who set out to prove telepathy.

Prince died without knowing that the last trumpet was about to sound in the case of the blue-eyed woman (and how he would have taken delight in hearing it!). The ASPR published a report that Dudley's conclusions were baseless and that "Walter's" thumbprints in "Kerr" dental wax were not those of any living person, including "X" or "Kerwin," the pseudonym for Margery's dentist, Dr. Caldwell.[24] Only idiots and babes in arms would have failed to see the clear implication in the report that Dudley had substituted the dentist's prints for "Walter's." Much to Dudley's disadvantage, the affair seemed settled in America — only to be unsettled because the English were not content to let the matter rest.

In view of the dispute over the prints, the SPR in August allowed Professor Harold Cummins, an American expert on "dermatoglyphics," to inspect "Walter's" left thumbprints which had been left impressed in wax and in the custody of the SPR after Margery had held sittings there. The object of the inspection was to determine if the prints were identical with the living person "X" or "Kerwin." Cummins' conclusions were that "Walter's" thumbprints were identical to "Kerwin's."

1935

Frederick Bligh Bond, the editor of JASPR, got wind of the Cummins finding and, anticipating its publication by the SPR, realized rightly that such publication would do great harm, not merely to the Margery mediumship but also to the reputation of the Society which had been her advocate. He believed that the only way to forestall this damage and to save face would be to publish the Cummins conclusion in JASPR and acknowledge the facts at once.[25] But the ASPR under Button, its president, did not share his apprehensions and denied his request to have a free hand to proceed with the publication.[26]

When, as Bond expected, the English published the Cummins report,[27] it was fuel for the fire. It incited the leading members of the ASPR, including George H. Hyslop and Gertrude Tubby, to demand that the facts be published. It was a question of moral justice. Dudley had been accused of the crime of substitution of evidence. Now his innocence had been shown and he ought to be vindicated.

Bond knew better than to make any dewy-eyed pleas for justice in the expectation that the ASPR officials would be sympathetic and would allow the facts to be published. His feet were on the ground, not in the clouds. He took affirmative action and, in May 1935, presented the Cummins findings in JASPR and stated to readers that Dudley had been vindicated by the report.[28]

This action did not put out the fire; it only added more fuel. The ASPR officials, who seemed to have entwined the fate and reputation of the ASPR with that of the Margery mediumship, immediately discharged Bond as editor and claimed that ASPR members and the public had been victimized by the publication as a conspiracy of Bond and some ASPR members. The publication was condemned as fraudulently representing the views of the ASPR. The earlier ASPR report suggesting that Dudley had been guilty of substitution of evidence was reaffirmed and his vindiction by Bond repudiated.[29]

The Cummins exposure of Margery and Bond's martyrdom might have been expected to wreck the ASPR. They resulted in the resignation of some of the membership, but the ASPR did not collapse because of the Margery scandal or the discharge of Bond. Actually, its president was able to gloat that the affair had gotten rid of many retrogressive influences.[30] The ASPR toward the end of 1935 continued, as if nothing had happened, to praise "the wonderful phenomena . . . that have been produced in the Margery mediumship" and to report sittings showing that the dead "Walter" had spoken through her.[31]

Well to the south of New York City, there were less dramatic but more significant developments in Durham, North Carolina. "Parapsychology" was the term now adopted to mark off the field being investigated with Rhine's methods at Duke. The unit in its Department of Psychology that was doing the research in this field was designated the Parapsychology Laboratory. It was the first of its kind in America and the first concerted effort by the members of an American university's Psychology Department to test the problems of telepathy and clairvoyance. Two Walter Franklin Prince Fellowships in Psychology were created there.

1936

J. Gaither Pratt, a graduate student at Duke, joined the Parapsychology Laboratory as a full-time research assistant. His experimental studies of the medium Eileen Garrett, entitled "Towards a Method of Evaluating Mediumistic Material," were published by the BSPR. This publication demonstrated how such material could be subjected to quantitative methods.

In spite of the "hit" made by Rhine's *Extra-Sensory Perception*, the publications of the ASPR had never mentioned or reviewed it, an understandable omission since the monograph had been published by the rival BSPR and the "too skeptical" Prince. But when Jocelyn Pierson, daughter of the ASPR secretary, was permitted to have a hand in the material presented in JASPR, her coverage of research specifically acknowledged and described Rhine's experiments at Duke and his book and even the ASPR's rival by whom it had been published. She also warmly approved an article by Gardner Murphy which described his ESP experiments at Columbia University and Rhine's at Duke.[32] Her article suggested more than a growing awareness by ASPR authorities and members that there was something else to write and read about than spirit communications: It indicated that a new crew member had come on board who might one day put the helm hard over and lay a new course for the ASPR. In 1936, however, President Button of the ASPR was still proclaiming Margery to be "undoubtedly . . . the greatest medium in existence."[33]

1937

The *Journal of Parapsychology* was founded at Duke with J.B. Rhine and William McDougall as coeditors.

C.E. Stuart and J. Gaither Pratt, two members of the Duke Department of Psychology staff, published *A Handbook for Testing Extra-Sensory Perception,* the first handbook on test procedures in parapsychology.

The Institute of Mathematical Statistics validated Rhine's method of statistical analysis.

1938

With a Foreword by Gardner Murphy, René Warcollier's *Experimental Telepathy* was published by the BSPR. Murphy was also permitted to conduct ESP experiments at the ASPR and to use its members as volunteer subjects.

In September at Columbus, Ohio, the American Psychological Association held an ESP Symposium organized by the severest critics of the Rhinean research at Duke, or, in the words of the target of their attacks, "a heresy trial." When it ended, however, these attacks lessened considerably.

On November 28, William McDougall, who had held professorships of psychology at Harvard and Duke universities and under whose aegis parapsychology and Rhine began and continued at Duke, died.

The history of American parapsychology during its first two periods was largely an account of the character, motives and efforts of two men: Richard Hodgson was the storm center of the first period, James Hervey Hyslop that of its second. The third period, however, becomes one of dispersion as new figures appear and parapsychology is partitioned among them. These figures included two men whom Rhine, as he looked back from his own period, called "the two leading figures in American psychical research at the time"[34]: Walter Franklin Prince and William McDougall. Their life stories follow.

Walter Franklin Prince: A Portrait

"Little girl, if you will hold up your head while I take your picture," said the photographer, "I will give you a penny." In 1894, a penny went a long way and would buy a chocolate cream pie or even a Foxy Grandpa (colored marshmallow on a stick that sometimes had a penny concealed in it as a prize), so a generous offer had been made to the five year old in her pretty dancing dress and a white bow in her hair. The sweet child was obviously pleased by the attention she was getting and, oh, how she wanted that penny! But she was so timid. Tittering, she kept her head down, too shy to hold it up for the man behind the camera. Then, suddenly, her entire expression and manner changed. She placed her hands behind her back, her lips pouted to show her pique, her eyes turned to one side, and she said indignantly, almost defiantly, "The idea of taking a penny to have your picture taken!"[35]

Walter F. Prince

Sixteen years later when this child, now a disturbed and unhappy young woman, came to an Episcopal Church in Pittsburgh to meet, first, the wife of its rector, and, later, Walter Franklin Prince, the rector himself, it was an encounter with destiny. The girl became his outstanding achievement in one of the most extraordinary cases of multiple personality ever studied. She was also the springboard that catapulted him into parapsychology as one of its foremost investigators.

Early Life, Degrees, Pastorates, Character and Rehabilitation

In 1649, Thomas Prince sailed from one port city named Gloucester in England to another of the same name in Massachusetts. Eight generations later, on April 23, 1863, Walter Franklin Prince came into the world, and, more specifically, into Detroit, Maine, the son of Walter M. Prince and his wife, Elmira J. Pray. His education began in a rude schoolhouse constructed in 1839 whose windows and door latch were always broken. Its two rows of desks and seats marked by a variety of designs made by the jackknives of little boys accommodated three or four pupils each.[36] But there were no books and Prince craved them.

It is recorded that, in order to borrow and read some, he would walk ten miles. His older brother used to complain that even when Prince came to help dig potatoes in the field, he was never without a book.[37] Fortunately, his parents craved books, too. A good library—poetry, history, travel, biography—was assembled by them and read and reread so avidly by Prince and his brother and sister that their mother had to keep sewing on the covers of the books.

When not reading or working in the fields, Prince loved to walk from spring to fall hunting wild flowers. Geology and mineralogy interested him, as did a favorite parrot named Lora who could speak some English and Spanish and sing some melodies that Prince sang.

There are no indications in his early life of psychic experiences, either his own or of members of his family, which might have stimulated an interest in the subject-matter of parapsychology. His brother recalled one incident, however, that tends to suggest some openness to the subject. When Prince was fifteen, a schoolmate admitted being afraid to walk through a graveyard after dark. Prince replied that he had already been through a graveyard at night and wanted to see a ghost.

Early he heard the call of the ministry and attended the Maine Wesleyan Seminary from which he was graduated in 1881 at the age of eighteen. That same year he met Lelia M. Colman of Newport. They were married in 1885 and remained so for forty years. She died in 1924, for all those years his loving helpmate.[38] She was to be an instrumental factor in his encounter with destiny and with the troubled young woman.

Following his graduation from Maine Wesleyan Seminary, he became pastor at Methodist and Episcopal churches in Maine but felt the need for more study and self-development. He went on to Yale, where he took his A.B. degree in 1896 and was a member of Phi Beta Kappa; he studied at Drew Theological Seminary where he received a Bachelor of Divinity in 1897; and he obtained a Ph.D. from Yale two years later at the age of 36. "Multiple Personality" was the subject of his doctoral thesis.

When forty, he took up the ministry once more and was pastor of Methodist Episcopal churches in Maine and Connecticut. In New York, Pennsylvania and California, he served as pastor at Protestant Episcopal churches. In 1910, he was rector of All Saint's Church in Pittsburgh and, in 1916–1917, director of psychotherapeutics at St. Mark's Episcopal Church on the Bowery in New York City.

No one is sure of the exact meaning and origin of the term "Yankee," but, whatever they are, there was a quality about Prince that induced people to apply the term to him.[39] He impressed his friends as honest, gentlemanly, scholarly, sincere and fussbudgety. He wore old clothes and, when he talked, made faces, chuckled and barked. Author Fulton Oursler thought that his friend Prince resembled the picturesque type of character Dickens would have created.[40] Prince was, in fact, so much like a Dickensian character, that, on a visit to London, he refused to stay at a hotel near Liverpool Station where some of the people from the English SPR were staying because it had not been mentioned in Dickens.[41]

Prince also had an old-fashioned conservatism and respect for authority and morality as demonstrated by his becoming field secretary of the Connecticut Temperance Union in 1899 and by his having been assistant secretary of the Connecticut Law and Order League for five years beginning in 1899.[42]

Prince wrote three important monographs during this period: *A Critical Study of Peter's Blue Laws* (1899), *The First Criminal Code of Virginia* (1900), *The Great Slave Conspiracy Delusion* (1902).

Yes, Prince had heard and responded to the call of the ministry, but, like the song of the siren which lured seafarers to their deaths, it seemed to destroy him. In 1912, after he had left Pittsburgh to become rector of St. John's Church in San Bernardino, California, he seemed a desolate, bewildered man who felt his genius was being smothered and whose writings would never be published, perhaps never even written. It was then, when he was nearly 50 and his soul was sad and sick and growing more so, that he performed one of his two great acts of rehabilitation—his own. He conducted this experiment on himself which would:

> ...consist wholly in the direction of my thought. In recalling the past I would deliberately concentrate on all that was happiest and best and ignore the rest. In thinking of the present, poor and barren as my life appeared to me, I would fix attention on whatever was bright and pleasant in it, and lay hold of every opportunity to make myself useful and agreeable to my fellow men.... It was my resolution in regard to the future which was absurd. And yet it was this which changed my whole destiny. In thinking of the future I determined to regard every high hope and worthy ambition I had ever entertained not merely as possible of attainment, but as actually on the way to perfect realization. As I recorded these fond dreams in my note book I had to laugh at myself. Yet in looking back, all that I regret now is that I did not include more and aim higher.... After eight days I knew that the experiment had succeeded and with it both my outer and my inner life began again.[43]

When Worcester's book, *Body, Mind and Spirit* (1931) was published some years later, no line in it provoked as many letters of approval and inquiry as did his description of Prince's experiment. Hundreds of people were inspired by it and tried it themselves.[44]

Doris Fischer

Prince's second act of rehabilitation was of the troubled girl who had come to his church in Pittsburgh. It is ironic that the ministry which was his barren prison turned out to be his means of self-discovery and escape into a distinguished career, all because this girl, born in 1889, whom he called "Doris Fischer," came to his church.

She was one of 13 children, the daugher of "Emma Fischer," a loving, sensitive and tender mother, and of "John Fischer," a long, lean man given to alcoholic excesses and outbursts of rage, a man without love or consideration for anyone.

The first fifteen years of Doris's life were spent in an Eastern city in a slum smelling of limburger cheese and whiskey called "Rubberneck Row" because the women were always hanging out of the windows of the row of brick houses, i.e., "rubbernecking."[45] When she was three, her mother was about to put her in the parental bed. But John Fischer objected. He swore, seized Doris from her mother's arms and hurled the child to the floor. Emma Fischer picked her up and placed her on the bed of an older sister. It was then that the first dissociation took place. Doris later developed multiple personalities. The main one, Margaret, described how she came into being: "When Doris was three years old I came one night when she was lying on the bed crying as if her little heart would break because her father had thrown her on the floor, well I made her play with her fingers and toes and finally had her laughing and then she went to sleep...."[46]

When Margaret was asked to identify the photograph of the five year old girl in her dancing dress who pouted defiantly when the photographer asked her for her photograph, this personality said: "That is *me*.... I'm sure. I remember all about it. The picture-man offered the D. [Doris] a penny if she would hold her head up. She was bashful and wouldn't hold it up. Then I came, and I was mad. The idea of taking a penny for having your picture taken! So I put my hands behind me and *I* held my head up."[47]

In 1908, the Fischer family moved to a new house not far from All Saint's Church in Pittsburgh where Prince was the rector. In October 1909, a friend invited Doris to come with her to attend a Sunday School class there. Doris agreed and there met Mrs. Prince, whose kindness impressed the girl. The following Sunday Mrs. Prince brought Doris to the rectory to meet Prince for the first time. Although Doris was fascinated by Mrs. Prince, she seemed afraid of Prince and avoided him when they met occasionally in the house.[48] Busy with his work, Prince paid her little attention. Yet he could not help noticing "something odd about her."[49]

Her moods were mercurial. She would be jolly, she would be melancholy.

When talkative, she looked child-like, when "in the dumps" she looked weary. Even when she was jolly, she could not understand any form of humor, not even Prince's favorite joke. "Once at dinner I told a story of a man who put a linament [sic] on his wooden leg and it sprouted" but this only made the girl "unnecessarily perturbed"[50] and, for some time, she refused to take any meals at the table with Prince.

Eventually, the strain of looking after Doris began to tell on Mrs. Prince's health. Prince became alarmed and decided to share the burden. Doris was now visiting the rectory more often and sleeping there, sometimes in the afternoon, sometimes in the evening. She was persuaded to sleep on a lounge in Prince's study, near his desk, where he could keep an eye on her. He watched her for the first time on January 17, 1911.[51]

The following day Prince began to keep records of the case. Two days later, when the girl used "we" when "I" would have been expected and said "Doris is gone away," Prince exclaimed: "It now suddenly dawned upon me, accompanied by wonder that it had not done so before, that here was probably a case of dissociated personality."[52]

In the course of his watching and recording, he got to know intimately each alternating personality. There was Real Doris, the bright, dutiful, primary one; there was Margaret, the chief mischievous, childish personality who could be vicious toward Doris and who might attack her by scratching her or making her bang her head against the wall; there was Sick Doris, another personality who manifested after Emma Fischer's death and who was so called because the girl was always sick when she appeared, an illness from which she recovered as soon as Doris or Margaret came back.

Early in the therapy, Prince tried to get rid of Margaret, who had been punishing Doris for coming to the rectory in the afternoons by scratching her arms and face. On the evening of January 22, Margaret appeared and savagely scratched the left hip and neck. Prince was horrified:

> I remonstrated in vain, and held her hands only to see them snatched away and the vicious movements repeated. Stern commands to desist had no effect but to increase the manifestations. Attempting suggestion I began to say impressively, ("I am going to take away your power. You are growing weaker. You are losing your strength.") The struggles became weaker. Finally I said, ("Your strength is gone. You are powerless.") All striving ceased, the face changed, and she [Sick Doris] awoke.[53]

But the girl's life seemed to be ebbing. She was in a state "which made Mrs. P. and me think, not for the first time, that she was dying.... Under the spell of considerable emotion I was looking into her eyes, and presently her gaze fixed upon mine, and with parted lips she continued to look, not rigidly, but dreamily and peacefully, while we waited for the end which we thought so near."[54]

Not the end, however, but another personality came: wise, calm, authoritative. A new voice came from the lips of the girl: "You must get her

out of this. She is in danger. . . . Shake her. . . . Walk her! walk her. Prince carried out these orders and soon heard, "She is coming to herself now; she will
be all right soon."[55] She was. Sleeping Margaret, who appeared only when
Doris was asleep, had made her dramatic appearance. Doris slept until 5 a.m.,
when she awoke and returned home to prepare her father's breakfast.

   Prince was also introduced to still another personality, Sleeping Real Doris
who appeared when Real Doris was asleep and was different from the true
Doris—"a little crack in R.D."[56]

   Prince became increasingly worried about Doris's surroundings. Her
father drank heavily and, when drunk, was even more callous and brutal than
when he was sober. He abused Doris with violent language and with blows
from his stick or fist so that she was often forced to flee from the house in fear.[57]

   Then there were the responsibilities of housekeeping which also militated
against Doris. She needed rest and change. Prince took her out of her surroundings and adopted her. She became Theodosia Prince.

   Theodosia's case (we will continue to call her Doris) was extraordinary.
There were as many as 40 daily alterations of personalities. Sick Doris was victimized by Margaret who tortured her physically, destroyed her possessions,
undid her work and insulted her. Night was not a time for sleep but for "a
phantasmagoria of strange experiences." Her life was so full of sorrow that,
when the primary personality (Real Doris) received a note from two of the personalities (Sick Doris and Margaret) that she was about to die, she fell on her
knees in thankfulness.[58]

   To authorities like Walker, a professor of psychiatry at the University of
Pittsburgh, the case seemed utterly hopeless, all the more so because it was in
the hands of a clergyman who, although his Ph.D. thesis had been on multiple
personality, had no qualifications to treat, or practical experience with or
knowledge of, dissociated mental states. Yet, in the end, after Prince's
therapy, Sick Doris disappeared for all time in June 1911, Sleeping Real Doris
in April 1912, and Margaret in April 1914, when Prince declared a cure to have
been effected. He remarked, "It is, indeed, not so much of a marvel that she
was restored to psychical integrity in but three and a half years as that this result
was attained at all."[59]

   How had Prince managed to cure her? In the first place, he used, not hypnotism, but suggestion in the normal state. Murphy assumed that Prince was
unfamiliar with the hypnotic method,[60] but it seems rather that Prince
doubted that hypnotism would work and that he felt, in Doris's case, that it
was better to create an environment agreeable to Doris's real personality but
disagreeable to the others.[61]

   But Prince did more. Janet and Morton Prince had observed many cases
of multiple personality. But clinical observation is one thing while the actual
daily participation in someone's life is quite another.[62] Prince qualified himself
by his caring, sympathetic, deep human interest in Doris as evidenced by his
participation, by his adoption of Doris and his insights so that, although her
case seemed without hope at the start, she was rehabilitated.

Prince's careful records of the case, kept daily for three and a half years, culminated in a report of over 1400 pages which included 25 rare pictures of multiple personalities. It is the most detailed and prolonged case study ever recorded.[63] It differed from Dr. Morton Prince's study of the Sally Beauchamp case in that, instead of publishing only certain parts of the record considered important, as did Morton Prince, Walter Prince presented the full record to enable students of the case to reach their own conclusions. Gardner Murphy was of the opinion that, of all personality studies, Prince's record was the most rewarding and illuminating.[64]

The Kindling and Rekindling of Interest in Parapsychology

Prior to Doris, Prince's interest in parapsychology seems to have been kindled by his "one chief passion," puzzles. "All sorts of puzzles in boyhood, mechanical, mathematical, verbal. Later puzzles as to literary genuineness, the identity of handwriting, mooted points in history, etc. Then puzzles in psychology. And finally puzzles in psychical research."[65] These led him to read the SPR *Proceedings*, probably also to join the ASPR in 1908 and to "a desultory correspondence" with Hyslop thereafter.[66] However, he said, "active interest again subsided with the coming into consideration of puzzles in abnormal psychology."[67]

But during his treatment of Doris his interest began to shift in the direction of parapsychology once again. As he studied her, one by one, Sick Doris, Sleeping Real Doris and Margaret made their exits. But not Sleeping Margaret because Prince did not regard her presence as a detriment and did not try to suppress or remove her. Her cooperation was of great value in the eventual cure and her continuance of great benefit. She was also the most fascinating of all the personalities.

Sleeping Margaret knew what Doris and the other personalities thought, said and did and understood their struggles with each other. She was aware, and able to speak, of subjects of philosophy and psychology that transcended Doris's ability. Sleeping Margaret was what appealed to Prince: a puzzle. When he tried to suggest to her that she might be a spirit, at first her firm reply was, "No I am not,"[68] possibly because she remembered that Prince had told her that he "was not partial to the spirit theory."[69] But later she began to claim that she had come into existence when Doris was three in order to take care of and protect Doris[70] and on August 25, 1914, left no doubt when she wrote: "I am a spirit, so-called by people who live on the earth. I do not know whether I have a name or not. I only know that I was sent by someone higher to guard Doris when she was three years old."[71] Apparently, this "someone" sent Sleeping Margaret in response to Emma Fischer's prayers for the well-being of her last born child.

Prince does not seem ever fully to have accepted Sleeping Margaret's claim to be a guardian spirit. When, for example, Murphy discussed this aspect of the case with him, Murphy recalled that there was a half-smile on Prince's face as he wondered whether it was legitimate for anyone to consider such a hypothesis.[72] Speaking of her claim to spirit guardianship, Prince also made it clear that "I am not ready to make this formal admission, though much puzzled to account for certain of her characteristics on the theory that she is a dissociated fragment of [Doris's] own mind."[73]

This puzzlement probably led him to write to the only person who might be able to help him clarify his thoughts: Hyslop. An exchange of letters followed which resulted not only in Doris's recovery but also in the remaking of Prince.[74] As Worcester observed, with all its trials, the case of Doris Fischer proved to be the most significant factor in Prince's life because she turned it around and into abnormal psychology and parapsychology.[75]

In the Thompson-Gifford case, where Thompson, a goldsmith, painted in the manner of the dead artist Gifford, the cross-referencing mediumistic method used by Hyslop suggested a possible possession of Thompson by the deceased artist. When Hyslop learned of the Doris case of five multiple personalities, he rushed to see Prince in Pittsburgh in 1911 to investigate whether this might be another case of a discarnate influence. Prince remembered that Hyslop "paid me a flying visit of a few hours' duration, saw some of the phenomena of the Doris multiple personality case"[76] and was much impressed by it. But it was not another Thompson-Gifford case. It was a case of a nonspiritist influence more like that of Ansel Bourne studied by Hodgson or of Sally Beauchamp studied by Morton Prince. Hyslop, Prince said, "instantly recognized the importance of the Doris case to abnormal psychology"[77] and published Prince's record of the case in the PASPR.

Nor was Doris's case at this point one of mediumship, as a comparison with a true case of mediumship, that of the extraordinary English medium Mrs. Gladys Osborne Leonard will show. There were some similarities. Feda, Mrs. Leonard's control, was like Margaret in many ways: She, too, claimed to be a spirit (of a Hindu girl); she was a childish personality who spoke childish language; and when dominant and in control was antagonistic to Mrs. Leonard. But the differences between the cases were greater than the similarities. In the Leonard case, there was only one controlling personality. There were also discarnate communicators. But in the Doris case there were five personalities and no discarnate communicators.

The Hyslop visit not only caused Prince's genius to be revealed and gained for him a ranking as a first-class psychological investigator; it stimulated his thinking about parapsychology again, particularly about the attitudes of Christians toward its subject-matter. Thus, he published in 1912, in JASPR, a lengthy paper about this attitude, which he characterized as "one of the strangest paradoxes of the age."[78]

In this same year Prince had a personal experience that pushed parapsychology more to the center of his mind:

> I had lately moved three thousand miles to California. No biographical
> sketch had preceded or followed my advent in the little city, no *Who's*

Who or similar work was then available to give facts regarding my
parentage, and to not a soul there had there been any occasion to
allude to such. My wife and I were calling for the first time, without
previous notice, upon a young woman, wife of a local businessman. I
saw a planchette on the table and asked, "Do you operate that?" "We
have done so a few times," she replied. "Get anything?" "Mainly 'yes'
and 'no' to questions. And once we got 'Bill.' Laughingly I said, "Suppose we try our luck," and she, who was but languidly interested, and
I, put our hands upon the instrument. She did not cease talking with
Mrs. Prince, nor look at the planchette, nor was she, I think, aware that
it was moving until the following words were drawing to a close:
"W.M. Prince. Your father, W.M. Prince." These, W.M., were my
father's initials, and each of them might have been—of course not all
with equal chance—any one of twenty-five other letters.

My hand was indeed on the board likewise.... And, after she
became consciously interested, the lady, with or without me, got
nothing more of interest.[79]

A puzzle indeed. It pointed him toward critical inquiry and rekindled his
interest in parapsychology, an interest due to burn even more brightly as a consequence of sittings that took place in 1914, the year that Hyslop concluded
experiments after the death of Emma Fischer in which Doris, now apparently
normal and fully recovered, was the sitter and Mrs. Chenoweth, the medium.
When Prince edited and published this experiment, he said: "There has probably never been printed a more evidential group of communications than the
one here presented. The conditions under which it was produced could hardly
have been more nearly perfect."[80] (And on the flyleaf of PASPR containing this
case, which I have in my possession, Prince wrote in his own hand: "Science
is proud today of precious gems which it cast out upon the dump yesterday.
Walter Franklin Prince.")

After Hyslop died, George Hyslop said that his father had one concern
before his death: that a successor should carry on the work of the ASPR.[81]
Hyslop had made an effort to find someone in 1914 when he appointed Edwin
W. Friend as his assistant. But with Friend's resignation a year later, the search
for a successor was renewed. It ended in 1916 when Hyslop made Prince, who
had come to New York from California to become director of psychotherapeutics at St. Mark's Church, his research officer.

Hyslop and his appointee were similar in some ways. Both had been
students of psychology, and farming was in their youthful backgrounds. But
did they share a common belief in survival? In 1916, Hyslop affirmed this
belief. But Prince had never expressed any, in fact, was "not partial" to
spiritism. But Hyslop "did not seem to care," wrote Prince, "whether his assistant ever would [express an affirmative belief in survival], being satisfied with
a certain mental habit and that of laborious observation."[82] A contemporary
who knew Hyslop said that Hyslop chose Prince because he perceived in Prince
the same sterling qualities that had made Hyslop an invaluable investigator.[83]

Parapsychology was to become Prince's life as it had been Hyslop's, and, like him, Prince was an exceptional worker who maintained the highest standards of evidence. His own estimate of himself shows both frankness and humor:

Put me under the microscope as the bug some people think I am. Reputed to be excessively cautious, and regarded by the Spiritualistic religious cult as a hard hearted skeptic ... one to whom accuracy is a religion and minute analysis an obsession so that it is an agony to terminate the testing process and write a report; intolerably detailed in reporting and in presenting the subject in hand at every possible angle; alive by experience and study to the various pitfalls of illusion, delusion and deception – all this has made me a kind of a scrutinizing, analyzing and rationalizing monster, quite unpleasant to the tender-minded.[84]

When this monster was at work over a mass of papers, his vest covered with ash from the smelly cigar jutting out of one corner of his mouth, his eyes would brighten whenever the material he was reading could cause him to say, "See, I've got it: look it went wrong here. Then they had to fake it to get it fixed. Pretty bit of work. Just the thing we like, eh?"[85]

Hodgson's familiarity with the tricks of conjurers helped him expose fraud. In order to learn conjurers' methods and to apply his learning to detect trickery, Prince became a member of the Society of American Magicians. Soon he discovered how trance mediums claiming to have received their powers from the spirits of the dead used the methods and sleights-of-hand of magicians and how trumpet mediums working in the dark or under poor lighting conditions provided breathtaking results by using the methods of prestidigitators.[86]

Prince had common interests with McDougall, also. There were psychology and the ASPR, of course, in which they seem to have cooperated well when McDougall became its president in 1921 and Prince its editor and director of research. In addition, both were right-wingers. Their deep-dyed conservatism provides an interesting reminder that parapsychology, while attractive to the credulous and the occultist, also attracts the cautious skeptic and always has been a field of mixed and offsetting forces.

The JASPRs and PASPRs published during the five year period when Prince was associated with them contain many of his papers. Some of these, such as his "A Survey of American Slate-Writing Mediumship," which runs almost 300 pages,[87] demonstrated his monster-like power to scan and scrutinize that made him, like Hodgson, feared by fraudulent mediums. As Hodgson had shown Eglinton's slate writing to be totally unreliable as proof that spirits wrote on slates, Prince exposed the trickery of P.L.O.A. Keeler, acclaimed "the greatest of the slate-writing mediums." Prince succeeded in exposing Keeler by making careful comparisons of the writing of spirit messages with the handwriting of the deceased person in whose handwriting the messages were supposed to be. Apparently the medium did not take this very kindly and threatened to prosecute Prince on some charge, probably slander. Prince's response to this came in the form of a paraphrase: "No tallow cat chased by an asbestos dog toward the fires of Hades could be more alarmed than is any gentleman subsisting by fooling the public at the very idea of entering a court of justice."[88]

His work in the ASPR publications shows that Prince was a dangerous controversialist because he was a living and breathing encyclopedia of knowledge of the phenomena and literature of parapsychology.[89] Prince was more than able to pick up the same cudgels Hyslop had used against critics who regarded parapsychology as subversive. He was particularly hard on scientists and scholars who insisted on confusing parapsychology with Spiritualism.[90]

Psychometry

Hyslop regarded the telepathic hypothesis as the only rival to the spiritistic one. In fact, he should have considered more seriously another rival which the deceased "Podmore" purportedly described to him through Mrs. Smead during a sitting in 1911:

> "Podmore": "different objects do carry their influence Hyslop more than you know . . . yes and in somm . . . some cases it is all from your side. yes. do u know I wish to convey the meaning S C I Cometry [Psychometry] . . . impressions of ours are left more distinctly on those things we have kept about our person con in.... ..tinually . . . but some times the owner of it is not present and yet you get information from them."
> Hyslop: "Can you get little incidents of their lives, that is, of the owners from the objects alone?"
> "Podmore": ". . . not I but some on your side H. can."[91]

In "psychometry" or token object reading, a sensitive, merely by using an object as a psychic link, seems to obtain information about the past history of people or events associated with the link, information unknown to the sensitive and sitters who are present. If, as "Podmore" argued, some on our side of death, through retrocognitive ESP, can derive this information from objects and not from spirits, a serious threat to the hypothesis of spirit communication is posed. It is also a threat to the hypothesis of reincarnation. C.T.K. Chari has, for instance, said that Ian Stevenson, the leading investigator of reincarnation, has underestimated this threat.[92]

The question is whether the faculty has been established by experiment. The work of Dr. Eugene Osty, a French physician, published in 1923[93] sometimes is cited as an example of experiments demonstrating this faculty.[94] Osty's method, however, which consisted largely of relating how French mediums seemed to display the ability, has been criticized as one which "hardly deserves to be called 'experiment'."[95]

It is to Prince that we owe the first two striking cases of psychometry. One was Mrs. King, his discovery, who was able to obtain paranormal information about 33 of 34 items contained in an unseen letter placed between her palms.[96] And both indirectly, in the sense of giving the experimenter an opportunity to bring it to the attention of American readers, and directly because he investigated it personally, Prince deserves credit for a more dramatic and continually cited experimental illustration of psychometry:

Gustav Pagenstecher, a German physician who lived and conducted his practice in Mexico City, where he was a surgeon in the American Hospital, had written to the ASPR in 1920 about experiments witnessed by members of the Medical Society of Mexico City which he had carried out with an extraordinary medium. Prince corresponded with him and asked many searching questions. Finally Prince wrote: "If your experiments, under the most rigid conditions, particularly guarding in some instances against the possibility that the medium could ever have handled the same objects before their responses in her consciousness are registered before a company of witnesses, continue to bring forth such results ... I have no doubt that we would wish to publish them...."[97]

Such results were brought forth and Pagenstecher's experiments were published in JASPR.[98] The English-speaking world learned that, after Señora María Reyes de Zierold was hypnotized by Pagenstecher and placed in a state of deep trance, she was able to report correct sensory impressions about various objects, such as pieces of pumice stones, while touching them with the tips of her fingers. In another test, she reported the sensation of an earthquake when a fragment of a lava bed of an extinct volcano was placed in her hands.

Was it possible that, as the Pagenstecher tests with pumice stones seemed to suggest, to be able to see, hear, smell and taste, it was not necessary to have eyes, ears, nose or tongue? Prince went to Mexico City in 1921 to judge for himself and to participate in further token object experiments with the Mexican medium. "When I arrived in Mexico," he confessed, "I was prepared, with *malice propense,* to suspect, as a method of procedure, anyone or anything having to do with the experiments."[99] Pagenstecher, at whose house he stayed for a time, disarmed him. The German seemed honest, candid, able, and open to any feature Prince wanted to introduce into the experiments.[100]

The medium struck him well, also, as "a woman of good sense and good education,"[101] a person belonging to the highest class of Mexicans whose father had been a general and governor of the State of Michoacán. Prince had eight sittings with her. Before each one, Pagenstecher used a polished metal button held in front of her eyes to hypnotize her, and, when the lady's eyes were closed, he used passes to complete the hypnotism. After she appeared asleep, the tests started.

The sitting of March 30, 1921, is of both human and scientific interest. A letter of January 31 had been sent to Pagenstecher by a friend in Japan on behalf of a woman who wished to know whether her Spanish husband was dead, or, because he had political enemies, was being kept in some prison in Spain. These facts, however, were not stated in the letter which contained two sealed documents that had been deposited on March 12 with a lawyer. The letter said that one envelope contained a paper written under emotional

circumstances, the other a description of the writer of the paper. The letter requested that the first envelope be submitted to the medium and that neither
sealed envelope be opened until the sitting was terminated. This letter was
given to Prince, then placed in the hands of Señora Reyes de Zierold. She
clasped her hands over the first envelope. She began to describe a ship at night;
many frightened, screaming people on board; they spoke English; they were
putting on life preservers; they heard an explosion. Then she described a man
in detail. He had a beard and moustache, black eyes and hair, and a scar over
his right eyebrow; he held a small notebook from which he tore a leaf; on this
he wrote as machine-guns and an explosion like a bomb were heard; he placed
the note he had written in a bottle and corked it; he threw it overboard; all
the people drowned.

Prince examined the sealed envelopes which contained the facts and
noted that the mucilage and the waxed seals were intact. The envelopes were
not wrinkled or otherwise suspicious. The seals of the envelopes were broken
only after the test and in Prince's presence. When the documents were opened,
they disclosed contents which no one present had known. The first envelope
contained a slip of paper appearing to have been torn from a notebook. On
it, in Spanish, were written these words: "The ship is sinking. Farewell my
Luisa, see that my children do not forget me your Ramon Havana May God
care for you and for me also farewell."

This note had been discovered in a bottle picked up on the coast off the
Azores. An investigation in Havana disclosed that a Spanish political refugee
using the name Ramón P. had left New York on a boat bound for Europe during the period when many ships were being sunk by German U-boats.
Although the name of the ship was not given, Pagenstecher's friend thought
it might have been the *Lusitania,* which was among the vessels the Germans
had sunk. Ramón P.'s wife was named Luisa and he had children. He had
black hair, black eyes, a full black beard and a pronounced scar over the right
eye.

Prince commented after the test: "It can hardly be denied that the appearance of the paper corresponds with the medium's description, even as comparison with the letters . . . has already shown that her description of the writer
was astonishingly correct."[102] Yet the skeptical Prince still was on his guard and
he tried one of his "mean tricks." In the midst of a sitting, without warning,
he gave a note to Pagenstecher to read to the hypnotized medium. It instructed
her to admit that, before the sitting, the doctor had told her about the
drowned Ramón. The note was read in Spanish to the medium by the hyp-
notist with, Prince believed, conviction. But she shook her head and denied
that it was true. Prince was convinced: "Uttered as the words were, and considering the established *rapport,* there would certainly have been an admisison
had there been any ground for it."[103]

Telepathy is no explanation for token object reading when, as in this case,
Prince and the other experimenters had no knowledge of the facts in the sealed
documents. In fact, Prince dismissed telepathy altogether in his work with the

medium because of another experiment with an object he picked up on the beach at Vera Cruz which looked like the seed of a marine plant. But when he put the object between the tips of her fingers, she described tall tropical trees growing in a forest near water. "In my ignorance," he said, "I was telepathing to her, if anything, that the object was picked on the beach, whereas she referred it to a tropical forest; that it was the seed of a sea-plant, whereas she associated it with an inland tree."[104] When the seed was examined later by professional botanists, both confirmed that it came from a tree like the one described by Señora Reyes and that the seed frequently falls into a river and finally ends up on an ocean beach. Prince, the only one who knew what object had been used in the experiment, had the wrong idea about it. Yet the medium's impression, different from what was in his mind, was the correct one.

As telepathy was no explanation in the case of Ramón P., neither was communication with the medium from Ramón's spirit. Rather, in the medium's supplying of correct information unknown to her or anyone else present which she derived from an object, there is the suggestion that the faculty of paranormal cognition, like the super ESP of antisurvivalists, may really exist.

Prince's investigation of the Mexican medium was an extremely important experience for him. He told Hans Driesch that his work with Pagenstecher had converted him. He had gone to Mexico a skeptic and come back a "psychist."[105]

Psychometry has been used to justify different theories. Johnson thought that it indicated "a psychic aether" which provided some sort of conveyor of thought-images between mind and matter.[106] Roll proposed a "psi-field" theory[107] which holds that a physical object is surrounded by a field force in which are registered events in its neighborhood. These events may be detected subsequently by sensitives. Prince had a word of advice and caution for theoreticians both of his time and of ours:

"What we at present want is facts, facts, and yet more facts. It really is not of much use to propound theories until facts of every kind within the scope of the species of phenomena have accumulated and been viewed from every angle and subjected to the most searching analysis."[108]

International Congress

Prince hoped to create a network among parapsychologists in different parts of the world. After Mexico City and as representative of the ASPR, he went to the First International Congress on Psychical Research organized by the Danish Society for Psychical Research and held in 1921 in Copenhagen. A who's who of parapsychology attended. Among them: from England, W.H. Salter, Helen Salter, and the Rev. C. Drayton Thomas; from Germany, Albert von Schrenck-Notzing; Gustave Geley and René Sudre of France; H.J.F.W. Brugmans of Holland; and from the United States, Prince and Hereward Carrington.

Prince delivered a paper on telepathy versus spiritism and shared in the discussion at the Congress. Since, in his view, there were too many terms used in parapsychology for the same phenomenon and too many different meanings attached to these terms, he proposed a resolution, passed unaninously, which called for the preparation of a standard glossary of technical terms used in parapsychology and to be employed the world over. Charged with this responsibility, Prince undertook correspondence with people in fifteen countries.[109]

When in 1923 a further Congress was held in Warsaw, Gardner Murphy went as the ASPR's representative to pursue Prince's proposal to compile a glossary of terms,[110] but no agreement was reached. In 1927, Prince, in Europe to hold sittings with the physical mediums Rudi Schneider, Frau Maria Silbert and Jean Guzik,[110] attended as representative of the BSPR the Third International Conference in Paris. Bird of the ASPR was there also, as might be suspected, to play his role as Margery's untiring advocate. Prince's attempt to standardize terms again came to nothing as, indeed, have all such attempts since. According to JSPR, Prince delivered "an extremely valuable and interesting"[111] paper on how he had cured two cases of paranoia by talking to obsessing "spirits" "as a gentleman to a gentleman" and inducing them little by little to leave the patients. A Fourth International Congress was held in 1930 in Athens, but a fifth, scheduled for London in 1932, during the fiftieth anniversary of the SPR, was postponed because of the serious worldwide economic depression in the 1930's. Prince had no opportunity to take part in further attempts to organize parapsychology internationally.

Popularization, Margery and Resignation From the ASPR

The election in 1923 of Frederick Edwards as president of the ASPR really concealed the fact that the ASPR was now in the control of a group which intended to alter its policies and lower its standards. Proclaiming that "[t]he time has come for a great enlargement of our work,"[112] the new administration proposed to organize as auxiliaries to the ASPR state and local councils which were to do their own research and experiments with mediums and perform other functions.

Now the popularization of parapsychology does not seem an unreasonable policy if it will make people more aware of the field, bring them to the support of the operations of parapsychological societies such as the ASPR and, if these societies are not performing certain essential operations, allow people to supply competent personnel who will.[113] But here the policy made the ASPR's "activities dependent upon the deliberations of a sort of Town Hall Meeting."[114] It was the "Town Hall Meeting" trend which contributed heavily to the clash within the ASPR with those, such as Prince, McDougall, Murphy and Worcester, who urged the maintenance of rigid scientific principles and the new administration which seemed ready to lower or abandon them.

It was this same administration that offended Prince and others from the outset. An interesting document in the ASPR archives[115] discloses that, beginning with his first year in office, Edwards was sharply criticized by opponents who "felt that scientific standards were not being maintained." Edwards stood aloof: He "preferred a policy of silence." His sound program would speak for him instead, he believed. But it remained silent as a stone and the line of critics lengthened. Edwards did not require a seance with Margery to find out the identity of the chief instigator of the opposition. "Mr. Edwards felt strongly that Dr. Prince was responsible for the continued activity of this group of critics and Mr. Edwards frequently stated to members of the Board and others that such was the case." The Board stood by Edwards and tried to quell criticism which nevertheless persisted. By the end of 1924, the impression had grown among some Board members that Edwards "intended dispensing with the services of Dr. Prince" who, out of loyalty and a hope that affairs would come back to a sound footing, continued in his post through 1923 and 1924.[116]

It was not disappointment but frustration that plagued Prince as a member of the *Scientific American* committee organized to examine cases, frustration because of the arbitrary restrictions that had been placed by Dr. Crandon and Margery's other protectors on the investigation of her mediumship. Investigators' hands were held fast. Alleged phenomena took place in darkness eased occasionally by a red light, but only on "Walter's" signal. And, instead of being able to plan the kinds and durations of tests, investigators were at "Walter's" mercy as "he" alone decided when to stop a series of phenomena or to change them before investigators were satisfied that enough evidence had been provided.[117]

Among other hampering techniques was the requirement, noted also by McDougall, that Margery's husband be one of the controllers. Prince's verdict was that not one sitting with Margery was convincing and that every indication pointed to the normal and deceptive production of phenomena.[118] And he was not alone in his verdict. McDougall was inclined to believe that all phenomena had been produced by normal means, Comstock said no rigid proof had been furnished, and as might have been expected of a man whose mission in life seemed to be to expose mediums, Houdini said that everything that occurred was fraudulent. The sole dissent came from Hereward Carrington who was convinced by Margery.

As an organization, the ASPR had never taken any official position in the case but individuals connected with it had. Notwithstanding the adverse views of four of the five members of the *Scientific American* Committee and the inability of Dingwall to express his belief in the genuineness of the Margery phenomena, a strong faction inside the ASPR supported her mediumship. Bird, of course, had not been a judge on the *Scientific American* investigating committee. He, too, however, was convinced that Margery had produced genuine, not fraudulent, phenomena, and he became her avid defender. With the conclusion of the *Scientific American* investigation in 1925, Bird left his editorial post with the magazine to be welcomed warmly by the ASPR as research officer to investigate physical phenomena. Prince was to remain as research officer in charge of mental phenomena.

But Prince could not endure this defender of indefensible phenomena. He regarded Bird as totally unreliable, and, indeed, had warned Rhine to be careful of Bird.[119] The Margery affair was the proverbial straw that finally broke the camel's back, a back that, for two years, had been straining and sagging under the weight of a popularization policy against which Prince had railed and which he described in a letter to George Carey:

> The new president tried to 'democratize' one of the most technical and difficult of all types of research, brought a 'section' composed for the most part of credulous, vaudeville seeking amateurs, into the very building with the ASPR, made the contents of the *Journal* puerile, neglected American Research for the publication of foreign matter, in fact nearly stopped research in order to carry out his futile schemes, put research work, calling for expert judgment, under a lay committee, etc., etc.[120]

The *New York Times* of March 6, 1925, summed up Prince's actions when the camel's back finally broke:

DR. PRINCE RESIGNS OVER MARGERY ROW

Chief Investigator of Psychical Research Society Forced Out, Friends Say J.M. Bird Succeeds Him

> Antagonisms which have long been smoldering in the American Society for Psychical Research have resulted . . . in the resignation of Dr. Walter Franklin Prince . . . [A] clique headed by Frederick Edwards, President of the Society, had practically forced his resignation by stripping him of all authority. . . . Dr. Prince is regarded by the Edwards group, so his friends asserted, as being "too skeptical."

Prince's "friends" would have included Worcester, McDougall and others, but never Bird who, no doubt, was pleased by Prince's departure because, said Bird, "aside from [Prince's] brilliant success in making himself obnoxious to the Crandons, he had demonstrated more conclusively in this than in any preceding case his weaknesses of temperament and procedure."[121]

Prince's connection with the *Scientific American* did not end after its investigating committee had rendered its verdict on Margery or after his resignation from the ASPR. Following Bird's exit from the publication and the controversy over Margery, Prince became one of its editors corresponding with readers interested in paranormal phenomena. He also contributed articles on telepathy, spirit photography and automatic writing, published in 1927 an outline of the history of ESP investigations,[122] and, in 1933, when the *Scientific American* conducted tests for telepathy among its readers, Prince examined the data and helped arrive at conclusions.

Progress of the BSPR

When Worcester and other disaffected people abandoned the ASPR, he established the BSPR with McDougall's help. In his Presidential Address to the Society, Worcester explained the importance of Prince to its formation:

> I regard Dr. Prince as one of the foremost investigators in the whole field of psychic research both mental and physical, if not the foremost investigator now living. In fact, without the promise of his services this Society would not have come into being, for the group of men and women interested in psychic research and dissatisfied with its status in America, out of which our Society sprang, knew of no other man available capable of fulfilling its ideals and of maintaining the lofty standards of Dr. Hodgson and of Dr. Hyslop.[123]

Besides McDougall and Prince, Worcester was able to call on advisors such as professors Newbold and Gardiner and to convince Gardner Murphy, then in the Department of Psychology at Harvard, Professor Francis L. Strickland of Boston University and the psychiatrist Dr. Frederick Peterson of New York, to join the BSPR's Council. The initial years of the organization passed in attempts to perfect the Society, frame its policy, write its Constitution, gather its members and justify its existence with highly constructive and critical scientific contributions in parapsychology.[124]

A chill of disappointment must have been experienced as some of these goals were not reached in spite of Prince's reputation as "the foremost" figure in parapsychology. Not even his presence and services were enough to attract many members to the BSPR. Three years after its formation, for instance, it could boast of only 192 members,[125] almost the number of members the ASPR had at its low ebb in 1906 when Hyslop took it over.

But, in the summer of 1926, Prince did entice a pair of visitors to the office of the BSPR at 346 Beacon Street in Boston, and, when J.B. Rhine and Louisa E. Rhine made their way to Boston and found Prince, it was as if three drops of water had come together. Prince immediately liked Louisa well enough to salute her as "The Doctoress"[126] and with Rhine seemed at once to find a common bond in Margery at one of whose seances Rhine, also, had noted suspicious circumstances. Prince was impressed by Rhine. "I early learned," he said of Rhine, "that he was keen to discover the indicia of deception within the field of psychic research...."[127]

Prince was always on the lookout for younger people to succeed him—he was then 63 years old—and he hired the Rhines at $12 a week to conduct what turned out to be disappointing experimental sittings with Minnie R. Soule (Mrs. Chenoweth) in Boston. Something might have developed from their relationship, but the Rhines could not resist Thomas' offer to send them to Duke with his mediumistic material and to pay expenses.

Rhine wrote to Prince: "It was at once a chance to study under Professor McDougall and an opportunity to continue learning something of psychic phenomena."[128] After his arrival, the exuberant Rhine sent Prince this letter: "I am glad to have come here and I expect it to be one of the great years in my life."[129]

As Prince's presence did not lure members, neither did it draw from others high quality papers for publication by the BSPR. Apart from his own writings, the Society published only two works of the first rank. In 1927, when Estabrooks was ready to publish the results of the card-guessing experiments he had conducted at Harvard with McDougall's support and which recorded a large number of hits indicative of telepathy, Prince seized Estabrooks' offered paper and published it at once.[130] Seven years later, Prince was able to publish, and wrote the introduction for, Rhine's famous monograph *Extra-Sensory Perception*.[131] Prince also sent hundreds of complimentary copies of the book to scientists, mathematicians, psychologists and others.[132]

In terms of research, investigations or experiments, the progress of the BSPR was slow and it accomplished little. The membership was little concerned with such matters. Meetings during 1928 at the rooms of the Society may be taken as typical of the interests of the membership. In the course of this year, members observed healing mediums controlled by a spirit, "Doctor Bede," make medical diagnoses and listened to papers on music, mysticism and the psychic practices of American Indians.[133]

In 1929, however, Prince involved the members in a pioneering experiment. The ESP experiments conducted at Harvard by Murphy and Estabrooks under McDougall's sponsorship had dealt with telepathy. Clairvoyance had not been investigated in America up to 1929. Prince had a hand in this effort although the primary impetus for it came from across the Atlantic. Card-guessing experiments to test for clairvoyance had been carried out in England by Ina Jephson.[134] The successful results were suggestive of clairvoyance until S.G. Soal noticed several difficulties with the experiments which arose principally because most subjects in the experiments used their own cards and did so in their own homes.

In 1929, Soal, along with Theodore Besterman and Miss Jephson, decided to repeat a series of experiments under more controlled conditions. One of the series was conducted in America by Prince in Boston with 95 members of the BSPR. In these experiments, sealed envelopes containing playing cards were sent to subjects who, within a week of receiving them, were to return to the experimenters the unopened sealed envelopes with a record of guesses of what the concealed cards were. The experimenters opened the envelopes and, against the guesses of the subjects, entered the actual cards. The 2031 guesses in the Boston experiment produced negative results with no evidence of clairvoyance.

The same was true of the joint experiment as a whole and the conclusion was that the series did not confirm the hypothesis that clairvoyance is a commonly possessed faculty.

BSPR Bulletins and Proceedings

In terms of publications, the BSPR's output was about equal to that of the SPR. More important than quantity was the quality, which also was on a par with the publications of the English organization. Wrote the proud Worcester: "Our Bulletins and Proceedings are regarded as among the most judicious and keenly critical documents which psychic research possesses."[135] They were the fruits of Prince's labors. With him, it seemed, the impairment of one sense stimulated the others, for he was deaf and therefore unable to be an effective investigator of seances in which physical phenomena occurred. This was "a tragedy"[136] for Prince because it made him an easy target for criticisms which the supporters of Margery, gloating over Prince's inability to hear or check direct voice phenomena in her seances, did not miss. But his other faculties remained or were made sharper and his literary work was never affected.

Under his editorship, the BSPR issued 17 *Bulletins* which he wrote or edited. Among the more interesting were the BSPR *Declaration of Principles* and Prince's *Inaugural Address*[137]; a discussion of a record made of phenomena in a "haunted house" not far from the BSPR's office on Beacon Street[138]; a resume of papers presented at the Third International Congress held in 1927 in Paris to which the BSPR had sent Prince[139]; a study of the indicia of physical mediumship resulting from sittings Prince had with some of Europe's best physical mediums, such as Frau Silbert and Jan Guzik — in no sitting with them was Prince able to evaluate object movements or raps as of paranormal origin; a study of 13 sittings with Rudi Schneider, who had persuaded Baron Schrenck-Notzing and other investigators of his psychic powers, in which no results worthy of mention took place[140]; a discussion of psychical experiences for which Prince wrote a Foreword and added notes[141]; a discussion of psychic experiences both spontaneous and experimental[142]; a study of two cases of multiple personality in which paranormal phenomena were produced[143]; two *Bulletins* discussing the results of a questionnaire sent to 10,000 people whose names appeared in *Who's Who in America* and who reported spontaneous experiences, including dreams[144]; a discussion of the telepathic experiments described in Upton Sinclair's *Mental Radio*[145]; a study of physical phenomena[146]; a discussion of "drop-in" communicators[147]; and a further consideration of "Walter's" thumbprints in the Margery case.[148]

From Prince came four of the BSPR's *Proceedings*. Besides coauthoring the Leonard and Soule experiments with Lydia W. Allison in 1929 which discussed sittings with Mrs. Soule in which Prince and Doris were sitters, he produced four of the chief works published by the BSPR during its existence: *Psychic in the House* (1926), *The Case of Patience Worth* (1927), *Noted Witnesses for Psychic Occurrences* (1928) and *The Enchanted Boundary* (1930).

The Psychic in the House

Although the title of this work of nearly 300 pages suggests that the book deals with a psychic in one house, the mysterious footsteps, raps and crystal visions which it chronicles occurred in three houses in which Prince resided: on Bellevue Street in Montclair, New Jersey; 27 Forest Street also in Montclair; and on Beacon Street in Boston. The psychic was not Prince or his wife. It was their adopted daughter, Theodosia (whom we have been calling and will call Doris).

The book is noteworthy on two counts. First, although rappings are not uncommon and were noted both in England in the Parsons house on Cock Lane, London, in 1762 and, in America, where rapping phenomena increased greatly in the period following their outbreak in the Fox residence in Hydesville, New York, in 1848, Prince's book was the first sustained record of these phenomena to be kept carefully, methodically and over a long period of time. There is no presentation like it in the literature of parapsychology.[149]

This book should also be considered in relation to the belief of many researchers today that an altered state of consciousness — hypnosis, meditation, sensory deprivation — is conducive to psi. Prior to Doris's cure in 1914, when Margaret, the mischievous, fun-loving, child personality, was banished for good, a few incidents had occurred, some telepathic, some involving Doris's feeling that her dead mother was present. Twice she saw her mother's apparition, and, on one occasion, Margaret appeared to obtain paranormally the contents of a letter Prince had written to Dr. Morton Prince.[150] Evidently in her dissociative condition, Doris had some psychic abilities. But they were not really brought out, or, as Prince said, "only stray gleams of psychism were manifested in this disintegrated state."[151] But, following her cure, psychic gifts which had been blocked became unblocked and matured. After 1914 Doris began to do automatic writing, saw visions in a glass or silvered ball or frequently saw apparitions — some evidential — felt beds and chairs vibrating or shaking.[152]

Nor can the experiments Hyslop conducted in 1914 to attempt to reach the dead Emma Fischer be overlooked. Doris, now cured, went to New York to sit with Mrs. Chenoweth and Hyslop during the experiments. If evidential communications were in fact received from Doris's mother, as Prince believed, it may have been because Doris and not Mrs. Chenoweth was the psychic. Eleanor Sidgwick urged the theory "that the sitter plays some important part in bringing about the results obtained"[153] because it is the sitter who, without knowing it, may be in telepathic communication with a deceased communicator. The medium only receives telepathic impressions from sitters and like a mirror gives them back to the sitters by way of speech or writing.

The Psychic in the House should be reread today because it brings out beautifully the increase in Doris's psychic gifts in the years subsequent to Margaret's last appearance. As Prince wrote:

Take the psychic of this volume and the various houses in which she has lived. She had lived in seven houses, and spent periods in others, without hearing mysterious sounds. But in the subsequent three residences she has heard them. It is highly improbable that say ten houses should successively have utterly lacked a quality which the next three possessed. It is intelligible that something in her developed. . . .[154]

The first of the three residences in which Doris heard strange sounds was the house in Montclair, New Jersey, occupied by the Princes and their adopted daughter four years after her cure. Never before had she heard raps or footsteps. Now, however, beginning with the two house in New Jersey and later in the one in Boston, she did. Even Prince who "never in my life had heard such sounds, though I had lived in twenty-six houses, have heard them in the subsequent three."[155] He attributed these sounds to the development of something in Doris which stimulated their production.

The Doris case of dissociation — certainly one of an extremely altered state of consciousness — would seem to indicate that such a state is not necessarily psi-conducive but, on the contrary, psi-preventive since Doris's "stray gleams" of psi abilities seemed to grow more powerful and constant only after her recovery from this state and her reassociation.

"In brief," Prince summarized, "when Doris was plainly dissociated in an abnormal way and degree she gave little manifestation of psychism; as she progressed toward normality . . . a true psychism began to develop; and now, at her acme of physical and mental well-being, she is strongly psychical and gives evidence from time to time of the supernormal."[156]

In Prince's psychometric experiments with Mrs. King and Señora Reyes de Zierold, mediums obtained information from objects through paranormal means. It was as if this information lay buried in the objects and was unearthed by psychics as they were stimulated by the objects. A similar phenomenon seems to have occurred in *The Psychic in the House,* and Prince did not fail to notice that what he called "psychogenetic centers" might exist: places and especially houses which, at times, can rouse and stimulate psychic abilities. In other words, it is likely "that the something in the psychic and the something in the house react upon each other."[157] That there may be a "something" in an object which persists even after a person who had been associated with it is dead or absent is strongly suggested not only by the case of the Mexican medium whom Prince investigated but also by the classic experiment with clock cards carried out by D.J. West and G.W. Fisk. West believed, from prior ESP experiments he had conducted, that he was a jinx doomed to get only null results. In the clock card experiments, packs of cards were made up by West and Fisk and sent to subjects who did not know which of the packs had been prepared by West. The scoring for Fisk's section was significant but not for West's.

The experimenters concluded: "The fact, if fact it be, that the person who actually prepares the lists of random numbers, arranges the cards in the packs, and finally assesses and marks the score sheets, should have some influence on the result is very mysterious and surprising."[158] But it is not mysterious or surprising if West left "something" in the cards which continued to jinx his section. *The Psychic in the House* presaged this.

The first residence on Bellevue Avenue in Montclair seemed to arouse Doris's psychic abilities because in it were manifested the largest number of paranormal happenings—as if a Fisk had lived there before and left "something" in the house which got significant results. Yet despite "the fact that strong expectations had been raised in [Doris's] mind that the most striking group of the Bellevue Avenue phenomena would be continued at Forest Street, it utterly ceased there"[159]—as if a West had been a former occupant and had left "something" which jinxed Doris and had a dampening effect on her. At the Boston house, although Doris had no expectations of anything peculiar occurring, it did—possibly because this house, unlike the one on Forest Street, had "something" left in it by a previous owner which aroused Doris again.

Although published three generations ago, Prince's *The Psychic in the House* belongs in the library of anyone who wishes to try to understand the paranormal.

The Case of Patience Worth

In this publication, Prince presented a comprehensive discussion of the remarkable case of a 31 year old housewife whom he had observed closely. She was Pearl Lenore Pollard who lived with her husband, John H. Curran, in St. Louis, Missouri. Before her marriage, she had lived in Mound City, Illinois, where she was born in 1883, and later in the Ozarks, in Texas and in Chicago. She left school at 14, took music and voice lessons, worked for music companies and Marshall Fields department store. When Prince questioned her, she admitted to having read no poetry as a child. The extent of her literary reading was "Black Beauty" and "Ichabod Crane." She thought Don Quixote was a Spanish poet. Her knowledge of history was equally limited. She knew that America had been discovered in 1492, but Prince found that she could tell him nothing of Guy Fawkes, James I or James II. She thought that Henry VIII had been beheaded. To Prince's question concerning Mrs. Curran's opportunity to read books she replied:

> There were no cyclopedias, books on antiquities, ancient customs,
> histories of literature and the like in father's house that I
> remember.... All the books I have had in my own residence I have
> now; you may see them. I never lived in a house that had a well-stocked
> library.... I never frequented public libraries, never even had a library
> card until Mr. Curran's last illness, when we took cards to bring him
> novels to read.[160]

Her skill at literary composition was described in this response: "I remember only two attempts, except for some valentine single verses, to write poetry, and these were when I was about fifteen. They were poor stuff. . . . I never wrote anything in prose but little school compositions."[161]

Yet, in 1913, Mrs. Curran began to receive communications apparently from "Patience Worth," a personality claiming to be a seventeenth century English girl who had come to America and been killed by Indians. From "Patience Worth" there came, through the ouija board on which Mrs. Curran's fingers were placed, literary compositions of the highest quality framed as long tales, aphorisms and poems of a superior order and proverbs, all delivered in archaic English and with a spontaneous literary genius. On many occasions, after being interrupted by a question or by a telephone or doorbell, or after laying it aside for weeks or months, the ability to go on with a complex story or imagery was unaffected. Once, within three hours, 5,000 words dealing with a dramatic and difficult point in a narrative were composed. "All this," Prince observed, "involves phenomenal memory, phenomenal speed and phenomenal complexity of mental operations."[162] Combine this with an ability to pass from archaic English to a more modern language, to make instant responses to groups of people, and with a literary production amounting in all to three million words, and one can see why Casper S. Yost, editor of the *St. Louis Globe-Democrat* decided to publish the case of "Patience Worth" in 1915. When he saw the tremendous response caused by his articles, he published a book about her in 1916. The public interest thus created was stimulated even more by what was to follow.

In 1917, *The Sorry Tale,* a novel purportedly dictated by "Patience Worth" was published. It depicted Jesus and the places and people in the Holy Land during his era. Critics called it as dramatic as *Ben Hur.* W.T. Allison, professor of English literature at the University of Manitoba, said, "No book outside the Book of Books gives such an intimate picture of the earthly life of Jesus and no book has ever thrown such clear light upon the manner of life of Jews and Romans in the Palestine of the day of our Lord. . . ."[163]

Telka, another novel that took place in the Middle Ages, was also published. William Marion Reedy, editor of *Reedy's Mirror,* knew literature. He found in *Telka* "hundreds of words of strictly Anglo-Saxon origin. . . . [T]hese communications are literature. . . . They are wonderful . . . thoroughly consistent in form. . . . There runs through them all a sort of musical fugue . . . passages of bewitching beauty, of rare high spirits, of pathos — and all in a language of an indescribable simplicity and felicity, though strange."[164] After still another novel, *Hope Trueblood,* was published, the *New York Times* commented: "No teller of tales who studied his craft could read this story without the keenest admiration for the finished technique with which Patience Worth handles this story;" and the *New York Tribune* was of the opinion that: "[w]hether in the body or the spirit, the author of 'Hope Trueblood' is singularly gifted with imagination, invention and power of expression. The psychological analysis, and invention of the occult, the dramatic power displayed in the narrative are extraordinary, and stamp it as a work approximating absolute genius."[165]

Here, then, was the case of an ordinary housewife of very limited education, reading and literary ability who produced over a period of many years amazing pieces of literature in an archaic English supposedly written or dictated by an English girl of a bygone era. It is not astonishing, therefore, that the case was a sensation among the American public. Yet it is astonishing that the case was all but passed over as devoid of interest by people who should have known better. Of course, it was not totally ignored. Dr. Morton Prince looked into the case to a limited extent. Hyslop, ever alert to cases suggestive of survival, read and reviewed *The Sorry Tale*. But he put it down in disappointment because he thought that there was "no scientific interest in the book save the method of getting its contents"[166] from a deceased English girl for which conclusion, in his opinion, the book gave no evidence.

It was not until Prince became research officer of the ASPR that the case was subjected to a thorough investigation which led him to say: "I am very certain that had Dr. Hyslop lived and had the time and opportunity to go into the case as I have done, or even to become cognizant of the fruits of my labors, he would have become greatly interested. . . ."[167]

Prince went to see Mrs. Curran in 1924 and, impressed by the quality and quantity of the material she presented to him, returned to St. Louis in 1926 to conduct experiments with her and to put her "in the witness box." In addition, he obtained from her the names and addresses of people who had known her intimately, went to the Ozarks where Mrs. Curran had lived to interview them and even printed an appeal in a mass-circulation periodical for more information. His efforts culminated in *The Case of Patience Worth*.

The mere writing by way of the ouija board was not interesting to Prince. One of the principal questions was: Could the case be acounted for on any normal basis? Were the literary productions the result of powers Mrs. Curran consciously possessed and manifested? It soon became apparent to him from her testimony and that of others that Mrs. Curran, who had never been conscious of literary skills before the appearance of "Patience Worth" beyond writing some school-girl doggerel, with her educational background, her limited knowledge of history and even more limited library and access to libraries, had never consciously possessed or manifested intellectual powers sufficient to make her the author of *The Sorry Tale*, *Telka*, or *Hope Trueblood* in which "Patience Worth" demonstrated not only literary genius but also much correct historical knowledge of the circumstances, color and details of the periods in which the stories were set.

Through Mrs. Curran's autobiography and interviews with people who knew her, he built up a picture of a woman who had never been east of Chicago or south of Fort Worth and who spoke only the colloquial language of the Midwest where she had been born, a picture altogether incompatible with the English dialect used in the writings and inconsistent with the language used in *Telka*, which contained 90 percent Anglo-Saxon words and 10 percent Old French words.

But it occurred to Prince that Mrs. Curran could have memorized her material before the sessions and then poured it all out during them, especially since sometimes a verse or fiction would come through the ouija board in such final form that they needed no alteration; or sometimes they would stop incompleted in one session to be picked up perfectly without delay or difficulty at the next. So, as he had done with the Mexican medium, he tried one of his "mean tricks." He gave "Patience Worth" two themes which she was to address, one with a verse entitled "The Folly of Atheism" for a few lines, the other with a dialogue between a lout and a wench at a fair for a few lines, and then she was to go back and forth between them until poem and dialogue were completed. With no confusion evident, the tasks were accomplished.

To this point Prince makes it appear that the writings manifested a knowledge and a genius beyond the capabilities of the average American woman playing with her ouija board. New questions arose. Were the knowledge and genius that of the dead girl? The spiritistic hypothesis would hold that they had come from her. Or did Mrs. Curran possess the requisite subconscious powers to be the author of the astonishing writings without conscious awareness? An alternative hypothesis would hold that "Patience Worth" was a secondary personality which had developed its literary genius and needed only the ouija board to express it.

Prince was no stranger to cases of split personality, of which none could be more outstanding than that of Doris Fischer to which he had devoted years of study. If the case were like Doris's, there would be no discarnate communicator. In support of the split personality theory, one need only recall that "Patience Worth" claimed to be a simple seventeenth century peasant girl. It would be extraordinary for such a girl to know and to be able to express herself in an obsolete tongue of earlier epochs, to be able to write with a detailed knowledge of the histories of these epochs and to be able to perform remarkable feats of memory and intellect. Isn't it more than probable that the author was Mrs. Curran?

Those who prefer this theory tend to be quite cranky with Prince because they think that his book avoided the split personality theory and was deliberately "designed to bolster the case for spiritualism."[168] If it was so designed, Prince would have been travelling in good company. The eminent British Cambridge psychologist and parapsychologist Robert H. Thouless, wrote: "As evidence for survival, the Patience Worth writings are unique in kind. . . . It is a case that we cannot afford to forget in an all-round view of the evidence for survival."[169] The difficulty with the spiritistic hypothesis is not so much the strength of the split personality theory as that the "Patience Worth" character was never identified as a real person who actually lived. This failure does not mean, however, that the split personality theory is right and that "Patience Worth," the philological marvels and the full grasp of history were all produced by Mrs. Curran. From the details of her life which Prince was able to put together, it is not possible to see any source to which she would have had access in order to derive her knowledge of history or of English words and dialect belonging to eras prior to and during "Patience Worth's" life, some of which words were unknown even to scholars at the time they were written or dictated.

There are difficulties with either hypothesis. Any criticism of Prince's book as pro-spiritist is wrong because, in reality, he was just as confused about the correct interpretation of this case as we are. The cautious and open-minded position he finally took may be one to which many of us would assent:

> For ten months my time has been mostly devoted to the study of this case by all the methods possible for me to employ. No single discovered datum has been omitted, no clue or hint from any source neglected. It is not possible for any fact that shall come to light to disconcert me, since I am not wedded to any theory. . . . If there should be reason I will retreat as cheerfully as I have advanced, but, after the arduous and unremitting labor now drawn to a close, am not sanguine of having the opportunity to retreat from or to modify this proposition: *Either our concept of what we call the subconscious must be radically altered, so as to include potencies of which we hitherto have had no knowledge, or else some cause operating through but not originating in the subconsciousness of Mrs. Curran must be acknowledged.*[170]

Noted Witnesses for Psychic Occurrences

Within that disorderly dust-cloud floating about the orderly facts of established science which cannot be fitted into science's neat system are, in parapsychological nomenclature, "spontaneous cases" — peculiar reports from daily life which tell of premonitory dreams, of apparitions of dead people, of messages from the spirit of a deceased person, of someone knowing the thoughts in another's mind when no normal channel of communication exists between them. From the beginning of parapsychology in America, there has been a desire to see whether the experiences of ordinary men and women furnished any real evidence of extrasensory perception or spirit survival. When Barrett spoke to scholars during his tour of America in 1884 to express his idea for forming a society to look into these phenomena, he outlined the aims of the SPR and said: "out of alchemy came chemistry; out of astrology, astronomy. There may be much in these extraordinary accounts of second-sight, thought-reading, apparitions, and so forth, fit only to ridicule; but if there are any facts at the bottom, we want to find them."[171]

These words were still ringing in their meeting-halls in Boston and Philadelphia where Barrett had spoken when scholars, headed by James, established the ASPR in the winter of 1885 to subject the accounts to rigorous scrutiny to be certain that any facts at the bottom of the cases could be corroborated by independent testimony. The ASPR's aims were similar to those of the London Society as were its lines of inquiry: into spontaneous cases, including telepathy (thought-transference), apparitions and haunted houses. The first committee report made by the new ASPR was by a committee set up to look into telepathy.[172] Another committee on apparitions and haunted houses was constituted.[173] Hodgson's and Hyslop's absorption in mediumship meant that little attention was paid to spontaneous cases, but Prince, convinced of the importance of such cases, published reports of them, including his own dreams, in JASPR until 1923 when he was replaced as editor.

Prince added to the case for extrasensory perception and spirit survival when he compiled the psychic experiences which had been reported by more than 170 people whom he described as "noted witnesses."

These experiences were wide-ranging: telepathy, visions of the dying, raps, apparitions, out-of-body experiences, clairvoyance, hauntings, premonitory and simultaneous dreams, other premonitions, mediumistic communications, odd auditory and visual experiences.

Since all reports of spontaneous cases are essentially fallible human testimony, the initial questions always are: How reliable is the reporter and how far can the report be corroborated? To answer these perennial questions Prince selected the experiences of "noted" people—men of science, lawyers and doctors, high-ranking officers in the Army and Navy, statesmen and diplomats, poets, playwrights, novelists, artists, theologians, people such as Luther Burbank, Augustus de Morgan, Arthur Balfour, Robert Browning, Mark Twain, John C. Fremont, Goethe, Oliver Wendell Holmes, Victor Hugo, William R. Newbold, Carolus Linnaeus, Alvaro Obregon, John Ruskin, Alfred Tennyson. Why people of prominence? It is a question of veracity. William Moggs of Sheboygan, Wisconsin, may be a good man, indeed the very best of men, but, since we don't know him, his alleged experience is not very convincing. But few of us would doubt that declarations by people whose careers have been in public view and whose deeds and writings are known are at least honest.[174]

The class of persons Prince had brought together had another importance. The same William Moggs of Sheboygan might receive some satisfaction, attention and publicity from the invention or unconscious exaggeration of a story. But it is far less likely that a prominent person like a Mark Twain or Luther Burbank, with nothing to gain from narrating a strange experience, had been guilty of invention or exaggeration.

Before 1928, no collection of the spontaneous cases of famous and brilliant men and women had been made. Prince's, therefore, was new and was a further step in the study of this category of the paranormal. This collection of experiences continues to be worthy of our attention today. Murphy gives one reason:

> They compel the reader to face and work through for himself the prob-
> lem of "coincidence," decide what he is going to mean by this term and
> what degree of correspondence there must be between impressions and
> the authenticated facts to warrant their being taken seriously in
> psychical research. The reader can then settle down to the study of their
> taxonomy, their grouping, their organization, the psychological con-
> currences and uniformities that bind certain groups of cases together,

and the possibility of a physiological or psychological glimpse into their meaning.[175]

Critics of parapsychology who think that the beliefs of parapsychologists are shaped by a "will to believe" might want to consider Prince's book. They might try to account for the curious fact that Prince's book does not describe a single report by a parapsychologist, English or American, of a psychic experience. Prince wrote:

> I have not found in the whole task of preparing this book, and at the moment I cannot remember, with a single exception, any person of prominence in professional psychic research who is generally regarded as scientific in his modes of approach, and who has admitted having had in his own person, a spontaneous psychic experience. It may be that there are such and that I ought to recall the instances, but they must be few indeed.[176]

Who the "single exception" was Prince did not say. It might have been himself. Not only was his father's name spelled out on the planchette in California, not only had he heard raps and observed other phenomena in the Bellevue Avenue and other residences in which he and Doris had lived after her cure, but Prince had also reported several precognitive dreams. The most striking was a horrible dream on the night of November 27–28, 1917 of a pretty, slender, light-haired woman of about 35 years of age who brought him an order for her execution and who was beheaded. At the time of her execution, her hand gripped his hand. His hand felt the bloody hair of the severed head while the fingers of his other hand were caught in its teeth as the mouth opened and closed several times. Within twenty-four hours, a pretty, slender, golden-haired woman of about 31, and whose name was Sarah Hand, calmly lay down on the tracks of the Long Island Railroad and was decapitated by a train running over her neck.[177] She believed that her head would continue to live after decapitation, and to Prince the severed head had seemed alive.

But Prince was one of the rare well-known parapsychologists to have reported a psychic experience. Another exception was Hodgson who told James that one night in bed in 1884 he felt a hand seize his arm. Yet, more than any other group, parapsychologists who are absorbed by ESP and PK should have recorded in far greater numbers personal incidents involving such phenomena. One would have expected Lodge or Myers, Hodgson or Hyslop, all of whom believed in spirit survival, to have witnessed apparitions of dead persons or have heard strange footsteps after midnight in the halls and on the stairways of their houses. But they told of no such experiences. Instead, the narrators of these experiences were people such as the brilliant English lawyer Lord Chancellor Erskine and Carl Schurz, a United States Senator. So critics who say the "will to believe" accounts for the beliefs of parapsychologists might try to answer Prince's question:

> If the will to believe has its deadly control of [parapsychologists'] whole trend of thought, why did not suggestion, auto-suggestion, illusion and morbid hallucination, which are supposed by the same critics to ac-

count for the peculiar mental phenomena of more obscure folk, induce in [Myers, Barrett, Lodge, Hodgson and Hyslop] also peculiar spontaneous experiences?[178]

The Enchanted Boundary

Because of its variety of quotations and pronouncements which show up an attitude toward parapsychology which has not changed over the years, namely, sneering resistance and rejection, *The Enchanted Boundary* continues to have a present day relevance. Collective parapsychology was established in England in 1882 and in America three years later. When we take into consideration the phenomena it studies, "of which," said Sidgwick in his Presidential Address to the SPR, "it is quite impossible to exaggerate the scientific importance, if only a tenth part of what has been alleged by generally credible witnesses could be shewn to be true. . . .";[179] and when we also take into account the illustrious character of the people who have been connected with it — the Sidgwicks, Myers, Barrett, Crookes, Lord Balfour, Lodge, Schiller, William James, and others — as rational people we would have every reason to believe that the subjects to which they devoted themselves would not be rejected scornfully, especially by individuals of intelligence. And when people such as James, Sidgwick, Henri Bergson, Hans Driesch, and those whose lives are depicted in this book have studied the evidence for over a century and are satisfied that it is a subject meriting study, it seems presumptuous and unscientific for intelligent people who never studied it to ignore and dismiss the subject.

Yet, in *The Enchanted Boundary*, Prince presents an array of writings and pronouncements by over 100 people prominent in science, academia and other fields, all hostile to parapsychology. His book made the point that, regardless of intelligence, training, learning or standing, hostile critics seem to display an ignorance or disregard of facts which, in their own fields, would be unthinkable and never tolerated. Prince's title for the book was apt, for it seems that when even the best minds cross the enchanted border into the region of parapsychology something strange happens. Prince described the effects:

In other fields they are prudently silent until they have acquired special knowledge, but they venture into this with none. Elsewhere they test their facts before they declare them, but here they pick up and employ random statements without discretion. Elsewhere they use a fair semblance of logic, but here their logic becomes wondrous weird. Elsewhere they generally succeed in preserving the standard scientific stolidity, but here they frequently manifest and confess a submission to emotions ill befitting those who sprang from the head of Brahm. Elsewhere they observe the knightly etiquette of the lists, but in this field think it no shame to decline the fair encounter, and, from the safe shelter of the barrier, to jeer about the presumptive quality of their opponents' brains.[180]

It is more than likely that parapsychologists will agree that not all critics who cross the enchanted boundary are adversely affected and that, when they are informed and fair and make valid objections, their objections must be recognized and discussed. Prince's book makes us realize, on the other hand, that critics often can be irresponsible, uninformed and untruthful in their treatment of the subject and that with them dialogue is impossible and may do more harm than good. The interesting question is why are they so? Because, said Prince:

> The zeit-geist, particularly in America, is at present unfavorable to psychic facts, and for many the vane is set, from childhood, against liking them. In some cases the dislike is so great that it prevents one from making any understanding examination of the evidence and at the , same time betrays him into making declarations based on manifold misapprehension.[181]

The vane may be set in America where at one time Spiritualism claimed 11 million adherents and parapsychology is confused with that feared and suspect creed. It is probable, too, that parapsychology is considered a threat to many belief systems. Perhaps only a reincarnated Prince could explain what it would take to convince some critics to abandon their irresponsible hostility to it.

The SPR

Prince was elected twice, in 1930 and 1931, to the presidency of the SPR. Described in the SPR *Journal* as "one of the most experienced, persevering and distinguished students of psychical research," he was welcomed by the Society, which looked upon his presidency "as further evidence of the cordial relations which have always existed between serious psychical researchers in the United Kingdom and the United States."[182]

In July 1930, Prince went to England to present his Presidential Address in which he made a distinction between the "will-to-believe" and the "will-to-prove." When critics parrot the "will-to-believe" as a sneer in order to disparage serious studies in parapsychology, this "peeping behind the scenes to discover a will-to-believe is silly." If the basic facts are there and the interpretation and argument emerging from them are valid, if they and not desire produce the will-to-prove, they are their own vindication.[183]

Prince also entered what he called "A Plea for Sweetness" which is not out of place today. In spite of the fact that parapsychologists have been atacked by criticisms and ridiculed, they must try to keep all discussions on a calm and intellectual plane. Even though they are accused of being a sort of Guy Fawkes gang plotting to blow up everything, parapsychologists must still keep their tempers, control their pens and tongues and reply in terms of reason and not emotion.[184]

Tributes

Prince had one guiding principle, that of every scientific investigator: "What we at present want is facts, facts, and yet more facts."[185] But are the accumulation and presentation of facts, even if done with the greatest thoroughness, the sole marks of the ideal parapsychologist? When Prince addressed the symposium held by Clark University, he added other qualifications. He defined a parapsychologist "as a person of evident intelligence and cultivation, whose writings reveal acquaintance with and employment of critical method, who has had much experience in this field, and who is interested in the fixation of facts, and not in propaganda...."[186] Prince himself, of whom Worcester said, "His name is known wherever psychic research is known and it is honored by the honorable and feared by others,"[187] was a man of such qualities and, by his own definition, the ideal parapsychologist.

While some of his works appeared in the *Scientific American,* two in the *American Journal of Psychology* and two historical monographs were published by the American Historical Association, his major labors, including "The Doris Case of Multiple Personality," his great contribution to abnormal psychology, remain unknown (except perhaps to students of abnormal psychology) because they were published by the ASPR and BSPR whose publications are rarely read outside the charmed circle of parapsychology. Nevertheless, first, all represent a devotion to parapsychology not exceeded by Hodgson or Hyslop. Second, all display what Murphy described as "the capacity, as no other American has had since William James, to study the normal and the supernormal in exactly the same spirit, with the same enthusiasm yet with the same lack of awe and excitement."[188] Finally, so "scrutinizing" and "rationalizing a monster" was Prince and so "scared to death of being caught in an error"[189] that, although his books and reports were written over three generations ago, they still have value for us, and it is as difficult now to mount justifiable critical attacks against them to show their flaws in scientific method or reasoning now as it was when they were written.

The variety of his work suggests that, in contrast to Hodgson and Hyslop, Prince was not overly occupied with the survival issue. His interest in parapsychology was broader, comparable in breadth to his travels, which took him to Antigonish, Nova Scotia, to investigate poltergeist phenomena,[190] to St. Louis and the Ozarks to study Mrs. Curran, to Mexico to investigate psychometry and to Europe to encourage international cooperation. In the end, what impressed him most? What were his final conclusions about the subject-matter of parapsychology? William James's "white crow" was Mrs. Piper. Prince said, "Mrs Soule ('Chenoweth'), Sra de Z., Mrs King and the singular happenings in my own residence during many successive months, are the particular 'white crows' of my experience."[191]

A few weeks before he died, he answered questions about his beliefs: What did he think about clairvoyance and telepathy? They were proved, he said. What of the survival question? Prince was cautious. He thought he believed in survival; still the "final clincher" was lacking and he felt that judgment could be too easily blinded by desire.[192]

Prince's death came on August 7, 1934, at his home at Hingham, Massachusetts. Of him, Rhine wrote: "I have been proud to claim Dr Walter Franklin Prince as my teacher, and I strongly hope that his splendid critical poise and his ruthless logic will continue to influence the subject he did so much to advance along sound lines in America."[193] Twenty-five of his friends and colleagues in parapsychology published similar high tributes to his memory,[194] and a Walter Franklin Prince Memorial Fellowship was created at Duke to encourage research in parapsychology. Perhaps the greatest tribute to his memory might have come from someone who contributed nothing to the published tributes—his adopted Doris who "loved him not merely as a devoted daughter, she adored him almost as her God, in that he had saved her from hell and had, one might almost say, given her a soul."[195] Prince's attitude toward his adopted Doris has been described as "Christlike in its patient love and sacrifice. . . . She was the support, the joy of his declining years."[196] Prince himself told Irwin: "And since my wife died, [Doris] has taken care of me. And she has been all that a daughter possibly could be."[197] Irwin added, "There were tears in all our eyes."[198] And Prince went to his grave in the sweet, sure knowledge that he had cured his daughter.

But when the God on whom she had relied for direction and support died, why had Doris not added her tribute to those of the others? Worcester went to her after Prince's death and found that she had "sunk into a pitiable condition of grief and despair."[199] Doris now lived alone in Hingham in a bungalow by the sea, her only companion a black spaniel, her nights filled with horrible dreams, her automatic writing dominated by frightening messages ostensibly from evil communicators. Worcester tried therapeutic conversations with her in order to rescue Prince's "great work from final shipwreck."[200] He thought that he, too, had restored her to health but Worcester deceived himself. With Prince's care and love gone forever, Doris was unrestorable. She died insane, the miserable inmate of an institution.[201]

Whether Prince knows that his friends paid their tributes and that present day parapsychologists continue to hold him in esteem, depends on whether there is survival after death and communication between this world and any other. If there is and Prince is aware that he is considered one of the great masters in parapsychology, does it all mean anything to him if he is aware also that his brave effort to save his dear Doris failed in the end?

William McDougall: A Portrait

In Greek mythology, the evils oppressing the human race are blamed on the beautiful woman called All-gifted or Pandora. She was made by the gods

William McDougall

at the command of the vengeful Zeus, angered after Prometheus stole fire from heaven. Although his brother had been warned by Prometheus not to accept gifts from the gods, Epimetheus accepted Pandora from Zeus. Her curiosity led her to open a strange box belonging to Epimetheus and from which, according to some accounts, every worldly ill escaped.

As many see it, however, not all evils were let loose. Every "superstition" invented by parapsychology—that a human mind, without the mediation of the senses or rational inference, can become aware of objects, past, present or future events or the contents of another mind whether it is still in a physical organism or has continued after the organism's death; or that a human mind, without the mediation of physical force, can influence or move physical objects—these evils still remain in Pandora's box and must not be allowed to fly into the world to set back civilization to a darker age.

Among the uncompromising critics of parapsychology are the psychologists of the university world of whom none was more opposed to notions of extrasensory perception or a death-surviving psychical entity than John Watson, the leader of behaviorism which, he said, had

> effectively expelled all such pseudo-concepts as sensation, perception, images or will, and rooted out every theory that involved such relics of Judaic superstition as mind, consciousness, or soul. . . . No one has ever touched a soul or seen one in a test-tube; and what can be neither touched nor seen and so eludes objective verification must be dismissed as non-existent.[202]

For psychologists who followed Watson, the expulsion of the pseudoconcept of perception meant the denial also of perception in its extrasensory form and, equally, the rooting out of superstitions like mind and soul meant the denial as well of their postmortem continuation.

Joseph Jastrow, who had been professor of psychology at the University of Wisconsin, was also a spokesman for academic psychologists hostile to parapsychology. Proclaiming his loyalty to the spirit of science, he opposed to the "last ditch" the conclusions and animus of parapsychology.[203]

Watson and Jastrow may be gone from the scene but new apostles of the opposition they represented have arisen in the persons of C.E.M. Hansel of the University of Wales and Ray Hyman of the University of Oregon. Not all contemporary academic psychologists are as rational and vocal as these critics, but most would agree with their opinions that parapsychological experiments and findings are marred by fraud, statistical flaws, failure to preclude sensory cues or other experimenter incompetence, would consider the parapsychologists' will to believe to be more powerful than their judgment and would not support research in parapsychology that might one day open Pandora's box.

During the first quarter of the twentieth century, however, one prominent psychologist cried out in protest against this unrelenting negativism and hostility. By his own admission, he was a nonconformist. "I have never fitted neatly into any social group. . . . I have participated in the life of many groups, scientific, medical, academic, and social, but have belonged to none."[204] But nonconformity for the sake of nonconformity was not behind William McDougall's protest. It was motivated initially by his criticism of the behaviorism of Watson and of Gestalt psychology which neglected the very fundament in the nature of the living organism whether human or animal: purpose. For McDougall's was a purposive psychology, or a "hormic" psychology, as he called it, to express his belief that in every living thing there is a vital factor which does not work in accordance with mechanistic principles but has its own peculiar nature and strives toward goals. That factor is *mind*. The psychologies with which he had struggled were defective because, while their doors were open to mechanistic biology, they swung shut against the purposive or theological aspects of mental life and biological processes.[205]

Not only did these psychologies neglect these aspects but also the equally obscure problem of the mind-body relation. It was to this relation that McDougall thought light might be brought by the methods of parapsychology.[206]

One reason for the opposition to parapsychology was the materialistic view of the world that induced psychologists and scientific thinkers to stand aloof from parapsychology with a sneering "there is nothing to it." McDougall disagreed with this stance:

> [I]f any man of science is convinced of the essential truth of
> Materialism, he is yet under obligation to approve and to give at least
> moral support to Psychical Research. For only by a well-organized and

long-sustained course of scientific investigation into the phenomena of
Psychical Research can it be proved that there is "nothing in them."[207]
Opposition to parapsychology came from another source, a Pandora box
syndrome described by our rebel:

> Men of science are afraid lest, if they give an inch in this matter, the
> public will take an ell and more. They are afraid that the least display
> of interest or acquiescence on their part may promote a great outburst
> of superstition on the part of the public, a relapse into belief in witch-
> craft, necromancy, and the black arts generally, with all the moral evils
> which must accompany the prevalence of such beliefs.[208]

Yet those who opposed parapsychology at the start of the century as well
as those who assail it today as pseudoscientific handmaiden to ESP, PK and life
after death, neglect to realize that research in parapsychology, in McDougall's
language:

> does not really add to the risk of relapse into barbaric superstition;
> rather it is our best defence against it. For Pandora's box has been
> opened, the lid has been slightly lifted, and we are bound to go on and
> to explore its remotest corner and cranny.... It is the policy of sitting
> on the lid of the box that is risky; a danger and threat to our
> civilization.[209]

McDougall was no soft-headed sympathizer with parapsychology. He
always insisted that he belonged to the right, not the left, wing of parapsychology; and not merely the right wing but "the extreme right."[210]

Suppose that other right-wing parapsychologists, after rummaging through
Pandora's box, should come up with negative research results and should
therefore conclude that what critics had feared might be in it—ESP, PK and
survival after death—did not exist at all? McDougall knew that "we may
ultimately find the box to have been empty from the first.... [Even if that oc-
curred] I should maintain that the work of [parapsychology] in boldly exploring its recesses and showing its emptiness to the world had been of the very
greatest value. But I do not anticipate this result, though I do not dread it."[211]

The box may indeed have been empty insofar as the survival hypothesis
is concerned, for the evidence for it continues to be highly ambiguous and controversial. The evidence for ESP produced by spontaneous experiences and
laboratory research, however, has been mainly positive. McDougall believed
that if and when telepathy should be established, all the achievements of all
the university psychological laboratories would be outweighed by the importance of the phenomenon for science and philosophy.[212] Others, such as
G.N.M. Tyrrell,[213] have shared this belief.

Youth, Education and Career

William McDougall's life was a divided one in several senses. It was spent
partly in the nineteenth century and partly in the twentieth, partly in England

and partly in America, partly in psychology and partly among the evils of parapsychology which the rest of his profession wished to keep under the lid of Pandora's box.

As Scottish as his name, McDougall was born on June 22, 1871, in Chadderton, Lancashire, England, almost close enough to the border for the sound of bagpipes to be heard. He rated as spirited and original his Scottish paternal grandfather who had eloped across the border with an heiress to settle in northern England where he founded a chemical factory.[214]

McDougall's father was the same kind of fiery Highlander, very extroverted, dark, small, even something of the Mediterranean type,[215] who inherited his father's originality—and the chemical factory. McDougall considered his mother an excellent example of the fair, introverted Nordic type, an ideal mother but without her husband's fire and originality.[216]

McDougall, therefore, considered himself a mixture of the Mediterranean and Nordic races and for this reason, "I have never felt myself to be altogether and typically English and altogether at home in the English social atmosphere."[217]

He thought of himself as "introverted, reserved, outwardly cold and arrogant, severely disciplined and absorbed in abstruse intellectualities."[218] It was an arrogance that was displayed early. At five years of age he was a brat, quick of tongue and nimble of mind, as precocious as a child could be, but still a nasty brat who delighted in domineering over boys of his own age, perhaps because "it was early made plain to me that I was expected to distinguish myself."[219] The brattishness received a considerable setback when he made the mistake of pulling the ear of a boy older and bigger than he and received a thrashing he did not soon forget.[220]

He attended a private boys' school where, without difficulty, he mastered Euclid, Latin and French, and, before he was 14, he was reading Huxley and the English novelists. His parents saw to it that Hume and Gibbon were in the library of their home for him to read, as well as the best magazines.[221] When he left the boys' school at 14, his parents, proud as could be of their bright son, sent him to Germany because of its reputation for learning. But this turned out to be a mistake. Instead of making more academic progress, he made less because of the language problem and because the German method of teaching was so different from the English.[222] So, after a year in Weimar, he came home in 1866 to a father who was making plans for him to become a future Lord Chancellor of England or another Michael Faraday. But McDougall "was so arrogant"[223] that he disdained the English bar and chemistry as careers and elected one in pure science.

At 15 he entered the University of Manchester, where he was attracted to biology, and, before his graduation in general science two years later, had read Spencer, Darwin, Huxley, Lyell and numerous scientific works. For him, however, the university was too provincial. Cambridge and Oxford, with their great academic and social prestige, appealed to him—but not equally. He decided that first-rate minds went to Cambridge while Oxford was the home of the second-rate.[224] In 1889, he was offered and accepted a scholarship at St. John's College, Cambridge. A year later, at the age of 19, he began his studies there in physiology, anatomy and anthropology.

During his freshman year his mother died of cancer, an event which was definitive in fixing his attitude toward religion. At 16, he had wavered between taking the Christian teaching very seriously or regarding it as "a monstrous system of delusions."[225] Mainly, he tended to be skeptical. The term "agnostic" described the path he followed.[226] When his gentle mother, whose life had been full of self-sacrifice, died of an agonizing cancer, this "unforgivable outrage" absolutely destroyed what little remained of his belief in a kindly Providence[227] and made him see that only through personal effort, not prayer, could one's lot be ameliorated.[228]

He passed the final examination, or "tripos," in natural sciences with highest honors in 1894 and obtained a University scholarship at St. Thomas's Hospital in London. McDougall was as ambitious as the next man but contemptuous of moneymaking. Neither business nor the law nor medicine seemed to him worthy vocations.[229]

Then why should he have elected in 1894 to study at Cambridge for another four years in order to take a medical degree? Because he felt it would be the best and most intimate way of working in the sciences concerned with people. While a medical student and, later, physician making his rounds through the wards and laboratories of St. Thomas's Hospital, he read for the first time William James's *Principles of Psychology*. It opened his eyes to investigating human nature through psychology and philosophy as well as through neurology and physiology.

He applied for and received a fellowship at Cambridge in 1898 and soon abandoned his medical career in favor of the broadest research into the nature of the human being. The next year found him accompanying the Cambridge Anthropological Expedition to the Torres Straits. A few months later, he went to Borneo to survey tribes of head hunters and found field anthropology extremely interesting. Years later, when he wondered why he had not pursued it as a career, he recalled "that my conscious ground of rejection was characteristically arrogant. I said to myself, 'That field is too easy for me'. . . ."[230]

James's work probably contributed to this rejection, too, and to McDougall's decision to assault the mysteries of the nature of the human being by way of psychology. He read Wundt, Ziehen, Muensterberg, Stout, Lotze. It seemed to him wise to spend time with Sigmund Freud, Pierre Janet and other of the best psychologists in Germany. But he decided against them and went to Göttingen instead to learn laboratory methods from G.E. Muller, especially experiments in color-vision. His reason for this curiously unexpected choice was more romantic than rational. McDougall had fallen in love, become betrothed and thought that quaint and quiet Göttingen would be a lovelier place for a honeymoon than Vienna or Paris. Actually, it is surprising that he ever allowed marriage to enter into his life. For it had been one of his self-imposed rules that no man should marry, and surely not before he reached the age of 40, if he was to cultivate his intellectual abilities to the fullest.[231] But even cold, reserved, disciplined and intellectual McDougall was human: "nature was too strong for principles."[232] This mismatch between nature and principles proved fortunate for him because McDougall "learned more psychology from [his wife's] intuitive understanding of persons than from any, perhaps all, of the great authors."[233]

In 1900, McDougall accepted a position at University College in London, where he taught laboratory methods while he carried on with research in the field of vision. Two years later, he became a reader in experimental psychology there. His research in this period culminated in papers which contributed later to his election to the Royal Society in 1912, the year he also became a fellow of Corpus Christi College. While he was teaching at University College, he also helped to found the British Psychological Society in 1901 and to create the *British Journal of Psychology*.

His appointment as Wilde Reader in Mental Philosophy at Oxford came in 1904, a post he was to hold for 15 years. His lectures covered the entire area of psychology, and when his topic was hypnotism, his listeners crowded in to hear. But, said McDougall, "I was neither fish, flesh, nor fowl."[234] As far as the scientists were concerned, he was not a scientist but a metaphysician, and the philosophers saw him as standing for a nonexistent brand of science. Even the students were wary of him. One of Professor E.R. Dodd's recollections of McDougall was that this professor was one of the men whose lectures he was advised not to attend because psychology was "a new-fangled extra-curricular subject which ought to be taught, if at all, only by philosophers trained on Aristotle."[235] Even the founder of the Wilde Readership tried to get McDougall expelled from his post. At these times McDougall thought of going back to medicine. Nevertheless, he was able to continue, and did continue with research and teaching in whose value he believed.

Several books now followed: *An Introduction to Social Psychology* (1908), *Body and Mind: A History and Defense of Animism* (1911), *Psychology, the Study of Human Behavior* (1912) and *The Pagan Tribes of Borneo* (1912). *Social Psychology*, considered by many a landmark book in psychology, was thought by McDougall himself to be his most outstanding and original contribution to the field.[236] For anyone in parapsychology, however, *Body and Mind* holds the greatest interest. It attacked mechanism and expressed McDougall's conviction that all living organisms possess a factor with its own endowments and which works independently of mechanistic principles. In the final chapter of the book McDougall argued so effectively that the soul should be accepted seriously as a scientific hypothesis that John Beloff was led to say that "the animistic position which [McDougall] so well stated still remains the most logical one for those who take their parapsychology seriously."[237] *Body and Mind* also contained a chapter on parapsychology. In it, McDougall discussed the cross-correspondences in the context of his attack on mechanism. He wrote that the

keenest critics of the view which sees in these writings the expression
of the surviving personalities of deceased persons, are driven to postu-
late as the only possible alternative explanation of some of them the
direct communication of complex and subtle thoughts between persons separated by hundreds and even thousands of miles.... [W]e
stand before the dilemma—survival or telepathy of this far-reaching
kind. The acceptance of either horn of the dilemma is fatal to the
mechanistic scheme of things.[238]

The Great War, in which McDougall served first as an ambulance driver
in the French Army and then as a major in the Medical Corps of the British
Army, intervened. When soldiers suffering from shell-shock came under
his care, he used hypnosis as a method of treatment, all the while feeling like a father caring for children who were helpless and grateful to
him. For a psychologist, he said, "[i]t was a wonderful experience.... I
was giving my whole time and energy to work that was indisputably worth
while."[239]

In 1919, he received a Doctor of Science degree from the University of
Manchester, returned to work at Oxford, published *Group Mind,* and then
received from America "in every way a very flattering"[240] invitation.

Parapsychology, Harvard and America

Elwood Worchester tells how McDougall came to be invited to Harvard:
I happened to be a member of the committee on philosophy and
psychology at the time, when, after Dr. Hugo Münsterberg's death, it
became necessary to appoint his successor. Naturally, we felt that Harvard was entitled to the greatest English-speaking psychologist living.
After deliberation, Doctor McDougall was the man on whom we all
agreed. The recommendation was made to the overseers and the call
was extended. In Doctor McDougall's reply he stated that he would
favorably consider it if it were recognized that his interest in Psychic
Research was second only to his interest in general psychology.[241]

How did this son of the owner of a chemical plant, this man who was
preoccupied with intellectualities, who started a medical career and became a
psychologist, find his way into parapsychology and make his interest in the
field a condition of his acceptance of the Harvard invitation? Even before
McDougall developed his idea of purposive psychology, before he rejected
materialism and estimated the possible value of showing the emptiness of Pandora's box, and while he was still an undergraduate at Cambridge, he was exposed to parapsychology. At Cambridge, he remembered, "I attended lectures
by Henry Sidgwick"[242] and in all probability became acquainted with the other
intellectuals at Cambridge who were members of the SPR. By 1900, when
McDougall taught at University College in London, we find him saying: "I also
became interested in psychical research."[243] He also tells us:

What then of my dabbling in *Psychical Research?* . . . I was led to make
some study of this field by my desire to know the truth. Here, it seemed
to me, was a body of ancient beliefs all of which Science seemed utterly
to deny. Yet . . . [h]ere were phenomena alleged to occur in all times
and places, an allegation supported by a body of strong testimony.
And Science frowned upon it all and said: "Such things cannot happen." As usual I was thrown into rebellion against this orthodoxy. Further, I saw in the Society for Psychical Research a body of earnest
seekers after truth, conscientiously using methods which might reveal
truth; and these researches were largely in the field of psychology. . . .
And it seemed to me a scandal that psychologists should refuse to lend
a hand or at least moral support to this heroic effort.[244]

Every important question for McDougall could be passed through a filter
and reduced to the single essential inquiry: Is the mind nonphysical? It was
this question parapsychology proposed to attack. If mind transcended matter,
somehow, somewhere, direct evidence of its transcendence should be obtained
by using scientific method and by the observation of phenomena. This proposition McDougall saw underlying parapsychology.[245]

When he met William James in 1906 in Rome and was visited by him in
1908 — "[o]ne of the greatest pleasures of my life"[246] — their conversation probably drifted into parapsychology and stimulated McDougall's interest even
more. We know that McDougall attended at least three seances. During a dark
seance in 1906 with one Craddock, the medium's spirit control, its face glowing
dimly, emerged from the cabinet and made its rounds slowly past the circle
of seated sitters. When it reached McDougall, he stood, grabbed the spirit's
head and dragged it, with the struggling body of Craddock attached to it, into
the next room where the gaslight was on. McDougall reported the result in
terse language: "There was a scene of some confusion while the 'medium' and
his agent received corporal chastisement."[247] Three years expired before
McDougall's next seance with Francesca Carancini, a physical medium from
Italy. She had been invited to England to give seances for Henry Sidgwick, Sir
William Crookes and others. McDougall was present at two of these, both
suspect because they were held in complete darkness and there was evidence
that the medium had cheated.[248] Understandably, McDougall became extremely skeptical of all physical phenomena. He believed in the reality of
telepathy, however, and when Gilbert Murray, the Oxford scholar, conducted
telepathic experiments, mainly as a parlor game, McDougall was among the
participants along with Arnold Toynbee, the historian.

Appointed a Council member of the SPR in 1913,[249] McDougall was
elected its president in 1920,[250] the year he went to Harvard, and was reelected
in the following year.[251]

McDougall's acceptance of the invitation from Harvard was dictated by
several considerations other than the fact, indicated already, that he never
looked on himself as the typical Englishman and was uncomfortable in the
atmosphere of England. Of course, the post as head of the psychology

department at Harvard had been occupied by James and Muensterberg. This tenure plus the reputation Harvard enjoyed made McDougall see the chair there in psychology "as the premier post in America."[252] But McDougall had other reasons for wanting to go to America:

> I had always felt the lure of life in America as a land of romantic possibilities. . . . [I]t had always been my principle to accept whatever challenge life might bring. Harvard would be a stimulating adventure; whereas at Oxford I might too easily subside into inactivity. . . . [W]e had recently lost a child from rheumatic fever; and I was savage against the English climate, which also I blamed for total deafness in one ear. . . . I accepted and put myself in full harness for the first time in my forty-ninth year.[253]

If it had been any other university, the frank admission of an interest in parapsychology by an invitee might have been sufficiently disenchanting to chill a committee on philosophy and psychology and to cause an invitation to be withdrawn. But Harvard was not any other university, as McDougall must have known. It was the first university to show any interest in the field of parapsychology. As early as 1857, three professors from Harvard were part of a committee appointed to investigate the rappings that were heard when the Fox sisters purported to act as mediums.[254] William James of Harvard was instrumental in the establishment of the ASPR and three of its original officers—Pickering, Bowditch and Minot—were Harvard men. In 1912, a Richard Hodgson Memorial Fund was established at Harvard to encourage the study of parapsychological phenomena, and, in 1916–1917, Leonard T. Troland of the Harvard Psychology Department, helped by Gardner Murphy, conducted ESP experiments at the Harvard Psychological Laboratory.[255]

When McDougall came to Harvard in 1920, he brought to it a wide range of views in medicine, psychology, anthropology, a rebellious spirit, a desire for truth—and for the study of parapsychology. Only once before an American university had sponsored the investigation of ESP. Stanford University in California had been given $50,000 in 1912 by Thomas Welton Stanford to encourage parapsychological research. A few years later, a research fellowship was awarded to John E. Coover, a psychologist, who investigated telepathy and, in 1917, published his results. Now it was Harvard's turn. In order to sponsor research there, McDougall activated the nearly forgotten Hodgson Memorial Fund. With his support, Gardner Murphy was endowed by the Fund and, from 1922 to 1925, sought gifted subjects for ESP experiments, the results of which, however, did not deviate from chance expectation.

In 1923, McDougall received a letter from a young man who said that he had been attracted by the kind of investigations being conducted by the SPR and wondered if McDougall knew of any available position or fellowship which would permit him to support himself and carry out studies in parapsychology. McDougall replied that the "Hodgson Fellowship" was filled (by Gardner

Murphy).[256] The young student to whom the note was sent was Joseph Banks Rhine. What was to be had to wait four more years.

In 1927, however, the Hodgson Fund was available and, again with the support of McDougall, George H. Estabrooks carried out card-calling experiments in telepathy at Harvard.

McDougall had still another interest which he pursued at Harvard: research into the Lamarckian view of organic evolution which McDougall felt had been rejected only because of the mechanistic dogmas in biology. He put to use equipment for animal psychology he found at Harvard to conduct a continuing experiment to resolve the hypothesis advanced by Lamarck that acquired characteristics are transmitted by parents to children. McDougall used and trained 49 generations of white rats and was satisfied that this procedure over nearly twenty years confirmed the Lamarckian view.

McDougall and his family came to America with the highest hopes and expectations, so high that they could not fail to fall after his eager response to the "lure" of American life. He discovered Harvard dominated by Watsonian behaviorism. His book *Group Mind* received "very hostile reviews." The graduate students at Harvard, ingrained with mechanistic psychology, "looked upon me and my outlandish theories with suspicion. . . ."[257] L.E. Rhine, who was on the scene, observed: "Among psychologists in this country he's a lone wolf too. They jeer at him for being 'religious.' He does have an appreciation for the deeper and more intangible *reality* which they are too narrow-minded to grasp."[258]

The American press was also hostile to McDougall because "I incautiously lectured on national eugenics."[259] When these lectures were published in 1921 as "Is America Safe for Democracy?" they seemed racist and were seen to raise ugly racial issues.

Critics of his book and lectures and outlandish psychological theories didn't like his other views, either, and ridiculed him as a Victorian antique because of his narrow-minded opinions about sex relations and the place of women.[260] So it was refreshing and confidence-restoring for McDougall who, by this time, might have been reconsidering whether the English atmosphere had been so bad after all, when, one night at dinner, the kind Louisa Rhine read to him from a friend's letter in which she said she had loved one of McDougall's books. The praise produced in McDougall a glow of pleasure[261] which may have made America seem somewhat a brighter place.

Margery

It is said of Bostonians that they are Americans, broadly speaking. It must also be said of Boston that it is unique among American cities, psychically speaking. For from it came great mental mediums such as James's "white crow," Leonora Piper, and Hyslop's Minnie R. Soule (Mrs. Chenoweth), and from it came a blue-eyed woman from whose body and head ectoplasm issued and in whose presence incredible marvels took place. So did McDougall, with faint praise, damn Boston which

> has long had the reputation of being, above all other cities and places, the home of new things, the very fountain head of new religions, of new cults, new methods of healing, new wonders of all sorts. It has always been in the van, and it would be a strange thing if in this [Margery] controversy Boston had been left out. But Boston has not been left out. Boston has risen to the occasion. It has produced "Margery" ... [who] has preserved the ancient reputation of Boston.[262]

The Margery question, which helped to alienate many important people from the ASPR, propelled its research officer, J. Malcolm Bird, into an attack against McDougall whose opinions about the medium were antithetical to his own.[263] The *Scientific American* investigation in which McDougall had taken part was now behind him. He had had enough of a subject which had aroused so much ire and he wanted to leave it there. His reply to Bird was plainly painful for him: "I am unwillingly forced into recording my testimony in this matter,"[264] he said, but it was "my scientific duty"[265] to do so.

In his response to Bird, McDougall did not recapitulate his part in the *Scientific American* investigation. Instead, he described some sittings during the Dingwall investigations which McDougall attended along with Elwood Worcester and Margery's husband, Dr. Crandon. During several of these sittings in darkness, Margery wore luminous bands around her head, the cuffs of the sleeves of her bathrobe and her ankles. Her hands were controlled, the left by Dingwall, the right by Dr. Crandon. While she was thus restrained, ectoplasmic phenomena appeared, a cold, clammy material that made violent movements of various kinds on the table at which McDougall and the others were seated. He observed these movements but was totally dissatisfied with the sittings because, so far as he was concerned, Margery's right hand, supposedly controlled by her husband, was not controlled at all.

McDougall was not permitted to control her hand because in 1923 and 1924, when he had done so, the medium had complained that he had held her hand too violently. Once, when Worcester was able to control the medium's right hand, ectoplasm issued from her body and lay on the table connected to the medium's thighs by a strong ectoplasmic cord. In the brief sequences of red light, McDougall strained to see if it made the same movements as it had when Crandon controlled his wife's right hand. The ectoplasm moved about one quarter of an inch. In McDougall's opinion: "Since the cord was tautly stretched between [the ectoplasm and Margery's thighs], it is obvious that these movements may well have been produced by some action of [the medium's] muscles and that, therefore, they are entirely without evidential value."[266] The contrast with the free movements of earlier sittings when Margery's right hand was "uncontrolled" supported the suspicion that this lack of control had been the cause of the phenomena.

McDougall had another strong feeling about what seemed to be an ectoplasmic hand. He suspected that it might be "the lung, or part of the lung, of some animal, artificially manipulated to give it a crude resemblance to a hand . . . [and] the cord attached to it closely resembles the trachea or windpipe of an animal."[267] When photos of the "ectoplasmic hand" were submitted for examination by independent experts, McDougall's suspicion was confirmed.[268]

McDougall and Dingwall did not see eye to eye on Margery as appears from a letter written by McDougall to the English investigator: "I expressed some difference of opinion with you about the policy you are following in the present conduct of the Margery sittings. . . . [I]t is premature to throw aside the question of the evidential nature of the phenomena (as you have seemed inclined to do during the last few sittings) and to proceed at once to the further question of the exact *modus operandi* and process of production of the ectoplasm, regardless of controls."[269] Dingwall disagreed because it "was part of a definite policy of action which secured just that evidence that was most important."[270]

Good physical mediums are rare today. If they exist at all, they avoid serious investigation. Should an exception be discovered, future researchers may wish to determine whether or not Dingwall's policy was right. If the *modus operandi* is such that it is possible for a medium to cheat, then the phenomena produced at a sitting are valueless as evidence. If the controls and procedures have made it impossible to cheat, the phenomena may be considered genuine. In either case, the question of *modus operandi* seems the primary and not the "further" question.

McDougall's letter to Dingwall also takes the tone of a senior partner addressing a junior:

> My testimony [as to the reality of the Margery phenomena] would, I venture to think, carry considerable weight, even in the scientific world; whereas a favorable report by you, if not supported and confirmed by me, might fail to do so. Secondly, it seems to me that you need my support in your own self-defense. . . . [W]hen you report the ectoplasmic phenomena to be genuine, you will be accused by the scientific, or by some of them, of being an accomplice, of being in collusion with Margery. Your best defense aganst this would be my concordant testimony and support.[271]

This letter surely demonstrates the arrogance which McDougall often confessed. But have we here also a surprisingly emotional and unscientific side to the Professor who prided himself on being a cold, disciplined man of science? An ugly attempt to have the SPR investigator fail to report the case as he saw it and even affirm the genuineness of the Margery phenomena, an attempt to dictate to Dingwall in order to avoid embarrassing public disagreement and to make a show of unity?

It is the purest speculation whether McDougall succeeded in influencing Dingwall, but, at the time of his letter, McDougall believed that Dingwall had been convinced. When Dingwall finally issued his report, however, he confessed his inability to reach a final conclusion in the case,[272] a report Crandon denounced as placing the SPR "in a ludicrous position of straddling, in order always to be right."[273]

Le Roi Crandon was also no slouch when it came to defending his wife against McDougall. The professor, he said, "when he sees ectoplasm, is in the state of mind of the well-known farmer faced for the first time by a giraffe: 'They ain't no sech animal.'"[274] Anyway, argued Crandon, why must ectoplasm move to be valid when "its mere production as an inert mass is a psychic phenomenon of the utmost importance?"[275]

Moreover, the validity of the Margery mediumship was not based on the question of ectoplasmic phenomena. There were other phenomena—scales which worked against gravity, an electric bell-box which rang, the thumb prints attributed to the dead "Walter." McDougall had not been able to condemn them all as fraudulent although they had been placed in sharp dispute by Dudley's charges. Yet perhaps the evidence of other paranormal happenings was very strong. Still, McDougall had the last and most important word, as pertinent in the Margery case as in any other case of physical mediumship. The reality of the phenomena does not commit us to the spiritist theory. "[T]here is a long step between the acceptance of the facts of the phenomena and the theory of the spiritist...."[276]

Spiritualism

Parapsychology owes much to British Spiritualism. The founding and work of the Society for Psychical Research were largely directed by Spiritualists. Although Henry Sidgwick, Frederic W.H. Myers and Edmund Gurney all had been interested in investigating psychic phenomena and had done so prior to 1882, they had had "disappointing results"[277] and "had become somewhat discouraged."[278] It was the stimulating force of Sir Edward Barrett, a Spiritualist, who renewed the interest of these non–Spiritualists and led to the formation of the SPR. Other principal figures behind its formation were Spiritualists such as Edmund Dawson Rogers and the Rev. Stainton Moses. For the first five years after the organization of the SPR, it was controlled by a Council two-thirds of whom were Spiritualists.[279] In later years, some of the most impressive evidence for survival came from the mediumistic experiments of the Rev. Drayton Thomas, a Spiritualist.

It is the opposite side of the coin in America where Spiritualists have displayed none of the qualities of their counterparts in Britain and have failed to be supportive of parapsychology. Indeed, in an address delivered in Boston in 1922, McDougall had words for Spiritualists:

> For experience shows us that, of all those who enter upon the path
> of Psychical Research, a considerable proportion become lost to it,
> by passing over into this hostile camp. Having become personally

convinced of the truth of the main tenets of Spiritualism, these persons cease to be interested in Research and devote themselves to propaganda.[280]

McDougall chose the creator of Sherlock Holmes as an example of this kind of Spiritualism. He said of Sir Arthur Conan Doyle: "instead of supporting Psychical Research, he is indifferent to it; or rather, he is not merely indifferent, he is actually hostile to it."[281] Conan Doyle expressed his

> amused surprise at reading Professor McDougall's estimate of my views upon psychic research. . . . [I]f Professor McDougall means by psychic research that school which always rivets its attention upon the negative rather than upon the positive, and which imagines that medium-baiting is the most important part of this great new development, then I freely grant that he has judged me right.[282]

But there is a great difference between concentrating on the negative and recognizing that only one case in every one hundred comes up to the standard of evidence required by parapsychologists. Recently, the author spoke at a public meeting in Miami on the need for obtaining strong evidence of survival after death and further pointed out the need for separating the chaff from the grain and for considering alternative explanations for some of the experiences narrated by the audience. Hostility in its most vociferous form came from listeners who proclaimed themselves Spiritualists and who reproached me for being "skeptical" and "out to disprove" life after death. So there continue to this day on the part of most Spiritualists in America the same indifference and opposition to parapsychologists on account of their criticalness that existed in McDougall's time.

Should parapsychology lower its evidential standards to please the Spiritualists? How can parapsychology overcome the Spiritualist attitude? McDougall offered a solution that still seems correct: Do not lower our standards of evidence or relax the strictness of rules of investigation. Continue to regard research as of the first importance. For, if what Spiritualists:

> would teach are truths, further research will establish them more firmly; if they cannot be verified by further research, they are not truths and ought not to be taught. . . . [W]e confidently say to those who are personally convinced of some or all of the tenets of Spiritualism — "Do not desert Psychical Research; stand by us, give us at least your moral support. Do not be impatient with our slow methods. Do not be offended by what seems to you our excess of caution, our obstinate skepticism. For our road is the only sure road. . . ."[283]

The American and Boston Societies

Immediately, on his election as president of the American Society for Psychical Research (in the same year that he arrived at Harvard), McDougall performed two acts. First, he formed an Advisory Research Council, which included some distinguished scholars and academicians holding varying opinions about the value of the work done by the ASPR and the interpretation of the phenomena investigated. Their function was advisory and was to help the ASPR carry on research with a critical spirit and with the most exact methods possible. The notion of such a body which might inspire greater confidence in the future work of the ASPR was laudatory, yet Prince could not conceal his anxiety. On May 24, 1921, he wrote McDougall:

> If the members of the Council do not fully understand that they are advisors only . . . to the President and his subordinate executive assistants, we might have a situation which practically destroyed the usefulness of the first American Society, wherein a topheavy academic control brought about the fatal disease of dry-rot.[284]

McDougall's second act was to change Hyslop's publication policy which had been based on the belief that readers wanted details not brevity. On May 22, 1921, McDougall penned instructions to Prince concerning what should be published in JASPR and PASPR. After advising against rushing anything into print, McDougall said:

> I feel that quality is so much more important than quantity. Few readers will find time or energy to read lengthy reports, of inconclusive tendency. I know that many admirers of Dr. Hyslop felt that he made a mistake in publishing at so great length, & I am inclined to agree with them.[285]

McDougall's election to the ASPR presidency made him the only person to have presided concurrently over both the English and American societies — a distinction destined to be short-lived. In 1923, "to the utter surprise"[286] of McDougall and by the unanimous vote of the ASPR Board of Trustees, Edwards replaced McDougall as president. Historians Mauskopf and McVaugh believe that it was a "coup" in that McDougall was given no "notice of the crucial April meeting; if true, this strengthens the possibility of an organized coup."[287] In fact, however, the unanimous vote of the ASPR Board of Trustees came, not at a special and sudden April meeting of which McDougall was ignorant, but at the annual meeting of the ASPR held in January, which McDougall surely knew about.[288] A stronger possibility for McDougall's ouster is that it grew gradually out of his sharp attack on Spiritualism and its leading exponent, Conan Doyle, which may have ruffled the feathers of Spiritualists among the ASPR's leaders and membership. It may be significant that McDougall was replaced in the same month that his attack appeared in the January issue of the ASPR *Journal*, that the April issue published a rebuttal by a representative of the London Spiritualist Alliance who felt "justly irritated" by McDougall's criticisms, that in its May issue the *Journal* carried not only a defense from Conan Doyle who expressed "regret to see that in this instance this distinguished psychologist has shown such a sad want" of accuracy in his statements[289] but as well two articles on the matter by Frederick Edwards. He had heard Conan Doyle lecture at Carnegie Hall and, in his first article, lauded him as "intelligent and masterful . . . a distinguished visitor and an earnest godly man."[290] His second piece mocked McDougall's claim that there had been any leakage from parapsychology into Spiritualism: Some members of the ASPR might have left parapsychology because they were angry or could not afford membership dues "but none say they are leaving because they have become Spiritualists. We are sorry to put an end to what promised to be a lively scrimmage. It turns out to be only a pillow fight."[291]

Besides the Spiritualist faction, which could have considered itself injured by McDougall, there was probably another in the ASPR which did not care for his attempts to bring the organization closer to the academic community as evidenced by his insistence on the creation of an Advisory Council, five of whose seven members were academics. Indeed, after Edwards succeeded McDougall, the Council was allowed slowly to wither away and disappear.

With McDougall's replacement, the popularization of the ASPR's work by the new administration and its departure from the standards established by Hyslop and which McDougall had endeavored to maintain convinced Worcester "that the only way to perpetuate scientific Research in America was to establish a new Society in Boston,"[292] where he had been rector of Emmanuel Church, a great Episcopal church in the city and the home of his healing ministry called the Emmanuel Movement.

"It was largely by the help of Professor McDougall...," said Worcester, "that I was able to found the Boston Society and to supply it with scientific and technical advisors."[293] McDougall became a member of the Council of the new Society and was instrumental in the preparation of a Declaration of Principles and a Constitution to which every member was required to assent.[294]

It is close to impossible to know McDougall's real feelings produced by the harsh reception his books and views were given in America, by his unpleasant involvement with Margery, his disagreements with Dingwall and his abrupt dismissal as ASPR president. Did he regret having left England to "dabble" in American parapsychology? When, in 1930, he looked back at his dabbling, he answered: "[T]hough my contacts with the field in America have brought many very disagreeable incidents, I do not repent."[295]

University Study of Parapsychology

William James's discovery of Leonora Piper in 1885, his knowledge of the SPR *Proceedings* and the work of Gurney and Myers, whose brilliance he admired, and his respect for the critical intellect of Sidgwick all combined to impress upon him the importance of parapsychology. Yet neither in his role as a leader of the early ASPR, nor in his major criticism of science for its aloofness from parapsychology nor in any of his other writings or letters on the subject did James ever suggest making parapsychology a subject of study on the university level. As for Hyslop, the idea would never have occurred to him and, if ever it had, it would have been driven out of his mind by the bitterness he harbored against the academic world and his conviction that it did not have, and would never have, any interest in parapsychology.

It remained for McDougall to propose the idea of including parapsychology as a subject of university study. The time was December 1925, and the place, a symposium on parapsychology held at Clark University as a result of a lively disagreement about mediums and psychic phenomena which had taken place the year before between McDougall and Harry Houdini while they were having lunch at the Bancroft Hotel in Worcester. Carl Murchison of Clark University, who was also present, had suggested that the whole subject be thrashed out in a series of public lectures.[296] When the lectures were given, McDougall's, most probably a reaction against the Margery mediumship and the ASPR's determined policy of popularization, stressed that all future research in parapsychology should be taken out of the hands of local lay groups and enthusiasts who controlled the parapsychological societies and put instead in those of the universities. McDougall emphasized that opposition to university acceptance of parapsychology was based largely on the false understanding of university functions. One of the main ones is the education of young minds. While parapsychology can offer no established truths and no firm conclusions, it teaches students patience and discipline in observing and recording phenomena and reasoning in order to draw conclusions from the phenomena observed.[297]

A second function of any university is to find out into what areas knowledge can or cannot be extended. For this reason, parapsychology belongs within a university because if, after using all of its methods to find solutions to problems which now defy scientific laws, it still can provide no answers or thoeries, then we should have to admit that there are gates to which we have no keys: "and, though Science might then turn aside, baffled and discouraged, it would at least have given some respectable foundation for the cry Ignorabimus [we cannot know] and have made some real contribution to our knowledge of the limitations of human knowledge."[298]

A third function of the university is to guide public opinion on obscure questions that affect our intellectual outlooks and moral lives. In parapsychology, universities might find the light that is needed.[299]

McDougall issued a clear call for parapsychological research within university gates and gave telepathy as an example of one problem which would be a suitable research task.[300] By clear inference parapsychology definitely did not belong within the walls of amateur groups calling themselves parapsychological societies. But, although to its everlasting credit Clark University pioneered a symposium on the subject of parapsychology, McDougall's arguments did not persuade it to take any steps beyond the symposium. Nor did any other American university at the time seem ready to be convinced to accept parapsychology within its gates. Only at Harvard did McDougall have success in the promotion of some research.

The developments over the six decades since the symposium at Clark University, however, seem likely to be traceable to McDougall's lecture;[301]

furthermore, it seems likely this symposium was the stimulus for a shift away from research by enthusiasts and toward the study of parapsychology in universities. What McDougall said was, in Pratt's view, "the hinge upon which subsequent research in parapsychology has turned."[302] And it is a view that seems warranted because, besides the introduction of parapsychology into universities in other parts of the world, such as the University of Edinburgh in the United Kingdom, Freiburg in West Germany, Utrecht in Holland and Andhra University in India, American colleges and universities which have accepted parapsychology include the City College of the City University of New York, the University of Pittsburgh, St. Joseph's College, John F. Kennedy University and West Georgia College.

Duke and the Rhines

In 1926 McDougall published another book, *Outline of Abnormal Psychology*. In that year, also, the new Duke University, an outgrowth of Trinity College in Durham, North Carolina, supported by the benefactions of the Duke Brothers (of American Tobacco Company fame), needed a head for its department of psychology. Duke's president, William Preston Few, solicited McDougall's opinion about eligible psychologists. In spite of his having come to America for the specific purpose of assuming the chair of psychology at Harvard, McDougall declared himself ready to accept the post at Duke, if offered to him. It was so offered in July 1927 and, within a couple of months, McDougall left Harvard.

It is a curious fact that McDougall's autobiography omits any explanation of his decision to leave Cambridge. It could have been caused by his discovery that Harvard had not informed him about a committee it had organized to reorient the study of psychology.[303]

This decision meant both an end and a beginning. It finished parapsychological research at Harvard and consigned the Hodgson Fund once again to inactivity. It started parapsychological research at Duke and led to the creation of a Parapsychological Laboratory there and the introduction of parapsychology into a university setting in keeping with the doctrine McDougall had urged in his lecture at Clark University. This same lecture, plus the defense of animism he had published in 1911, led in another way to research at Duke because they had been read by two young people seeking their destinies. As McDougall described them:

> The Rhines, in pondering the question—What is most worth doing? To what cause can we give ourselves?—had come upon my *Body and Mind* and upon others of my writings, especially my plea for *Psychical Research as a University Study;* and had determined to join forces with me at Harvard.[304]

J.B. Rhine had come to Cambridge in June 1926 to see McDougall. Unfortunately for Rhine, McDougall recalled, this was "at the moment when I had completed the bestowal of my family and worldly possessions in two tax-icabs, with a view to begin a journey round the world. . . ."[305] So forces could not be joined until the fall of 1927 when, at Duke, the Rhines finally caught up with McDougall and their destinies.

It was John F. Thomas, an assistant superintendent in the Detroit Public School system, who facilitated this joinder. He had been a graduate student at Duke's Department of Psychology and had worked there under McDougall. During this time, he had assembled a great many notes which had been taken, after the death of his wife, at proxy sittings with the medium Gladys Osborne Leonard.[306] Although Thomas had interested the Rhines in evaluating the material, he wanted as well the evaluation of a psychologist, and not just any psychologist, but McDougall, whose interest in parapsychology and in investigations of its phenomena relating to the transcendence of mind were well-known.

Fearful that the big package of mediumistic material might be lost or neglected by the busy psychologist just taking over the duties of his new post, Thomas entrusted it to a man he was confident would make doubly sure that it would not be ignored. That messenger was J.B. Rhine.[307] When McDougall consented to the Rhines' coming to Duke for a semester to study Thomas's material under McDougall's direction, Thomas provided the money which enabled the Rhines to travel to Durham — and stay. Thomas himself would receive from Duke in 1933 a degree of Doctor of Philosophy for a thesis en-titled, "An Evaluative Study of Mental Content of Certain Trance Phenomena," the first time a university had accepted as a doctoral dissertation a report on mediumistic records.

The many reasons for the beginning of Rhine's work at Duke University and its continuance there will be explored when his portrait is presented, but the presence of McDougall and his sponsorship of the work were dominant reasons. McDougall was forever being diverted by problems in psychology and was much too preoccupied with his Lamarckian experiments with rats to do much in the way of ESP experiments or to dictate to Rhine which experiments in telepathy or clairvoyance were to be conducted. Nevertheless, McDougall found time to "sit in" on Rhine's experiments on a number of occasions,[308] was ever willing to offer appropriate guidance to Rhine, to examine the evidence[309] and to provide Rhine with inspiring leadership.[310]

McDougall became coeditor with Rhine of the *Journal of Parapsychology* which was created in 1937 and wrote an editorial for its first issue.

Parapsychology and the Monadic View of Personality

Myers conceived of personality as divided territory. On one side of the line of consciousness or threshold (limen) was the supraliminal self (above the threshold), on the other, the subliminal self (below it). He made us aware that the human personality was not a simple entity. Parapsychology has tended to justify this concept by showing that subliminal operations, which include the use of psychic abilities, can be inhibited by the conscious part of our personalities.[311]

McDougall, on the other hand, defined in other terms the internal environment of the personality. He conceived it as twofold, as both unitary and composite. It is first the activity of a unitary being endowed with the faculties of knowing, feeling and striving, the ego, soul or self.[312] But don't cases of divided personalities destroy the concept of a unitary ego? It would seem that, where a self has been divided and each division has all the faculties of mind, here is a suggestion that the stuff or stream of consciousness is not a unitary thing but is divisible into parts and capable of being reassembled. In defense of his conception, McDougall argued that each of us may be possessed of more than a single stream of consciousness which knows, feels and strives, and that each stream may not only be separate from but sometimes in conflict with another. Each of the streams in us is the activity of a unitary self and in each of us there are many such selves. The McDougall who spoke to Rhine, like the I who writes these lines, was the dominant self with whom subordinate selves generally cooperate for the good of the whole organism while the dominant self is strong. But when the dominant self becomes

> weak and irresolute, if I do not face the problems of life and take the necessary decisions for dealing with them, then conflict arises within our system, one or more of my subordinates gets out of hand, I lose my control, and division of the personality into conflicting systems replaces the normal and harmonious co-operation of all members in one system.[313]

The Sally Beauchamp case and the case of Doris Fischer can be explained as rebellions by subordinates who had dominated the ruling self. Dreams may also represent a cessation of control during sleep and the coming into consciousness of thoughts and purposes alien to the dominant self.

McDougall's view of the composite makeup of the personality has a number of considerable implications for several subjects that fall within the domain of parapsychology. He based it on Leibniz's monadology. Leibniz had followed the Cartesian proposition that substances cannot interact; hence, one of Leibniz's monads could not have any causal relation with another. The appearance of interaction between them was explained as a "preestablished harmony" arranged by God between the active monads. Monadology, remarked Lord Russell, was like clocks which all strike at the same hour, not because they interact but because God made them keep perfect time.[314]

McDougall's monadic view of the human organism as consisting of a hierarchy of many monads with a dominant ego and subordinate selves which normally work in harmony for the common good of the organism is no Leibnizian denial of interaction. The interaction is real and not just apparent. But what is the nature of this interaction? Myers had been unusually obscure on this point. Since telepathy is an ability limited by him to the subliminal self, no telepathic interaction with the supraliminal self would be possible.

McDougall, however, is quite clear on how monads stay in touch with one another: "communication between the members seems to be direct, that is to say it seems to be of the nature of reciprocal telepathic rapport. . . ."³¹⁵ Indeed, it is hard to conceive of direct interaction without telepathy. McDougall's conception, therefore, makes the acceptance of the probability of telepathy taking place within us somewhat easier. At the same time, it opens up the additional possibility of further telepathic connection between the monads in one organism and other monads external to them whether the others are still within a living organism or have survived the death of that organism.

McDougall's monadic hierarchy may provide a further theoretical framework for some of the mysteries of telepathic communication. Sometimes this process is thought of as a union. Speaking of reciprocal dreams, for example, where two or more people have simultaneous dreams that are similar and have no discernible external cause, Eleanor Sidgwick said: "I think the kind of union of minds, the thinking and feeling together, here shown may be regarded as the type or norm of telepathic communication to which all other cases conform in varying degrees."³¹⁶ The same principle of unity may be present in paranormal healing as a healer and healee unite psychically. It may be present as well in clairvoyance where a human mind merges with a distant event or object.

If this principle is correct, questions arise such as: How can one single personality encapsulated within a physical body abandon that body to go out beyond its limits and merge with another personality or an object? Calling the process "ESP," "telepathy," "paranormal healing" or "clairvoyance" does not explain how a physical body can be deserted by its personality. No explanation was offered by Eleanor Sidgwick in her description of spontaneous dreams, by Rhine who maintained that a mind went out to another, or by Thouless and Wiesner who argued that in ESP and PK a *shin* went out to interact with another *shin,* or external object. No light is shed on the problem by the rigid conception of a single personality within a single physical body. The McDougall theory, however, allows the possibility that one of several subordinate egos which has the ability to merge with external egos or objects, has managed to slip from the organism while the dominant one is asleep, in an altered state or otherwise not in control.

The out-of-body experience in which experients believe that their consciousnesses have separated from their bodies raises the same question of abandonment. The theory that assumes a single stream of consciousness is incapable of supplying any basis for understanding how a body can be left devoid of its consciousness. The McDougall notion of two or more streams of consciousness functioning separately makes the OBE more comprehensible.

And, should the survival hypothesis be supported by data, McDougall's monadic view would be of great importance to our understanding of the kind of environment in which one survives. Will it be a place where the spirits of deceased persons play harps all day except for the time they take out to ring up people on earth with messages of love and sundry advice? Is the spiritual world to be understood in terms more glowing than those used in travel brochures and pictured as a glorified Hilton in a paradise where the air is without smog and one can drink the water? The theory advanced by McDougall suggests what the basic organization of a postmortem world might be like.

In his conception of the human organism:

> I and my associates are all members of one body; and, so long as the whole organism is healthy, we work harmoniously together, for we are a well-organised society, the members of which strive for a common good, the good of the whole society.[317]

In our internal operations, as in our external lives, our work is done and our goals are achieved in a social setting in cooperation with others. So it must be for our future lives:

> it would seem to follow that . . . hereafter [I can] hope to live richly and satisfactorily only by entering into and playing an active part as a member of some other society which will demand my faithful co-operation and service. For we are essentially social beings; outside of and apart from such intimate communion, our selves would have no meaning and no value, and perhaps could not be said to live or be conscious in any intelligible sense of those words.[318]

So, instead of heavenly musical recitals by free spirits living in a spiritual Hilton, we can look forward to a postmortem communist state in which individuality has been lost and discarnate entities dutifully carry out specialized functions for the welfare of the group in the tradition of ants and bees devoted to their nests and hives. McDougall was in every sense the impartial and cold scientist who carried his theory to the end no matter how unpleasant.

Final Verdicts

As 1938 drew to its close, McDougall was named Honorary Fellow of St. John's College in Cambridge, the last honor he would ever receive. For he was now 67 and dying of the same cancer that had made his mother's death an outrage. Karl E. Zener, then a member of the Duke Department of Psychology, recalled how McDougall's

> great courage and strength of character were brought into relief during his last months. Very weak, and suffering from a painful cancer, he wrote the final chapter of his last book lying on his back, and, until physically unable, walked to the laboratory to run final control trials in his Lamarckian experiment.[319]

McDougall managed to finish his book, *The Riddle of Life,* and when he could not walk by himself any longer, Rhine would come to his house on the East Campus of Duke University to assist him in short walks on the campus.

Then, on November 28, 1938, it was all over. Louisa Rhine was deeply affected by his death:

> Dr. McDougall died last night.... [I]t is as if someone who really belonged to us had passed. I had hardly realized how much affection for him, as for a father, I had.[320]

Some years before he died McDougall seemed satisfied with how he had lived and what he had tried to do: "[I]n the main I have lived hitherto the sort of life which in my youth I judged to be the most desirable; and that perhaps is all a man can properly demand."[321]

But one's opinion of his own life and contributions counts for very little. What verdict does history pass on McDougall? An obituarist wrote: "Future historians of mental science will either hold William McDougall in high esteem or leave his name to sink into oblivion."[322]

How long must we wait before the verdict of history can be rendered? If one is permissible now that fifty years have passed since his death, it would have to be that McDougall's name has been allowed by the historians of mental science to sink beneath the waters of Lethe. He was a great defender of animism, Driesch's vitalism in biology, and dualism in psychology, as well as a great critic of "dogmatic materialism" and the mechanistic assumptions of science. Animism, vitalism and dualism, however, are still high on the list of prohibited doctrines prepared by the Church of Science, and materialism and mechanism have not been dislodged from scientific thought. As John Beloff, until recently senior lecturer in psychology at the University of Edinburgh wrote: McDougall must be considered "more of a tilter-at-windmills than a slayer-of-dragons ... [and] his image has faded fast. Both biology and psychology have continued to become more, instead of less, mechanistic with every fresh advance."[323] And Professors Hansel's and Hyman's continuing and devastating attacks against parapsychology are eloquent testimonies to the failure of McDougall's hope of enlisting the support of psychologists to this effort. The final blow comes from McDougall's twenty years of experiments with rats which convinced him that Lamarck's hypothesis had been supported. They have not convinced anyone else; "subsequent work has failed to confirm his findings which are now ascribed to methodological defects."[324]

And what of the verdict of the higher court—one uses the phrase with some irony—of parapsychology itself? McDougall was reasonably content with his life. But toward the end of his days what did he think of parapsychology? How did this "dabbler" in it measure his value to parapsychology? In his valedictory message to the SPR, he continued to talk of "the importance which seems to me properly to attach to all good work in this field." But he did not place a very high price tag on his work in the field for he felt "great regret that I have not been able to do more to promote" parapsychology and he lamented "the small bulk of value of my contributions."[325]

How should we measure his contributions? Probably McDougall is remembered principally for his sponsorship of Rhine and the investigations at Duke. Nevertheless, as Rhine said, McDougall was, without question, one of "the leaders of the day in psychical research" he admired most.[326] He was, Rhine stated in another place, "one of the greatest minds I have ever met, either in life or literature."[327]

J.G. Pratt also admired him as "a key figure"[328] in the story of parapsychology. Even many years after McDougall's death, Pratt "often spoke appreciatively of McDougall, the only one of his teachers whose photograph he kept in his office at the University of Virginia."[329] In tracing the development of parapsychology over the years since McDougall, Pratt used an interesting metaphor: the genealogical chart. In his drawing of the family tree, McDougall was listed as "the great-grandfather" of parapsychology,[330] and, indeed, he had contributed to its growth in a number of ways. Although there had been many scientists in parapsychology up to 1920, there had been few psychologists and only one, William James, had ever been elected to the presidency of the SPR. William McDougall's defiant entry into the field as the leading psychologist of his time, his assumption of the presidential office of the SPR, and, later, of the ASPR, his role in the Boston Society for Psychic Research and at Harvard and Duke, are all historical events that cannot fail to be connected to the subsequent entry into parapsychology of other psychologists, including Thouless and Beloff in England, Rao in India, and, in America, Murphy, Schmeidler, Pratt, Krippner and others.

In addition to encouraging research at Harvard and sponsoring Rhine at Duke, McDougall was the first and most influential advocate of parapsychology as a university study and were it not for his Clark University lecture "parapsychology would have had a different history."[331] And future researchers may find fruitful, as a working hypothesis for ESP, the out-of-body experience and survival, his conception of the organic human being.

Contrary to the opinion of the judges in mental science, perhaps McDougall's descendants in parapsychology will remember their "great-grandfather" in the way that Rhine advised his daughter Sally to remember McDougall: as "the greatest man you will ever know."[332]

4
Storms and Reorientation
(1939–1980)

Commentary

The seed of American parapsychology was first planted long ago and far away: In antiquity, in primitive cultures, in the New and Old Testaments, where and when holy men had the power to effect miraculous cures, people had strange dreams of events still in the future and tales of ghosts and hauntings, telepathy and clairvoyance were told around camp fires, in tents, forests and castles across the centuries. The seed developed in England when the SPR was founded in 1882 to investigate such reports and was borne by Barrett to America during his tour in 1884. His contact with James and other scholars allowed parapsychology to take root in this soil.

Its growth through three periods ending in 1938 was along the same two traditional lines followed by the SPR in London but with a pronounced emphasis on one: mediumship. James had given initial impetus to interest in mediumship with his sittings with Mrs. Piper. Hodgson and Hyslop added to the momentum during their tenures, and it went almost out of control when Margery enchanted Bird and the ASPR. A second line of development was the collection, recording and attempts at authenticating anecdotal reports of psychic experiences to see if they would stand up as evidence of telepathy, hauntings or apparitions. The ASPR of James's era undertook these investigations, as did Prince who surveyed the spontaneous experiences of "noted witnesses," prominent people listed in *Who's Who*.

The fourth period of American parapsychology was to see a reorientation in its development. The trend was very definitely away from mediumship. There was, however, a continuing insistence on the value of anecdotal reports of life experiences although a sharp divergence of views on what exactly this value was. But primarily the focus of the fourth period would be on packs of cards, statistics and laboratory games.

Telepathy was taken out of the hands of tellers and believers of marvelous stories and out of the American vaudeville circuit and placed in the laboratory by a mop-haired ex–Marine sergeant named Joseph Banks Rhine. His presence at Duke University would make Durham, North Carolina, one of the two great

centers of parapsychology in the United States. He was one of the two
dominating personalities of the fourth period, which ended with his
death.

Even though Rhine started his card-guessing experiments at Duke in
1930, this reorientation had to wait until the fourth period beginning in 1939
because, until his *Extra-Sensory Perception* reported them in 1934, the public
and scientific worlds were unaware of them. With its publication for the first
time his work was exposed to public gaze, yet there was no radical change in
the situation at that time. Certainly the monograph created a public furor—
although it was not the sensation that Margaret Mitchell's novel *Gone with the
Wind* would be in 1936—but by the standards of 1934 it was a "hit." Some
wide-eyed, open-mouthed people compared the publication of the work to the
Copernican revolution.

Mail poured in from ordinary people who wanted to tell Rhine about their
own psychic experiences and from psychics who wanted to be tested in order
to display their gifts.

But the reaction of parapsychologists and orthodox academicians was
quite different. The parapsychologists were not ready to accept extrasensory
perception and abandon their traditional lines of inquiry, at least not
until Rhine's methods could be tested and replicated. In the eyes of orthodox academicians, Rhine's monograph was a "miss" and served only to
provoke attacks and controversy. It was not until 1937 that assaults on
Rhine's mathematical methods were effectively repulsed and not until 1938
that criticisms of research methods were blunted after an ESP symposium
held by the American Psychological Association. It would be in the period
beginning in 1939, after all the uproar and attacks had been quieted
down, that extrasensory perception would be taken seriously by parapsychologists and attention diverted from the old approaches to the experimental
one. "Parapsychology," which would replace "psychical research," would
be born.

The events at the laboratory at Duke University kicked up such a cloud
of national interest as almost to conceal the second great center of American
parapsychology in New York where the Margery bomb had helped to drive
away McDougall, Prince and others. There a medium founded an organization
to assist scientific investigation of paranormal phenomena and there a teacher
and researcher in parapsychology whose name was as Irish as a brogue became
the second dominating personality of this period.

Gardner Murphy would start to play his role almost simultaneously with
the ending of the unforgettable story of the blue-eyed woman which was also
the story of the ASPR during the third period. Under him a new chapter would
start for the ASPR characterized by a reorientation of aims and the collaboration
of gifted and productive workers, and a new era would also begin for parapsychology which, as a result of his influence, would gain greater prestige and
acceptance.

Chronological Narrative

1939

The *Journal of Parapsychology* passed to Gardner Murphy and Bernard F. Riess, who became coeditors in order to give the publication a "new look" which might appeal to psychologists.

On December 27, Dr. L.R.G. Crandon, Margery's husband, died. He had defended and supported her mediumship and had been in the center of controversy after controversy over her. With his death the one person in the world except for Margery who knew the truth about her mediumship passed into silence. The era of Margery was about over.

1940

Pratt, Rhine, and three other members of the Duke Parapsychology Laboratory (B.M. Smith, C.E. Stuart and J.A. Greenwood) coauthored *Extra-Sensory Perception After Sixty Years* as a source-book for experimental and evaluative methods. This book surveyed all the experimental data bearing on ESP that had been collected and examined all the major hypotheses that had been suggested in criticism. The harshest critics of parapsychology were invited to express their criticisms in the book. After its publication critics were effectively silenced. The book can be looked upon as the end of a period of controversy over, and the start of a new one for, experimental research.

The BSPR lost Elwood Worcester to death. He had founded it as an independent organization committed to strict evidential standards after the ASPR deviated from them.

1941

When Murphy and Riess relinquished the coeditorship of the *Journal of Parapsychology*, Rhine, Pratt and Stuart assumed its editorial control. Dorothy H. Pope, a staff member of the Parapsychology Laboratory at Duke University, became managing editor and, in later years, would become its coeditor and consulting editor.

Finis was written to an extraordinary mediumship which had made and destroyed reputations, when Mina Crandon died on November 1 from the effects of chronic alcoholism. A short time before her death, the parapsychologist Nandor Fodor interviewed her about her mediumship as the controversial Margery. ". . . [G]o to hell," the bedridden alcoholic said, "all you 'psychic researchers' can go to hell. . . . You'll all be guessing . . . for the rest of your lives."[1] Almost five decades later we are still guessing because, with

Mina Crandon, went the knowledge of whether all or any of the phenomena she produced were genuine or fraudulent.

There is a tragic irony in the fact that Margery's demise was not even noticed by the ASPR which had been her ardent champion while she lived. Although the dominating faction of the Society was grief stricken when Dr. Crandon died and the Society's *Journal* paid a sensitive tribute to him, the death of the principal figure in the drama of Margery's mediumship evoked not one word in the pages of JASPR. This unexpected silence was not the result of ingratitude. The explanation is that Margery was simply part of an era that was past and to be forgotten by the ASPR.

An analogy can be found in what happened in America after the end of the American Revolution. For about 10 years following Independence, America was governed by Articles of Confederation. But it was split into 13 quarrelling states, was virtually bankrupt and on the verge of civil war. By 1787 it needed and was ready for a strong central government. Out of the Constitutional Convention in Philadelphia came the Federal Constitution with this government's powers and functions spelled out in a political document that has stood for 200 years. On July 10, 1788, a New York paper, *The Public Advertiser,* carried news of the termination of the old era with an article entitled, "Ship News—Extra." It reported the entry of the good ship *Federal Constitution* whose master was Perpetual Union and whose passengers were Messrs. Flourishing Commerce, Public Faith and National Energy. Also reported was the clearance of *Old Confederacy,* whose master was Imbecility, with its cargo of paper money and discord.[2]

In 1941, a similar "Extra" might have reported the beginning of a new creative era for the ASPR which, for more than a decade, was the scene of discord and was bankrupt in terms of scientific prestige. The entrance could be noted in this year of the good ship *Reorientation,* master Scientific Standards, and the exit of *Seance Room Phenomena,* master Popularization and a cargo of credulous amateurs and abandoned scientific principles. In modern terms, there was at the American Society what was called "a palace revolution."[3]

The origins of this revolution reach back into the long period prior to 1941 which began when McDougall was ousted from the presidency of the ASPR, Prince and others left it, and it failed to command the respect of serious investigators. Internal discontent with the firm policy of the ASPR to democratize parapsychology, to act as Margery's advocate and, most of all, with its myopic research which could see no further than the seance room, had built up. But it took leading figures to bring pressures to the bursting point. They were those who had caught the Rhinean fever, realized the value of laboratory experiment and were determined to have the ASPR sail on an entirely new heading.

Historians of the period have identified Jocelyn Pierson as one of the new pilots.[4] Having assumed the editorship of JASPR, she had used its pages, from 1936 to 1940, to pay increasing attention to the experiments which Gardner Murphy and his assistant, Ernest Taves, were carrying on at Columbia.[5] The second pilot was Adele Wellman, the ASPR's executive secretary, who was instrumental in stimulating interest in Murphy's ESP experiments which were conducted later at the offices of the ASPR itself.[6] A third pilot was Murphy and ironically, a fourth, who may have helped inspire the revolt, was William H. Button, the ASPR president against whose administration the revolt had been launched. For it was Button who permitted Murphy to conduct his ESP experiments at the ASPR and then praised them, thus unwittingly increasing Murphy's stature as the most important figure in parapsychology in New York.

The revolution took place at the annual election on January 28, 1941, and was completely successful. The incumbents, whose terms were up but who sought reelection, including Button, were defeated and an entirely new slate elected. With this inpouring of new blood, the members of the Board of Trustees whose terms were not up all resigned.[7] George H. Hyslop, now a neurologist and son of the ASPR founder, was chosen as the new president. At the same time Gardner Murphy was elected to the Board of Trustees and also became chairman of the Research Committee. Others elected as new trustees included Lydia Allison, a member of the BSPR Council, and Waldemar Kaempffert. Jocelyn Pierson gave up the editorship of JASPR in anticipation of her coming marriage although she agreed to become a trustee. The *Journal*, now to be edited under the supervision of a publications committee, was changed from a monthly to a quarterly publication.[8] Laura Abbott Dale, a gifted and vigorous worker, became a research associate.

The reorganization went further. The ASPR Board and the Council of the BSPR decided to amalgamate. In Lydia Allison's letter to the ASPR she explained: "As conditions in Europe have naturally limited the distinguished work that has been carried on there, it appeared self-evident that united effort in this country was necessary."[9] But actually since Prince's death and then Worcester's, there had been no leadership in the BSPR. Moreover, its membership was divided between Boston residents and residents elsewhere, and, as is clear from correspondence that passed between the BSPR and Lydia Allison,[10] the organization was having financial troubles, was contemplating dissolution and turning over its library and archives to the Boston Medical Library. So when the opportunity came to amalgamate with the ASPR, it seemed a very prudent thing to do. Amalgamation was accomplished on May 1. The two societies would work as one and would be called the American Society for Psychical Research.

The SPR, which had regarded the ASPR during the third period in the same way that the Victorian upper class looked down upon the lower, could not restrain itself on hearing the "gratifying news" and at once sent the revitalized ASPR its "heartiest" congratulations.[11]

With the name of Hyslop again associated with the organization, it set out to resume the scientific standards on which its founder had insisted. As part of its reconstruction, it would investigate the phenomena traditionally accepted as parapsychological, would publish reports which measured up to the standards on which any other branch of science would insist, and would not

in the future devote its resources to unnecessarily controversial subjects or en-
dorse the claims of any mediums.[12] There would be no more Margerys for the
ASPR or for parapsychology.

1942

Invited to do so by Edwin G. Boring, Gardner Murphy offered a seminar
at Harvard on parapsychology which awakened an interest in the field on the
part of the clinical psychologist Gertrude R. Schmeidler. With his advice, she
began to conduct card-guessing experiments to explore the correlation between ESP scoring and ESP beliefs. It was the start of pioneer research that
would disclose two categories of subjects, "sheep" who believed in the reality
of ESP and "goats" who disbelieved in it, and would be one of the true advances in parapsychology. Her "sheep" and "goats" were to pass into the
vocabulary of parapsychology.

Margaret Mead and J.B. Rhine became members of the ASPR Board of
Trustees. Laura Dale became editor of JASPR. Gardner Murphy was elected first
vice president and continued as chairman of the Research Committee. Serious
contributors were invited to provide articles for JASPR which would be worthy
of scientific attention and articles were written by such persons as H.F.
Saltmarsh and Whately Carington.

1943

Experiments in psychokinesis which had been conducted at Duke by
Louisa and J.B. Rhine as early as 1934 were published in the *Journal of
Parapsychology*.

1944

William H. Button, who had served as ASPR president for 10 controversial
years, died.

1945

One of the figures who played a courageous role in the ASPR's history died.
Frederick Bligh Bond, editor of JASPR, who had been discharged in 1935, was
dead in Wales on March 8.

Gardner Murphy made a significant contribution to the survival question
when, in three papers,[13] he reviewed and evaluated the types of evidence,
outlined the difficulties confronting the hypothesis, and presented a guiding
field theory to include survival as well as psi phenomena.

1946

Gertrude Schmeidler was appointed research officer of the ASPR, where she continued her exploration of "sheep-goat" effects.

1947

Laura Dale resigned as editor of JASPR in order to devote more time to the conduct of experiments in ESP and PK with Gardner Murphy and Ernest Taves. The Publications Committee with Lydia Allison at its head edited the *Journal*.

1948

A Medical Section of the ASPR consisting of physicians whose purpose was to apply a clinical approach to parapsychology was created. Montague Ullman, Jule Eisenbud, Jan Ehrenwald and others were its members and Laura Dale was made secretary.

The *Journal of Parapsychology* turned the eyes of parapsychologists toward life experiences and their bearing on laboratory experiments. J.B. Rhine emphasized that such experiences were not evidence of the reality of ESP or PK and did not confirm theories about paranormal phenomena. Spontaneous experiences, however, might provide leads to guide future experiments and hypotheses to be tested. At the Duke Parapsychology Laboratory Louisa E. Rhine began a case study of thousands of reports of experiences from everyday life. It was the first major project of its kind in America.

The Reverend Frederick Edwards, once ASPR president, died on October 6.

1949

Gardner Murphy became the third American after William James and Walter F. Prince to become president of the SPR.[14]

1950

At the age of 91, Leonora Piper, the trance medium who impressed William James, Hodgson, Hyslop and the greatest savants of her era and produced valuable evidence of survival, died on July 3. Her death shut the door on what had been a notable, if not the most remarkable, phase in the history of American parapsychology.

1951

Eileen J. Garrett, who shared with Mrs. Piper the record in America as the most intensely investigated trance medium of all time, founded the Parapsychology Foundation in New York and so increased its growing importance as a center of parapsychology. Gardner Murphy was appointed general research consultant. The aims of the Parapsychology Foundation were, through financial support and conferences, to encourage an interdisciplinary approach to many special fields of parapsychological inquiry. In future years, the Foundation would supply grants for a variety of qualitative and quantitative studies by many individual researchers and promote international conferences and meetings on a number of themes.

1952

Gardner Murphy, who had spent the previous year in India as a consultant to the United Nations Educational, Scientific and Cultural Organization, returned to the United States to become director of research at the Menninger Foundation, Topeka, Kansas. His participation in the affairs of the ASPR continued but on a more limited basis.

The A.W. Mellon Educational and Charitable Trust, donor of the National Gallery of Art in Washington, D.C., supplied financial support for research into "psychological physics" by Professor Robert A. McConnell, a research assistant professor in the Department of Biophysics at the University of Pittsburgh. Over the next years, the Trust's funding of his research into extrasensory perception and psychokinesis would amount to $840,000.

1953

Under a grant from the Office of Naval Research, J. Gaither Pratt at Duke University conducted research to test whether homing pigeons use ESP.

The search for spontaneous cases was one of the first great efforts of the SPR and resulted in classics such as *Phantasms of the Living* and "Census of Hallucinations." Murphy emphasized the importance of studying cases of spontaneous telepathy, clairvoyance and precognition to throw light on the study of human personality[15] and in 1953 attended an International Conference of Paraspychological Studies held at Utrecht and sponsored by the Parapsychology Foundation.

1955

As a result of a recommendation made at this conference, another was organized by the SPR in Cambridge in 1955. Once again the sponsor of the conference was the Parapsychology Foundation, which would bear the costs of many more international conferences on divers themes. The Cambridge conference was on spontaneous cases. Murphy gave the opening address to stress their importance. On his return to America a broad net was cast by the ASPR in succeeding years to catch new cases and Laura Dale and Rhea A. White would be key workers in the surveying and investigating of spontaneous psychic experiences.

1956

Two parapsychological laboratories were created, one in Philadelphia at St. Joseph's College under the supervision of Carroll B. Nash, the other in Plainview, Texas, at Wayland College, to be directed by John Freeman.

1957

With the production by Rhine and Pratt of *Parapsychology: Frontier Science of the Mind,* the first textbook on parapsychology appeared.

The Parapsychological Association, a professional organization for workers in parapsychology, was founded upon the initiative of J.B. Rhine. The objectives of the organization, as set forth in its charter, were to promote parapsychology as a science, integrate its findings with other departments of science and disseminate information concerning its work. The *Journal of Parapsychology* was chosen as an affiliated periodical.

A Division of Research was established by the Parapsychology Foundation. Karlis Osis, who had been on the staff of the Duke Parapsychology Laboratory, was appointed director of research. Among the projects to be investigated were survival after death.

The Duke Parapsychology Laboratory established the William McDougall Award ($1,000) for Distinguished Work in Parapsychology.

1958

Gertrude Schmeidler and Professor R.A. McConnell coauthored *ESP and Personality Patterns,* which summarized—for those who wished to scrutinize ESP research from a strictly scientific point of view—research in the field to date, statistical analyses and the famous experiments conducted by Dr. Schmeidler between 1942 and 1951 to explore the relation between ESP successes and ESP beliefs.

The Mind Science Foundation was established in San Antonio, Texas, to conduct scientific studies of the human mind. Over the years, while other avenues of research were to be followed—into creativity, psychoneuronimmunology and Alzheimer's Disease—research into three aspects of parapsychology would be investigated also: remote viewing, or the clairvoyant ability to perceive objects and events at a distance, and psychokinesis with respect both to living systems and to random-number generators.

1959

The Parapsychology Foundation began the publication of the *International Journal of Parapsychology*, a quarterly review in several languages in which research reports and scholarly papers relevant to parapsychology were published.

Lydia Allison, who had a great interest in both mental and physical phenomena and was an energetic worker in both the BSPR and the ASPR, died on March 25.

1960

The editorship of JASPR was assumed by Rhea White.

The Psychical Research Foundation was established in Durham by Charles E. Ozanne to carry out, under the directorship of William G. Roll, research into the survival question.

1961

The most important primer on parapsychology yet to appear was *Challenge of Psychical Research,* published by Gardner Murphy with the collaboration of Laura Dale. It presented and discussed experiments and cases representative of parapsychology.

As part of the investigation into the survival question carried on by the Parapsychology Foundation's Division of Research, Karlis Osis's monograph on observations of dying patients by physicians and nurses was published. Osis would be one of many authors, besides Gertrude Schmeidler, Hornell Hart and Joseph H. Rush, whose monographs on different subjects the Parapsychology Foundation would publish.

With grants from the Ittleson Family Foundation in New York and the Scaife Fund of Pittsburgh, Montague Ullman, chief of psychiatry at the Maimonides Medical Center in Brooklyn, New York, established a Dream Laboratory there to conduct research into sleep and dreams in relation to ESP. Stanley Krippner, an experimental psychologist, later would become director of the Laboratory and, in collaboration with Dr. Ullman, would conduct experimental telepathic dream studies using electrophysiological recordings to monitor dreams.

1962

The 21-year ASPR presidency of George H. Hyslop, reelected to his post year after year during which the organization was free of controversy, came to an end when Hyslop decided to transfer the responsibility of the presidency to someone else. Gardner Murphy was elected on March 21.[16]

Along with this change Karlis Osis, having left the Parapsychology Foundation, joined the ASPR as director of research. Laura Dale resumed the editorship of JASPR and, in the years that followed, was to make it a model among parapsychological publications, esteemed for its high standards.

When Duke University signified that it would not continue the Parapsychology Laboratory after Rhine's mandatory retirement, he established in Durham the Foundation for Research on the Nature of Man.

1964

J. Gaither Pratt left Durham for a new association with Ian Stevenson in the Department of Psychiatry at the University of Virginia.

John F. Kennedy University was founded in Orinda, California, and eventually offered an accredited graduate program in parapsychology in its Graduate Program in the Study of Consciousness, a division of the School of General Studies.

1965

After 40 years of involvement in the affairs and activities of the ASPR, George H. Hyslop died.

1967

At the University of Virginia School of Medicine, a Parapsychology Research Endowment Fund, established by an anonymous donor, permitted a Division of Parapsychology to be created and a research professorship in psychiatry to be established whose holder was to carry on research in parapsychology. Ian Stevenson, M.D., was appointed to this chair. This marked the second time parapsychology had been able to get a purchase on the American academic world.

1968

Chester F. Carlson died on September 19. The inventor of the Xerox process and drawn to the survival problem and investigations into the recesses of human nature, he had been a generous donor to parapsychology. His financial support almost doubled the ASPR endowment, largely maintained its research budget and provided money for Karlis Osis's questionnaire-survey of physicians and nurses in his investigations of death-bed visions. Carlson's generosity also supported the reincarnation studies of Ian Stevenson.

In Carlson's memory the ASPR named its new laboratory the Chester F. Carlson Research Laboratory.[17]

1969

After Margaret Mead argued in its favor, the Parapsychological Association was admitted as an affiliate member of the American Association for the Advancement of Science.

A prolonged illness ended the life of one of the ASPR trustees who had served on the Board for 18 years and had contributed many important writings to JASPR and other publications. C.J. Ducasse was one of the few major philosophers who analyzed paranormal phenomena and considered that the empirical approach was the only valid approach to the survival problem.

1970

The death of Eileen Garrett took place in September. She had founded the Parapsychology Foundation, supported research in parapsychology and submitted her mediumship to experiments by eminent scientists in the search for answers about survival, ESP, psychology — and herself.

1971

The Survival Research Foundation was established by Susy Smith, the author of books on parapsychology, to conduct investigations into the possibility of the survival of the conscious mind after bodily death.

The Gardner Murphy Research Institute was founded to promote the relevance of parapsychological research to other disciplines and areas.

Montague Ullman replaced Gardner Murphy as president of the ASPR. Although plagued by ill health, Murphy continued as a member of the Board of Trustees and adviser to Ullman.

The fortunes of the ASPR were affected literally as the result of a holographic will made in 1946 by a grizzled prospector who, three years later, went, pick in hand, into the Arizona hills and never returned. Apparently disdainful of lawyers, James Kidd decided to write his own will. Taking up a pencil, he wrote,

This is my first and only will and is dated the second of January, 1946. I have no heirs and have not been married in my life and after all my funeral expenses have been paid and $100. one hundred dollars to some preacher of the gospel to say fare well at my grave sell all my property which is all in cash and stocks with E.F. Hutton Co Phoenix some in safety deposit box, and have this balance money go in a research or some scientific proof of a soul of the human body which leaves at death I think in time their [sic] can be a Photograph of soul leaving the human at death, James Kidd

It all seemed simple enough to Kidd, but when it came to light that he had left $270,000, numerous claimants appeared in the courts of Arizona. As Kidd had not named any specific legatee, the field was open to all, including the ASPR. Batteries of lawyers and 130 litigants clashed in a lengthy contest. After a judicial decision favored the Barrows Neurological Institute, which intended to use the legacy for brain research and expressly disclaimed any interest in the existence or fate of the human soul, the ASPR and other disappointed claimants appealed to the Arizona Supreme Court. The decision of the lower court was reversed, the case was retried, and the outcome was an award of one-third of the legacy to the Psychical Research Foundation and two-thirds to the ASPR. The ASPR's share went in part to subsidize Osis's investigations of deathbed visions in concert with parapsychologist Erlendur Haraldsson and, in part, to other ASPR research.

The Science Unlimited Research Foundation was set up in San Antonio to study psi through computer experiments.

1973

The Institute of Noetic Sciences was founded by Astronaut Edgar D. Mitchell to support research into the mind/body problem. In 1971 Mitchell, while a member of the Apollo 14 lunar expedition, had conducted a telepathic experiment with four people on earth.

Pratt published a survey of all ESP investigations, including his own, which had been conducted over 10 years with the remarkable Pavel Stepanek of Czechoslovakia.[18]

The name of the Dream Laboratory at Maimonides Medical Center was changed to the Division of Parapsychology and Psychophysics as its research programs were extended beyond sleep and dreams to other areas. Charles Honorton joined the program as research assistant.

1976

Although concerned psychologists who criticized J.B. Rhine's work had succeeded in working together long enough to hold a "heresy trial" in 1938, the opposition to parapsychology had never been brought together into a cohesive group determined to strike hard and often at claims which alarmed it. In this year, however, a band of philosophers and scientists headed by Paul Kurtz, a professor of philosophy at the State University of New York at Buffalo, organized the Committee for the Scientific Investigation of Claims of the Paranormal. Reacting sharply to what it perceived as a wave of fantastic and pseudoscientific claims that threatened to drown the minds of the young and undermine the scientific outlook, CSICOP listed parapsychology and its assertions concerning psychic powers as among the occult claims and beliefs that were a danger to reason and science. Its journal, *The Zetetic,* and its popular magazine, *The Skeptical Inquirer,* fired the first shots in this fourth period of American parapsychology in what was to become a deadly barrage of criticisms of parapsychology and its evidence for the paranormal.

1977

Russell Targ and Harold Puthoff, two scientists at the Stanford Research Institute in Menlo Park, California (not to be confused with nearby Stanford University), described, in *Mind Reach,* "remote viewing" experiments. This book was sensationalized in the press but its real importance lies in the fact that the experiments which strongly suggested the existence of clairvoyant abilities were not conducted by parapsychologists with a "will to believe" but were based on physics and conducted in a prestigious laboratory.

K. Ramakrishna Rao, professor of psychology at Andhra University in India, was appointed director of the Institute for Parapsychology in Durham.

1979

Although in 1940 *Extra-Sensory Perception After Sixty Years* laid to rest criticisms against the case for ESP, ESP and parapsychology were still not recognized and accepted. Academic psychologists still continued to view parapsychology as crackpot research and, in the postwar years, were joined by magicians, writers of science columns and members of a highly skeptical scientific community who labelled parapsychology a pseudoscience and placed it in the same class as Big Foot.

In January 1979, at a symposium held by the American Association for the Advancement of Science, the latest assault against parapsychology's claim to be recognized as a legitimate science came from Dr. John A. Wheeler, a prominent physicist from the University of Texas. He compared parapsychologists to conjurers and confidence men and suggested to the Board of Directors of the AAAS that the Parapsychological Association be disaffiliated because "it is time to drive the pseudos from the workshop of science." His appeal, however, was not entertained.

The SPR elected J.B. Rhine as its president.

The death of Gardner Murphy ended brilliant chapters in the stories of both psychology and parapsychology. Murphy was an honored teacher and scholar in the former and, while not a successful experimenter in the latter, was what he called "big brother" to the most brilliant investigators. He was also a powerful leader whose influence and prestige were felt both within and outside of parapsychology.

J. Gaither Pratt, formerly associated with Rhine at the Duke Parapsychology Laboratory, and later with Stevenson at the Division of Parapsychology in the Department of Psychiatry at the University of Virginia, died on November 3. He had been coexperimenter in two historic card-guessing experiments while at Duke, coauthor of the first textbook on parapsychology and of the first survey of experimental and evaluative methods in ESP.

James S. McDonnell, who had merged his aircraft company with the Douglas Company to produce jet fighters, cruise missiles and commercial airliners, also had founded the James S. McDonnell Foundation. In 1979, the Foundation, which had supported Stevenson's studies in apparitions and reincarnation and Osis's out-of-body investigations, established the Psychophysical Research Laboratories at the Forrestal Research Center in Princeton, New Jersey. With Charles Honorton as its director, the Center was to conduct laboratory research into extrasensory perception and psychokinesis by using the Ganzfeld, or sensory deprivation technique, for the former and random-number-generator techniques for the latter.

1979 also saw half the financial support for parapsychological research in the United States provided by the Foundation in a single grant to Washington University in St. Louis. The sum of $600,000 was given for the creation there of the McDonnell Laboratory for Psychical Research. Peter R. Phillips was its director.

1980

J.B. Rhine died on February 20 at the age of 84. Sometimes called the "grandfather" or "father" of parapsychology, he had devoted himself for 50 years to parapsychology, both as researcher concerned with the establishment of ESP and as leader concerned with the recognition of parapsychology by official science. Whether he succeeded in achieving either goal is still problematical.

Louisa E. Rhine succeeded him as president of the SPR and became executive director of the Foundation for Research on the Nature of Man.

Arthur C. Twitchell, Jr., replaced Montague Ullman as president of the ASPR. Twitchell, a theatrical producer, became interested in parapsychology after he saw an apparition in the barracks of a German prisoner of war camp in which he had been interned. He had served on the ASPR Board of Trustees from 1962 and had been generous in his financial support of parapsychology.

James S. McDonnell, president of McDonnell Douglas Aircraft, whose philanthropy had supported the Parapsychological Association and many centers of parapsychological research, died in St. Louis.

The death of J.B. Rhine ended the fourth period of the development of parapsychology in America on which he and Gardner Murphy, as the major figures of the era, had the strongest influence. Full-length portraits of their characters and work are presented next, along with a cameo of J. Gaither Pratt, who made a distinctive contribution and also died within the fourth period.

Gardner Murphy: A Portrait

Gardner Murphy straddled two worlds, psychology and parapsychology, and was a giant in each. A gentle, patient giant, but one with a problem which his closest friends, associates and students never suspected.

His problem cannot be ascribed to his birth on July 8, 1895, in Chillicothe, Ohio. No charge can be laid against his father. Edgar Gardner Murphy, an Episcopal minister, who struggled against child labor and wrote on issues of race relations and education, was the best of fathers. Up to his death, in 1913, he poured "out an affection which I reciprocated,"[19] said Murphy. Was Maude King, Murphy's mother, to blame? She was the daughter of fine New England stock in Concord, Massachusetts, had attended Vassar, been elected to Phi Beta Kappa and had to gone to Texas to teach. In San Antonio, she stayed at a boarding house operated by Jeannie Gardner Murphy, met Edgar Gardner Murphy there and married him.[20] But, until she died at the age of 92, she was Murphy's close and constant support.[21] Nor can the problem be blamed on Murphy's older brother, DuBose, with whom he also was close.

The problem started when Murphy was still a very little giant and the Murphy family went to live in his mother's home town of Concord. "Gran'pa" and "Gran'ma" King were "extraordinarily loving" and the Emerson, Thoreau, Alcott world that was Concord was one to which he felt he truly belonged.[22] But in all towns there were railroad tracks which constituted a line both of steel and snobbery between good neighborhoods and slums and minorities. In Concord, it was the tracks of the Boston and Maine Railroad which passed through the center of Concord. Murphy's problem as a small boy began with them and with his discovery that, in Concord, the Irish were assigned a low status.

> On one side the people were so-called Anglo-Saxons, Republicans, businessmen, Protestants and commuters to Boston and on the other side of the tracks they were mostly Democratic, Irish, Roman Catholic, wage laborers and did not go often to Boston. And I discovered in school and elsewhere that these people from across the tracks—they were called . . . people from Texas—were sort of behind us in various ways.

Gardner Murphy at 75.

There was no hate but there was a good deal of derogation. My name classified me as belonging to quote Texas quote....[23] The problem ... arose from the fact that [I] belonged to the majority group on the "good" side of the tracks, but [my] name placed [me] spang in the middle of "Texas." This problem of divided loyalties, and uncertain identity, has been with me for a lifetime.[24]

As a result, he developed an antiaristocratic way of looking at things and people. He was always for the Democrats rather than the Republicans, intentionally sided with the Pats and Mikes of this world instead of the Emersons and Thoreaus, to whose world he felt he belonged,[25] and regarded mavericks and minorities "my kind" of people.[26] He became unofficial defender of the underdog—literally, as one of his earliest recollections shows. When he was about six years old in San Antonio he befriended a stray dog with big floppy ears. When he found that no one would feed it, he took his entire spending money for one week—a dime—and bought food for the dog. And in like manner, in later life, when he was awarded an honorary degree from the University of Hamburg, he said, "They are atoning somewhat for what they did to Jewish psychologists."[27]

Even though Gardner Murphy's good old Irish name created problems of identity and loyalty, his initials became a passport which identified him clearly to others who came to know him and who used these initials to create nicknames for him. "God Murphy" the undergraduates at City College of New York were wont to call him when he was chairman of the Psychology Department there in the 1940s.[28] A "great man" his colleagues called him, in whose presence, as one of them wrote, "lesser men do not want to waste time."[29]

But those of us who never knew Murphy may ask, as James asked of Hodgson, "Who is this Gardner Murphy?" My task is to establish his identity as well as to show to whom, besides his mother and wife, he was devoted, what challenged him, what he loved, why he had a double life and what he did with it.

James and Murphy

Since indifference and hostility toward parapsychology among American psychologists have limited sharply the number of them who have been active in parapsychology in the last century, can we think of any Americans who, in their own eras, simultaneously were notable in psychology and devoted themselves to parapsychology? In spite of having achieved prominence as a psychologist, McDougall is disqualified from running for this office because he was a Scot. Prince, although an outstanding psychological investigator, was not a trained psychologist and had no academic reputation. There were only two men who achieved renown in psychology and were willing to make lifelong commitments to parapsychology. One was creative, eloquent William James, the other incisive, scholarly Gardner Murphy. This rather tenuous tie between the two men may have been no accident of history. It may have been the last link in a chain of subtle yet stronger affinities of interest, temperament and mind between them.

Murphy seems to have regarded James as a kind of hero. "My devotion to William James began very early," he wrote.[30] How early we cannot be sure, but 1910 or 1912 at Bad Nauheim, Germany, are possibilities. Its famous baths had drawn not only William James, who sought in them a cure for his poor health, but also Edgar Gardner Murphy, whose heart condition sent him to Nauheim in 1910 and 1912 when he took Gardner Murphy and the rest of his family with him.[31] It is certain, however, that in 1916 Murphy read James's *Varieties of Religious Experience* and the two volumes of *Principles of Psychology* in 1920, read aloud James's collection of letters which had been published by his son Henry, and Ralph Barton Perry's biography of James in the 1940's. Murphy taught courses on Jamesian psychology. At every literary opportunity, Murphy wrote on James—the foreword to *The Letters of William James and Théodore Flournoy*[32]; Murphy's own *Historical Introduction to Modern Psychology*[33]; and his *Personality: A Biosocial Approach to Origins and Structure.*[34] James was the subject of Murphy's essays published in JASPR[35] and JSPR.[36] And Murphy coedited a selection of James's letters, reports, lectures and book reviews in, and wrote the introduction and epilogue for, *William James on*

Psychical Research.[37] Finally, said Murphy, "I used James constantly in connection with psychical research."[38]

Some clues to this hero worship suggest themselves to the biographical sleuth. Murphy's maternal grandfather, George King, had been the attorney for Mrs. Piper, James's "white crow," and, Murphy recorded, "William James came out to lecture in my home town of Concord, Massachusetts, and was admired and loved by those close to me."[39] But the strongest clue for the attraction that James had for Murphy may be that whenever Murphy looked at a picture of James, Murphy saw an intellectual double of himself. Murphy's views on so many subjects in psychology and parapsychology are so close to those of James that often it is hard to tell when Murphy, and when James, is speaking.

There were many other resemblances between the two men. Sir Oliver Lodge, who had studied the evidence for survival for twenty years and was absolutely convinced of the continuing postmortem existence of the human personality, said that his office boy contradicted him. It is not recorded whether his office boy continued in Sir Oliver's employ after that. But if James and Murphy (both of whom probably would have sided with the office boy) had been contradicted by some adverse opinion or fact on any issue, neither would have scorned it or have reacted defensively. For both were teachers who had patient, tolerant minds ever open to fresh ideas even contradictory to their own, from students and others. Intimate colleagues were struck by this same comparison between James and Murphy. One observed that Murphy "possessed a certain Jamesian 'tender-mindedness,'"[40] and Gertrude Schmeidler that James and Murphy "so resembled each other . . . in large part from . . . intellectual generosity, this willingness to incorporate new ideas and new facts."[41]

Murphy was willing because he felt strongly that real education required discussion and the confrontation of incompatible facts[42] and he readily admitted to "my broad or eclectic or tolerant or flexible" beliefs.[43] But he was more than merely tolerant. As Laura Dale, who collaborated with Murphy in the ASPR from 1941, wrote of Murphy, "I have never known him to be anything else than interested in the other fellow's ideas even when he by no means agreed with them."[44]

There are more parallels between James and Murphy. Both came in packages that contained psychology and philosophy, for Murphy, too, had his philosophical side. In one writing, he expressed his philosophical position,[45] and in *Western Psychology*,[46] coauthored with his wife Lois, Murphy made a bold attempt to interrelate psychology and philosophy and to show how psychological thought evolved by presenting selections from great philosophers throughout the intellectual history of the West, from the pre–Socratics, through the Greek classical period, the Roman era and the periods of the Renaissance and Enlightenment, through Darwin and Nietzsche and ending, of course, with Murphy's hero, James. Even in matters of health there is a similarity between the two men. Both lived as semi-invalids for years.

James had a heart condition and sought every cure suggested by his doctors from the baths at Bad Nauheim in Germany to the clean air of Switzerland. Murphy's health became poor after he had a severe case of influenza in 1925 and, during the nine years that he was sickly and almost disabled, he tried every treatment prescribed by conventional medicine.[47]

Psychology and Teaching: A Challenge and a Love

James, although a medical man and philosopher, was primarily a great psychologist, as proved by his monumental *Principles of Psychology* published in 1890. Murphy followed in James' tradition as an author of textbooks and as an inspiring teacher in the field. Both shone as the brightest stars of their times in the firmament of psychology. But there had been no psychologists in Murphy's family. His mother was a teacher, his grandfather a lawyer, his father a minister. Why didn't Murphy choose the ministry, for example? "I accepted without any question at all," he said, "the main contours of Christian, specifically Episcopal Church belief, and I loved Sunday school and church."[48] After graduation from elementary school in 1908, he was

> more and more overwhelmed with religious preoccupation and this wasn't all Episcopal Church either.... I got interested in religion at many levels—interested in a personal sense of concern with Jesus and with the personal relation which is emphasized in all evangelical approaches. And interested in the fellow-feeling group-life that goes with membership in a religious body.[49]

Murphy "became what my elder brother, DuBose, later called an 'evangelical Catholic.'"[50] Everything "guided me for some years towards the life of a missionary."[51]

After the Murphy family moved from Concord to Branford, near New Haven, and then on to New Haven itself, the years from 1905 to 1910 became ones of intellectual curiosity and growth.[52] During this time, also, while he played center on a football team and participated on a debating team, he learned Latin and Greek and so loved the latter that he was able to integrate it with his religious interest when his father gave him a copy of the Greek New Testament.

After two years in high school he received a scholarship to attend the Hotchkiss School from 1910 to 1912. Although he worked at odd jobs, such as cleaning blackboards and waiting on tables, he was able to maintain his grades sufficiently to keep at the head of his class for these two years.

"All the dice were loaded," said Murphy, "in favor of my going to Yale."[53] After taking the college entrance exams he entered Yale in 1912, took a classical curriculum and sang second bass in the freshman glee club. A crucial course for him was English, which taught him the craft of expression. When he joined the debating team, he learned the crafts of public speaking and teaching.[54] His missionary ambitions were deemphasized in college when his interest shifted to medicine. He thought of becoming a heart specialist so that he could take care of his father who was suffering from heart disease. But then he had a second thought when, in his freshman year, he developed an intense interest in psychology and made the decision to study the mind and become a "brain specialist," in part to help his fellows and in part to establish the independence of mind or personality from the brain.[55] The second part must have weighed more heavily with him than the first since, at that time, his religious interests were as strong as ever. He acknowledged that the "motivation for [the decision] was mainly religious" and that he wanted to prove the transcendence of mind over mechanistic concepts.[56]

But there was something else that pushed him in the direction of psychology. That something was parapsychology[57] in which, at this time, he had an interest supported by his evangelical convictions.[58] Indeed, the final element that entered into his decision to major in psychology at Yale was his determination to get ready for parapsychology.[59] This subject had convinced him that there existed "a vital challenge"[60] in psychology.

It was during his junior year at Yale that his world views began to form and their gradual formation produced "an erosion of my religious beliefs."[61] He took a course in anthropology offered by A.G. Keller which taught the classical Darwinian evolutionary point of view with an emphasis on blind, or fortuitous, and not purposive, dynamics. This was, he said, "a thing that would weaken one's faith and it certainly did mine—more than any other single thing. . . . The big effect was the consistency of the global agnostic, materialistic, what-have-you conception of the universe, without any steering mechanism . . . what Clarence Darrow called being a deck-hand on a rudderless boat."[62]

His religious faith, though not crushed, was badly crippled. While his friends were going to the ministry, his qualms prevented him from doing so. He received his B.A. degree from Yale in 1916 and in September entered graduate school at Harvard where he studied with Muensterberg, Yerkes and Holt, and where he underwent an intellectual turmoil like that which had made Hyslop cry like a baby and perspire like a horse:

> I found myself in this year at Harvard thinking through with genuine desperation, headaches and insomnia, the question of religious values and meanings and whether they could be made to coincide with the monistic, or if you like, materialistic world view which Keller had made so absolutely convincing. I decided, after much writhing, at 2:00 one March morning in 1917, that I would have to give up my religious faith.[63]

This decision could not, however, break Murphy's father's heart as it had Hyslop's, because Edgar Gardner Murphy's diseased heart already had stopped beating.

Also in 1917 war was declared on Germany. Murphy, who had just received his master's degree from Harvard, suspended his graduate study to go overseas with the Yale Mobile Hospital Unit as part of the American

Expeditionary Forces. He returned in 1919 to take up his graduate work again, this time at Columbia where, in 1923, he received a Ph.D. He also attended courses at the New School for Social Research. At Columbia were Ruth Benedict and Margaret Mead with whom he formed close friendships.

In 1920 he followed both his mother and William James into a teaching career. He became an instructor in psychology at Columbia as James had been at Harvard.

Murphy had had "two light intense puppy-love affairs" in elementary school, had fallen in love in his senior year at Hotchkiss, and again in his second year at Yale.[64] But when, in 1924, he met Lois Barclay, then a student at Union Seminary, it was the start of a different world for Murphy.[65] They discovered mutual interests in education, clinical psychology, comparative religion and the same philosophic and esthetic concerns. They were married two years later. Their son Alpen was born in 1930 and their daughter Margaret, in 1932.

At Columbia, where he later became associate professor of psychology, Murphy's course, entitled "The History of Modern Psychology," culminated in 1929 in the book *Historical Introduction to Modern Psychology* in which Murphy described the evolution of psychology. Here James's hand helped to guide Murphy's pen again. "I encountered [James] in new contexts when working on" the book.[66] It was a remarkable feat for Murphy to have completed this book, since his health had failed in 1925. He could not see so that the "book was written by dictation, with never a chance to see what I had written"[67]; yet, despite this extraordinary difficulty which would have defeated most, and perhaps with James as coauthor behind the scenes, Murphy's book was praised by Edwin G. Boring, profesor of psychology at Harvard, and by other psychologists.[68]

In the same year, Murphy edited his *Outline of Abnormal Psychology*. His early perspectives of psychology appear in his *Historical Introduction to Modern Psychology*, in the introductory chapter to *Experimental Social Psychology*, coauthored with his wife in 1931, and in the introduction to *A Briefer General Psychology*, in 1935. These works expressed many components of his beliefs and approaches, such as that it is by the study of their origins and growth that things are understood and that it is only through arbitrary compartmentalization that psychology is separated from the social and biological sciences and that this separation is more harmful than good. At Yale, however, his teacher, Chauncey Brewster Tinker, who taught him English during his freshman year and the "Age of Johnson" in his senior year, taught him as well what became the center of all his convictions. It was the slogan "plus ultra."[69] Tinker had said that the slogan signified the new world that lay beyond the Pillars of Hercules in the straits of Gibraltar. The ancients had viewed them as marking the end of the inhabited world and before the epoch-making discoveries of Columbus and other explorers, the slogan had been "ne plus ultra." But after navigation through the straits of Gibraltar to the new world beyond, the phrase became "plus ultra": "There is more beyond." The idea was the crux of Murphy's philosophy: There could be no end of discovery or finality of knowledge for science. "Plus ultra" characterized his constant openness to fresh ideas.

His professional specialization was forming. Beginning in 1924 he offered at Columbia graduate courses in abnormal psychology and in social psychology, and a course in the latter at a summer session in 1927 at Syracuse University. A preoccupation in 1929 with students' Ph.D. dissertations in social psychology soon made him a specialist in the field. He felt that *Experimental Social Psychology*, of which he was the coauthor and for which he received the Butler Medal at Columbia, introduced him as a social psychologist.

With the support of the Columbia University Council for Research in the Social Sciences, Murphy created a project for the study of social attitudes in which Rensis Likert joined him. The result in 1938 was *Public Opinion and the Individual*, which Murphy and Likert coauthored.

Soon, however, his whole outlook on social psychology was to undergo a change. Lois Murphy's background in child and clinical psychology, and the empirical material on which she had been working, stimulated a growing interest in personality study and made Murphy aware of fresh concepts of personality. This new awareness led to the development of a field theory of personality. Books such as Ruth Benedict's *Patterns of Culture* and Margaret Mead's *Cooperation and Competition Among Primitive Peoples* further altered his perspectives. Somewhere during this period Murphy again "put [James] to use."[70] Now the sort of social psychology which gave a social basis to personality research began to have greater meaning for him.[71] His field theory contained one basic idea which he was later to apply in an unusual parapsychological context: "that the biological and the social are *literally the same events.*"[72] His concepts and the implications of the field theory were presented in 1947 in *Personality: A Biosocial Approach to Origins and Structure*, which Lois Murphy has called his "magnum opus,"[73] and, in 1958, in *Human Potentialities*.

The relevance of psychology to social issues concerned him and he became chairman of the Society for Psychological Study of Social Issues. The relevance of psychology to international relations and to war also occupied Murphy. This concern led to many lectures, active participation in the American Friends Service Committee and the editing in 1945 of *Human Nature and Enduring Peace*. In 1949, as a consultant to the United Nations Educational, Scientific and Cultural Organization, he paid a six month visit to India in order to study Hindu-Muslim conflicts. He also served with Lois Murphy on the Ministry of Education of the Indian government. Murphy's *In the Minds of Men: A UNESCO Study of Social Tensions in India* (1953) was the result.

His career at Columbia ended in 1940 when he became chairman of the Psychology Department at City College of New York, where he was offered the chance to do experimental research in the problems of perception and cognition which had not been given enough attention in psychology. The opportunity appealed to him because such research seemed to be at the heart of a complete personality system. For some years studies in this field were pursued at City College until laboratory methods seemed to attract fewer psychology students than did clinical psychology. So, in 1952, Murphy left City College to become director of research at the Menninger Foundation in Topeka, Kansas, where the experimental method, which Murphy considered the most important of all the methods, would be followed. This change in professional association did not alter in the least his steadfast devotion to James: he "found him standing nearby, always ready to be consulted, and often profoundly helpful in connection with studies at The Menninger Foundation. . . ."[74]

He considered certain ideas to be "really me." His field theory was one. There were as well autism—cognitive processes that move in the direction of need satisfaction—and canalization—as needs are satisfied in specific ways, they tend to become more specific.

Murphy had taught in college about three decades up to the time he made the professional shift to the Menninger Foundation. After retiring from the Menninger Foundation in 1968, he became visiting professor in the Psychology Department of George Washington University in Washington, D.C., and taught there until 1973. "I loved my teaching," he wrote.[75] This love seemed to be reciprocated for "in the anonymous balloting of class after class of graduating seniors at the City College of New York, Gardner Murphy had been designated 'best-liked teacher.'"[76]

Prior to 1940, there were but a few psychology majors at City College each year. Yet in the decade beginning in 1940, CCNY not only attracted more students capable of doctoral work in psychology but more graduates went on to their doctoral degrees in psychology there than in any other American college[77]—a tribute to CCNY and to Murphy's tenure as head of the Psychology Department.

Murphy was lionized by his former students and associates who, on his sixty-fifth birthday in 1960, presented him with a Festschrift, a many-layered birthday cake consisting of 26 contributions which recognized his character and convictions as a teacher and his role "as catalyst and fomenter of our ideas and research interests."[78] Murphy's standing as a teacher was also recognized in 1961 when the John Dewey Society invited him to lecture on his conception of the part the teacher plays in the teaching situation.

Murphy learned much from his exchanges with students and from his concern with Ph.D. dissertations at Columbia and with the Honors Research Studies at City College. But, in words reminiscent of McDougall's, who credited his wife with teaching him psychology, Murphy said, "I have learned a great deal more psychology from Lois than from any other living person."[79]

Many honors were bestowed on Murphy by his profession. He was president of the American Psychological Association, the Southwestern Psychological Association, the Eastern Psychological Association and chairman of the Society for the Psychological Study of Social Issues. The University of Hamburg in Germany and the City University of New York conferred honorary doctorates. In 1932, he was the recipient of the Butler Medal from Columbia University and, in 1977, the Gold Medal Award of the American Psychological Foundation.

Double Life

Murphy wrote that James gave parapsychology "a certain status, a certain intellectual respectability, which only his own immense prestige could have given it in the United States, in the era in which he flourished."[80] Murphy could have been writing about himself. For Murphy, the "great man" of psychology, notable scholar and honored teacher, by his very prominence compelled psychologists and scientists to be less hostile and more accepting of parapsychology. The support given by Murphy to parapsychology by his name, his reputation and standing and his university affiliations lent the greatest weight to parapsychology in America. The Parapsychological Association is a case in point. The PA, conceived in 1957 as a world-wide professional organization of parapsychologists, but bastardized by orthodox science, finally was accepted as legitimate in 1969 when the American Association for the Advancement of Science admitted the PA as an affiliate. But parapsychology's acceptance by the scientific community as a legitimate scientific enterprise came only after a debate in which Margaret Mead argued effectively for a favorable vote because the PA used scientific methods and, she said, it is methodology, not hypotheses, that determine what is a science. Behind her argument and the ultimate affiliation of the PA, however, was Gardner Murphy. As Lois Murphy said, "His friendship with Margaret Mead led to her forceful and successful effort to get the AAAS to accept parapsychology."[81]

That Murphy was known to some people only as a parapsychologist and not as a psychologist may seem incomprehensible in view of his prestige as a teacher and textbook author and his energetic activities in psychology. This identification followed because Murphy stood, as James had, with one foot planted in the world of parapsychology and the other in the world of psychology. As Murphy commented, "all through these years I was leading a double life, for psychical research was just as real and important to me as it had ever been."[82] In another writing, he said, "I led a double life, keeping a toe-hold on respectable psychology while carrying on the work of a 'quack,' as psychologists saw the matter." Not even his friends understood his commitment to parapsychology. They considered him a little "off" or "touched"[83] for wasting his time on such nonsense.

It is also hard to believe that he was able to lead a double life between textbooks, teaching, the Menninger Foundation and his numerous other honors affiliations. But, as Lois Murphy explained,

> One thing that I think is relevant to Gardner's productivity is the way he used his time. . . . [H]e has always had a clear sense of what was worth spending time on, so that material things didn't matter much

except for good records and pictures. It was his ability to make the best use of his time that enabled him to pursue two full-time careers concurrently, one in psychology and one in parapsychology.[84]

She also made it easier for him to pursue both careers during their 54 years of marriage. For Lois Murphy was not only a developmental psychologist who worked with him in psychology; she also had read about and was interested in the paranormal for many years prior to meeting Murphy.

In fact, although he had many qualities, Lois Murphy admitted that she had not initially been attracted by them. "I didn't marry Gardner for his brilliance and charm, although he had much more than the usual share of that, but for his guts and courage in support of psychical research." She had been "thunderstruck" by the courage he demonstrated in "bucking the establishment to pursue this taboo field."[85] And Murphy described the value of her support to him: "Her interest in psychical research, as a challenging pioneer field, was a primary factor in maintaining my own morale."[86]

Prince had observed that prominent parapsychologists did not seem to have psychic experiences. Was Murphy the exception and were his experiences the reason for his double life? According to Lois Murphy, "Neither Gardner nor any member of his birth family ever had any telepathic or other parapsychological experience."[87] She herself "had some experiences which [Murphy] considered parapsychological but since they occurred only under severe stress or illness"[88] neither she nor Murphy encouraged them and they were not the reason for his interest.

At this point one proximate cause of Murphy's willingness to do the work of a "quack" illuminates still another tie between James and Murphy. For it is fact, common to both, that parapsychology, like charity, began at home. Henry James, Sr., gave his son intellect, charm, fluency, Swedenborgian mysticism and after-dinner religious and philosophical debates which could not fail to provoke James later to a search for God in religious experience and immortality in parapsychology. In the case of Murphy, too, his family ignited sparks of interest in parapsychology. From the time he was eleven or twelve, Murphy heard about mediums and anecdotes about their contacts with the dead which aroused in both his mother and father an intense curiosity. Hodgson's sittings with Leonora Piper also challenged them, especially since Murphy's grandfather, George A. King, had been the medium's attorney. Yes, it was the general atmosphere of the home that contributed to his interest in parapsychology but Murphy could be more specific as to the time and place when that interest really began. It was in his grandfather's library when he was sixteen. There he read one of Barrett's books on parapsychology "and from that moment the quickened flame never abated."[89]

The cultural atmosphere of Concord permitted individualistic and heterodox opinions. When the family moved to New Haven, however, and Murphy entered Hotchkiss and Yale, the climate "was much less favorable, and of course the intellectual world into which I was immersed at preparatory school and college were utterly unfavorable"[90] to the flame that had quickened.

But it could not be extinguished and when Murphy decided to be a "brain specialist" and to major in psychology at Yale, it was really "in order to prepare myself for psychical research. This determination was never altered."[91]

After he was admitted to the Graduate School at Harvard in 1916, the atmosphere became more favorable for parapsychology. Murphy was able to work with Leonard T. Troland who, as recipient of money from the Richard Hodgson Fund, introduced Murphy to a large quantity of research material. Murphy began to realize that he could prepare himself for an academic career as a psychologist and, at the same time, carry on in parapsychology.[92] In addition, he was able to assist Troland in some telepathy experiments supported by the Hodgson fund.

The religious question which had made him "writhe" in 1917 also had a good deal to do with his continuing interest in parapsychology. "My knowledge of psychical research, however, was at this time considerable, and I made up my mind that I would pursue psychical research for its own intrinsic interest and for the very considerable possibility that it might ultimately reverse my decision regarding religion."[93]

The Hodgson Fund

When he was overseas with the American Expeditionary Forces in 1917, Murphy joined the SPR. On his return to Columbia he began to "read very hard, very long, and often read twice or three times" a program of reading that had been prepared for him by Isabel Newton, the SPR's secretary. This reading was not "iron discipline," Murphy assures us, "for I loved the material passionately. . . . [W]ith all the ardent intensity of youth I had found what I believed in."[94]

Throughout this systematic and prolonged reading, Murphy wrestled with a question that subsequently was to be the subject of brilliant writings. "I was, of course, during all this time, trying to decide whether I believed that the evidence for survival was strong enough to warrant conviction."[95] In June 1921, he visited London for three weeks to read unpublished material in the files of the SPR and to interview its officers. Later that year, Murphy made another trip. This time he went to Harvard to see McDougall. Did the British psychologist think that Murphy could obtain permanent employment by the SPR? It is interesting that Murphy did not ask about a permanent position with the ASPR of which McDougall was president nor did McDougall suggest the ASPR. Instead, McDougall

> wheeled his chair towards me with a sort of electrical intensity, snapping into action: "Why don't you come here?" He went on to spell out the availability of the Richard Hodgson Fund. I talked it over with my mother, thought it through, and decided I could do this without giving up the part-time position available at Columbia, and without risking my neck altogether on what might prove to be a dead end. I could identify myself with the Richard Hodgson Fellowship.[96]

In 1922, Murphy became a beneficiary of the Richard Hodgson Fund and until 1925 commuted weekly to Harvard from Columbia. While he taught elementary and abnormal psychology at Columbia, he conducted experiments with Mrs. Piper in Boston, telepathy tests at Harvard, and, at Columbia, cooperated in weekly long-distance telepathy experiments directed by René Warcollier, a chemical engineer and one of France's pioneer investigators of telepathy who published *La Télépathie* in 1921.

A Failure of Health

Nineteen twenty-five was a crucial year for Murphy. The ASPR's departure from the standards laid down by Hyslop caused him, along with Worcester, McDougall and Prince, to terminate the connection he had made with it around 1922, and to associate himself with the BSPR on whose Council he became a member. Because of encephalitic influenza he contracted in March and its "desperately distressing sequelae,"[97] he was forced to stop his experimenting, to give up the support of the Hodgson Fund and to see his preparations and plans for parapsychology checked for nine years during which he was virtually disabled. Even "[m]y eyes had failed me utterly in 1925."[98] When Clark University held its symposium in that year, Murphy, who was to have been a speaker, could not attend. His paper, "Telepathy as an Experimental Problem," however, was printed in its proceedings.[99] Ironically, his sickliness became a buoy for his determination to go forward with parapsychology: Murphy decided to leave orthodox medicine and to seek a cure from those whom conventional doctors regarded as quacks.[100] A month later he was healthy again. The lesson to him was that "[s]uch experiences with 'deviations' and heterodoxy were enormously and profoundly significant in their interaction with my belief that psychical research could be essentially sound although damned from the housetops by all the sound and sturdy intellects of an era."[101]

The Rhine Partnership

There have been many years of significance for parapsychology as the Chronological Narrative reveals. But 1934 was especially important, for in that year Murphy's health was restored so that he could return to parapsychology once again and in that year also Rhine's *Extra-Sensory Perception* was published. Other major developments ensuing upon its publication will be taken up more appropriately in Rhine's portrait, but for many leading figures in psychology, including the British psychologist Robert H. Thouless,[102] it opened the door to parapsychology.

Murphy, however, was already inside the gates. The monograph was no shock to him as it might have been to others in orthodox circles. Murphy knew of Rhine's work at Duke University and Rhine had written to him to recall to his mind that they had met in New York in 1923. In his letter, Rhine had asked not only if J. Gaither Pratt and Charles Stuart, two student assistants, could transfer to Columbia to finish their graduate work and to do parapsychological experiments there; he also told Murphy of the monograph and asked whether Murphy would review it. Murphy replied on June 8, 1934,

> I have been *deeply* impressed by your epoch-making studies in E.S.P. and am most eager to cooperate in every way I possibly can.... What your book needs is to [be] read and re-read, not reviewed. Hillbillies aren't made into evolutionists by reading reviews of *The Origin of the Species,* nor are psychologists going to be convinced of ESP by reading reviews of your book. However, tell me how I can help & I'll try to do it.[103]

Murphy reviewed Rhine's book, found it "overwhelming"[104] and wrote in the *Journal of General Psychology* what Rhine called "a splendid review ... introducing it to American psychologists."[105] In the fall of 1934, Murphy went to Duke University to visit Rhine and to meet Pratt and Stuart. Following the visit, Murphy wrote on December 7, 1934,

> I can't tell you how profoundly grateful I am for the time at Duke, for the opportunity to share in this most extraordinary quest and to know such an extraordinary person. You know that I speak simply and honestly; so that I can say without any indirectness that it has been an intense satisfaction to talk with so great a man and to glimpse some of his vistas of scientific worlds to conquer.[106]

It was the beginning of, in Rhine's phrase, "a partnership in parapsychology."[107] Arrangements were made for Pratt to be lent to Murphy for a period of time for experiments at Columbia. Pratt was to be supported by Murphy's royalties from one of his books, another indication of the verity of Montague Ullman's statement in the letter he addressed to Murphy after Murphy's death: "You were a truly generous man."[108] After Pratt returned to Duke in 1937, Ernest Taves, a graduate student of psychology, replaced him and, when Taves entered the army during World War II, Joseph L. Woodruff, who had received training in parapsychology at Rhine's laboratory, joined Murphy to continue work on ESP problems, this time in the Department of Psychology at City College. Murphy was again the beneficiary of the Richard Hodgson Fund but turned the income over to his collaborators.[109] Thus did Murphy receive academic support from Harvard for ESP research.

Scientific Showdown

In September 1938, in Columbus, Ohio, the American Psychological Association held a symposium with the title "Experimental Methods in ESP Research." Against the results of ESP tests which Rhine had published, many counterhypotheses had been proposed and many objections made to the methods he used. Rhine knew that it "was to be a sort of scientific show-down"[110] and, of course, he was there not only to participate in but also to witness this critical battle in a professional warfare that had been going on for years between those, such as the young psychologist John L. Kennedy from Stanford, who represented the strongest resistance to parapsychology, and those such as Rhine and Murphy who defended ESP research. Murphy was as unstoppable as the tide. He presented a paper in which Lois Murphy said he "vigorously defended"[111] parapsychology by showing that all weaknesses in methodology had been corrected particularly with reference to errors in recording and handling data. Aside from his paper, he debated with Kennedy and so complete was his refutation that Kennedy "who had come with the press announcement that he had the nails ready for the coffin of ESP . . . failed to get the nails driven home. . . . [H]e alone of the speakers declined to let the *Journal of Parapsychology* print his paper."[112]

The outcome of the APA meeting considerably brightened the sky over Durham, home of Rhine's Parapsychology Laboratory, and illustrates how Murphy's great prestige combined with his skill to allow parapsychology to become more credible and acceptable to psychologists and scientists.

At Murphy's urging, Rhine had applied for membership in the APA, and at this convention his application was to be voted upon by the Council. Just prior to the vote, however, Murphy discovered that Rhine's application would be rejected and so he had the application withdrawn. When Rhine's application was resubmitted to a new Council the following year, it was approved, by a margin of only one vote. Rhine said, "I am of course not proud of this vote to grace my record, but I am pleased beyond words at what my partner did."[113]

At this time Rhine felt that, in order to focus on laboratory research, it might be advantageous for him to break editorial connections with the *Journal of Parapsychology*, which began to be published at Duke in 1937. Murphy, along with Bernard F. Reiss, agreed to coedit the *Journal* in order to create editorial policies for it which would open up a channel of communication with psychologists. One outcome of the APA symposium was a Board of Review which Murphy had proposed. It consisted of committees of psychologists from various parts of the country. When Murphy became editor, the *Journal of Parapsychology* assumed a "new look," the papers it published being accompanied by the criticisms and observations of psychologists.

Boston Society for Psychic Research

After Prince's death, Rhine became honorary research officer of the BSPR. His office was short-lived, however. Like McDougall, he favored removing research from local societies and concentrating it in universities. Murphy, on the other hand, was committed to the BSPR and, after Prince died, tried to maintain it along with Lydia Allison and Worcester. René Warcollier joined the BSPR Research Commitee in 1935. Although the BSPR's stream of major publications ended with Prince, it did produce one more important book in 1938: Warcollier's *Experimental Telepathy* to which Murphy contributed a foreword.

Gertrude Schmeidler

In the summer of 1942, Murphy again encountered the influence of the ubiquitous William James. Up to that time, Murphy's teaching at Columbia and City College had been confined to psychology. To commemorate the centenary of James's birth, Boring of Harvard asked Murphy to give a course there on parapsychology. This course was followed by others in subsequent years at the New School for Social Research. The teaching opportunity thus given him allowed Murphy to enlarge his role as a catalyst in the field and to bring into it new young workers. And because of the James centenary Murphy discovered such a worker, a woman who became a monumental contributor to parapsychology. Murphy remembered her well:

> By far the most important thing about the [summer session course at Harvard] was the presence of Dr. Gertrude R. Schmeidler, a young Radcliffe and Harvard Ph.D. in psychology, who became fascinated with the psychology of the telepathic process, and whose long and brilliant experimental contributions require no description here.[114]

Murphy helped guide Dr. Schmeidler through the literature of parapsychology. She, in turn, credited him with converting her curiosity about parapsychology into a strong interest and with most of the thinking behind the ingenious "sheep" and "goat" research she was to do.[115] Once again, as Murphy had done for others, he used the income from the Hodgson Fund to guide Dr. Schmeidler's studies.[116] She also joined him and Woodruff at the Department of Psychology at City College.

ASPR: Reentry and Leadership

But Murphy's greatest contributions to parapsychology were yet to come. They begin with the "palace revolution" whose origins were suggested in the Chronological Narrative. Although Jocelyn Pierson has been mainly credited with the initiative that led to the reorganization of the ASPR,[117] the enterprise of Adele Wellman, executive secretary of the ASPR, should be noted. She had become interested in the experiments Murphy was conducting in his laboratory at Columbia and participated in them. Because of her interest and influence, other members of the ASPR also participated in Murphy's work in the spring and summer of 1938.

When Adele Wellman went to ASPR President William H. Button with news of the experiments and told him of Murphy's willingness to conduct controlled experiments at the ASPR, Button yielded. Murphy was invited to address the ASPR on ESP and returned for the first time to an organization he and other disenchanted people had left in 1925. Soon 15 ASPR volunteers were taking part in telepathic and clairvoyant experiments held at the ASPR offices on 34th Street in New York City. From November 1938 to March 1940, tens of thousands of calls with playing cards, colored cards, Rhine's ESP symbols and photographs were made.

The sudden appearance of the conservative Murphy and his apparently dull guessing experiments with cards and other materials under controlled conditions within the sacred precincts of the ASPR must have caused many raised eyebrows in that faction of the ASPR which was still enamored of the seance room, Margery-type phenomena and which was dominated by an overwhelming interest in the survival question. Some justification for Murphy's experiments had to be provided to grumbling ASPR members who objected to them as irrelevant and repetitious in the sense that they seemed needlessly to add more evidence of the existence of ESP which Rhine had already proved. Jocelyn Pierson, who had assumed the editorship of JASPR, impressed readers with the relevance of Murphy's experiments to their interest in survival. His ESP tests pointed to the existence in the human mind of a nonmaterial psychic faculty which was able to function through, yet independently of, the physical organism. The establishment of this faculty, she argued, would remove one of the greatest stumbling blocks to any scientific consideration of the survival hypothesis: the apparent dependence of memory on the physical organism.[118]

Had Button tried intentionally to turn the ASPR against the policy of his administration of concentrating on seance room phenomena and toward the experimental approach he could not have chosen a better method than to coauthor a laudatory editorial in the 1940 PASPR which published Murphy's report on the ASPR ESP experiments. Like Jocelyn Pierson, Button vindicated the ESP research done by Murphy and Taves as another step toward proof of survival.[119]

Jocelyn Pierson's determination combined with Adele Wellman's interest and Button's unwitting help produced in 1941 the "palace revolution" which Murphy seized immediately as an occasion "for a radical redefinition of the aims of the A.S.P.R. and a renewed dedication to vigorous standards."[120] Lois Murphy wrote, "Gardner was utterly committed to the highest scientific standards in psychic research and lifted the ASPR from a somewhat naive level to a serious scientific level."[121]

Another resemblance between William James and Murphy is now visible. As James had been a guiding force in the early formation of the ASPR, Murphy now played a leading part in the revitalization of the organization. Murphy wrote of James's "emphatic recognition and *insistence* that an organized type of research enterprise must be set up."[122] Murphy shared this view. As one of the ASPR's newly elected Trustees and now chairman of the Research Committee with a chance to bring about a needed restructuring of the organization, he "supported a vigorous research program."[123]

Murphy "'moved down' to the A.S.P.R., working there five or six mornings a week."[124] Part of his work included the restoration of prestige to the ASPR which he accomplished by persuading Margaret Mead, J.B. Rhine and William James's son Henry to become members of the ASPR Board of Trustees. He also assumed the chairmanship of the Research Committee, in which post he enlisted the energy, talents and productivity of several brilliant people: Gertrude Schmeidler, Montague Ullman, Ernest Taves, Joseph Woodruff and Laura Dale. They came into the ASPR only because Murphy recruited them. One of them confessed that they "would have been unlikely to develop parapsychology as a professional interest if it had not been for our close contacts with Murphy. In addition he recruited many others whose work was less prolonged, but who either contributed research projects which he designed with them or else helped the work of others."[125] The ASPR was to become in the east what Duke was in the south — another center of parapsychology staffed by skilled investigators. And it was there that Murphy continued to lead his double life as, in a large, private room at the ASPR, he helped Laura Dale and others with their work while, at the same time, he wrote on psychology and parapsychology and conducted experiments.[126]

Murphy had already done a considerable amount of experimenting. There were experiments with Troland at Harvard, those between 1922 and 1925 under the Hodgson Fund, and those during his collaboration with Pratt and Taves at Columbia. In addition to the transatlantic experiments with Warcollier and card-guessing experiments at Columbia as part of a series of experiments that Soal, Bateman and Ina Jephson were carrying out in 1929, he also conducted experiments with Laura Dale and Taves at the ASPR. He even tried experimenting with himself, but, as his wife commented, "Gardner had little success either as sender or receiver in telepathic experiences,"[127] and in the end, Murphy's opinion was that he was not the experimenter he thought he was:[128]

> what I hoped to do in experimental work gradually fizzled out. I tried dozens of experiments, some of which were briefly reported, as indicating slight or negative results, and a considerable number of which were not deemed worthy of even a brief report. What I was able to accomplish along experimental lines was due to my acting as big brother to many able investigators.[129]

One of these investigators whom Murphy counseled described what he did as "big brother." Murphy

> had a special gift for sparking research ideas from others, typically beginning with a statement of unfinished business which was so provocative and clear that it made it easy for them to see how the business should be continued, and yet to feel that the idea for furthering the work was their own. He gladly worked with them on the details of experimental controls, and often acted as one of their pilot subjects. He gave statistical, technical, and professional guidance. If necessary he wrote the papers reporting the research (though he always insisted as

being listed as the junior author). And in his lectures and writings he would heap lavish praise on those he helped, producing a warm glow that was likely to make them attempt still more.[130]

Among others to whom Murphy gave guidance were Schmeidler, Pratt, Taves and Woodruff in the conduct of ESP investigations and Edmond P. Gibson who, upon Murphy's suggestion, analyzed 313 cases from *Phantasms of the Living* to determine whether the motivation to initiate phenomena associated with apparitions was assignable to the appearer or to the percipient.[131]

Murphy was more than "big brother." He was variously described by his associates as "a dominant figure,"[132] "the leader of the ASPR [and] center of the Society."[133] Some thought "Murphy was the Society."[134]

During the period from 1941 to 1952, he published 25 seminal papers in JASPR and the PASPR as well as in the *Journal of Parapsychology*, including his three papers on survival and on personality and psychology vis-à-vis parapsychology. These were papers "with which I feel a deep identification."[135]

In 1951, he became general research consultant at the Parapsychology Foundation and one year later left for Topeka, Kansas, to assume his appointment as research director at the Menninger Foundation, where he became interested in biofeedback. Although absent from the ASPR and from the mainstream of parapsychology, he continued his role as "big brother."

He plunged back into parapsychology once again in 1962 when he became ASPR president. There was an upsurge of activity and enthusiasm in several areas. The ASPR membership, which had consisted of about 800 people in 1962, increased to 1200 by 1965 and twice that number three years later. An education department was established by Marian Nester.

Rhea White reorganized the Society's library. Attendance at lectures soared and research projects went forward. JASPR, taken over by Laura Dale when Rhea White was drawn temporarily into another profession, became a premiere publication.

Outside the ASPR, Murphy's influence was felt, also. When, for example, the Kidd legacy was the subject of protracted legislation in the Arizona courts, the one person who prevented the money, intended by the miner's will for survival research, from going to claimants who had no interest in this area of research was Murphy. "It was almost surely his testimony which determined the court's ruling that the money left by James Kidd in his will should be awarded to the A.S.P.R. rather than going outside of parapsychology."[136]

Failing health forced Murphy to relinquish the presidency in 1971. Dr. Montague Ullman who had been an ASPR Trustee succeeded him. We can measure Murphy's strong influence within the ASPR while he was actually guiding the policies of the organization from Osis's assessment of what happened to it when ill health greatly limited Murphy's active participation in its affairs after 1971:

> The Board and staff split sharply into two factions, each perched upon its own hill and holding fast to the truth of singular, narrow landscapes. More often than not, Murphy had been able to reconcile widely

divergent perspectives.... The post-Murphy differences in the ASPR were not reconciled, but were manifested in fights between factions and in behind-the-scene politics.[137]

The Revolving Mind

Murphy confessed a strong "resonance to William James."[138] Like James, his intellectual qualities included a willingness to tolerate new or incompatible ideas. But they embraced another aspect of intellect which the following passage, written by Murphy of James, brings out and which applies with equal force to the writer: "I believe that the highest contribution which James was able to give to psychical research was a disciplined, unfearing, ever inquiring, nervously revolving and reconsidering mind."[139]

In psychology, Murphy had demonstrated this same sort of mind as, like a cut diamond, it reflected many facets of the field: among others, the social and historical, studies of personality, international relations, perception and cognition, autism, all combined with a teaching career. When Murphy took up the leadership of the ASPR, too, winds from many quarters filled the sails of his thought and sent his mind sailing in many directions. Their number can be grasped from the fact that, on parapsychological themes alone, he contributed 50 pieces to JASPR, 8 to the *Journal of Parapsychology,* 11 to other parapsychological periodicals, and 22 to nonparapsychological periodicals; he also made 19 contributions to reference works and books, authored one book, and coauthored or coedited two more.[140]

A bewildering variety of parapsychological subjects flashed from the facets of his revolving, scintillating mind: trends in parapsychology[141]; plans for parapsychological investigations[142]; concentration versus relaxation in relation to ESP[143]; human needs and paranormal phenomena[144]; impediments to the paranormal[145]; ESP experiments with drawings[146]; the mind-body relation[147]; personality appraisal and the paranormal[148]; precognition[149]; the need to distinguish between telepathy and clairvoyance[150]; dowsing[151]; spontaneity in ESP[152]; current developments in parapsychology[153]; the natural, the mystical and the paranormal[154]; Indian and western views of paranormal phenomena[155]; qualitative studies of ESP[156]; creativity and ESP[157]; the question of whether there is a "law" of paranormal phenomena[158]; research in creativity[159]; contacts with the past and future[160]; gifted sensitives[161]; the question of solid facts in parapsychology[162]; the problem of repeatability.[163]

Six additional subjects to which Murphy devoted considerable thought are singled out for attention in the following paragraphs.

Survival and Murphy's Law

In 1885, after James' discovery of Leonora Piper, whose mediumistic powers defied all his attempts at normal explanation,[164] he became utterly fascinated by the question of human survival after death and continued, throughout his life, to be interested in hauntings and apparitions and to engage in extensive sittings and studies of mediumistic research. He wrote a lengthy report on communications purporting to be from Hodgson received through Mrs. Piper.

Murphy followed James into the arms of the survival question. The attraction had already begun when he was a child of six in San Antonio wondering how survival was possible. It continued in Concord where his intense evangelical Christianity and stories about mediumship paved the way. Although, as I have shown elsewhere,[165] virtually all modern parapsychologists have crawled away from the survival question and into a turtle shell of indifference, Gardner Murphy, like James, gave the subject his closest and most critical attention almost to the end of his days. As he said,

> "To see life steadily and to see it whole" includes looking honestly at death. Most of us not only fear death, we are afraid to talk about it, or to ask what there is beyond the biological termination of our . . . individual existence. . . . [But if the] concept of time proves to be different from what it is now, human existence in the form of recognizable individuality may be accessible after death to scientific investigation and communication. Is it not worth while then to investigate such matters?[166]

In its concept of the last judgment, Christianity teaches that Christ, like a shepherd, will separate the people of the earth into righteous believing sheep and cursed disbelieving goats. So runs the Gospel of Matthew.[167] Similarly, Schmeidler, at the start of her ESP experiments, categorized as sheep those subjects whose attitudes were favorable toward ESP and as goats those who rejected the possibility of ESP. This sheep-goat dichotomy has passed into parapsychological history and, in fact, allows attitudes toward postmortem survival to be placed in similar but more subdivided categories.

There are sheep who believe in survival because of devout religious faith, because they are Spiritualists or because it just makes them feel better. There are sheep who believe because of a philosophy or personal experiences, and there are sheep whose belief is based rationally on evidence. Some goats disbelieve because of the assumed a priori impossibility of it, because it clashes with scientific assumptions they accept, because, like the philosopher Broad, they would be "slightly more annoyed than surprised" if they found themselves continuing after death[168] or because, like Rhine, they think that the evidence has not ruled out other possible explanations.

Murphy, however, was the kind of animal who cannot be fitted neatly into our sheep or goat categories. He was a cross between the two species, a stubborn creature who could not reject the evidence of survival and yet could not accept it, a thoughtful, scholarly, yet vexatiously indecisive animal, who presents a problem of classification.

This putative third category, indecisives, can be subdivided also. Among them are those who never had an interest in the subject, or were interested but

never thought about it or studied the literature or data. Murphy fits in still
another subdivision. As early as 1921, he was an intensely interested student
of the subject who pored over all the pertinent published and unpublished
material he could find both in and out of the files of the London Society. Yet,
he, too, was indecisive. And he could justify his indecisiveness:

> Often a more appropriate attitude in science than belief or disbelief is
> to say: "It would be sheer chicanery to pretend that I have a right to
> an opinion." This is a point of view which may properly have a strong
> claim upon our allegiance in psychical research. We may well respect
> those who, like Drayton Thomas, have reached an honest conclusion
> in favor of full survival of personality after death, or those who, like
> Professor Dodds, wholeheartedly reject the hypothesis. But another
> position which is fully as defensible at the present time is that of saying
> that the case rests upon dead center, waiting for evidence *so good,* or
> objections *so sound,* as to warrant forming a judgment.[169]

In *Challenge of Psychical Research,*[170] Murphy finished his examination
of the evidence with this deep sigh: "To me, the evidence cannot be by-passed,
nor on the other hand can conviction be achieved. . . . I linger because I cannot
cross the stream."[171]

What could be more reminiscent of that great indecisive, William James?
After Richard Hodgson died, lengthy messages purporting to be from him ap-
peared in Mrs. Piper's trance mediumship. James undertook to study them and
write a report. Was it Hodgson communicating or a "spirit counterfeit" of
Hodgson? All James could say was "I remain uncertain."[172] And once more in
"The Final Impressions of a Psychical Researcher":

> For twenty-five years I have been in touch with the literature of
> psychical research, and have had acquaintance with numerous "re-
> searchers." I have also spent a good many hours . . . in witnessing (or
> trying to witness) phenomena. Yet I am theoretically no "further" than
> I was at the beginning; and I confess that at times I have been tempted
> to believe that the Creator has eternally intended this department of
> nature to remain *baffling.* . . .[173]

There were many difficulties which confronted and prevented Murphy
from crossing over into belief. In the first place, he thought it "improbable that
the issue has been correctly stated at all. I think it probable that five hundred
years hence the arguments both pro and con will sound childish and superficial, if indeed they sound relevant to the problem at all."[174]

Some of the other difficulties were:

(A) "As the biological evidence comes in, decade by decade, year by year,
[Murphy] cannot find any easy way to conceive of a soul, a spiritual entity independent of the living system known to biology, psychiatry and
psychology. . . . [T]he conception of an independent soul recede[s] more and
more into the land of the utterly incredible and unimaginable."[175]

(B) The biological evidence makes untenable any suggestion that the
process of consciousness could have a greater independence from the physical

body than the process of digestion. A living being is a psychophysical unity.[176]

(C) The nature of a postmortem existence without a body and any means of influencing an environment, or coming into contact with it, except perhaps through telepathic interactions with other bodiless entities, cannot be imagined.[177]

(D) Since a human personality is the outcome of social relationships, a culture, a period, that which survives, if it does survive, in radically different circumstances can hardly be called a recognizable personality.[178]

(E) The possibility cannot be neglected that mediums, through paranormal gifts, have the ability to sift telepathically among, and filch from, the minds of living people information desired by sitters, and the further ability to portray with great histrionic skill communications embodying this information, or the ability to derive it retrocognitively from the minds of deceased persons as they existed before death.[179]

A number of efforts to study and evaluate survival data have been made by Myers,[180] Hyslop,[181] Hart,[182] Salter[183] and Ducasse.[184] But no more determined or valuable effort to evaluate survival data has ever been made than Murphy's three papers on survival published in 1945 in which the examples of the main classes of survival evidence collected by parapsychologists, such as apparitions and mediumship, including proxy sittings and the cross-correspondences, were outlined.[185]

An equally valuable effort was made in the *Challenge of Psychical Research* in which Murphy also discussed survival evidence by devoting the lengthiest chapter in the book to spontaneous cases, mediumship and the cross-correspondences.

The method used by Murphy in his first paper on survival was to organize the evidence by starting out with classes of evidence for which counter-hypotheses might account and then to take up more and more complex cases resistant to these hypotheses. Having examined all points of view and the evidence dealing with survival, particularly that supplied by the mediumship of parapsychology's golden age between the 1880s and the early 1900s, Murphy summed up his position and again revealed that he and James were kindred spirits.

In one spirited writing, he said: "[W]e need more than verbal argument. We need new kinds of evidence."[186] He repeated his plea in *Challenge of Psychical Research:* "We need far more evidence."[187] James's need had been identical: "I . . . await more facts"[188] and "[I] still remain a psychical researcher waiting for more facts before concluding."[189]

One of the reasons for the general lack of interest in survival on the part of modern parapsychologists may be that Murphy's plea has not been met and no fresh evidence has been obtained. A few parapsychologists have gone on with mediumistic experiments and with the investigations of apparitions, but these types of evidence are not distinguishable from those in existence when Murphy considered them. No noteworthy findings have come out of research into out-of-body experiences. Few positive results have emerged from research into the experiences of the dying; my own recent research, for instance, has yielded negative results.[190]

Evidence dealing with survival is not limited to these classes. There are also cases in which after the death of the body there is an ostensible reembodiment of a surviving mind once contained in that body. Hundreds of cases of young children who identified themselves with personalities who lived before have been investigated by Ian Stevenson. Murphy, however, did not assume that these children actually were the people with whom they identified themselves and whose lives they recalled. For him, a likely alternative explanation for Stevenson's cases was that the children were sufficiently psychic to have used telepathy, clairvoyance or retrocognition to acquire knowledge about the dead persons they claimed to be.[191]

The position of the case has not changed during the last quarter century since Murphy's appeal. Still, a few researchers have tried to find new approaches.[192] Nevertheless, from the reservations and qualifications expressed by Gardner Murphy in all his analyses of the data on survival, we should probably find in him the same pessimistic spirit toward these schemes and proposals for new evidence as we find in the well-known "Murphy's Laws": "Anything that can go wrong, will go wrong," "A bird in hand is safer than one flying overhead," or "The light at the end of the tunnel is the headlight of an approaching train." Of course, the foregoing are not Gardner Murphy's laws, but he had his own special law, which was more or less that "everyone has a guaranteed plan for getting survival evidence that will not work." At least such plans would not satisfy Murphy because he had his own criteria for the kinds of cogent evidence that would convince him of the reality of survival.

First, it must be improbable that living people could have produced the evidence — for example, "the discovery of cases of collective veridical hallucinations occurring *long after death*" which would point to the probability of motivation and activity on the part of the deceased rather than to activities assignable to a group of living persons.[193] A case frequently cited in favor of the survival hypothesis is that of James L. Chaffin who, four years after his death, was said to have appeared by the bed of one of his sons to give information that permitted the son to have set aside a will that the father had made for the benefit of another son and to probate successfully a second will previously unknown to anyone.[194] It is doubtful, however, that Murphy would have accepted this case although the event occurred long after death and the case was veridical. He would have objected that the son might have obtained the information by ESP; or that he had had an ordinary dream and had not seen an apparition; and, if it was an apparition, that it had not been observed collectively.

What had struck him with considerable force, however, was the "Ear of Dionysius" case,[195] a cross-correspondence in which two deceased persons apparently made a plan for the transmission from the next world of evidence which would not crumble under objections that information had been obtained by telepathy from someone alive. He considered this case "one of the few generally recognized classics of survival evidence"[196] which led him to this answer to the question of what survival evidence would have the greatest cogency for him:

> The answer, I believe, is that it is evidence which by definition takes the form of post-mortem *interaction* of two or more communicators. . . . Let us say that Paul Kempton, of Tulsa, Oklahoma, Pierre Leclerc, of Pawtucket, Rhode Island, Angus MacGregor, of Stirling, Scotland, and Leslie Durand, of the Isle of Wight, meet on the "other side." They wish to give evidence to their families. Checking over their various life activities, they discover that they all had one thing in common: they all had made collections of rare old Wedgwood china. No living human being ever knew that they had this *in common;* it is the kind of fact that could be ascertained post-mortem, but not before.[197]

Years later, he had still not altered his view that this would be the "strongest survival evidence,"[198] and, as a concrete indication of his interest in this kind of evidence, Murphy proposed to Lydia Allison, when she went to England, that she conduct an experiment with the English medium Gladys Osborne Leonard to try to put his plan for survival evidence into motion.[199] Sittings were held with Mrs. Leonard but both Murphy and Mrs. Allison agreed that the experiment was not a notable success.

Murphy, the fence-sitter, created criteria for survival evidence that were not merely strict but were also apparently impossible since no case has ever met them and probably no case ever will. He presents us with what is—and is also the title of one of his books—the greatest "challenge of psychical research." If those keenly interested in resolving the survival issue would take up this challenge, meet his standards, implement successfully the kind of plan for evidence in the form of postmortem interaction that Murphy suggested, as he said, "it would be worth almost any amount of labor."[200]

Interpersonal Field Theory

The sheep-goat dichotomy can be extended to all other parapsychological phenomena: telepathy, clairvoyance, precognition, psychokinesis, poltergeists and out-of-body experiences. Both in and out of the circle of parapsychologists there are those who believe that the evidence has established the occurrence of these phenomena and those who do not; and, of course, those who, try as they may, cannot express any clear-cut opinion. It is, therefore, a cause for wonderment, as we stumble through this wilderness of differences and conflicting attitudes, to come suddenly upon a space as neatly manicured as a putting green and rid of all discord or uncertainty. There seems complete accord, particularly in the realm of parapsychology, that "the need for new basic insights is a paramount one and that acceptance of the findings of parapsychology by other scientists will not occur until a theory is available that 'makes sense' of psi phenomena."[201] In Murphy's view, the need to build a theoretical system for the findings was a "scientific challenge."[202]

The long absence of any comprehensive theory capable of bringing all or, at least, many of the phenomena related to ESP, PK and survival under one intellectual umbrella and of explaining them has prevented any understanding of how ESP or PK could possibly work and has created massive problems for the survival hypothesis. One of Murphy's greatest difficulties with this hypothesis, in addition to those mentioned before, consisted of imagining how there could be any kind of personal survival when there were no sense organs, no nervous system, no organs of movement and force, to make contact with the surrounding environment. He even asked his readers to try to imagine a personal existence without these indispensable devices and said, "Unless this effort is made — and unless some sort of intelligible substitute for life as we know it is offered — the attempt to schematicize the nature of post-mortem existence is likely to be a sorry product of wishful thinking."[203] Here perhaps is the heart of Murphy's inability to accept the evidence of survival: the absence of any theory that might make personal survival intelligible.

This lack of theory may be more responsible than the lack of fresh evidence for the general withdrawal of parapsychological interest in the survival question; and it may be to an explanatory theory that the dwindling number of survival researchers should address themselves instead of to the task of obtaining better evidence. For if the very idea of personal survival is not imaginable, then all the new evidence in the world will be pointless because it would not make the concept less meaningless or less puzzling. But if such researchers were to make the effort to offer an intelligible theory of personal survival, and succeed in that effort, then evidence would be cogent and have its place.

Early theories advanced have included concepts of "psychic ether,"[204] of telepathy as a "wireless" or "mental radio," or of "sixth sense" or of "psychons."[205] Later theories, such as Wasserman's[206] and Roll's[207] "psi fields" theories, also have been advanced. But not one provided a guiding hypothesis broad enough to include both psi phenomena and those related to survival. Murphy seems to have been the first to try to design an explanatory theoretical compass to guide us not only through the perplexity called the psi wilderness but through that labyrinth known as survival. To meet the scientific challenge he created a "field theory" for parapsychology — although the term also is applicable to other sciences. Kahn refers to Murphy's theory as "his most sophisticated and least understood concept . . . [yet] his most important legacy to psychical research."[208]

Murphy's interest in personality issues and the help given to his concepts of personality by Lois Murphy's research into child development went into his formulation of a field theory of personality. He also acknowledged that, before him, Myers, Warcollier and Eleanor Sidgwick[209] had conceived of some fusion and intercommunication of minds at a deep level. But we can see in his theory the shadow of William James falling again across his path. For Murphy's field theory bears a clear resemblance to a "mother-sea" theory James expressed as follows:

> Out of my experience, such as it is (and it is limited enough), one fixed conclusion dogmatically emerges, and that is this, that we with our lives are like islands in the sea, or like trees in the forest. The maple and the pine may whisper to each other with their leaves, and Conanicut and Newport hear each other's foghorns. But the trees also commingle their roots in the darkness underground, and the islands also hang together through the ocean's bottom. Just so there is a continuum of cosmic consciousness, against which our individuality builds but accidental fences, and into which our several minds plunge as into a mother-sea or reservoir.[210]

In Murphy's concept, also, we are to think of a transcendent reality which, from time to time, we can touch and which touches us to give rise to paranormal experiences,

> a cosmic system of psychical laws and psychical realities; the universe had to be the kind of a universe in which the paranormal could emerge. We may conceive the world of the paranormal as a sort of matrix from which proceed impressions which influence the specific psychological events which happen from day to day, and upon which they in turn make some impression.[211]

The evidence for the operation of this system can be found in telepathy, clairvoyance, retrocognition and mediumship.[212] Murphy's theory would have us abandon the idea that psi functions are the activities, properties or abilities of separate individuals. The "clue to the paranormal lies . . . in the relations between persons and not *in* the persons as such. . . . [T]he phenomena are, so to speak, trans-personal, just as they are, indeed, trans-spatial and transtemporal."[213] The effect of an undivided whole is greater than the individuals who are its parts and cannot be understood in terms of ingredient parts.[214] If individuals were to function as one impersonal entity, they might have "extraordinary capacity"[215] to make contact with the invisible matrix. It is our "psychological insulation" which prevents the interpersonal relations within this matrix that permit paranormal events to occur.[216]

Since Murphy goes on to refer to a deeper and more stable level of psi functions, the clear suggestion is an initial level of sensory, everyday functions. Our remaining on this level may also prevent paranormal contacts. Murphy argues, however, that relaxed states can remove our insulation, diminish the usual sharp awareness of ego and separation from others and bring us below the initial level of awareness to the deeper one where we become closer to one another. Murphy, in a paper coauthored with Laura Dale,[217] repeated the theme of relaxation in contrast to concentration as an aid to telepathy and revealed himself as one of the first advocates of the use of psi conducive states. Yet his suggestion for helping psi to function through altered states of consciousness was not adopted until some 30 years later.

But if there could be a merging of individuals at their deeper levels, the interpersonal points of contact would be called telepathic or clairvoyant, the theory states. The points of contact in the psychical field include those both of space and of time so that, through precognition, phenomena which will happen in the field in the remote future can be known and, through retrocognition, phenomena of long ago can also be known.

Murphy now took a long step toward applying his interpersonal theory to the survival problem. If there are good reasons for supposing that deceased people survive death, they will be as able as the living to participate with the living in the psychical matrix. They will be able to produce some effects within this reality, too.

Now, what is it that continues after death? Murphy's theory cannot mean the interpersonal field itself, for that seems always to have been in existence since in it are the traces of phenomena that occurred in the remote past which can be captured by retrocognition. It also contains future phenomena which can be precognized so that it gives every appearance of an everlasting, boundless reality encompassing every event that has been or will be. The theory suggests to us that what survives death are the psychical activities of an individual in time and space which an individual leaves in the field and which become aspects of the field.

Murphy responds to the following question on everybody's lips:

> Does personality survive bodily death or not? The question presupposes a rigidity, a sharpness, a distinctiveness, an encapsulation, which simply is not an attribute of the thing we know as personality. The field properties of personality from infancy to old age change profoundly as contacts change. With the change called death, there is every reason to believe that in so far as psychical operations continue, they must, as aspects of larger fields, take on new qualities, new structural relationships. . . . The simplest way of conceiving the matter might be to say that activity in time and space leaves a trace in a world which is not defined in terms of time and space.[218]

But what kind of postmortem existence would this be *sans* sense organs, nervous systems or organs of action? Can we ever say that this is the same old person we once knew? No, Murphy tells us. The person we knew was always dressed in clothes of flesh and bone and now that clothing has been removed. Our old friend was an individual with an independent existence in a certain cultural context and now all that is gone. Murphy's conception of survival is that "[e]very remaining and continuing psychical activity must tend to be articulated more closely into the complex structural whole of which it is an aspect."[219]

Surely there is here an unmistakable similarity between Murphy's theory and the idea of Merger with the One in Buddhism or the religion of the Brahmins in India. But don't be disappointed in the fact that personal survival as we know it or want it may not be possible. Take cheer. "We may well find," Murphy says, "as science has usually shown us, that the specific things that we want for ourselves are not waiting there in nature for our use, but that many undreamed things—often far more interesting—come to surprise and intrigue us."220

So the problem is not at all whether we survive death. It is in what sense we survive. There are two senses in which an entity may be said to survive in the interpersonal psychic field. The entity may be located in the field as a result of psychic activities left there sometime in the past, a "static surviving entity,"221 which "survives" only when retrocognized through the paranormal powers of the living and brought to "life" through dramatic impersonations by mediums.

Those who have had personal experiences or who have read the evidence suggesting survival in the literature of parapsychology may or may not agree with this conception. Or, the entity may not only have left traces in the past but may also actively participate in the interpersonal field with the living and maintain paranormal contact with them at their deeper and more stable levels of paranormal functions. In the latter sense, there could be "a continuing personal life articulated into an interpersonal existence."222

The concept of an "interpersonal field," still faintly understood, has not been explored by researchers. Until such exploration, we can only speculate on whether mediumistic material has its source in the retrocognition of a "static surviving entity" in the field or in a postmortem communicator. If, then, we ask in which of the two antithetical senses we survive, whether in the first, the passive, impersonal sense, or in the second, the active, personal sense, Murphy's answer is that this is a question which there is no way of answering at present.223 From Murphy's point of view, however, the only way to determine whether the impressions which survive in the interpersonal reality bear any resemblance to the memory and mind of a deceased individual who remains active and purposeful after death would be through those types of evidence which he considered cogent.

Murphy's conception of a realm in which we merge at our deeper levels should not be criticized even if it seems queer. As he said rightly, "Hypotheses should be bold, but methods of verification cautious."224

But the conception of an interpersonal realm creates two difficulties. One is the sheer discomfort one feels at the probability that, if in fact at one's deeper and perhaps more essential and intimate level one is constantly penetrated by and fusing with others, individuality, uniqueness and personal privacy are all illusions and impossibilities. It may be to protect and maintain these qualities that we raise psychological walls at our sensory levels to prevent merger.

The conception of a cosmic system of nonphysical psychical realities creates the second difficulty of understanding how clairvoyant events could occur in it. By definition, clairvoyance is ESP of physical objects as distinguished from mental events, and the system would contain no such objects. Clairvoyance can occur only if we grant that physical objects also leave their traces in the field. Nevertheless, although Murphy found too many difficulties confronting the survival hypothesis to allow him to accept it, he did not construct a nonsurvivalist theory. To the contrary, he was willing to erect a theoretical framework within which the idea of the survival of a human personality was made intelligible to him, and, if the evidence met his criteria, in which an active, personal survival might be shown.

Tertium Quid

In his Presidential Address to the SPR, Murphy resumed his theme of an interpersonal reality. He used the expression "tertium quid" to define a third principle, a something new and different, which invades the individual without warning and brings with it psychic experiences, such as that which happened to a college student who made 15 consecutive correct calls when she suddenly "saw," on a radiator in the experimental laboratory, the symbols from a deck of ESP cards held by Laura Dale, the experimenter in another room. In all further experiments the girl's scores were on the chance level. She sparkled once and not again.

For Murphy, parapsychology was full of such once-in-a-lifetime flashes which suggested to him that they may emerge from a deeper level in us where the paranormal is normal and which is in contact with all of space and time. For that reason he argued that psi phenomena are "strictly interpersonal. . . . [T]he world of interpersonal phenomena is a world which must be faced on its own terms; pursued in its own right; its laws made clear and recognized to be essentially different from those laws which apply to individuals. I would plead for the direct empirical study of the laws of the interpersonal; the functions of an interpersonal field."[225]

In this plea there is the important suggestion that parapsychology reconsider the total Rhinean commitment to laboratory data and mathematical evaluations and return to focussing on the human beings who have psychic experiences. Why they have these experiences and how they make contacts in the interpersonal field with other human beings at deeper levels are matters surely as important as whether what they experience is a hit or a miss. We should study human interpersonal relations and not conduct contests for archers or trapshooters.

If Murphy's argument that the laws of the world of the interpersonal are different from those of individuals is right, then here is a valuable insight which should not be lost. Perhaps the fundamental problems in parapsychology of predictability and repeatability have not been solved because Murphy's interpersonal field theory has not been sufficiently understood or applied. We cannot specify the conditions under which new phenomena will occur, nor can we duplicate conditions under which a repeatable experiment can be designed, as long as we fail to understand the difference between experiments with individuals and experiments with groups. Murphy's theory states that psi phenomena are transpersonal and will occur, or be repeated, only when a complex inter-individual whole of which the individuals are a part is specified or duplicated.

The "experimenter effect" is one of the theories and fields of investigation now favored by the current crop of parapsychologists. Experimenter influence seems to have received special attention in the well-known clock card experiments in 1953 in which, after subjects scored significantly on Fisk's cards but not on West's, the experimenters thought it "mysterious and surprising" that West should have influenced the result. But the idea of the role of the experimenter should have been neither mysterious nor surprising because its seed had already appeared in Murphy's perceptive paper.

The "experimenter effect" of which he treated may also explain why the evidence for the reality of ESP remains contradictory and, indeed, why one may question the scientific image parapsychology seeks to guard. If the Rhines, Schmeidlers and Dales are "successful" because they have liberated paranormal gifts in their subjects, and the Murphys and Wests are "failures" because they have inhibited them, how is it possible to presume that the subject matter of parapsychology can be approached and treated in an exclusively impersonal way and to maintain that parapsychology can be an entirely quantitative impersonal study? How can any investigation be truly controlled and scientific when results depend upon the investigator?

Personality and Parapsychology

Ralph Barton Perry, James's biographer, wrote that "James hoped that psychical research, like other studies of abnormal phenomena, might throw light on the central constitution and deeper causes of human nature."[226] A similar passage was written by Murphy in his comments on William James whose conviction was that "psychical research has epoch-making implications for the extension or understanding about the deeper levels of personality, and of the relation of personality to the universe in which it is placed."[227]

Murphy's attitude is essentially the same. His equal conviction that there was an undeniable relationship between parapsychology and the study of personality is reflected in several of his writings and is almost indistinguishable from James's thinking. Murphy's Presidential Address to the SPR, significantly entitled "Psychical Research and Personality,"[228] was a plea for "more explicit recognition that psychical research has a huge contribution to make to an understanding of human nature."[229] Murphy believed that "a profoundly revolutionary conception of human nature will come when unconscious interpersonal dynamics are more fully understood. . . . [P]arapsychology is one of the major neglected areas, the study of which might give us a fuller understanding of the nature of man"[230]; and he urged "more study of those deep resources of human personality of which Frederic Myers first made us fully aware. . . ."[231]

Murphy perceived splendid opportunities in the study of spontaneous cases[232] and in the psychology of mediumship[233] for discovering more information about the depth and range of the human personality. As more and more spontaneous cases are gathered, more and more light will be thrown on the complex factors which allow one person to convey information better than another or this person to receive impressions better than that person.[234] The capacity of sensitives to detach themselves from the sensory world as they carried on their paranormal tasks would make an intriguing study to determine the fundamental factors which make a medium sensitive to paranormal phenomena.[235]

Psychology and Parapsychology: A Strange Paradox

One of the aims of the ASPR that Murphy wanted redefined was the relationship between psychology and parapsychology and the desirability of applying psychological methods and data to paranormal phenomena. For a decade the policy of the Button administration had been to appeal to the laity and to avoid shrinking "into a merely academic body for the benefit of a comparatively small circle of the learned."[236] Within this circle were the psychologists with whom the dominant faction of the ASPR wanted no links, as was clear from Button's Presidential Report in 1939:

> Any such ideas as those promulgated by Dr. Rhine were not at all acceptable to our psychological friends. They are in the unfortunate position of living in a house something like one of the prehistoric dwellings perched on poles in a remote European swamp. They are not pleased to be told that a lot of their foundations are rotten — hence one source of opposition is that they might have to hire other quarters, possibly at increased rental.[237]

In 1939, far from estranging the psychologists with ridicule such as this, Murphy was coediting the *Journal of Parapsychology* in order to provide a forum for a dialogue between psychologists and parapsychologists. After the "palace revolution," the need Murphy perceived for the 1940s and thereafter was for closer, not more remote, contact with psychology. This closer contact, however, was going to be difficult, for it was obvious to him, as it had been to McDougall, that official psychology ignored parapsychology. Yet Murphy also knew that this attitude constituted "a strange paradox" because while, on the one hand, psychologists were disinclined to touch parapsychology, on the other, every problem in parapsychology involved a straightforward problem in psychology and, further, parapsychology was a psychological discipline that used psychological discoveries as technical adjuncts to the tasks it pursued.[238]

It was Murphy's conviction that there is "the need for an organic unity of psychology and psychical research, in which each will throw light upon the other" and "[j]ust as psychology cannot get along without psychical research, so psychical research cannot get along without psychology."[239] Yet

parapsychology involves paranormal events that may require more than explanations limited to physical and physiological events in the life of an
organism. Psychological data and assumptions may explain these events to a
point, but, beyond this point, a dualistic theory missing from psychology may
be needed. "Let us not prejudge this issue,"[240] however, he warns. Only
research, not speculation, will resolve it.

While sex and death—formerly subjects decent people never talked
about—have been taken off the taboo list, parapsychology, still without scientific respectability, remains high on it, and conventional parapsychologists will
do their utmost to discourage young psychologists interested in parapsychology
from making it a focus on their research interests. But Murphy was not the conventional psychologist. He was concerned about the young person who wanted
both to do parapsychological research and, at the same time, to get a stable
academic position. Murphy made several realistic suggestions for the solution
of this still unsolved problem.[241]

Giving Scientists and Parapsychologists
A Perspective on Parapsychology

To introduce parapsychology to general readers Murphy wrote a book
which still remains a major work in the field and which should be read by
anyone who wants to gain a clear perspective on the subject. Murphy dedicated
Challenge of Psychical Research,[242] written in collaboration with Laura Dale,
"in gratitude" to Myers, Eleanor Sidgwick and Prince. This recognition of the
efforts and accomplishments of his predecessors in parapsychology is similar to
Murphy's acknowledgment that others before him had groped toward the conception of a deeper interindividual reality when he formulated his interpersonal field theory. As Emerson said, "There is properly no History; only
Biography."[243] It is in the lives of all those who have gone before that we
discover the real history of this (or any other) subject.

Murphy flatly disclaims having written *Challenge of Psychical Research* to
convince anyone. His object in writing the book was altogether different and,
because of it, the book continues to be valuable and stimulating not only for
the professional scientist and thoughtful lay persons for whom it was written
but as a tonic to revive many parapsychologists who, in their concerns with narrow aspects of their field—anpsi, random number generators, PK or Ganzfeld
studies, educational or ethical issues, or methodological problems—have
forgotten how broad their field is and the principal types of subject matter it
embraces. It was Murphy's aim "to try to show what psychical research is . . .
[and] to offer exhibits of data; to suggest ways in which the data may be interpreted; and to leave the reader to decide—or to decide not to decide—what
to make of it all."[244]

He placed parapsychology in clear and full perspective through the selection and documentation of examples of the kinds of data available in the six

main areas which he considered representative of the total field: spontaneous cases of telepathic dreams, experimental telepathy, experimental clairvoyance, precognition, psychokinesis and survival.

It appears to have been Murphy's idea to present what he considered the core of parapsychology. Following the tradition of the American and English societies, of Rhine's Laboratory at Duke, and of investigations conducted at universities such as Harvard, none of which studied the human aura, suspended animation, stigmatization or the out-of-body experience, he did not include these subjects in his book. Today, however, one might be willing to enlarge Murphy's concept of what constitutes parapsychology and include the out-of-body experience, which has been the subject of recent invest- igations by Karlis Osis; psychic photography (or thoughtography), investi- gated by Jule Eisenbud; unorthodox healing; biofeedback; altered states of consciousness, including dream experiences, investigated by Montague Ullman and Stanley Krippner; and the experiences of the dying and nearly dying.

The arrangement of *Challenge of Psychical Research* is instructive because it demonstrates which, in Murphy's view, are the simpler and which the more complex problems in parapsychology. The subject matter, beginning with telepathy and clairvoyance, and followed by precognition, psychokinesis and survival, seems to progress in logical order from the more philosophically ac- ceptable phenomena to ones less and less philosophically acceptable, as if the mind of the reader were being gently but gradually stretched with each chapter. Murphy himself, who seemed prepared to accept the first four types of phenomena studied by parapsychology, was unwilling to participate further in the stretching process. His acceptance stopped at the issue of survival after death.

He attempted, however, neither to grind any axe nor to gloss over any problem. His treatment of his samples was absolutely impartial. In a final chapter he dealt with the psychological character of psi phenomena as expres- sions of unconscious dynamic principles and with the attributes which ap- parently favor the exercise of psi abilities and will. He presented this cautious appraisal of the investigations and studies made by parapsychology of its major types of material:

> We are dealing with the first steps that will lead *up* to the gateway of science; not with a single step within the hall *beyond* those gateways. We have no science of parapsychology; no theoretical system tightly and beautifully organized in the manner of the architect; no solid beams of repeatedly confirmed findings, reproducible by a careful ex- perimenter who can exactly follow the specifications, sure of the general trend of the results that he will get.[246]

Someday parapsychology may take a step beyond those gateways and be granted recognition as a science. In the meantime, it is probable that it will remain as is suggested by the title of Murphy's book, a challenge, and, as he describes it at the conclusion of his book, a "'thorn in the flesh,' necessitating

some basic rethinking in basic new research, and playing a large role in the
functional shift to a new way of looking at life and mind."[247]

Spontaneous Cases

Prince was missing from the international conference which met in 1935
in Oslo to try to create an international parapsychological network. He had
died in 1934. Then World War II intervened to stop such conferences until
1953 when, to renew international consultations, an International Congress on
Parapsychological Studies was held at the University of Utrecht in the
Netherlands. Murphy, now director of research at the Menninger Foundation,
who had gone to Warsaw in 1923 as a mere delegate of the ASPR, was made
chairman. There were several working groups established at the Congress, one
to deal with qualitative phenomena.

One of the important steps taken at the Congress was a recommendation
that a conference be organized in 1955 at Cambridge under the auspices of the
SPR for the discussion of spontaneous cases. As a result of this recommendation, such a conference was organized and attended by Lydia Allison, Laura
Dale and Murphy, who gave the opening address to stress that spontaneous
cases should remain an important area of parapsychological investigation.

The early parapsychological researchers had looked to such cases in the
hope of obtaining tangible results. Prince's *Noted Witnesses for Psychic Occurrences* was an effort in this direction. Before him, James took time from his
mediumistic sittings, as Murphy tells us, to be "eagerly and actively concerned"
with spontaneous cases.[248] Even before the SPR Conference, Murphy, like
James, was eagerly and actively concerned with such cases. It seemed to him
that the fragmentary material consisting of anecdotes of visions, precognitions,
collective apparitions and more should be pieced together to build a systematic
picture of human potentialities just as a geologist pieces together reports and
studies of riverbeds, oceanic currents and crags in the mountains to construct
a science of geology.[249]

He was determined to cast out a broad net in order to catch fresh cases.
But neither he, Laura Dale nor Rhea White could do it by themselves. Hence
his plea:

> What we need above all else are eager participants who begin to catch
> the importance of a broad survey of these powers of human person-
> ality.... We need people to collect, we need people to analyze, we
> need people to point out ways of building bridges between spon-
> taneous and experimental cases. Aside from those able actually to take
> part in the research, we need an intelligent audience which will move
> with us in the understanding of the importance of the challenge and
> will support us through the difficult steps on the way.[250]

Manpower for the collection of cases was and remains necessary. It seemed
easy and quick simply to make appeals for cases in the pages of professional

journals or to advertise in newspapers. But neither advertisements nor radio broadcasts seemed to persuade people to send in accounts of their experiences to either the SPR or the ASPR. Murphy and the ASPR, therefore, decided on "more radical methods." Arrangements were made for a staff writer from *This Week* magazine, a syndicated Sunday supplement, to conduct a series of interviews with Murphy on the importance of the cases. The publication in 1957 as a result of these interviews of three newspaper articles brought in 1200 letters. The great majority were of no value as evidence of paranormal phenomena, but, after analysis of the best cases by Murphy and Laura Dale, 17 were found to meet criteria established for authentic spontaneous cases.[251]

Although Prince and Murphy, and their predecessors in parapsychology, were convinced of the importance of investigating spontaneous cases, interest in such cases has diminished. Largely because of the quantitative research done by Rhine, the choice now seems to be for material that can be statistically evaluated rather than qualitative experiences which are not susceptible of this kind of assessment. As a result, the subject has become one of sharp disagreement. The remaining supporters of the study of spontaneous cases urge a return to it. They maintain that such cases furnish clear-cut evidence of paranormal phenomena. Further, spontaneous cases provide a natural and logical field of study of telepathic and related phenomena as compared to the artificial conditions of a laboratory. Murphy supported the investigation of spontaneous cases:

> I believe, actually, that of the two methods in psychical research, the experimental and the spontaneous, the experimental has made greater advances in the last few decades than the study of spontaneous cases. I think this is paradoxical. It seems to me that in an undeveloped science, like parapsychology, the spontaneous must inevitably play a very large part, perhaps the greater part in our total endeavor.... [W]e have grossly neglected the enormous riches which are to be learned [from the study of the spontaneous cases].[252]

Opponents, composed chiefly of those leaning toward the experimental method, object that the evidence collected by these cases is weak and falls far short of proof, especially because percipients are not sufficiently interested to make a careful record of their experiences and soon forget them, because all relevant facts cannot be known or authenticated and because questions of chance coincidence, fraud or hallucination always surround such cases. Generally, further investigation turns up defects in the evidence or unsuspected circumstances which make untenable the conclusion that a case is genuinely paranormal. Probably the heart of the opposition argument is that, if parapsychology is worried about the opinions of the outside world and its aim is to gain the respect of orthodox science and psychologists, it should concentrate only on that work which has the best chance of being respected, namely, laboratory investigations.

Both arguments are strong. But it may not be necessary to choose between

them because this is not an "either-or" situation. The alternatives are not between spontaneous cases on the one side and experimental work on the other.
Students of parapsychology must pursue both. Rhine would never have started
his card-guessing experiments to test telepathy or clairvoyance if he had not
heard of these phenomena occurring in the daily lives of people. For this
reason, many experimentalists, including Rhine, are willing to concede the
value of new observations of spontaneous cases as suggesting new problems for
experimental investigation. Murphy, however, would not have been comfortable with this compromise, either, and would have continued to urge the
study of spontaneous cases for their own sakes:

> I firmly believe that psychical research will be able to create a systematic
> and intelligible picture of what happens in the deep-level interactions
> of human beings, under the heads of telepathy, clairvoyance,
> precognition, whether we happen to be smart enough to document
> these things in the laboratory or not. If we can document them in this
> way, fine. I don't think that this means that the *only* purpose in spon-
> taneous cases lies in the preparation of laboratory tests.[253]

The Last Ballet

With Prince and McDougall gone, only Gardner Murphy had the stature
to be considered with Rhine, to whom the fourth period from 1939 to 1980
belongs in part, the supreme leader of American parapsychology. Murphy's
right to be recognized a coequal leader has been challenged. For instance, it
is a surprise to see that Pratt, a competent and critical researcher, did not
devote any discussion at all to Murphy in his 1973 book, *ESP Research Today,*
which purported to be "an excursion over the field of modern parapsychology"[254] since 1960. While historians Mauskopf and McVaugh acknowledge that Murphy might have been a threat to Rhine's leadership in the field,
they go on to say that "Murphy was simply not temperamentally capable of
doing so even had he wanted to."[255]

But leadership is not always a question of temperament or desire. Like the
kingship which is bestowed naturally by some primitive tribes on the man who
has certain powers esteemed by the people, such as making rain to fall or the
sun to shine, Murphy was made leader by force of his own qualities. He was
a scholar, teacher, scientist, a responsive human being who was a natural leader
in his own right. His qualities were beautifully expressed by Osis:

> Whenever he walked through the door into the ASPR's headquarters,
> I felt the presence of a giant who could see further and deeper than
> could I. Everything he considered was raised to a higher plane, the
> larger landscape of thoughtful humanness. His social touch was warm,
> considerate, and deeply understanding. He shaped the ASPR like a
> gardener who loved his plants.[256]

Murphy was helped to leadership by various factors: his prominence among empirical psychologists and other scientists which made them, as in the case of Margaret Mead, less hostile and more supportive of parapsychology than others in their circles; his stimulation of student interest at Columbia and City College of New York, not only in psychology but in parapsychology; his encouragement and counseling for researchers, such as Pratt, Taves, Woodruff, Schmeidler and Dale, and his ability to supply financial assistance for them either from his own purse or from the Hodgson fund; and his connections with the BSPR and his dominant role in the ASPR which lifted it back to scientific standards.

Murphy, who had recovered his health in 1934, suffered a series of severe setbacks in the 1960s. He developed Parkinson's disease, which made it hard for him to write and made him tire rapidly. In 1973 he was forced to resign from the faculty of George Washington University, and in 1975 he broke his hip, suffered from complications during surgery and developed pneumonia. A tracheotomy was performed. His last years "were extremely difficult and painful."[257] They were brightened to some extent because Murphy received letters of encouragement and affection from all parts of the country written by people who had once been his students. He died on March 17, 1979, at George Washington University Hospital in Washington, D.C. His heart had simply given out after he had settled in his chair at home to watch on television a ballet he particularly liked. It was an appropriate exit for the "great man" whose career was like a lavish and spectacular ballet. Whether costumed as a scholar, scientist, teacher or leader, he danced beautifully on the stages of psychology and parapsychology and stepped, turned, and leaped from creative research ideas to brilliant lectures and writings with the ease, alacrity and virtuosity of a Nijinsky.

One fundamental difference between ballet and Murphy's life is that ballet is an art that ceases once the ballerina or the *danseur noble* leaves the stage. But Murphy's artistry will not cease because he is gone. Thus we come to a final indication of the close similarity between William James and Murphy.

James continues almost eight decades after his death to be America's voice in psychology and philosophy because his *Principles of Psychology* (1890), *Will to Believe* (1897), *Varieties of Religious Experience* (1902), *Pragmatism* (1907), *A Pluralistic Universe* (1909), and other writings in philosophy and psychology, and his reports, essays and lectures in parapsychology, such as "Final Impressions of a Psychical Researcher" (1909), still must be read and reread as examples of moving thoughts, powerful arguments and striking prose.

Murphy is the other vibrant voice which continues to sound through his writings. Because of his publications in psychology, Eugene Hartley wrote, "he has influenced countless thousands."[258] His *Historical Introduction to Modern Psychology*, updated in 1949 and 1972, was and is a text for contemporary psychology. The influence of *Experimental Social Psychology* still is felt, while

Personality: A Biosocial Approach to Origins and Structure continues to be assessed as "the best book ever written in psychology."[259] The research and theoretical papers he authored and coauthored in the 1940s which helped give psychology a "new look" in perception still are cited. He was a model teacher who "ranks second only to Freud in the frequency of listing by a sample of America [sic] psychologists of the individual most influential in leading the respondents into work in psychology."[260]

His books and contributions in parapsychology, consisting of more than 100 published papers, not only reflect the many facets of his revolving mind but also have the highest standing in the field. After 40 years, they are still cited in important books and periodicals on the subject as writers and researchers see in him a rich mine of ideas. In the JASPR, for example, there are over 400 references to him as compared to approximately 500 for Rhine, the acknowledged "father of parapsychology." In a significant book, Benjamin Wolman's *Handbook of Parapsychology* (1977), which the editor dedicated to Murphy "with affection and appreciation," there are 38 references to Murphy. That his ideas continue to be fresh and useful is also evidenced by an anecdote Gertrude Schmeidler narrates:

> A couple of years ago, I set as part of a take-home final examination, in a doctoral seminar on parapsychology, this question. Take any one of . . . (here I specified a half-dozen of Murphy's old articles); show which points are no longer valid; and show what additions should now be made. It was an exercise in one-upmanship. These sharply critical doctoral students would, as it were, score a coup each time they could effectively contradict one of Murphy's early arguments. But when they wrote their exam papers, even they could see little or nothing to criticize. They cited newer research which should be included if the articles were to be republished, but almost always the new findings were confirmatory of Murphy's thesis.[261]

It is appropriate to end this discussion of Gardner Murphy with Dr. Schmeidler's comparison between James and Murphy: "It is striking to reread what either wrote and find it still retains that stimulating, provocative, enlarging quality. Certainly both men were ahead of their time; and the times have not caught up with either."[262]

Joseph Gaither Pratt: A Cameo

He thought of himself as a "professional revolutionist" — a fighter without a beard or a bomb, caught in a bloodless struggle to change and advance thought. The revolution was carried on by a science called parapsychology which sought to establish through laboratory methods that mind can meet with mind without the instrumentalities of the senses or can influence matter without physical contact.

Joseph Gaither Pratt

Youth and Commitment

Pratt was born in 1910 in Winston-Salem, North Carolina, into a family of farmers. The direction of his career appeared to be fixed at an early age. He was committed to the Methodist Church and proclaimed to family and friends his intention to become a minister. This determination persisted through college and brought him into graduate study at the Duke University School of Religion.

In 1932, he passed through the same intellectual storms which had beset Hyslop and Murphy. He could not contemplate a career which required that an answer to the question of the relationship of the human being to the cosmos be based on faith. The old commitment was abandoned. The desire to find out about the true nature of the human being took its place. With this change in plans came the change in courses. He left the School of Religion and began study in the Psychology Department at Duke.

McDougall, Rhine and Murphy

At Duke Pratt met a teacher whom Pratt came to designate "grand-father" in his genealogy of parapsychology: William McDougall who had become head of the Psychology Department. Pratt became his admiring grandson.

In the same year that Pratt entered the Psychology Department, J.B. Rhine, then conducting ESP experiments at Duke in the Psychological Laboratory there and on the teaching staff of that Department, invited Pratt to become one of his Research Assistants, along with C.E. Stuart and Sara Ownbey, at 50 cents an hour. Pratt accepted and for the next four years tested subjects while he went on with his studies. In 1933, he received his M.A. and in 1934 met Gardner Murphy to whom Rhine lent him to do ESP research at Columbia University in New York.

Up to that time, parapsychology had been only an avocation. In 1936, the year he received his Ph.D., Pratt made the decision to be a "revolutionist" by accepting a position as a full-time member of the Duke Parapsychology Laboratory. In so doing, he became only the fifth person in the history of American parapsychology, besides Hodgson, Hyslop, Prince and Rhine, to burn his bridges behind him and to hinge his professional and economic future on parapsychology.

After two years with Murphy, Pratt went back to Duke to assume his duties as a research associate in the Parapsychology Laboratory which had been established. He does not seem to have regretted his decision to become a full-time "revolutionist" because he did not revoke it, although he might have done so, once when he was offered a position in the Duke Psychology Department and twice during World War II when he left Duke and could have remained either with General Motors, by whom he had been employed for a while in war work, or with the Bureau of Naval Personnel which the government wished to continue.

But with the termination of the war he "could not get back to Duke fast enough"[263] – although he certainly did not stay in parapsychology for the money. In 1954, for example, Stanley Krippner was visiting the Parapsychology Laboratory in Durham. While talking with some of Rhine's research associates there, including Pratt, one of them tried to sell Krippner his car because he was desperate for money. Krippner says it made him "realize that parapsychology was one of the most financially hazardous of professions."[264]

Pratt undoubtedly realized it, too. In spite of this hazard, he remained at Duke as research associate until 1964 when he left to become Ian Stevenson's colleague in the Department of Psychiatry at the University of Virginia School of Medicine in Charlottesville (the Division of Parapsychology there had not yet been created). Pratt's departure raises the question of why, while still a determined revolutionist well below the retirement age and in good health, he should have left Duke after 30 years? In 1957, Rhine was thinking of retirement and declared that, in two years, Pratt would succeed him.[265] Nineteen fifty-nine came and went, however, and Rhine still had not stepped down in favor of Pratt. Whatever understanding the two men may have had, any expectancy Pratt nurtured of becoming Rhine's successor was never fulfilled. Loyally, however, Pratt stayed on. So what precipitated his departure five years later? Pratt's intimate friend and associate, Ian Stevenson, provided what seemed a knowledgeable answer to the question:

> It will not take long to explain why Gaither came to the University of Virginia from Duke. He believed—with his teacher William McDougall—that parapsychology belongs in universities and that its pursuit in private societies and institutes isolates parapsychologists from other scientists—to the detriment of all. In the early 1960s, Rhine thought that universities were still not ready for parapsychology, and when the time came for his retirement, he chose to withdraw parapsychology from Duke and establish a private institute. Gaither took his chances at the University of Virginia.[266]

The reader may find interesting a rather different version of the event contained in a letter written on October 18, 1963, by Laura Dale to Dr. Jule Eisenbud:

> Guess you've heard that the Great White Father [Rhine] threw Gaither Pratt out on his ear after 30 years.[267]

Pratt had just spent three hours with Laura Dale venting his hurt and bitterness as he told her why, after three decades, he was now forced to think of a new association.

Historic Experiments

During the 1930s, while he worked at the Duke Parapsychology Laboratory as a graduate student, Pratt trained new researchers, tested people to see who might be gifted with ESP abilities, and made two historic contributions.

Flaws which many critics saw in some of the early experiments at Duke created the general impression that all the experiments were valueless as evidence of ESP. Pratt was to be the key experimenter in two classic experiments, the Pearce-Pratt series and the Pratt-Woodruff series, whose results could not be attributed to loose conditions.

In the 1933 distance experiments called the Pearce-Pratt series,[268] the results were phenomenal (one in a billion). Rhine and Pratt were coexperimenters and Hubert Pearce the subject. Pearce and Pratt met briefly on the Duke campus, synchronized their watches and agreed on the exact time the test would begin. Pearce then walked across the campus to the library at Duke and sat in a cubicle in the stacks. One series was carried out when Pratt and a pack of ESP cards were in the Medical School and another when Pratt was in the Physics Building, distances of 250 and 100 yards, respectively. In this experiment, Pratt kept all cards face down throughout and did not see the target symbols. Even if he had seen them and had called out (or unconsciously whispered) what the targets were, it would have been impossible for the information to have been transmitted to Pearce. In these experiments Rhine was the second experimenter to whom Pearce delivered a copy of his call record and Pratt a copy of his record of the order of the cards. This experiment, therefore, excluded all sensory clues and its other precautions excluded, also, other counter-hypotheses skeptics had urged, such as errors in recording of the data and experimenter incompetence. The Pearce-Pratt experiments have been called "the climax of the clairvoyance tests."[269]

In the Pratt-Woodruff experiments in 1939[270] use was made of the Screened Touch Matching procedure for each run of 25 ESP cards. In this procedure, a vertical screen was placed on a table between a subject who sat with a pointer on one side and Woodruff who sat on the other and shuffled and handled a face down deck of cards. Because of the screen the subject was unable to see the cards.

In back of the subject sat Pratt, observing and recording. On the side of the screen facing the subject, five ESP cards were suspended to display five different symbols. Pratt changed the order of these cards after each run so that Woodruff would not know their arrangement. On the table below the key cards were five blank cards. Upon a signal from Woodruff, the subject pointed to a blank card beneath the suspended key card which the subject guessed corresponded to the top card in the deck that Woodruff held. Woodruff was able to see the tip of the subject's pointer through an opening at the bottom of the screen. When he saw it, he took the top card from the deck and placed it face down opposite the blank card at which the subject had pointed.

The safeguards adopted did not permit Woodruff, who handled the target cards, to be aware of the order of the key cards and prevented Pratt, who arranged the key cards, from being involved with the target cards. Each experimenter kept a separate record which, when completed, was deposited in a locked box to be scored later by a third individual. The number of hits were scored jointly by the experimenters. The score for each run was entered by each experimenter in a personal record and the records checked independently by the Laboratory's secretary. In 2400 ESP runs with undergraduates from Duke and eight adults, 489 hits were scored above chance expectation. The chance probability of such results was one in 500,000.

This series of experiments is considered the high-water mark in the development of ESP research methods. Its elaborate experimental and recording controls met all the counterexplanations having to do with sensory cues. The procedures used for independent recording by two experimenters were safeguards against errors, manipulation of data or the incompetence of experimenters.

Mediumship

While at Duke, Pratt was placed in charge of devising a method of evaluating objectively the verbal statements made by mental mediums. Normally, such statements are nonquantitative in that they depend largely on the subjective judgment of sitters. Pratt developed a method of determining whether chance could be excluded as the hypothesis for information presented by mediums. Under the method, records of the medium's statements were shown to several subjects who did not know which of the records were intended for them and were to select which of the records corresponded to their cases. From their responses a value was arrived at.

Pratt's study of Eileen Garrett's abilities while she was in trance discussed this method at some length. It was published by the Boston Society for Psychic Research in 1936 and republished in 1969 by the Parapsychology Foundation.[271]

Pigeons

Pratt was a fancier of pigeons, but he was not interested in homing races. He was intrigued by the question of how birds are able to find their way during migratory flights over thousands of miles or on shorter homing flights, and whether ESP or sensory abilities were at the bottom of this puzzling ability. Under a contract made between the Office of Naval Research and Duke, Pratt attempted a number of experiments with pigeons over a period of a dozen years beginning in 1951.[272]

No experiment satisfied him that pigeons do not have some kind of inertial guidance system, such as that used in a submarine, that allowed them to know landmarks. He contrived one test which called for a pigeon loft located on a ship in the open sea where no landmarks were possible. If pigeons which learned to fly to and from such a loft were released at some distant point in the ocean while the loft was moved to another point on the ocean, and then if the pigeons returned to the loft at its new location and not back to the spot on the ocean where it had been, ESP would be indicated and would be an important test passed with flying pigeons.

Pratt made great efforts to secure a ship. William Cox, Pratt's closest colleague at the Duke Parapsychology Laboratory, said, "I recall how regretful he was that a ship captain whom he had contacted could not arrange to provide a 'moveable loft' for pigeons to return to in a different part of the ocean."[273]

Similar failures were recorded in other efforts Pratt made to obtain a ship, and his crucial experiment remains a dream waiting to be fulfilled by future researchers. Their opportunities to fulfill it seem vastly greater today than in

Pratt's time. Not only are the pigeons still there, but so are fleets of idle and rusting supertankers.

Poltergeists

When, with a sigh of regret, Pratt relinquished the investigation of pigeon-homing to the Zoology Department at Duke University, he found a new area of investigation which he was not only able to complete but in which he was to leave the mark of his competence: poltergeist disturbances consisting of noises and happenings in households for which no normal explanation could be found. With William G. Roll in 1958 he investigated a poltergeist case in Seaford, Long Island,[274] to which the New York Times gave considerable coverage. It was a case in which household disturbances, such as flying figurines, were taking place. Careful explorations were made which failed to discover pranks, fraud, group hallucinations or physical causes as explanations for the occurrences. Pratt traced the center of the disturbances to an adolescent and to the possibility that they were instances of recurrent spontaneous psychokinesis (RSPK) or spontaneous outbursts of "mind over matter" emanating from the boy.

The Seaford case was only exploratory and not conclusive, but Pratt felt that it "marked the turning point in research on the poltergeist."[275] It was perhaps the most comprehensively studied poltergeist case up to that time and showed the importance of firsthand investigations of such cases. It showed how these cases can be the "necessary link between the uncontrolled, question-raising events of the natural life situation and the controlled, question-answering events of the laboratory experiments on PK."[276] Pratt joined Roll in another poltergeist investigation in Miami in 1967.

Stepanek

A Czech citizen is recognized (even by the Guinness Book of Records, in 1970) as having had the largest number of successful ESP trials under laboratory conditions. His name is Pavel Stepanek.

Pratt himself set some sort of record by conducting experimental investigations of Stepanek over a period of ten years either in Prague or at the University of Virginia. And from these experiments in which the target cards, with one green side and one white side, were placed in black envelopes that were placed in turn in opaque envelopes, considerable evidence of ESP was elicited and a "focussing effect" noticed in which Stepanek's ESP seemed to focus more effectively on some and not others of the cards presented to him. Pratt published an overview of the work that had been done with Stepanek by various investigators, including himself, and an interpretation of the reports of research with him.[277]

Russia and Kulagina

What more appropriate place for a "revolutionist" to go than to Russia, particularly when he had heard, as Pratt had, that the Russians also were doing ESP research? In 1962, Pratt went to talk with Professor L.L. Vasilev, head of the Telepathic Laboratory at the University of Leningrad, and to exchange information with Russian scientists about current work. Pratt was deeply impressed. He found the Russians "eager to talk"[278] and said that, after thirty years in the ESP field and participation in discussions of parapsychology with other scientists, he had "rarely found another group with whom [he] felt as much at home or had as much in common."[279]

This rapport opened the way to more trips and conferences in 1963 and 1968. In 1968, the "high-point of the conference" was a film showing Nina S. Kulagina using psychokinetic abilities to move static objects, such as wooden matches, an empty match box and a glass, without physical contact and by conscious will alone. Pratt could reach no scientific conclusion from the film but was determined to investigate the case further. In 1970, Jürgen Keil, a friend of Pratt's from the University of Tasmania, arranged for such an investigation. Pratt and another member of the Division of Parapsychology at the University of Virginia were able to watch Kulagina in a hotel room as she moved a match box and a compass placed on the table. But scientific procedures did not control the demonstration and it lasted only a short time.[280]

Pratt and Keil, therefore, agreed on the necessity for making a more rigorous study. In 1971, they returned to Leningrad after having made "what seemed to be adequate arrangements with the Soviet citizens concerned"[281] for the tests and were confident there would be no problems. Pratt's initial impressions of the Russians, however, must have been set back severely when he encountered what seems to be a common experience of foreigners: delays and frustrations. Cooperation was required and Kulagina would not see Pratt at the time. Pratt and others, including Montague Ullman, who had been permitted direct observations of Kulagina, published a survey of the scientific observations that had been made of this challenging physical phenomenon.[282]

Personality

> Pratt's colleagues knew him well. Gertrude Schmeidler described him as such a good, solid, steady person. So far as I know his interest was in growing plants and vegetables, and of course in his family. Idiosyncrasy? Loyalty. He was a wonderful subordinate.... Work: steady and patient, careful. Words like steadfast and dependable are the kind to use for him and honest. Everyone who knew him trusted him.[283]

Cox called him "the most careful and cautious researcher"[284] and Stevenson "the gentlest and most considerate of persons."[285] The opinions of the subjects with whom he worked may be even more interesting. In a letter from behind the iron curtain, Pavel Stepanek said that Pratt's death

means for me a great personal loss. I am losing in him my great friend. I liked him very much, especially for his very good nature, honest and friendly attitude, and moral qualities. I could always rely upon him, he never disappointed me, and he was a very good representative of America.[286]

But, in fact, Pratt did disappoint Stepanek. In a letter written to Stepanek on October 3, 1979, he had made a promise: "Never, never think that I have forgotten you.... About my book: all I can really say is that I'm working on it in my mind. I'll do it—you just wait and see!"[287]

But he never kept this promise to write about his life's work. A few weeks after writing Stepanek and while he "was working in his garden with Ruth [his wife]," said Laura Dale in a letter to William Cox, "[h]e told her he felt dizzy, fell to the ground, and was gone in an instant, presumably of a heart attack."[288] Thus was Pratt's 43-year career as a full-time active "revolutionist" terminated at the age of 69 on November 3, 1979.

Major Writings

Pratt authored or coauthored several books or monographs, including "Towards a Method of Evaluating Mediumistic Material" (1936); *Extrasensory Perception after Sixty Years* (with J.B. Rhine and others) (1940); *Parapsychology: Frontier Science of the Mind* (with J.B. Rhine) (1957); *Parapsychology: An Insider's View of ESP* (1964); *ESP Research Today: A Study of Developments since 1960* (1973); *The Psychic Realm: What Can You Believe?* (with N.A. Hintze) (1975). He contributed a chapter on "Soviet Research in Parapsychology" to B.B. Wolman's *Handbook of Parapsychology* (1977), 40 papers to JASPR, 59 to the *Journal of Parapsychology* and 12 to periodicals on bird orientation and on psychology.

Joseph Banks Rhine: A Portrait

In 1911, the White House was creaking under the ponderous bulk of William Howard Taft, America's 27th president. Henry Ford had begun manufacturing the Model T. And in February of that year, Samuel Ellis Rhine and his family were on a train chugging west from their mountain home in Pennsylvania. With him were Elizabeth Ellen Vaughan, his wife; Myra, their 18-year-old daughter; and four younger, black-haired sons.

How Sam Rhine decided to pull up stakes was almost ridiculous. But, of course, he had always been a man on the move. He moved about 16 times in

J.B. Rhine

Pennsylvania, then to New Jersey, then returned to Pennsylvania. He was a man of many trades: teacher in a country school, merchant, farmer, an ambitious man who believed that greener pastures always lay over the hill. He thought he saw a green pasture when he read an ad in a farm paper, *The Rural New Yorker*. Some man in northern Ohio had a truck farm for rent and Sam Rhine was interested. The advertiser, whose name was Weckesser—German, like his own—sent snapshots of the place and of his family, including his freckled daughters. The man's letter also mentioned horses.

To Rhine's sons, especially the oldest, tallest and most serious, 16-year-old Joseph Banks Rhine, or Banks as he was called by his family, the freckled daughters were of no interest. But the prospect of horseback rides was exciting and distinguished this move from all the others. Otherwise it was just another move to a strange town and new people, a circumstance that prevented him from ever getting to know anyone and left him with what he described as his "only handicap": his shyness.

For he was a mountain boy.[289] A log house in Waterloo, in the lonely Pennsylvania mountains, had been his birthplace on September 29, 1895. For his first five years his only companion was his sister. The neighbor's children were too far away to be playmates. This situation made him "shyer than a wild turkey and about as ignorant of the world." This shyness had its positive effect. When the bashful child began school at the age of five and continued his education through 11 sundry schools which he attended up to high school, he tried for recognition, with his father's constant encouragement, through his schoolwork. It was easier for him than for most mountain children attending rural schools. Unlike their fathers, his was a literate man who had in his home what no other house in the mountains had: a small library. And when his father was teaching, young Banks, beginning at the age of four, accompanied him to school and learned to read.[290]

But outside of class Banks' bashfulness in every new school and town made him a figure of fun for the other boys, a target to be teased and taunted. Young Rhine, however, had spirit and used his fists to stop them, the first sign of a plucky soul willing to fight when necessary.

When Rhine was about 10, one of his father's moves took the family to a town in New Jersey. The opportunity to live there for two years and to become one of a gang of companions transformed him. The innocent, shy mountain boy in that "modern little Sodom" — Rhine's own words — became "wicked," revelling in the vice of the town, worse than the worst evildoer among his chums and "a brazen young lady-killer." Later he said he realized that he had been an amorous fool [at the age of 10!] and then and there made up his mind that only the girl he would marry would have any claim on his attention in the future.

When he was nearly 12, he had a moving religious experience. Bible stories he had heard years before from a pious aunt had intrigued him. After his father got him a book about the Bible, he plunged into it repeatedly, his eager eyes scanning every line. There he found Jesus, whose life, deeds and teachings inspired him. He felt Jesus near him and that he was destined to work for Jesus. When the Methodists held one of their open air religious meetings not far from the town where he lived, he stood up at the altar to pray and to tell the gathering that his life was committed to Jesus. Now his plan was to follow in the steps of brilliant American evangelists such as William Vaughn Moody and Thomas deWitt Talmadge. It was a plan that brought the sparkle of delight into his mother's eyes, for the ministry was what she had planned for him. Rhine could recall that when she took him for baptism at the age of four, she told the preacher some day her son would be a preacher also.[291]

The change from the air of New Jersey to that of the Weckesser farm in Marshallville, Ohio, did not change his plan to be a Methodist minister. He became active in the village church, a reader not only of the Bible but of other books on religion, a speaker at prayer meetings and a devout believer ready to argue the case for Christ with the Bible as supreme authority. During his attendance at high school, one of his odd jobs included selling *The Story of the Bible* by Hurlbut.

One of the girls in the snapshot Weckesser had sent Sam Rhine was his 19-year-old daughter, Louisa Ellen. She was not at all freckled as the inferior

1911 snapshot had showed her to be. But she was older than Banks Rhine who "was attracted to her mind alone." He said, "We used to hold long, juvenile discussions of religion and our philosophical perplexities, and in the course of them became attached to each other."[292] Very soon, however, they discovered that their viewpoints clashed. She hated discrimination against women; he saw nothing in the Bible concerning the rights of women. She advocated the theory of evolution; he found no proof for it in the Bible. She tended to be irreverent, critical of religious creeds and ministers, and she pitied the credulous young man who had been taken in by them. Religion became a constant theme of their arguments.

Banks Rhine worked hard in high school. He was studying six subjects instead of the usual four or five. He appeared at school at the opening bell, remained after classes ended and left only when the caretaker locked up the building in the late hours. He completed the four year high school course in three[293] and went on to join Louisa Weckesser at summer school at Wooster College. A stimulating teacher there made them both start to think of new and exciting issues. His attendance at church became less frequent. But Louisa Weckesser's reasoning and personality had the strongest influence on him. It is not that he began to have second thoughts; she made him have first thoughts about something that he had taken on trust.

At 19, with the hearing in one ear and the sight of one eye impaired and the senses of smell and taste lost as a result of the measles,[294] Rhine went to Ohio Northern, a college in Ada, where he worked his way through as a waiter in a dining room. It was not a religious school and soon, in his letters to Louisa, now attending Wooster College, it became clearer and clearer that his old time religion was being attacked by doubts and developing critical faculties. A terrible struggle was going on in him during this period: "This rupture of my faith and shattering of my ideals and ambition has completely broken my mental equilibrium. I am left with no definite purpose."[295] Louisa persuaded him to join her at Wooster College where, whether in library, laboratory or church, they were always together.

But Wooster College did nothing to help Rhine's religious predicament. In fact, he found the heavy religious atmosphere of the place unendurable. When the semester ended the world seemed as purposeless to him as when the semester had begun. He left Wooster with no future, no plans, and went to one city after another where he got odd jobs, a roaming blue-collar worker with no thought of anything except a day's wages.

A little later he was on the verge of going to Michigan Agricultural School to train to become a forester—he had always loved the outdoors with its mountains, woods and hills—but the Germans changed his mind and gave him a purpose he had never considered. In 1916, President Wilson was still convinced that the United States would bring peace to war-torn Europe. But after the Germans decided on a policy of merciless submarine warfare and sent American vessels to the bottom in February and March, 1917, war was declared on Germany in April. "Over there," Rhine would find some light to clear up his perplexities. He wanted action and tried to enlist in the Army but was turned down because of his defective hearing and sight. The Navy refused him because of hammer toes. After one rejection, the Marine Corps accepted his enlistment after Rhine challenged the Marine physician to a hike.[296]

Although he served in the Marines from 1917 to 1919, he did not see the action he wanted in France. He served in boot camp where he trained and drilled. From there he was transported to Santo Domingo where, between mess calls, there was only monotony on that sunny tropical island.

In 1919, now a sergeant, he trained in New England for the National Rifle Matches. He entered the competition, outshot over 700 expert marksmen and won a gold medal as "Military Rifle Champion" and a congratulatory letter from President Wilson. But there was something even better in store for him: Louisa. They were married the following year.

Botany and Parapsychology

Out of the Marines with no money, no future, no training, Rhine went to work as a door-to-door salesman of pots and pans until the fall of 1920 when he and his wife went on to the University of Chicago. Rhine explained:

> As we grew older and had to decide what to do with our lives, we turned by common consent to the field of professional forestry. The woods seemed to offer a free and natural life, one in which we might hope to escape the fog of an increasingly dubious philosophy and work out at least a practical formula for existence.[297]

Preparation for a career in forestry required Rhine to start his studies in the Department of Botany. (Louisa had already gotten a degree in botany and was doing graduate work.) He obtained an M.S. degree in 1923 when Louisa received her Ph.D. and went on to work for his own doctorate. Yet something was very wrong. Botany was not satisfying him. "I can't see what it's all about. I don't doubt that a lot of facts are presented, but to what do they lead? What help is it to know them?"[298] There had to be some connection between research and science and human values. Where was this connection in botany? Then, Rhine recorded, "before we completed our studies in that sphere our imaginations were caught by the possibilities of useful work in the borderland science of psychic research."[299]

The borderland of parapsychology! It may seem curious that it had not crossed his anxious, searching mind before to enter this borderland for answers to his philosophical and religious perplexities. Yet from his earliest childhood in Waterloo, he remembered that the mountain people believed in the paranormal.[300] It was also in his boyhood that his mother told him a story of her dying brother who heard the sounds of sawing and hammering on his coffin at the time it was being made, sounds he could not have heard with his normal hearing. These mountain beliefs and his mother's stories, however, had little influence on him because his father was a dyed-in-the-wool skeptic and "he taught me to dismiss them as superstitious nonsense."[302]

But his imagination was titillated by an article in *American Magazine* on spirit photography which made Rhine wonder if it might be possible to obtain objective evidence of the existence of the spiritual world he was not willing to take on trust.[303] Also, as a graduate student at the University of Chicago, he had been impressed when one of his professors gave an account of a woman who dreamed that her brother in another village had gone into a barn and killed himself with a pistol, his dead body thereafter being found with the pistol just as his sister had described it.

Rhine remembered that story for a long time afterward, for the professor was a man he respected and an honest man, he believed. What puzzled Rhine was not so much the story of the sister's experience or even that it had been confirmed, but that the professor could not explain it and lived his life doing nothing to satisfy his curiosity about it.[304] There were many such stories, many supported by independent witnesses and documents. Why, Rhine wondered, why is it that such strange happenings in the realm of mind were not being studied by psychologists as eagerly as new bugs are studied by entomologists?[305]

But what really trapped him was the net cast by Arthur Conan Doyle who was on a lecture tour of America. Conan Doyle, who created Sherlock Holmes with such reality that people still write to the great detective at Baker Street in London, was speaking to convince his audiences that he had received communications from his deceased son. Rhine, still retaining some of his father's skepticism, went "with many reservations, almost to scoff," in 1922 to hear Conan Doyle's lecture "Proofs of Immortality," but left it saying, "clearly if there was a measure of truth in what [Conan Doyle] believed . . . it would be of transcendental importance. This mere possibility was the most exhilarating thought I had had for years."[306] His interest in parapsychology was piqued. He wanted

> to find a satisfactory philosophy of life, one that could be regarded as scientifically sound and yet could answer some of the urgent questions regarding the nature of man and his place in the natural world. Dissatisfied with the orthodox religious belief which had at one time impelled me toward the ministry and dissatisfied, except as a last resort, with a materialistic philosophy, I was obviously ready to investigate any challenging fact that might hold possibilities of new insight into human personality and its relations to the universe.[307]

This interest and Conan Doyle's lecture did not mean that Rhine had been completely entrapped by Conan Doyle's sincerity and had been led into the fold of Spiritualism as had Frederick Edwards who heard the lecture in Carnegie Hall in New York. For Rhine was a scientist and not a clergyman and was too critical to accept at face value Conan Doyle's claims. But they made him act. He was driven to the library at the University. Since Conan Doyle had referred to several scientists, such as Sir Oliver Lodge, who were persuaded of survival after death, Rhine read Lodge's book entitled *The Survival of Man* and found it important.[308] Rhine also read the SPR publications and discovered the existence of the ASPR.

But still he wondered whether it was wise "to meddle" in the borderland of parapsychology. Louisa shared this doubt with him. Was she ready to meet the challenge of new facts? Fortunately for Rhine and parapsychology, she was. Her support and encouragement made it easy for him to decide.[309]

The first step in carrying out the decision now made was to write letters to the ASPR, McDougall and Joseph Jastrow. On June 6, 1923, Rhine's letters went out with the basic message that he was trained in plant chemistry but wanted to inquire if any position or fellowship were open for him to be trained in the field of parapsychology in which he had become deeply interested. Edwards of the ASPR, with no position open for Rhine, advised him to stay in his own field of training. Jastrow proffered the same advice. McDougall was forced to tell Rhine that Gardner Murphy occupied the Hodgson "Fellowship."

Around the time of this disappointing correspondence, Rhine and his wife received and accepted an offer to become plant physiologists for a year at the Boyce Thompson Institute for Plant Research in Yonkers, New York. But that proved more hope-balking than the replies Rhine had received to his inquiries about opportunities in parapsychology. Instead of being asked to do research, they were called on to sweep out shavings left by carpenters and to keep bookshelves tidy. But the year was not totally wasted. The proximity of the Boyce Thompson Institute to New York City gave Rhine the opportunity to go to a seance there and to have an interesting encounter:

"It was around 1923 that I first met Gardner [Murphy], one night in New York City, as he was investigating a medium; it was incidentally the first demonstration for me of a professional type."[310] This meeting was to be the start of what Rhine liked "to call a partnership in parapsychology."[311]

When the year at the Boyce Thompson Institute ended, Rhine went to West Virginia University in Morgantown in 1924 to teach plant physiology, although he found time in that year to send a check along to the ASPR in payment of his first membership fee.

The Learning Experience

Rhine's correspondence had the peculiar tendency to be sent at critical times. His 1923 letters were sent in the year that McDougall was ousted as ASPR president. His next letter in March 1925 to Bird of the ASPR was mailed in the very month that Prince resigned from the organization. As Margery had been a causal factor in Prince's being driven out of the ASPR, she was behind Rhine's letter to Bird. Rhine had not failed to notice Bird's articles about her in *The Scientific American*. If there were any measure of truth in her claim to spirit communications, Rhine wanted to know. His inquiry to Bird led to a dialogue with the ASPR research officer and, when Bird discovered that Rhine knew

German and French, he offered Rhine a chance to do reviews of foreign periodicals for JASPR.

Slender and of average weight, Bird differed from the powerful and ponderous giant of a figure Conan Doyle presented. But from Bird exuded the same sincerity and the same ability with words. And so when Bird began to tell Rhine that Margery was a genuine medium and that McDougall and Prince had not merely failed to see her unique powers but had tried to convert her into a shoddy vaudeville act, Rhine listened and believed. Bird knew that he had a ready helper. In May 1925, Bird wanted to know what Prince and McDougall were up to in Boston and, especially, to read a pamphlet Prince had written. Would Rhine do some "detective work" and get it from Prince for him? Rhine agreed and, after requesting it from Prince, received it as well as a caution from Prince who regarded Bird as unreliable. It was a caution Rhine ignored, for he was convinced of Bird's rectitude.

In the summer of 1925, Rhine went back to the University of Chicago to complete the requirements for his Ph.D. degree. By September he had resumed teaching at Morgantown, but the constant thought of Margery once more directed a letter to Bird. Would it be possible to arrange a sitting with the medium in Boston if Rhine should come the following year? After the affirmative response, and in spite of an assurance of elevation in rank and salary at Morgantown, Rhine turned his back on botany in June 1926 and faced toward that borderland of parapsychology which had challenged him. He sold his furniture and, with his wife and a few dollars they had saved, left for Boston and the seance which Bird had arranged for July 1 at the Crandons' well appointed home at 10 Lime Street.

The Rhines were there that night for dinner and social conversation with the Crandons and half a dozen other people. After dinner, the gay party ascended to the dark, curtained seance room on the top floor of the house. The Rhines had been told at dinner not to expect anatomical marvels such as the eruption of teleplasmic hands from Margery's body. But other things were in store for them. "Walter" speaking from the grave was one of Margery's feats as he has not only chatted wittily but also whistled. Now, instead of holding a hand over the medium's mouth, or filling it with peanut butter or water, which might have been the simplest way to assure sitters of the independence of Walter's voice, Dr. Mark W. Richardson, an ASPR vice president and Boston physician who had investigated Margery, and who surely qualifies as the Rube Goldberg of her coterie of admirers, designed a "voice-cut-out machine." The contraption he devised consisted of a U-tube, one arm of which entered Margery's mouth by means of a flexible gas pipe made of metal with a glass mouthpiece. Upper and lower holes in the mouthpiece were to be covered by the lips of the medium. When Margery blew through the pipe, two luminous corks would start floating at a certain level in each arm of the U-tube. To keep them afloat the medium's tongue had to keep the floats up and thus would show that she could not produce "Walter's" talking or whistling. When this experiment was performed for his benefit, Rhine noticed that the medium's

neck had not been fastened to prevent her movement forward. He thought
that she might have been able to move her head forward sufficiently to allow
her hands, although fastened, to take the tube from her mouth after she had
blown through it to position the floats and then to hold her thumb over the
end of the tube.

Another phenomenon which impressed all of Margery's sitters was the
pair of chemical balances used in her seances. The balances were made of brass.
There was a steel balancing edge with a set screw and two wooden pans. One
pan would be weighted with three to six checkers, the other would have no
weights. "Walter" would use some sort of psychic substance to make the two
pans balance. The balancing phenomenon would be visible during a few
seconds when a red light was on. The Rhines observed that Margery's husband
acted as "stage manager" for the experiment. He, not "Walter," seemed to
flash the red light to allow them to see the pans in balance. Now balances such
as these were no mystery to Rhine who had taught classes in chemistry. Following the sitting, he looked at the rider on the balance to see how it slid laterally
when he applied some pressure to it. He discovered that it did not respond to
his push. A small set screw held it in place, but, with his fingernail, he could
turn it without difficulty, move the rider to the other side and reset the screw.
He realized that the rider, whose position had been on the heavy side of the
scale at the start of the seance, had been moved to the other side to force the
lighter pan down. No sooner had he made this discovery when his annoyed
host, Dr. Crandon, came up to him and ordered Rhine not to tamper with the
balances.

It was the day of the crooners who projected their Tin Pan Alley songs
through megaphones. Not to be outdone, "Walter" used a megaphone, too,
to carry on a lively conversation with sitters. Tonight was to be no exception.
Only this time, as Rhine said in a report he coauthored with his wife,[312] he saw
Margery's foot "kicking the megaphone over within reach of her hand."

Immediately after the seance when he had left the Crandon home with
his wife, Louisa Rhine described his reaction: "When all was over and Banks
and I were alone outside, and I, still confused and uncertain, Banks burst out
with something like, 'Oh, Louie, Louie, what fools we've been!! That was the
most fantastic fraud I ever could imagine!'"[313]

Rhine wrote to Bird and to the ASPR Trustees. He was "disgusted" to find
"the falseness of it all"; "Crandon engineered the play"; "the wholesale fraud
we were witness to"; "I do not wish my name to even appear in the *Journal*
again until it shows a change of attitude on this dirty business"; "when I found
this poor bunch of tricks at the back of all these investigations and publications, it was a tremendous jolt."[314] Interestingly, all the members of the ASPR
Board of Trustees did in response to Rhine's letters was to write cranky letters
of their own to the disillusioned and bitter botanist who thought he knew more
about Margery than they and their research officer. But neither Bird nor any
of Margery's supporters ever used the pages of the ASPR *Journal* to rebut Rhine's
"exposé" of Margery although they never failed to use the *Journal* as a kind of

blunt instrument to smash her other critics. However, Conan Doyle, as strong a supporter of Margery as Bird, was more forthcoming. After he read Rhine's published report from England, he lashed out at the writer by taking out an ad which appeared in one of the Boston newspapers: "J.B. Rhine is a monumental ass!"[315]

McDougall and Prince had had the competence and background to judge the Margery mediumship after many sittings and observations of numerous happenings, and, if they questioned her, their judgments were entitled to respect. But Rhine, who was a tyro and, in 1926, as "ignorant as a wild turkey" about mediumship as he had been about the world when a boy in the Pennsylvania mountains—of what value was his judgment? Even if not a novice, was a single seance enough to make a judgment damning Margery? The basis for the judgment is, on analysis, extremely weak. It consisted of inferences and suppositions concerning the balances and voice machine. The only evidence he had worthy of mention was Rhine's observation of Margery kicking the megaphone "Walter" was to use. But it is evidence that needs to be approached with caution because it has many faults.

Rhine's claim was entirely unsupported by any of the other six sitters who attended the seance and, if there were corroborative statements, Rhine failed to include them in his report. It is natural to expect that, if a fraud had been committed, Rhine would have made an immediate objection at the seance. But there is no indication of any timely complaint except to his wife afterwards.

Even if Margery did kick the megaphone within reach of her hand, Rhine's contention that she used it for trickery is no more than his conclusion, for he never observed her actually reach for or use it. In cases of this kind, as in every courtroom, we need to distinguish between a fact and an opinion or conclusion drawn from the fact. Rhine's claim that Margery was a fraud, therefore, is based on evidence of the flimsiest kind and seems to be the case of a novice hastily giving an opinion and coming to a conclusion.

But inexperienced and hasty or not, Rhine's conclusion in the case made this episode, in Louisa Rhine's words, "in more ways than one a learning experience,"[316] one with the greatest implications. First, it made Rhine think that Bird, who had more opportunities than Rhine to discover Margery's fraudulent mediumship, had misled him and that Bird was either an incompetent scientist or Margery's confederate. Rhine may then have remembered Prince's warning about Bird. Second, it made Rhine realize that Prince, denounced by Bird, had been correct all along in his critical view of the Margery mediumship.

The other probable effect of his disillusioning experience with Margery on Rhine's future course and that of parapsychology in general should not be lost. Whether saint or whore, the genuine article or a clever charlatan, the blue-eyed sensation must receive credit for helping Rhine pioneer experimental parapsychology in America.

Margery did not destroy his interest in the question of whether the human personality continues beyond the grave — later events would show that. But she made him realize the futility of research with mediums and investigations of spirit communications in the poorly controlled, darkened seance room. She moved him out of it and into the laboratory where, with experimental methods and under experimental safeguards, hypotheses could be tested. And, because of Margery, Rhine found Prince an ally who, in 1934, published his monograph *Extra-Sensory Perception* whose concepts and methods became paradigmatic for parapsychology. At that time the only other para-psychological society that might have published his work was the hostile ASPR and it was more than likely that every psychological journal would have rejected it.

McDougall, Thomas and a Wonderful Lady

As we have seen, Rhine had written to McDougall at Harvard in 1923 because the year before, the former had read McDougall's *Body and Mind* and "Psychical Research as a University Study." Rhine considered McDougall the foremost exponent of purposive psychology with its emphasis on mind.[317] At that time Rhine had wanted to see if an exploration could be under-taken into the unknown regions of mind and its psychic capacities[318] but found that the Hodgson Fund was not available. Thereafter, Bird had made him believe for a time that McDougall's unjustified attacks on Margery made him, like Prince, a person with whom Rhine did not want to associate.

Now, however, the shock of the Margery episode showed Rhine the falseness of this belief. He decided to go to Cambridge at once to see McDougall. He did not write or telegraph beforehand nor did he telephone ahead for an appointment as he might, and as it turned out, should have done. This, after all, was Boston in 1926, not Waterloo in the mountains of Penn-sylvania where a telephone might not have been found, and so Rhine's decision must have been an impetuous one — and, as it turned out, a wrong one. He arrived just when taxicabs, loaded with the baggage of the British psychologist and his family, were waiting to start them on their trip around the world. Per-force, the meeting lasted only minutes, enough for McDougall to suggest that Rhine see a Harvard professor about a Hodgson "fellowship" and for Rhine to say goodbye as McDougall sped off on his journey. It was their first meeting but would not be their last.

After the professor suggested by McDougall seemed puzzled about Rhine's wanting to leave botany for parapsychology and evasive about the Hodgson Fund, the next name on Rhine's list of people to be seen was Prince, who had been slandered by Bird and now vindicated by Rhine's own judgment in the Margery case. When Rhine brought the Margery fiasco to Prince's attention, he also brought himself to Prince's attention as a skeptical investigator. Prince gave Rhine employment for the summer as a researcher of Mrs. Soule with whom he had sittings. To supplement the $12 a week Prince paid the Rhines, and to pay the rent at their rooming house near Massachusetts Avenue in Boston, Rhine taught carpentry at a kindergarten and took care of the furnace in the house while his wife cleaned the toilets and halls.

Through Prince, John F. Thomas found them in Boston that summer. He told them of his wife's death a few months before and of sittings with Mrs. Soule that made him believe that his wife had communicated with him because facts had been given that were known only to her and to him. The shock of the Margery failure and Rhine's subsequent dismal sittings with Mrs. Soule might have soured him toward any claims of spirit communication and made Thomas's visit to the Rhines as badly timed as had been Rhine's to McDougall. But Rhine listened eagerly to what Thomas said. Of course, he would help if he could. Thomas, however, was going to England for more sittings. Any active help Rhine might give would be postponed until Thomas came back.

Rhine left Boston; money was needed. He returned to Ohio to sell pots and pans once more. And then, in September 1927, Thomas ended the waiting with an attractive offer. He had collected stenographic records of what seemed evidential communications from his dead wife through English mediums such as Gladys Osborne Leonard. He was willing to send the Rhines with the material to Duke and to defray their expenses there for a semester in order to have Rhine and McDougall study the material to see whether it showed real spirit communications. "To us," wrote Louisa Rhine, "this promised to be the Real Thing at last and we accepted the offer at once."[319]

So they were off to Durham—by way of New York City (because Rhine wanted to see and speak with Gardner Murphy)—in their Model T. Evidently Rhine had learned nothing from his experience with McDougall because he did not telephone or otherwise get in touch with Murphy before his arrival. According to Lois Murphy

> That fall of 1926 when Gardner was not well, J.B. Rhine appeared at the door and said he would like to talk to Gardner Murphy. I told him that Gardner was sick. J.B. then explained the purpose of his visit: "I just want to know one thing—does he really take telepathy seriously? Because I'm considering making a commitment to spend my life at it." I assured him that Gardner was deeply and permanently committed to psychical research and expected to devote a good part of his time to it.[320]

And Rhine thereupon resumed his trip to Durham. The detour, however, was fortunate because it uncovered animal psi as a further area of study. A newspaper picked up at a roadside tourist stop reported that a horse named Lady in Richmond, Virginia, had correctly picked the underdog, Gene Tunney, to beat Jack Dempsey for the heavyweight championship of the world in their title bout in Philadelphia. After arriving at Duke in the fall of 1927,

starting on the Thomas records and auditing McDougall's classes and seminars
on psychology, Rhine arranged to see Lady later in the year and in 1928.

Claudia Fonda, Lady's owner, advertised the "mind-reading" horse to
bring paying customers into Mrs. Fonda's backyard tent. As Rhine and others
looked on, the horse's ability to give the right answers to questions asked by
the public by using her muzzle to make contact with alphabet or numbered
blocks after the order "Work, Lady, work," seemed to present an impressive
example of telepathy between the animal and her owner. Even when all possible cues by Mrs. Fonda or Rhine himself were prevented, Lady seemed to read
minds. She did as well when McDougall accompanied the Rhines to watch. But
like a skyrocket that flashes momentarily and then fizzles, the case of Lady
burned out for Rhine. When he observed the horse again in 1928, it was clear
to him that the trainer's movements with whip or body were directing Lady's
responses. Thus disillusioned, Rhine seems not to have observed the horse
again. Nevertheless, for two decades more, the horse now known as "Lady
Wonder" went on to predict horse races (who should know better?), the election of Truman against all odds and even to detect the location of a missing
child's body[321] so that, before Lady Wonder died at the age of 31, she seems
to have confirmed Rhine's original opinion of her remarkable psi abilities.

By the beginning of 1929 Rhine had been offered an assistant professorship at Duke to give courses on the history and methodology of sciences and
the approaches of various scientists to the mind-body problem. He also was to
do research, some on Thomas's mediumistic material, which Thomas was willing to support for another semester, some on helping McDougall with his
Lamarckian rat experiments.

The reputation of rats as marauders and bearers of disease is well-known;
to Rhine, however, McDougall's laboratory rats were special. He was enchanted
by the young ones especially, pink, white and soft babies whom he called
"symphonies in innocence" and when their tiny pink noses brushed him
delicately, he knew that this was "how fairies feel."[322]

But it was from the Thomas records that Rhine might know whether a
human being survived death. They were impressive enough to convince
Thomas—with such recondite facts as that he had been a gum-chewing addict
until his wife made him stop—that they presented a clear picture of his dead
wife's personality. But for Rhine, although chance, fraud or inference could
be dismissed, whether the knowledge shown by the mediums was obtained
from Thomas's dead wife or by telepathy from Thomas's mind was the problem. It was Rhine's unwillingness to yield to Thomas on this question that
finally terminated their connection.

Rhine had another problem besides Thomas. The borderland of parapsychology had excited both Louisa and him as a challenge that would keep
them active and fighting for something. But now his situation at Duke seemed
to be pushing him further and further away from that something. He was
becoming a campaigner without a campaign, a "strawy-minded professor"
afraid that his "'bearings will rust out with waiting,' that his impetus, his 'head

of steam,' his interest will seep away and be dissipated if he is forced to wait and divert his energy—into teaching, for instance."[323] The next year, however, solved the problem and rust-proofed his bearings.

Parapsychology Gains a Foothold

In books whose object is to disparage parapsychology, the complaint is made that "occultism, under the guise of scientific research, is invading the precincts of our most distinguished universities."[324] For such critics, "parapsychology" is "occultism" and hence sheer nonsense. But for others the subject matter of parapsychology is not nonsense and its experimental investigation by competent researchers in universities appeared necessary if the valid and credible were to be distinguished from the reverse. For almost 50 years, however, although James had occupied the chair of psychology at Harvard, Hodgson had been a Cambridge man and lecturer, and Hyslop an academic from Columbia, there had been no university research. All did their investigations outside a university as did Prince. Although McDougall sponsored Murphy and Estabrooks at Harvard, the fact is, as Rhine stated it, "In 1930, no American university was investigating extra-sensory perception."[325]

It is probable that in no American university other than Duke would parapsychology have been able to gain a foothold. At Duke it became possible largely because of McDougall, with his hormic psychology, his rejection of behaviorism, his belief that the human mind possessed a nonphysical element, and his interest in parapsychology that went back almost 30 years. When he became head of Duke's Department of Psychology no consent other than his was necessary for Rhine to come and remain at Duke.

The mediumistic records provided by Thomas and with which Rhine had come laden in 1927 to McDougall's Department of Psychology led Rhine directly to one of McDougall's favorite research topics. The records had raised an issue in Rhine's mind which he could not resolve: Were they spirit communications or were they telepathic communications from Thomas which the mediums presented to Thomas as spirit communications? Rhine proposed to address experimentally the question of the existence of telepathic communications among human subjects. This was precisely the question McDougall had posed in his Clark University lecture years before when he talked of those problems which would be suitable for a university research department: "Does telepathy occur? That is to say—Do we, do minds, communicate with one another in any manner and degree otherwise than through the sense-organs and through the bodily organs of expression and the physical media which science recognizes?"[326]

McDougall, therefore, was fertile ground for the seed of parapsychology. And so were others. Duke's president, William Few, was also interested in the general subject, as were the two other staff members of the Department of Psychology, Helge Lundholm and Karl E. Zener, who were Rhine's colleagues.

In 1930, supported by a $400 grant from Duke for research in parapsychology, Rhine began with the active cooperation of his colleagues, Lundholm handling the hypnotizing of subjects to be tested for telepathy, and Zener, in keeping with his training in sensory perception, devising distinctive symbols for target cards. Rhine also received the enthusiastic collaboration of hundreds of undergraduate students who acted as subjects.

There was at Duke an administrative and departmental interest, some funds and the spirit of excitement that came from doing something which might add to scientific knowledge, all of which contributed to what McDougall called the "naturalization" of parapsychology.[327] We have noted McDougall's role in creating this highly favorable situation, but Rhine's should not be overlooked. In McDougall's words,

> The manifest sincerity and integrity of Dr. Rhine's personality, his striking combination of humane sympathy with the most single-minded devotion to truth, have induced in his collaborators a serene confidence in the worthwhileness of the effort, and have set a tone which, to the best of my judgment, pervades the group....[328]

Novel Technique

Rhine was familiar with card-guessing experiments that had been done by the SPR. In 1929, Ina Jephson's experiments in England were repeated by Besterman, Soal and Jephson again. Gardner Murphy at that time carried out one of their series of experiments with Rhine as a participant.

In the summer of 1930, Rhine used cards to conduct tests with children. The cards, stamped with numbers, were held hidden in his hand. That fall he made 10,000 trials. At Zener's suggestion cards were placed in sealed envelopes and given to 63 students at Duke to guess the numbers or letters stamped on the cards. Rhine also worked with Lundholm. Students were tested while they were in a hypnotic trance induced by Lundholm or after being placed by suggestion during hypnosis in a mental state favorable for testing.

These early trials were sufficiently encouraging to cause Rhine to proceed—but with a different method. This method had been used first by a physiologist at the University of Paris. Charles Richet applied the mathematics of probability in 1884 during experiments with playing cards enclosed in opaque envelopes.[329] No Americans paid attention to his procedure, however, until Coover and Troland conducted their experiments in 1917 and Estabrooks his in 1927. When Rhine followed a procedure in the 1930s to obtain mathematical evidence of the existence of psi, therefore, it was not novel. But his collaboration with Zener to devise a different and practical kind of technique that allowed ESP test results to be evaluated easily was novel.

Where Richet, Coover and Estabrooks had all used ordinary playing cards in their telepathy experiments (Troland had used a test machine), Rhine and Zener designed the "Zener cards," later called "ESP cards," a pack of 25 cards marked with five symbols which could be imaged more readily than playing cards. There were five different symbols—a plus, a rectangle, a circle, three wavy lines and a star—each marked on five cards in the deck. Otherwise the cards looked like regular playing cards.

Rhine initiated a procedure which he admitted was almost as childish as it was monotonous[330] to obtain mathematical evidence that ESP occurred. He and a subject sat facing one another at opposite sides of a table. Rhine shuffled and cut a facedown deck of 25 ESP cards whose order in the deck was not known. When the subject attempted to guess the symbol on the top card, Rhine recorded his guess and removed the card to allow the subject to name the symbol to the next one. After all the cards were called, the guesses were compared to the true order of the cards.[331]

Yes, it was monotonous and as simple as could be, but it provided, said Rhine, "a highly satisfactory method of investigation and, ultimately, of proof."[332] It was not merely that the cards were simple to use and required no prior training; they were valuable because they were a practical and easily applied method for researchers to use to record a subject's ability, to allow an accurate statistical evaluation to be made of the results, and to see if Rhine's successes could be replicated. For each series of 25 calls, five correct ones would be the average to be expected on a chance basis. This permitted Rhine to determine the extent to which the actual results exceeded chance. By subtracting the chance expectation from the number of actual scores made by the subjects used in the experiments, the difference produced a deviation. To be sure that a deviation might not also be caused by chance alone statistical methods were used to decide the odds against chance as the cause.

Using the ESP cards in his experiments, Rhine worked with students at Duke. The results were encouraging but not spectacular until 1931 and 1932 when two remarkable subjects were discovered. One was A.J. Linzmayer, an undergraduate student in psychology. During Linzmayer's first session, Rhine picked up a pack of ESP cards and, as he glanced at each card, asked Linzmayer what it was. The subject made nine successive correct calls. "Here was something amazing!" Rhine exclaimed[333] because the odds against this result were about 2 million to 1. This sensation was repeated the following day only to be eclipsed by another experiment Rhine conducted with Linzmayer in Rhine's parked car when, with Rhine placing ESP cards facedown on a notebook in Linzmayer's lap, the subject made 15 correct calls in succession and made six more hits besides. His 21 correct calls out of a possible 25 were against odds of one in 30 billion.[334]

The second subject was Hubert Pearce, a nervous, sensitive young divinity student at the Duke School of Religion whom Rhine discovered in the spring of 1932 when Pearce described his mother's paranormal experiences. Naturally enough, Pearce was induced to take part in tests with Rhine's ESP cards, and he achieved some steady results though never the long successive runs which Linzmayer had produced—except for one episode Rhine thought well worth the telling. Pearce came by the laboratory one day and was induced by Rhine to try some calls. Pearce obliged him but called incorrectly the first five cards in Rhine's pack. Rhine teased him by asking if Pearce were in a hurry to go somewhere. When this little provocation seemed to cause Pearce to call correctly the next three out of five cards, Rhine tried to provoke him some more. "'I'll bet a hundred dollars you can't get this one,' I said banteringly. He did. 'Another hundred on this one,' I told him. He got that card right too." Pearce went on to get 25 hits in succession which meant that Rhine lost one hundred dollars on each bet. Despite his huge debt to Pearce, Rhine declared that this series of "calls was the most phenomenal thing I have ever observed. If there is anyone in the world who can believe that it was due to sheer luck, that would be another phenomenon almost equally startling. The odds against his feat having been due to pure and undiluted chance are 1 in 298,023,223,876,953,125."[335]

Did Rhine pay Pearce the $2500 he had won? "I need only say," added Rhine, "that the sum approaches an average college professor's yearly salary [in 1932] which ought to be a satisfactory reply."[336]

In 1932 and 1933, Rhine struck a rich vein of excellent subjects.[337] They produced results that were impossible according to the rules of chance so that the only course seemed to be to publish the experiments with the conclusion that indisputable evidence had been provided of the existence of an antichance factor at work and of the ability of the human mind to obtain information without the use of the recognized senses.

The Momentous Study

Prince who died in 1934 did not know how prophetic he had been when, in the Introduction to Rhine's monograph *Extra-Sensory Perception,* he called it a "momentous study." Although, for reasons soon to be made clear, one may question the wisdom of having put it into print at all, it was "momentous" on a number of grounds. It told the world that for six years a university had been actively and continuously investigating telepathy and clairvoyance. Long before the publication of the book and, like the English psychical researchers, American investigators had been collecting stories and spontaneous cases as the primary method for establishing the reality of paranormal phenomena. There were some experiments in telepathy, but they were the exception, not the rule. In fact, Hyslop was firmly set against experimenting: "It may be gravely questioned whether we can expect to perform experiments in telepathy."[338]

So Rhine's monograph is not important because of the new terms, concepts or theories it coined, because of the special kinds of cards or mathematical methods of evaluation used, or because of the design of his tests to separate pure telepathy from pure clairvoyance. Its major importance lies in the heavy emphasis it placed on rigorous experiments as the method by which to confirm the existence of a specific group of paranormal phenomena—telepathy and clairvoyance — and in its making the experimental method as fundamental in parapsychology as it was in other sciences.

The problem with many of the ESP explorations undertaken during the first 50 years of American parapsychology was the unconsidered question of how far psychic experiences or experimental results could be explained by chance. The approach described by Rhine's book, on the other hand, which determined what average might be expected from chance factors, made it possible to understand the extent by which actual results exceeded chance. Moreover, although fifty years of parapsychological research conducted by able scholars and scientists had preceded this monograph, nothing even came close to the sheer volume of experiments reported here with Linzmayer, Stuart, Pearce and five other subjects who had been not merely excellent but spectacular. There had been 85,724 trials which produced 24,364 hits, 7,219 more hits than could be expected according to chance. Some phenomenon caused this result and that something was a mode of perception which Rhine named "extra-sensory perception" or ESP,[339] an ability to be aware of something outside of one's self, the five senses or rational inference.

The objective of Rhine's experiments was to see if mathematical evidence of the existence of ESP could be produced and not to determine how widespread the ESP capacity was. But the work reported, nevertheless, bears on that question and makes the monograph additionally impressive. The remarkable number of successes which it reported and the estimate that one subject in every four or five displayed ESP capacity ran counter to the belief at that time that psychic talent was a rare gift; ESP seemed as common to people as the common cold.

The book also had domino effects. Any one experiment needs only to provide good enough data to stimulate an advance beyond its own first advance, and, if each succeeding experiment offers an improvement, the advance continues.[340] Rhine's monograph provided evidence good enough to bring on the next advance. It also led to constructive criticisms which, in turn, led to tighter ESP experimental situations in order to meet critical counterhypotheses.

Hullabaloo

"This is the book that started all the hullabaloo,"[341] wrote Rhine of his *Extra-Sensory Perception*. R.A. McConnell, research professor of biophysics at the University of Pittsburgh, was "inclined to think that the matter-of-factness of [Rhine's monograph] was a major, successful tactic in his plan to attract attention."[342] Of course, the purpose of publishing a book is to expose its subject to public gaze and consideration, but it is doubtful whether Rhine had ever planned originally to attract attention, certainly not the kind of uproar his monograph received. He had written the book, he said, only after "considerable deliberation" and "the results began to be so striking as to move some of my interested friends to urge publication."[343] Even then the volume was "obscurely published"[344] by a small parapsychological society in Boston whose literature was unknown and unread except by those who lived on the small and remote island of parapsychology.

Then, as Louisa Rhine recorded, "to everyone's surprise and probably to Banks' most of all, this supposedly inconspicuous little report was picked up and practically advertised nationally"[345] when the science editor of the *New York Times* of Sunday, May 20, 1934, dedicated the lion's share of his column, "This Week in Science," to telepathy and clairvoyance and Rhine. Waldemar Kaempffert said:

> From Duke University comes a report published by the Boston Society
> of Psychical [sic] Research, that gives an account of the most important
> study ever made of what is variously known as telepathy, mind-reading
> and clairvoyance communication. . . . [N]ever before has the Duke
> scale been even approached and never before has such analytical
> acumen been brought to bear on the results. . . . The man who under-
> took the formidable task of making 90,000 tests was Dr. J.B.
> Rhine. . . .[346]

Readers may wish to pause here to ask themselves what might have happened to the work in the Duke Department of Psychology if the right man had not been in the right place at the right time. That man was not Rhine; he was Waldemar Kaempffert, a member of the ASPR Board of Trustees, a friend of Hyslop and Prince, a strong ally of parapsychology who, at the crucial moment that *Extra-Sensory Perception* was published, was science editor of the most prestigious and influential newspaper in the country. If it had not been for Kaempffert's interest in the subject, and his willingness to read the publications of the BSPR, Rhine's monograph might have suffered from the same public neglect and scientific yawns that were the fate of Prince's Doris case that remained unknown because it was published by the ASPR.

It is perhaps to Kaempffert's lengthy and authoritative comments that the national attention Rhine's work received subsequently can be attributed. A review praising *Extra-Sensory Perception* appeared in *The New York Times:*

> At last Duke University has come boldly forward and backed Dr. Rhine
> in conducting the most important research of the century in his sub-
> ject. His approach to the subject of parapsychology is all that is to be
> desired. With the scientific care and precaution of a Pavlov he has made
> over 100,000 tests checked by competent assistants and recorded in the
> form of case reports, part of which are compressed into illuminating
> mathematical tables and charts. . . .[347]

The public eye was opened further in 1935 when *Man, the Unknown,* written by the French scientist Alexis Carrel, cited the work done by Rhine at Duke as establishing ESP: "Clairvoyance and telepathy are a primary datum of scientific observation. . . . [K]nowledge of the external world may come to man through other channels than sense organs."[348] In 1936, public interest was excited when *The Literary Digest* headlined its story: "Scientific Tests for Telepathy—Duke University Professor Finds Way to Entrap and Judge the

Frail Magic of 'Hunches' and Intuition. . . ." and went on to declare that: "Astonishing experiments have progressed to a point where private home tests are invited [with] a deck of twenty-five cards. . . ."[349] Public attention mounted even more as the *Times* again included Rhine's work in its "Topics of the Times Section"[350] and as another long article entitled "The Case for Telepathy—A Record of Some Remarkable Experiments" appeared in the glossy and respected *Harper's Magazine* with the exciting news that

> It is hardly too much to say that we may be travelling toward a revela-
> tion in the realm of mind more or less comparable to the revolution
> effected by Copernicus in the universe of matter. We may possibly be
> on the brink of marvel.[351]

Somewhat sensational perhaps, but understandable because in the 1930s science writers in America were on the lookout for new scientific topics that John Q. Public could assimilate. The success Rhine achieved at Duke and the remarkable paranormal capacities demonstrated by his subjects were exciting, startling and raised the question of whether everyone had psychic abilities. People wanted to know.

When Rhine got over his surprise at the surge of public interest in his work, he was as excited as the winner of a lottery. In one letter he wrote, he was especially pleased to notice that "'Epoch-making' seems to be a favorite word"[352] and that the world seemed "ready for the truth about mind and its larger meaning in the universe. It will be thrilling to be a part in the system of discovery that reveals it!"[353]

Since the general public seemed eager for education in the ESP experimental work at Duke, Rhine was prompted in 1937 to publish a popular version of *Extra-Sensory Perception.* His new book entitled *New Frontiers of the Mind*[354] was a description of the research that had been done at Duke. Rhine hoped that the readers of his book would "share something of the genuine excitement and joy of adventure"[355] which his work had brought him. To add to this excitement, and almost simultaneously with the publication of his new book in the fall of 1937, the Zenith Broadcasting Company started a series of broadcasts which Rhine helped to plan and which offered a vast listening audience ESP tests and dramatized stories in science.

At the same time, the Zenith broadcasts and the bookstores which carried *New Frontiers of the Mind* promoted Rhine's ESP cards, which were sold in packages reading "E.S.P. Cards for Testing Extra Sensory Perception, developed in Parapsychological Laboratory at Duke University, patent applied for by J.B. Rhine." Imagine mingling fun with science just by using these cards at home to see if one's mind could take the place of Western Union! The public loved the idea. Demand for the cards grew as thousands of people wanted to play this marvelous new parlor game to see how psychic they and their friends were. Rhine's book was a Book of the Month selection and became a national best-seller.

Eileen Garrett

The "hullabaloo" caught the ear of the Irish medium Eileen Garrett. She had met McDougall when, in her early days of apprenticeship, she was studying at the College of Psychic Science in London. Anxious to find out about the mechanics and meaning of her own psychic abilities, she offered herself for testing by Rhine. McDougall accepted her offer and, with the help of her sponsor, Frances Payne Bolton, she came to Durham in the spring of 1934. The medium was more than curious about her psychic abilities: She wanted to know whether her "controls," such as Uvani, who purported to be the spirit of a long dead Arab, were what they claimed to be or were "split offs" from her own personality. Hers was an attitude of absolute cooperation. She told the researchers: "I will do anything you ask if it is not harmful to me."[356] For his part, Rhine was interested to know how a first class medium with a world-wide reputation for honesty and psychic gifts would act when the experimental spotlight was turned on her.

The study of Mrs. Garrett proceeded along two avenues. One was a series of card-guessing tests for telepathy and clairvoyance while the medium was both in her trance and waking states. In the telepathy tests, use was made of different senders, sometimes in the same room with her, sometimes in another room. The results of these ESP tests, as might be expected, compared favorably to Rhine's best subjects. She did not, however, score well on the tests for clairvoyance; they were monotonous; packs of cards were cold, so unlike the sitters with whom she worked normally; and so, although after some days her scoring level was raised, it still remained below that of Rhine's subjects.[357] In the other branch of the study, Mrs. Garrett was tested for mediumship. In controlled sittings conducted by a graduate student in psychology named J.G. Pratt, there was a blind checking of records of Mrs. Garrett's statements and an application of mathematical criteria for judging the results which suggested ESP at work.

Of particular interest to Rhine was that, when Mrs. Garrett was in trance and Uvani was her control, his scores approached those of Mrs. Garrett in her normal state. Uvani scored high in the telepathy tests and low in the tests for clairvoyance. This suggested that he was, indeed, a "split off" from her own personality and that his psychic abilities were hers. Of equal, if not greater significance, the card-guessing experiments, especially in telepathy, showed how a medium's ESP could be used to obtain information and cast considerable doubt on the hypothesis that a medium's messages come from the spirits of the dead.

Rhine looked on the Duke experiments with Mrs. Garrett as "a turning point"[358] in the young history of parapsychology because it represented the first effort by an American university to test a medium under controlled conditions and because the experimental studies of her made Rhine even sourer toward claims of spirit communication than he had been after his disappointing encounters with Margery and Mrs. Soule.

Internal Storms

The sky over Duke's Department of Psychology had begun to darken even before Rhine's monograph was published. His colleagues, including Lundholm and Zener, were vexed because they believed that he was a danger to them in their work in the Department of Psychology. In April 1934, they wrote privately to McDougall, as head of the Department, that Rhine was making graduate students believe that their progress at Duke was conditioned on an active interest in parapsychology and was making his work and himself more important than the psychology program and the Department. McDougall was asked to take some steps to ensure that the Department would not be endangered and that students would not neglect psychology in favor of parapsychology.

On his discovery of this letter that was never meant for him to read, and which might have destroyed his work at Duke, Rhine's feelings were severely wounded. With a commendable avoidance of the frustration and shock he probably felt, he wrote to his complaining colleagues to express his awareness that "men of your position and culture must indeed have been violently alarmed, or else unendurably irritated, to have taken the action you seem to have done, especially to have done it in the secretive and circuitous way you selected." He tried to be as diplomatic as possible: "That I, my actions, or my fortunes should have engendered, however unwittingly, this unhappy result, is enough to warrant this concern of mine, and to move me to ask your cooperation in the interests of mutual satisfaction and general departmental good feeling."[359] He went on to assure them that he was willing to meet with them to settle all differences.

McDougall was inclined to agree with the complaint, suggested to Rhine that suitable precautions be taken against the danger and some of the storm clouds dissipated. But their threat and uncertainty over what other plot his colleagues might undertake to destroy his work forced Rhine, if he could get McDougall's support and that of the administration, to take shelter in a dream: the establishment of an institute for parapsychology which would be separate from the Department of Psychology yet would be part of Duke. Rhine persuaded the wealthy Frances Bolton, who was interested in parapsychology, particularly the survival question, to finance his dream. A fund to pay some of Rhine's salary, that of a research assistant and other expenses, was started in 1935 with money she supplied. In addition, through a suggestion of Worcester's, Rhine was able to obtain in the same year funds from Ellen A. Wood of Boston for the creation at Duke of two Walter Franklin Prince Fellowships in Psychology which would be used for the prosecution of some of the work of Rhine's project.

A base had been laid but a research organization with a special designation more or less independent of the Department of Psychology had yet to be constructed. Then another storm of resentment developed among Rhine's colleagues who now suspected that he had behaved unscientifically by promoting much of the "hullabaloo" himself. Scientists generally adhere to a standard of ethics that requires all research results to be reported initially to colleagues by means of scientific or scholarly publications and not first through the news media to the public. It was this standard that Rhine's cranky colleagues saw he was violating by going over their heads with reports directly to the press. They saw the publicity he was promoting as converting Duke University to the "University where Rhine is."[360]

So in 1935, Rhine was going to win no popularity contests judged by his colleagues in the Department of Psychology. It was now that he decided to ask the University administration and McDougall for permission to distinguish his research from the work his colleagues were doing.[361] He drew on the German word *Parapsychologie* — the principal term used in Europe to mark off the field — and, with McDougall's approval, the term "parapsychology" became the name for Rhine's ESP work. His laboratory was an anomaly. It was in the Department of Psychology but it did no teaching, offered no courses, gave no academic credit. Its research was carried on by an enthusiastic group of graduate students in psychology who were his assistants, including Pratt, Stuart and Sara Ownbey, but was conducted mainly with student workers who came and went. Yet, since it had been in existence as a going laboratory for several years, the "Parapsychology Laboratory" was not actually created at this time. Rather, its designation as such was approved at this time.

Although later, in 1947, the authorities at Duke finally agreed to sever the Parapsychology Laboratory from the Department of Psychology and to set it up as a separate agency with Rhine its Director, it was at this moment in 1935 that parapsychology became a recognized function within university walls in fulfillment of both McDougall's and Rhine's dreams.

It was as important to Rhine as it had been to Hyslop to have a means through which the work done by his organization would appear in print. Rhine wanted a scientific organ within the structure of Duke which would serve as a vehicle for first-quality research papers and find its way regularly into the libraries of academicians. It was to be a publication that would not only educate them but gain their respect for parapsychology. McDougall agreed and, when a private donor arranged to subsidize the publication, the *Journal of Parapsychology* was founded in 1937. It was the first initiative Rhine was to take in his desire to see parapsychology professionalized. Although he stood down as the *Journal's* editor in favor of Murphy in 1939, Rhine continued on its editorial staff for 40 years.

New Frontiers of the Mind, which Rhine wrote in 1937 to satisfy the popular demand for knowledge about ESP, is particularly interesting in that it reveals the charitable aspect of Rhine's nature. Although Zener and Lundholm had conspired against him, virtually threatened the continued existence of his laboratory and accused him of violating one of the fundamental rules of ethics in science, his book opened with an acknowledgment of the debt he owed them.

External Storms

The storm of dissension that confronted Rhine within the internal operations of the Department of Psychology was accompanied by another outside the Department, one triggered in part by the sensation caused by Rhine's work, in part by the supposition abroad shared by Rhine's colleagues that he had promoted the publicity, and in part by the general negative reaction to parapsychology by so many psychologists.

Rhine probably anticipated that some psychologists would be indifferent, especially those who considered ESP too trivial to waste time on when other subjects needed attention. He probably expected a positive reaction from Gardner Murphy and was not disappointed. And his preface to the monograph indicates that he anticipated a negative reaction to his introduction of his work to psychologists: "It is to be expected, I suppose, that these experiments will meet with a considerable measure of incredulity and, perhaps, even hostility from those who presume to know, without experiment, that such things as they indicate simply cannot be!"[362]

But he could not have foreseen the force of the storm of criticisms which fell in torrents on two principal areas: the mathematical methods he used to evaluate results and the conduct of the experiments.

Mathematical Methods

The mathematical techniques used by Rhine in the antichance evaluation of test results were not novel. Mathematics of probability had been used in the physical and biological sciences for years without objection. Moreover, in the development of his techniques, Rhine had the assistance of the Duke Department of Mathematics. Yet there were objectors—interestingly, all psychologists. Not a single mathematician questioned Rhine's methods.[363] Certain psychologists objected that the mathematics of probability used to evaluate the probability of the test results having been caused by chance were wrong and that chance had not been excluded as an explanation for the production of phenomenal scores by Rhine's subjects. They urged that, if the mathematics were not wrong, they were inapplicable, and, if right and applicable, then the mathematical statistics used for determing the deviation from chance were unacceptable. They said that statistics prove nothing, or, alternatively, that they can be used to prove anything, or that the test results had no statistical significance.

All the criticisms relating to mathematics and statistics, however, were largely laid to rest in 1937 by the Institute of Mathematical Statistics. Dr. Burton D. Camp, president of the Institute, released the following statement:

> Dr. Rhine's investigations have two aspects: experimental and statistical. On the experimental side mathematicians of course have nothing to say. On the statistical side, however, recent mathematical

work has established the fact that assuming that the experiments have been properly performed, the statistical analysis is essentially valid. If the Rhine investigation is to be fairly attacked it must be on other than mathematical grounds.[364]

Rhine was relieved:

> I have come to feel as much security in the general soundness of the research as is good for an investigator in science to have. . . . Among mathematicians the best authority is with us. . . . It is difficult to see what further mathematical criteria can be applied to evaluate the results of our tests. . . . Whatever we have claimed to be beyond chance has stood the tests and is safe.[365]

Conduct of the Experiments

So the mathematical storm subsided, but another had begun gathering. It is doubtful that Rhine was prepared for it. McDougall, who was acquainted with all the experiments, probably had disarmed Rhine when he wrote "my impressions are entirely favourable" and "the experimenters have been at special pains from the beginning to exclude, by the conditions maintained, any possibility of deception, conscious or unconscious."[366] But the storm broke in 1935 when Raymond R. Willoughby[367] of Brown University and others offered critiques of Rhine's work. Some of the critiques were unrestrained and made little if any effort to conceal their prejudices. Chester Kellogg of the Department of Psychology of McGill University wrote:

> Since Dr. Rhine's reports have led to investigations in many other institutions, it might seem unnecessary to prick the bubble, as the truth eventually will out and the craze subside. But meanwhile the public is being misled, the energies of young men and women in their most vital years of professional training are being diverted into a side issue and funds expended that might instead support research into problems of real importance for human welfare.[368]

There were British critics too. Eric Dingwall, for example, reached the conclusion that the American investigators were for the most part enthusiastic amateurs, who unfortunately lacked the necessary training to conduct experiments. . . . [O]ur colleagues in America should try to pay a little less attention to the statistical analysis of their results and should try to take the trouble, however arduous it may be, to train themselves properly to conduct [the experiments analyzed].[369]

Obviously, Rhine's work could be regarded as convincing and the conclusion warranted that ESP occurred only if there were no defects in his experiments. When we inquire of Rhine's monograph whether there were adequate safeguards, it lapses into a strange silence. One critic who reviewed the book complained that it was impossible to discover what the experimental conditions had been for any particular experiment.[370] Skeptics had not been persuaded because of Rhine's curious omission to demonstrate plainly the precautions taken and the conditions prevailing in the experiments. Questions were raised. Were errors made in recording? Were the experimenters trustworthy or competent? Were experiments carried out when the cards were visible to the subjects? If the backs of the cards were visible to them, could the symbols on the face of the cards have been identifiable somehow by looking at the backs? Thouless raised this last question so, in 1936, Rhine sent him two samples of one type of ESP card used in the experiments. On the blank faces of the cards had been stamped or stencilled the five familiar symbols. The backs of the cards were decorated in green with gilt and white borders.

When Thouless examined the packs one seemed acceptable to him. The other was highly objectionable, however, because, although the backs did not seem to have identifying marks, with a light shining on the backs of the cards their symbols could be seen through the backs. Thouless was able to identify nine cards with the light from a window, 14 by using a lamp with a 60 watt bulb hanging five feet over the table where the cards were placed, and 20 cards by using a 1000 watt projection lamp.

C.V.C. Herbert, the research officer of the SPR, examined another type of ESP card, produced by a card manufacturer and offered for sale to the public, on which symbols had been added by a lithographic process. When the cards were held at a certain angle in daylight, the symbols on almost every one were easily readable. The research officer commented that "critical examination of these cards shows that they fall very far short of the high standard which might reasonably have been expected."[371]

Defective ESP cards! Worthless results! Rhine responded to the attack at once. If he had described the method he and Zener had used at the beginning of their ESP experiments, the criticism would have been disposed of easily. Their method was to seal the cards in opaque envelopes and hand them to students who were invited to try to call the cards in the envelopes.[372] Clearly no sensory cues were possible when this method was followed. Unfortunately, in his later tests, Rhine often neglected to follow this precaution. All he could say therefore in answer to Herbert was that none of his conclusions about ESP had been drawn "without the security of covering series of tests in which the subjects had no sensory contact with the backs of the cards."[373] All well and good, but Rhine's reply seems insufficient because the research officer's criticism was not limited to experiments in which subjects were prevented from touching or seeing the cards. Rhine's experiments would be equally flawed if the experimenters themselves were able to read the symbols through the backs of the cards because they might, even inadvertently, whisper or otherwise convey information to the subjects.

Responsible criticism of research methods in parapsychology was and is extremely useful. The SPR research officer's observations are an excellent illustration of criticism which revealed serious shortcomings in Rhine's procedure prior to 1934 and made it necessary in future years to conduct ESP card tests in which better precautions were taken.

Rhine had no illusions about the American Psychological Association Convention in 1938 which was to discuss research methods in ESP. He saw it as "a heresy trial." "To mainstream psychologists, the idea that extrasensory knowing could occur was blatant heresy."[374] But Rhine, accompanied by Pratt and Joseph Greenwood, a mathematician, could not fail to appear in his own defense. In front of the hostile audience, Rhine seemed unusually nervous and spoke haltingly. His equally nervous wife who was present "thought from the point of view of structure, organization, and delivery, it was about the poorest speech I ever heard him make."[375] Yet his honesty and sincerity must have impressed his listeners because they applauded him more vigorously than anyone else who spoke.

As the storm over mathematics had ended after meetings of the Institute of Mathematical Studies had produced a favorable judgment in 1937, so the tempest over sensory leakage and errors in records was abated after Rhine and his critics discussed his experimental methods. The greater precautions of distance and the use of wooden screening and opaque envelopes against sensory cues satisfied some of the more vociferous critics. Other measures, such as conducting experiments in different buildings or separate rooms and checking and recording independently, also had a quieting effect. After the meeting, "The fact that the research staff returned to Duke with renewed confidence made it clear that the meeting was a victory for the new science."[376]

When we review Rhine's failure to use more rigorous methods, do we see another example of the hastiness demonstrated in his verdict on Margery? Rhine himself could not understand his failure. "As one looks back, he wonders continually, 'Why did we not see such and such a weakness?' Perhaps others in the same situation would have seen it. No one will ever know."[377]

Since Rhine's experiments were so loosely conducted, should the tests of the early 1930s be dismissed as worthless? Rhine himself raised the question.[378] To dismiss them all, however, would seem to be another act of hastiness because, although many of these experiments were done too rapidly in order to involve hundreds of subjects and complete thousands of trials, and many were exploratory only, many more reported in Rhine's monograph were sufficiently controlled to avoid the skeptic's damaging counterhypotheses. The more conclusive of Rhine's findings were based on the better tests of clairvoyance over which a strict control was maintained. The Pearce-Pratt experiments and the Pratt-Woodruff series, described in Pratt's cameo, are in this category. They remain a highly evidential part of the scientific case for ESP which even the most resolute and vocal critics of the present-day seem reluctant to attack.

In the Aftermath of the Storms: New Roles

In the decades following the 1930s storms of controversy, Rhine altered his role in the field of parapsychology. The pioneer experimentalist became author, lecturer, organizer.

In 1938, the Nazis annexed Austria and Franklin Delano Roosevelt was in his second term at the White House. For Rhine, that same year was "one of the hottest in the controversy between psychology and parapsychology"[379] because of the "heresy trial." It was this "trial" which probably brought about his transformation. It affected him so markedly that, after the APA symposium, his wife noticed that he had changed and he himself said "that since last September at Columbus . . . something vital [has] gone out."[380]

Rhine tried to find this something and found it both in filing cabinet drawers and in laboratory data which had been collected years before and in conferences with his staff on how best to counter the arguments against ESP which the APA symposium had forced into the open. Three important publications were the outcome of Rhine's search. Five years before the symposium, Rhine had begun precognition experiments in which the subject was to predict before the cards in a deck were shuffled the order they would be in after the cards were shuffled.

The ability to predict events before they have occurred seems to involve the impossible concept of an effect taking place prior to its cause. If backward causation is really involved in precognition, it is, in Rhine's words, "truly astonishing that science neglected the problem so long. Until the Duke research began in the fall of 1933 no systematic experiments on prophecy, so far as I am aware, had ever been conducted."[381] It was now in 1938 that Rhine decided to publish these significant experiments.[382]

In 1939, Rhine, together with Pratt and three members of the staff at the Parapsychology Laboratory, began preparation for an important work which would attempt, by collecting previously published material and careful and thorough analyses of it, to address the many objections against the acceptance of ESP. By 1940, with J. G. Pratt as the senior author, the Rhine group had produced *Extra-Sensory Perception after Sixty Years*.[383] Since its publication, a criticism of the book is that it is not easy to search out specific information in it yet it remains a major American work in the field. It presented for researchers mathematical tables and an explanation of experimental methods and methods of evaluating tests, and dealt with the controversial subject of ESP by reviewing all the experimental evidence together with 35 counterhypotheses.

Of particular interest in the monograph was its inclusion of the comments of leading critics who had been invited to express their criticisms. Their critical comments and the responses to them offered by the book gave interested readers a broad range of views. The book presented various experiments which met all counterhypotheses and rated the Pratt-Woodruff experiment as the best on the experimental list. The book was also interesting because of its report on the Ownbey-Turner ESP tests which, over a distance of 250 miles, achieved a 40 percent success rate compared with a 31 percent success rate over a lesser distance. These tests were significant, too, as examples of real or "pure" telepathy in that the subject was able to apprehend an agent's thought without any object present or used.

Rhine's work on clairvoyance, which implied some influence on a subject by an object, had suggested the possibility of some influence on an object by a subject. It was this reasoning that led to the experiments at Duke in psychokinesis, or the influence of "mind over matter." Or they could have been suggested by a man who came to Rhine's office one day. A gambler, he claimed that he could not only use his will power to influence the dice he threw so that he would win but that he could also influence others so that when they threw they lost. He then demonstrated some of his skill to the unbelieving Rhine. The name of the gambler has since passed into oblivion, but his visit started Rhine on psychokinetic experiments. He and Louisa Rhine worked on them together. Their experiments began as early as 1934, and from the start the scores were above chance, yet the results of the experiments were not published by the Rhines[384] until nine years later. Why weren't these experiments published earlier? Because, said Rhine, "Much as we desired to interest others in repeating the tests, we decidedly wished to avoid any publicity about our PK work. At the time, 1934 to 1937, the storms of controversy were rising over the ESP research reported in 1934, and we thought it best to withhold the PK work until that subsided...."[385] Louisa Rhine put it this way: "It had seemed a better strategy to let one bitter pill (ESP) be well swallowed before bringing on another."[386]

When Pearl Harbor was bombed, Rhine was ready to accept a commission in the Marine Corps. In May 1942 he went for a physical examination. It was not until the end of 1942 that he found out that he had been rejected. Disappointed, he went back to his work: more writing. In 1947, he published another popularization of his methods and findings in *The Reach of the Mind*.[387] Still wincing from the APA trial in 1938, he described his account as "heretical." Rhine began with a central question: "What are we human beings, you and I? No one knows.... Where does human personality belong in the scheme of things?"[388] Rhine described step by step the researches at Duke to establish ESP and PK as fundamental nonphysical properties of the human mind which transcend space and time and show the mind to have a wider reach into the universe than formerly supposed. Then he came to his real message: "Science does not ... accept ESP and PK as established ... there is simply no alternative to acceptance.... No other phenomenon in all the history of science has had so little recognition for so much experimental research [as ESP]...."[389] It was a message he was to repeat to the end of his life.

In the 1950s, Rhine gave frequent addresses. He spoke at the Royal Society of Medicine in London, at a chemical society in Chicago, and spoke frequently on college campuses. Stanley Krippner invited Rhine to lecture at the University of Wisconsin in 1953. After the invitation was accepted and the Forum Committee had agreed to bring Rhine, psychologists on the faculty were open in their hostility to the lecture. A professor of psychology told his students: "If you are interested in ESP, you might as well hear about it from the horse's mouth — and from the biggest horse's ass of them all." In spite of this hostility and a furious Wisconsin snowstorm, a thousand students packed the lecture hall to hear Rhine. After Krippner introduced him and Rhine spoke about his work with ESP, he received what he said "was one of the greatest ovations of his career."[390] This kind of enthusiastic response was not unusual. Although, as his critical wife noted, he was not a good lecturer, being "neither funny nor fluent" and generally talked too long,[391] Rhine had that sincerity and that something that captured his audiences.

In 1953 he attended a conference in Cambridge, England, on spontaneous cases and presented a paper there on research that had been done on them at Duke. From his point of view, however, as an experimentalist using objective methods of evaluation, these cases had limited weight. The value of any qualitative experience requires a subjective judgment which any other personal opinion can contradict. The only value he could see in spontaneous cases was that they provided a basis for experimental investigation of the experiences and for confirming in real life what the experimental data showed.

In 1953, also, Rhine wrote his fourth book, *New World of the Mind*.[392] This book was concerned with more than the mere evidence for ESP and PK and past and future research in these areas. It was an ambitious attempt to relate the findings of parapsychology to physics, biology, psychology, mental health and religion. In *Reach of the Mind,* Rhine had argued that the association between parapsychology and religion was theoretically "much the same as that of physiology to medicine, or that of physics to engineering."[393] He carried this theme forward ambitiously in *New World of the Mind* by arguing that the methods of parapsychology should be used in religion as a basis for faith. He maintained that all of religion's important problems were within methods of scientific inquiry. The efficacy of prayer, for example, could be tested empirically and falsified or verified. Rhine did not, however, show how one of religion's important claims, namely, life after death, could be tested. Indeed, he admitted that this was an area not amenable to experimental investigation. Nor did Rhine attempt to demonstrate how such investigation could possibly falsify or verify the existence of God.

The year 1955 quickly dispelled any thought that Rhine was safe from further criticism merely because the storms of the thirties had subsided and *Extra-Sensory Perception after Sixty Years* had, in 1940, rounded up all criticisms. George R. Price, a research associate in the Department of Medicine at the University of Minnesota, published an article in *Science*[394] in which he attacked Rhine and parapsychology. Following Hume, Price argued that, although fraud could not be proved in the claims made by Rhine, Soal, and parapsychology, it was more reasonable to think that fraud had occurred than that miracles had and that nature had gone out of her way. Whatever Rhine's real feelings about the charge, he struck a breezy pose in the reply he published in *Science:* "it is better to be attacked than it is to be ignored."[395] In addition, he wrote Price an explanation of his methods. Rhine's efforts evidently had the desired effect, for ultimately Price withdrew his allegations of trickery in a public apology.[396]

In 1957, Rhine, now known as JB to his colleagues and family, coauthored with Pratt *Parapsychology: Frontier Science of the Mind*[397] which defined terms, research methods, test procedures and statistical methods of evaluation, and was intended to fill the need for a textbook in the field of parapsychology. The book made assertions, such as: "It is, in fact, the manifestly nonphysical character of parapsychical phenomena that for the present constitutes their only general identifying feature and marks them off from the rest of general psychology"[398]; and "The evidence is now conclusive enough in parapsychology to leave no doubt that, so far as present concepts go, we are dealing with nonphysical principles and processes."[399] These observations gave Rhine a basis for rebutting materialism and giving human nature a transcendental quality. It was a revolutionary conclusion from which Rhine never retreated. But it was disquieting, especially for physicalists and reductionists in parapsychology who, rather than admit the validity of Rhine's conclusion, preferred to try to find explanations for parapsychological phenomena in the physical sciences, in particular and more recently, in quantum theory. They may or may not succeed. In the meantime, the jury is still out on the question of whether Rhine's assertion that parapsychological phenomena have been demonstrated conclusively to be nonphysical is valid.

In the same year that *Parapsychology: Frontier Science of the Mind* was published, Rhine again took the initiative to professionalize parapsychology as he had done some 20 years earlier in the creation of the *Journal of Parapsychology*. When, at the Parapsychology Laboratory, during the summer of 1957, he proposed to his students, staff and guest lecturers the idea of forming an organization for parapsychologists, Gertrude Schmeidler who was there said, "The idea was enthusiastically received.... An organizational meeting was held forthwith."[400] The Parapsychological Association, the first and only international professional organization of parapsychologists in the world, was formed. Cynics who believe that the organization was another instrumentality Rhine created in order to add to his own publicity, prestige and influence must be reminded that Rhine never accepted office in the organization and was content to remain its founder.

In the year that the PA was formed, Rhine had retirement on his mind. Louisa Rhine thought "that he's getting a little tired of the struggle of keeping the lab going. I would be very glad if he'd really turn over the reins and without regret when the time comes"[401] although he might continue to write or to guide research at the Parapsychology Laboratory.[402] And why not? His long-time colleague and assistant, J. Gaither Pratt, was there, waiting, ready to become his logical successor. But apparently the time for turning over the reins to Pratt had not yet come. Rhine was not ready to let go and more years went by.

In anticipation of his mandatory retirement from Duke as professor of psychology and in the face of an unwillingness by a now unfriendly Duke administration to allow the Parapsychology Laboratory to continue on its campus once Rhine had left, in 1962 Rhine founded in Durham the Foundation for

Research on the Nature of Man. He lodged the new research center, the library and equipment formerly used in the Parapsychology Laboratory, a staff, himself as executive director and his wife as director of research, in a big wooden building within hailing distance of Duke's campus. The FRNM's aim was the advancement of the understanding of the human being.

Rhine was deeply concerned that parapsychological research was moving at a very disappointing rate and that few young scientists were willing to enter the field on a full time basis.[403] Again, Rhine took the initiative, this time an educational one. Bright, young students were to be offered opportunities, through lectures by staff and guest speakers, review meetings and study programs to learn about research on psi problems. Through such meetings, which brought visitors from America and the world to Durham, and through such programs and research grants, Rhine was able to add to his stature as a leader in the field. He also conceived a research unit within FRNM to be called the Institute for Parapsychology which would be heir to the parapsychological program that had been carried on at Duke's Parapsychology Laboratory. Rhine saw it as providing a training ground for workers.

In 1965, the year of his retirement from Duke and a year after Pratt's depature, Rhine and his remaining associates published *Parapsychology from Duke to FRNM*[404] and in 1968 he coedited with Robert Brier *Parapsychology Today,*[405] which harvested papers presented at review meetings held by the Institute of Parapsychology as well as those which dealt with the significance of parapsychology for other fields. In 1971, he edited *Progress in Parapsychology,*[406] an extension of *Parapsychology Today* and another compilation of research reports presented at the Institute's review meetings.

At last, at 78 years of age, Rhine found a bright, enthusiastic youth to whom to turn over the reins. Walter J. Levy,Jr., was so devoted to parapsychology that he left medical school to work with Rhine. For three years, the young man conducted PK and precognition experiments with mice and birds at Rhine's laboratory. The positive results of these experiments were published in the *Journal of Parapsychology.* Levy showed not only competence as an experimenter but as an administrator as well. So in 1973, Rhine made him the director of his laboratory and retired officially—he thought. Unfortunately, Levy's competence included the ability to write a whole new chapter in the long story of fraud that began with the Fox Sisters and Madame Blavatsky and which was retold by the physical mediums from Eusapio Palladino to Margery—new because this time it was not the fraud of mediums but of an experimenter. For only a year after his appointment, and while using a computer and random event generator to test PK abilities in animals, members of the staff observed Levy doctoring data. The positive scores he had been reporting were the results of hits he had falsified. When Rhine was told he was "stunned."[407] It was, said Rhine, "the most distressing jolt I have had in many years."[408] Without hesitation, Rhine summoned Levy to his office. After he confronted Levy with the evidence which the latter was not able to refute, Levy resigned and left. Feeling great guilt at having put too much trust in his successor, Rhine forthrightly told the parapsychological community what had happened and disclaimed the scientific validity, not merely of those in which he had been caught, but of all experiments in which Levy had been involved.[409]

Unwillingly, Rhine resumed management of the affairs of his laboratory. But only temporarily, for in 1976 once again he turned over the reins of the Institute for Parapsychology, this time to K. Ramakrishna Rao, a psychologist and philosopher from Andhra University, who had worked on the research staff of the Duke Parapsychology Laboratory and, in 1965, had been president of the Parapsychological Association.

In 1977, a stroke hospitalized Rhine, but a year later he was able to appear in Washington, D.C., on the Smithsonian's program "Key Issues in Science Today" and to debate with Paul Kurtz, editor of the *Skeptical Inquirer,* in defense of parapsychology as a science.

In January 1979, at the annual meeting of the American Association for the Advancement of Science, John A. Wheeler, of the Center for Theoretical Physics at the University of Texas, proposed to AAAS authorities that they put "the pseudos out of the workshop of science" and, in a letter, asked them to disaffiliate the Parapsychological Association. When questioned, Wheeler supported his proposal by accusing Rhine, when he was a postdoctoral assistant to McDougall, of having intentionally altered the conditions in a Lamarckian experiment to produce spurious results. This incident of 50 years before was irrelevant to present day parapsychology. Moreover, Wheeler, like Price, eventually retracted his charge.

In the last year of his life, Rhine, following in the footsteps of James and Murphy, was elected to the presidency of the SPR.[410]

Six Last Questions

In this concluding section, we try to answer six intriguing questions which would engage all the resources of the Gallup poll for a year. One is: What manner of man was Rhine? He loved to relax with music, had a record library, played the accordion, violin, ocarina and mouth organ, and especially, liked to play "Meet Me in St. Louis, Louie," as he called Louisa Rhine. If Sara Feather, his oldest daughter, were asked, she would say admiringly that he was "an excellent model of the moral, healthy, and self-disciplined man. . . . I never knew him to do anything dishonest, unethical, or shoddy, nor to overindulge in any strong food or drink."[411] An interview with Elizabeth A. McMahan, for whom he was a friend and teacher, would describe Rhine as "a very kind and generous man . . . a believer in human dignity, justice, and the rights of the underdog."[412] Another interview with Jack Kapchan, who worked at Rhine's Parapsychology Laboratory, would underscore Rhine's kindness and generosity. Kapchan's father, an emigrant from the old country who spoke little English, for the rest of his life spoke of the great Rhine spending the entire day with him in gentle and gracious conversation.

But some — for example, one of his assistants who worked with him at

Duke for 30 years and who was said to have been summarily fired, or two highly trained parapsychologists whom Rhine brought from England to Duke on a three-year contract which he terminated abruptly after one year—might describe Rhine as a small and tyrannical idol placed on a high pedestal. A survey of four staff members who worked with him at the Parapsychology Laboratory, three of whom, Robert Morris, John Palmer and Rex Stanford, resigned, and one who was discharged in 1969, might corroborate this point of view. In the words of the one discharged, Rhine was "the most rigid, stubborn man I have ever known" and thought that a comparison between Rhine and Stalin was apt.[414] The following description, however, might characterize Rhine best. He liked to relate that Louisa Rhine was "the granddaugher of a German immigrant who was shipwrecked on Sandy Hook, clung to a mast all night, and lived to write a poem about his experience."[415] Rhine was a man who more than matched the stubbornness and grit of his wife's grandfather. For Rhine's life was, in effect, a determined clinging to the mast of parapsychology, a dogged spirit doing resolute battle, not with the elements but with hostile critics, resentful colleagues, the administration of Duke which refused further to support the Parapsychology Laboratory, a rebellious staff, charges of fraud and a scandal in his own laboratory at the very end.

Dictatorial, single-minded, resolute—J.B. Rhine was a powerful personality. He was for many a "charismatic father figure,"[416] a man of fire who lit fires in all those who came to his laboratory to work with or under him and who, because of Rhine, became leaders in the field. Dr. Rex Stanford, for example, although one of the young workers who joined the exodus of Rhine's staff in 1969, and today is a leader in parapsychology, admitted that "J.B. Rhine played a major role in my training. . . . Parapsychologically speaking, I owe my training both to independent effort and the wonderful encouragement and support provided me by JBR."[417]

Another question is: What was Rhine's impact and influence on parapsychology? Rhine did not invent the term "extrasensory perception." Others, including a German professor named Oskar Fischer, had used it before him. But, because of Rhine, ESP became and remains a household word. He placed Duke University on the map and still today, to the uninformed, Duke remains the center of parapsychological studies—although that would be a reputation it does not want. Just as "apple pie" is synonymous with "America" so does "parapsychology" suggest "Rhine." In Pratt's family tree of parapsychology, McDougall was the great-grandfather who urged the placement of parapsychology within the university.[418] Rhine, however, is the grandfather who brought the experimental side of psychical research to America, a man who, like his wife's shipwrecked grandfather, was autocratic and iron-willed, the very qualities that were needed to provide parapsychology, as he did, with its terms, concepts, theories, test procedures, research methods, statistical methods of evaluation and to give the field leadership. In Rao's language: "parapsychology is what J.B. Rhine did. It would be extremely hard, if not impossible, to imagine what parapsychology would have been if he did not exist."[419]

Rhine set out with his early subjects, ESP cards and statistics to prove the existence of an extrasensory ability to obtain knowledge that had been reported since antiquity but never really established. Our third question is: Has the existence of ESP been established? What is the consensus on this point? Many in parapsychology are now convinced of the reality of ESP. A large number of parapsychologists would agree with Rao: "The case for the existence of psi . . . is conclusive. . . . [T]here is no room for reasonable skepticism."[420] Senior parapsychologists, such as Thouless, are persuaded of the foolishness of trying to prove over and over again the reality of ESP.[421]

Yet today, a significant number of distinguished parapsychologists believe that there is no compelling evidence of ESP. John Beloff, for example, in his 1982 Presidential Address to the Parapsychological Association, said that one of the still open and most important questions was whether psi exists and that it "has tormented me all my life. . . . [E]ven the strongest parapsychological evidence is, by common consent, unsatisfactory and defective in one or more respects. Hence, until such a time as the evidence for psi becomes overwhelming, it will always be more rational to doubt than to believe."[422]

If it be granted that negative or controversial evidence which has fallen short of conviction for people in parapsychology provides justifiable grounds for doubting the existence of psi, then it becomes necessary to reconsider what might be called the majority view of the senior parapsychologists. It may mean, difficult as the pill may be to swallow, backtracking to Rhine's original goal of proving the existence of ESP by applying research standards higher than we have now so that evidence will be more airtight. The form of this research need not revert to mere card-calling again or even be traditional. But whatever its design, it seems highly profitable for those who study ESP to search again for outstanding subjects as did Rhine and to recognize that not since Duke has there been collected in one place and at one time such a spectacular array of gifted subjects whose successful scores were phenomenal.

So a fourth question arises now that students of ESP are aware both that ESP results are hinged to subject-experimenter relations and that Murphy theorized that paranormal events arise from an interpersonal psychical field which requires not only subjects but a happy combination of conditions and persons around them. The question is: Why did Rhine and his staff obtain positive ESP data from a higher proportion of subjects than has ever been obtained by anyone else either in America or Europe? What kind of interpersonal relations were there in those early years that we might recapture in order to make newer research more effective and future evidence more convincing? What in the atmosphere and in the work at Duke stirred in Professor McConnell "a little of the same awe and disbelief that I feel toward the Italian Renaissance?"[423]

If that ingredient was Rhine's dogged spirit, then it is gone forever. But we cannot be sure. For this reason his *Extra-Sensory Perception* continues to have a value for us. Why should we pay attention to this 50 year old book? And for whom should it have any value? Rhine himself answered:

> I should place the main value of the book in the fact that it reports a unique situation that needs to be re-examined by the student and worker in parapsychology today, young or old. It seems clear, to me at least . . . that we had in those early years at Duke a very special situation and it was largely responsible for the unusual and unequalled production of results in ESP experiments. . . . [The value of the report is that it tells us what we] want to know today—how in spite of the monotony of the procedure, how well . . . we were able to keep those early subjects scoring well . . . and what sort of program we had that kept so many productive for so long. What we would not give today for the like of that? I think any worker in the field today would say the same.[424]

In view of the unending debate over the reality of ESP, Rhine's monograph is one that should be read and reread not only because it reported spectacularly successful scores but because it continues to mirror for us an experimental environment filled with enthusiasm, confidence, team work and mutual friendships that may have been conducive to these scores. Where do we have such an atmosphere today?

A fifth question is: Was the establishment of psi the single aim to which Rhine devoted his life? It is not possible to study Rhine and still believe that the sole motivation of his work was the development of experimental and statistical methods for proving the existence of extrasensory abilities. On the contrary, he said of his work that it was "motivated largely by what may be termed an interest in its philosophical bearing—by what it can teach us of the place of human personality in nature."[425]

Rhine was convinced that at times the human mind is able to transcend physical limitations and that the human personality contains a factor which is nonphysical, not a "soul" in the theological or philosophical sense but what he called a "psychological soul."[426] Through scientific methods, a discovery had been made which thousands of years of preaching, theory and argument had not been able to make, and, for him, the discovery represented "the turning of the tide of three centuries of domination of our science of human nature by physicalistic theory."[427]

For the Bible-thumping teenage Rhine who later was caught in intellectual conflict over his beliefs and abandoned his plan to become a minister, the implications of this discovery were clearest for religion, whose fundamental teaching is that there is a spiritual element in the human being. Experimental evidence of this element, while perhaps unnecessary for the followers of religious authority, would be greeted warmly, he thought, by all intelligent people who had, as he had had, agonizing doubts about religion. The nonphysicality of the human mind might be extended to the hypothesis of a nonphysical world consisting of many such minds cooperating or even to a larger oversoul.

But if religion and parapsychology were to intersect anywhere it must be at the problem of what the former calls immortality and the latter simplifies into the question of whether some element of the human being continues for any length of time after physical death. I have called attention to the loss of interest in this subject by modern parapsychologists[428] which I think is due, in part, to an entirely wrong interpretation of their leader's attitude vis-à-vis survival. Such an interpretation is understandable since Rhine stated more than once that the "survival question is a very, very difficult one"[429] and because Rhine elected to focus only on experimental methods to study ESP and PK. Indeed, in the principal works he authored or coauthored, *Extra-Sensory Perception* and *Extra-Sensory Perception After Sixty Years,* the survival question is totally ignored. The appearance he gave of disinterest in the survival question was so convincing that even people such as Mrs. Bolton and Charles Ozanne, both of whom were keenly interested in survival, grew tired and impatient with him. Ozanne, for example, had promised Rhine a sizeable bequest for survival research. But, when he perceived Rhine using his laboratory at Duke for what seemed trivial nonsurvival areas of investigation, he used his funds in 1960 to create another organization in Durham which was to do survival research.

In reality, however, Rhine believed that the survival problem ought not to be neglected, for survival of any element of the personality for any length of time would be so consequential for human thought and emotion as to pale any other discovery into insignificance. He believed that the kind of evidence which had been collected by earlier investigators, such as Hodgson, Hyslop and Prince, merited close attention and made out a possible case for survival. "So important a block of evidence relating to so significant an issue constitutes in itself a starting point for research. Accordingly, we must turn to the problem of survival, even though we intend also to pursue with unabated energies the main lines of the psi investigations."[430]

While Rhine did not believe the moment was at hand for an *experimentum crucis,* and he was never willing to make any direct assault on the problem, he engaged in preliminary skirmishes with it. His ESP and PK researches were definitely flank attacks designed to wipe out some initial difficulties and to establish a beachhead for some of the factors survival involved. Rhine explained this intention clearly in passages which seem to have been overlooked.

> Consider first the favorable bearing of ESP-PK research on the survival hypothesis. If logic alone could be trusted, the evidence of ESP would go far to establish the survival hypothesis on logical grounds. . . . [W]hen ESP was found to function without limitation from time and space, this discovery was taken to mean that the mind is capable of action independent to some degree of the space-time system of nature. Now, all that immortality means is freedom from the effects of space and time; death seems to be purely a matter of coming to a halt in the space-time universe. Therefore the conclusion that there is at least

some sort of technical survival would seem to follow as a logical derivation from the ESP research. . . . We *can* say that the ESP research directly raises the question of the place of personality in the system of space and time, and it offers a positive suggestion in favor of survival. Even if there had never been a previous formulation of the problem of survival, it would have emerged from the ESP research.[431]

Rhine was a colossus who overshadowed the field of parapsychology for more than 50 years. It is understandable, therefore, that there should have been many accounts of his life and work, and that, as one circles a giant statue at dusk and sees its aspects change with each darkening moment, many different views of Rhine should be possible. These have been afforded by the historians Mauskopff and McVaugh,[432] by Rhine's authorized biographer,[433] by Louisa E. Rhine, his wife and partner,[434] and by his daughter and colleagues.[435]

This portrait of Rhine can be concluded with one more aspect. A few weeks before he died, I went to see him in Durham. It was raining when I arrived at the big old house and found Rhine seated and waiting in the solarium. He still looked powerful with his bushy eyebrows slanted over his eyes. As we talked, with Louisa Rhine silent but attentive in the room, it was plain that, in spite of his failing hearing and near blindness, the former Marine sergeant was still in charge and possessed a mind that was still active, critical and acute, yet thwarted, troubled and still grappling with a problem it had not been able to solve after 50 years: the nonacceptance of ESP and PK. In spite of all his work, science, as determined in 1979 as it had been many years before when he began his work, still refused to recognize these phenomena and persisted in regarding the frontier science investigating them as a pseudo-science. There was regret in his voice as he blamed himself:

"We overlooked many things. We failed to know how to convince people. We assumed it would all be accepted." Then he raised a challenging query which might be adopted as our own sixth question: "What does the world need to know to remove this blockage to acceptance?"

Rhine died on February 20, 1980. As she helped him into bed, Rhine's final words to Louisa Rhine were, "The work must go on."[436] It probably will go on but can be effective work only if we can answer Rhine's last question.

5

Harassment and Contemporary Parapsychology (1981–1987)

Commentary

The fourth period of American parapsychology ended in 1980. An account of significant happenings since then carries the history forward.

The current period is similar in many ways to the prior ones. Parapsychology continues to attract bright young workers as it had before, but, as before, funds are not sufficient to support them in the field and they are forced to carve out their professions elsewhere.

Parapsychology continues to be an outpost under seige but is even more beleaguered now than at any time in the past. CSICOP, its most formidable opponent whose *Skeptical Inquirer* has a circulation over twenty times that of the *Journal of Parapsychology*, consistently assails parapsychology as a "pseudoscience" and lumps it with UFOs, astrology and the Loch Ness monster. Professional magicians, such as James Randi, a founder of CSICOP, use conjuring tricks to test the alertness and procedures of parapsychologists and to expose them to ridicule and loss of financial support when the hoaxes are not detected. Parapsychology still encounters negative attitudes from academic psychologists which range from indifference to aloofness.

As before, parapsychologists are targeted for the same criticisms of experimental procedures that were aimed at Rhine, and, as before, many of their criticisms evidence the familiar forms of neglect or falsification of facts for which Hyslop denounced Muensterberg and Jastrow. But, in this fifth period of American parapsychology, the harassing fire and the determined attacks are from a new generation of psychologists who are more rational, systematic and deadly in their criticisms. Ray Hyman's detailed critique published in 1986 is an example. Even more serious for parapsychology is the fact that criticisms do not proceed only from strangers to the field who are not researchers, as in earlier times. Researchers themselves, such as Charles Akers and Susan Blackmore, have begun to pound parapsychology with criticisms of their own. Taken together, these battering criticisms pose in the fifth period a grave threat to the continued identification of parapsychology as a science as distinguished from a cult.

But to these discouraging differences encouraging ones may be added. "Remote viewing" and Ganzfeld methods hold out the prospect of meeting one of the chief criticisms of parapsychology by producing the repeatable experiment; computers make possible more accurate research; new models of psi and new hypotheses are being tested; fair and accurate surveys of research in parapsychology are beginning to find their way into highly regarded journals such as *American Psychologist;* attempts to form links with other disciplines are being made; the founding of the Koestler Chair of Parapsychology at the University of Edinburgh with its prospect of a new center of parapsychology in Europe offers a rare opportunity for broadening and strengthening contact between American and European parapsychology; a center to advance understanding of the field by making available information about parapsychology has been established; the Parapsychological Association grows with an emphasis on increasing international representation.

The record of fifth period events will be followed by cameos of Laura Dale and Louisa E. Rhine, both of whom died in this period, and by self-portraits drawn by Gertrude R. Schmeidler and Montague Ullman, two notables whom it was my good fortune to interest in writing autobiographical pieces for this section of the book.

The period which saw parapsychology established as a science and with growing prestige ended with the deaths of Murphy and Rhine. Although they died in the physical sense, their influence and impact continue in the research centers at Durham and New York and affect not only those who worked with them as colleagues but also those who came later into the structures where their presences still linger. Under them, or because of them, many of the current leaders in parapsychology were trained. In order to help readers keep abreast of contemporary figures and work in parapsychology, I sent inquiries for information about careers and interests to a sample of 30 members of the Parapsychological Association which included these leaders, those whose names are cited in the Chronological Narrative for the fourth period of American parapsychology, and others who have made or continue to make contributions to its development.

Of the 30, 27 (of whom 15 have been presidents of the Parapsychological Association) have answered. The personal and professional data supplied by these respondents are incorporated in brief portraits in Chapter 6, which follows the self-portraits of Drs. Schmeidler and Ullman. These portraits provide a representative and high level sample of professional American parapsychology, and will be useful in the fostering of regional and inter-regional networks for cooperation and sharing of ideas and information not only among other parapsychologists but interested readers outside of parapsychology, and also for improving communications with scientific and academic communities which lack information about the parapsychological community.

Chronological Narrative

1980

On the dissolution of the A.W. Mellon Educational and Charitable Trust, which had funded R.W. McConnell's work at the University of Pittsburgh since 1952, a final grant of $360,000 was made by the Trust to support his work.

1981

On the sudden death on October 25 of Arthur C. Twitchell, Gertrude Schmeidler succeeded to his post as ASPR president.

A need for useful information about parapsychology was filled when a Parapsychology Sources of Information Center was established in Dix Hills, New York, by Rhea A. White, who is its director. Its object is to collect, catalogue and index all English language books, journals and periodicals dealing with parapsychology as well as Jungian psychology, humanistic and transpersonal psychology and mysticism. The information center runs computerized searches of authors and subjects and compiles bibliographies for researchers.

Stanley Krippner, director of the Saybrook Institute in San Francisco, who had travelled in prior years to the Soviet Union to encourage dialogue between Soviet researchers and Western investigators, undertook another trip to the People's Republic of China with the same purpose. He and Harold Puthoff of the Stanford Research Institute, who accompanied him, were informed by Chinese researchers about the "extraordinary function of the human body," i.e., the ability of adolescents to recognize Chinese ideograms with their ears.

Among the objectives of *The Zetetic* and *The Skeptical Inquirer,* the official publications of the Committee for the Scientific Investigation of the Claims of the Paranormal, were the open and objective examination of all claims of the paranormal which were not to be rejected on *a priori* grounds. Within five years of the formation of the organization, serious questions were asked by some of its members about how fair, open and objective CSICOP's inquiries were and whether the inquiries were not controlled by a "will to disbelieve" to the same extent as the parapsychologists CSICOP attacked were controlled by a "will to believe." Internal dissension led to resignations, including that of Marcello Truzzi, a sociologist from Eastern Michigan University. He resigned as editor of *The Zetetic* and from CSICOP's Executive Council to establish a Center for Scientific Anomalies Research to encourage responsible scientific study and evaluation of claims of anomalies and paranormal phenomena. Its stated goal was "to promote open and fair-minded inquiry that will be constructively skeptical."

1982

This year marked the twenty-fifth anniversary of the creation of the Parapsychological Association by J.B. Rhine and the one hundredth anniversary of the SPR. To commemorate both anniversaries a Centenary-Jubilee Conference was held at Trinity College, Cambridge, England. Researchers from the Space-Medico-Engineering Institute of the People's Republic of China attended the conference to begin a dialogue with Western investigators and to describe experimental studies of the "extraordinary function of the human body."

Since the founding in 1976 of the Committee for the Scientific Investigation of Claims of the Paranormal, attacks against parapsychology had been mounted from platforms outside the field. Highly critical articles appeared in *The Humanist,* the organ of the American Humanist Association, and in *The Zetetic* and *The Skeptical Inquirer,* both publications of CISCOP. Direct confrontations between skeptics and believers in psi phenomena were rare, the only one reported having been a public debate on the scientific status of parapsychology conducted in Washington, D.C., in 1978 between J.B. Rhine and professor Paul Kurtz, cochairman of CSICOP and now editor of *The Humanist.* It was, therefore, a significant feature of the Conference at Trinity College that it provided critics, such as Professor Ray Hyman of the Psychology Department of the University of Oregon, with the opportunity to enter the precincts of parapsychology in order to confront parapsychologists directly with their case against it. In a crowded symposium, they stressed the constant and mounting criticisms against parapsychology: nonrepeatability of phenomena, the "experimenter effect" in which the data seem to be artifacts of some experimenters but not others, methodological and statistical flaws in experiments claimed to be convincing or conclusive evidence of psi. Although parapsychologists congratulated themselves on what they believed to have been a constructive dialogue with their critics, in reality no issues were resolved and critics were far from silenced.

Announcement was made of a Soviet-American exchange program established by Esalen Institute of Big Sur, California, to encourage scientific cooperation and sharing of parapsychological information between Russia and the West.

R.W. McConnell, research professor of biophysics at the University of Pittsburgh, began the direct distribution to scientists and libraries in the United States and sixty countries of books on parapsychology he had published. The purpose of the distribution was to advance the progress of parapsychology by making information about the field available to readers outside it. Within the next year and with some of the funds provided by the Mellon Trust, he would distribute 4800 gift books.

A new journal, *Psi Research,* was founded by Larissa Vilenskaya, a parapsychologist who emigrated from the Soviet Union to the United States and was published by the Washington Research Center and Foundation for Human

Sciences in San Francisco. The journal focussed on experimental results and theoretical papers with an emphasis on studies in the Soviet Union, Eastern Europe and China.

1983

Laura Dale, highly respected researcher at the ASPR and under whose long editorship JASPR grew to become a respected scientific organ, died on February 3.

Louisa E. Rhine, who came to Duke University with her husband and worked with him for 60 years, and who was the author of many scholarly papers and popular books on parapsychology, was dead on March 17.

Parapsychology Abstracts International, a semiannual publication of abstracts from both English and non-English journals and from articles on parapsychology in reports, theses and books and nonparapsychological publications, was founded by Rhea A. White and published by the Parapsychology Sources of Information Center.

1984

K. Ramakrishna Rao left the Institute for Parapsychology on extended leave to become vice chancellor of Andhra University. Richard S. Broughton became acting director of research for the Institute.

Internal critics now took their places on the firing line to take potshots at parapsychology. Charles Akers, who had worked in the Institute for Parapsychology, surveyed 54 of the most important ESP experiments and exposed methodological flaws in them ranging from recording and statistical errors to cheating by subjects and sensory leakages.[1]

Rhea A. White resumed the editorship of JASPR which, after Laura Dale's death, had been held by Carolee Werner.

Dr. Robert H. Thouless, an eminent British psychologist and honorary president of the Survival Research Foundation, who had devised a test to establish strong evidence of his survival after death, died on September 25. He left two messages, unbreakable by any rational process, enciphered with secret keys which he intended to communicate after his death.

1985

The most ambitious experiment conducted to investigate the question of survival after death was begun in this year by the Survival Research Foundation in an attempt to see whether Thouless's correct keys could be obtained in order to allow his messages to be read. A committee of academicians was appointed and offers of money prizes for the correct keys were broadcast throughout America and Europe.

The presidency of the ASPR passed from Gertrude R. Schmeidler to Howard M. Zimmerman, a member of the Board of Trustees.

Since much of the research in parapsychology either is presented inaccurately or not at all in writings by psychologists, it was a significant occasion when the American Psychological Asociation, through its organ, *American Psychologist,* permitted the publication of a paper critical of critics in psychology who were guilty of neglect or distortions in their writings with respect to parapsychology. The paper, by Irvin L. Child of Yale University's Department of Psychology, was illustrated by a description of how the dream telepathy experiments at the Dream Laboratory at Maimonides Medical Center had been ignored or misrepresented in the journals read by psychologists.[2]

But the gain afforded by the year was offset by a loss: 1985 became the year when parapsychologists, led by a conjurer, suffered the St. Louis Blues. James Randi (self-styled as "The Amazing Randi"), who called himself a "professional charlatan" and who maintained that parapsychologists were lax and not capable of establishing adequate protocols for their experiments, sent to the McDonnell Laboratory for Psychical Research established at Washington University in St. Louis other conjurers who posed as subjects. They were to test the laboratory in an experiment named "Project Alpha" carried out from October 1979 to January 1983. In 1983, Randi revealed to the press and on televison that he and his magician confederates had deceived the Laboratory into accepting spurious evidence of psychic abilities. The news media hailed the debunking as successful. In August 1985, financing for the Laboratory stopped, and it closed. The incident stressed the need for parapsychologists to impose greater precautions against fraud and to learn the tricks and techniques of conjurers.

Under the will of Arthur Koestler, the gifted author famous for *Darkness at Noon* and other writings, in 1983 a Koestler Chair of Parapsychology was endowed with £500,000 at the University of Edinburgh in Scotland. It was the first professorial position of its kind in Britain. In 1985, the first holder of the chair was an American, Dr. Robert Morris, until then senior research scientist at the School of Computer and Information Science, Syracuse University, New York. An opportunity arose for the fostering and strengthening of international links.

1986

Hard on the heels of this appointment came another. William George Roll, project director of the Psychical Research Foundation, assumed the post of professor of psychology and psychical research at West Georgia College, a senior college in the Georgia university system. The establishment of this professorial position represented a further extension of the grasp of parapsychology on the American academic community.

The interdisciplinary approach to the subject-matter of parapsychology initiated by the Parapsychology Foundation in 1951 was carried further by the Survival Research Foundation with its initiative to convert the question of the survival of consciousness after death from a relatively minor topic of investigation by a few parapsychologists working in isolation into an interdisciplinary and intercultural problem. Through the formation of its scholarly and scientific affiliate, the International Institute for the Study of Death, there was organized on an international scale the first institution whose purpose was to bring together professionals from different disciplines and cultures to interact on the premise that only through the multidisciplinary and multicultural study of the subject of death and the question of its survival that the possibility exists of developing new insights and innovative methodologies for attacking the problem.

With the publication of an article in the prestigious *Proceedings of the Institution of Electrical and Electronic Engineers,* Hyman again peppered parapsychology with damaging criticisms.[3] He argued that the best cases that seemed initially to offer evidence of psi have always been cast aside as later parapsychologists discover defects in them and replace them with new cases. New lines of research are continuously replacing old ones until the former also fade away. For over 100 years, he said, there has been no repeatability and the evidence is noncumulative. However, although he lashed out at several experiments which have been discredited by subsequent parapsychologists, such as S.G. Soal's, he struck not one blow against the Pearce-Pratt experiments or the Pratt-Woodruff series which parapsychologists continue to consider among the strong features of their case for ESP.

Before the year was out another internal critic fired away at the field in which she worked. After negative results over several years of ESP and out-of-body experiments, Susan Blackmore, a researcher from the University of Bristol, voiced her conviction that psi phenomena do not occur.[4]

Ian Stevenson, the holder of the chair created in 1967 at the University of Virginia School of Medicine to carry on parapsychological research, resigned from the Parapsychological Association, and the parapsychological unit, theretofore known as the "Division of Parapsychology," was now called the Department of Behavioral Medicine and Psychiatry.

1987

For three years, the Institute for Parapsychology was guided by Richard S. Broughton. However, K. Ramakrishna Rao returned from India in December to assume the Directorship of the organization. While in India, he was successful in establishing a new parapsychological research center at

Andhra University called the Institute for the Study of Yoga and Consciousness.

In the same month that Rao returned, the case against parapsychology, gradually strengthened by a series of systematic criticisms over a decade, reached its climax in a decision by the National Research Council, an arm of the National Academy of Sciences created to harmonize the work of engineers and scientists in government, industry and academia. All issues were resolved decisively in favor of the critics when a committee of the National Research Council promulgated a report, "Enhancing Human Performance," in which it was concluded that there was "no scientific justification from research conducted over a period of 130 years for the existence of parapsychological phenomena."

While this determination could not have been unexpected and arguably might even have been justified in view of the spirited attacks both from within and without against the quality of experimental parapsychological evidence, the judgment must be likened to that of a star chamber proceeding since it was rendered without any opportunity for the Parapsychological Association or any member of the parapsychological community to have a day in court. The only representation afforded parapsychology by the National Research Council was in the person of committee member Ray Hyman, who was its accuser and most vociferous critic.

Laura Abbott Dale: A Cameo

Background and Qualities

Laura Abbott Dale, the daughter of Dr. Lawrence Fraser Abbott and Winifred Buck Abbott, was descended from a famous New England family. Her grandfather, the Reverend Dr. Lyman Abbott, was coeditor with Henry Ward Beecher after the Civil War of the nondenominational religious weekly *The Outlook*. Her father took over publication of *The Outlook* after his father's death and persuaded his friend Theodore Roosevelt to become a contributing editor. He was also an acquaintance of Calvin Coolidge.

Between father and daughter there were ties of blood, not bonds of love, but from him she received poise, cultivation and a beautiful speaking voice and diction. In fact, her charm and stimulating conversation were so fascinating that it was thought that they had adverse effects on ESP test scores. Subjects who were greeted by and who talked with her before starting their experiments scored consistently below chance as if the experiments were to them unwanted intrusions on a pleasurable experience.

Laura Dale

A Career in Parapsychology

He was Hans, the musician, and she, a pianist and teacher of piano. They were in love and were to marry in the 1930s. Then, suddenly, he died, possibly of a brain tumor, and Laura Abbott was alone. Later she married and became Laura Abbott Dale. Divorced and childless, she accepted a positon with a rich woman in whose house she lived while she gave her patron piano lessons. Soon "loud cracking noises began to come from furniture, apparently in drawers."[2] These and other poltergeist phenomena induced Laura Dale to seek out Gardner Murphy in 1941.

On Saturdays she discussed parapsychology with him and others, such as Montague Ullman and Jule Eisenbud. She worked with Murphy on some projects and, under his guidance, started a serious examination of parapsychological literature, became a member of the ASPR staff in 1941 and thus began her long career in parapsychology. It was as if she left her old world behind.

Behind the reorganization of the ASPR after the "palace revolution" of 1941 loomed the figure of Murphy who returned to it its lost reputation and rededicated it to the standards of Hyslop from which it had deviated. Murphy would have been as effective in this process of reorientation, however, as a scissors with one blade if it had not been for Laura Dale. A follower of the high scientific standards set by the founders of the SPR (often she referred to "the glorious Eleanor Sidgwick"), Dale was the second cutting edge. Murphy acknowledged her role. "The most important thing about the revolution," he said, "was that it had brought into play the full intelligence and energy of Laura A. Dale, who became, and who has ever since remained, the primary research worker of the organization, to whose imagination, energy, and skill most of its effective contribution since that time has been due."[6]

Medical Section

From the weekly Saturday sessions that began in 1941, a Medical Section of the ASPR was organized seven years later to adapt clinical techniques to parapsychology. Among the psychiatrists who belonged to it were Jan Ehrenwald, Jule Eisenbud, Montague Ullman and others. Laura Dale was its secretary, its critic and its "catalyst."

Research

Laura Dale was a vigorous and productive researcher. In papers she coauthored with Ernest Taves, Joseph Woodruff, Montague Ullman and Gardner Murphy, she demonstrated wide-ranging interests: psychokinesis,[7] psychogalvanic response,[8] concentration versus relaxation in relation to telepathy,[9] attitudes of experimenters and subjects relative to ESP scores,[10] dowsing,[11] and current topics in parapsychology.[12] She collaborated with Montague Ullman in his pilot dream telepathy experiment[13] which led later to his work at Maimonides Hospital.

Laura Dale's name used to be associated with the myth of the greedy king of Phrygia who was granted by Dionysius his fervent wish to turn into gold everything he touched. Dale came to realize that she had the "Midas touch in reverse."[14] In this way did she describe the "decline effect," the sad experience of many experimenters, with which the literature of parapsychology abounds. If ESP evidence can be compared to gold, all Dale and other experimenters touched turned from initial positive (golden) results into dross—a decline from successful scoring to mere scoring at chance. The possibility was that this Midas touch effect was the result of elements at work other than chance, particularly psychological conditions such as a subject's boredom, trying too hard, or decrease in motivation. Dale urged further studies and herself undertook further investigations of these variables which might govern the reverse Midas touch.[15]

Spontaneous Cases

In addition to quantitative investigations, Laura Dale was interested in spontaneous experiences. In 1946, she examined spontaneous experiences reported by over 100 persons responding to a questionnaire sent by the ASPR in 1945, and she also discussed 110 cases of the "borderland" type presented in *Phantasms of the Living.*[16] Some years later, Dale examined more psychic experiences that had been selected out of approximately 1,000 that had been reported to the ASPR after an article on ESP appeared in *This Week* magazine in March 1950.[17] She also discussed other cases from time to time.[18]

She was present in 1955 at Cambridge when Murphy called for a resurgence of interest in spontaneous cases and joined with him in casting out a net for fresh ones. The 17 best cases, culled out of the 1200 letters received in response to articles published in a Sunday supplement which appeared in 1957, were analyzed and reported by them.[19] The collection of these cases was the culmination of skillful investigations. As Dr. Schmeidler said,

> Laura's investigations of spontaneous cases were superb. Success in following up a spontaneous case requires the difficult combination of friendly persuasion (to obtain further important information from witnesses) with hard critical thinking (to know which questions need answers), and careful wording of those questions so that none should be leading. Laura's delightful letters, so appreciative and concerned and so clear in their inquiries, elicited the details that were needed; and her charm and interest elicited similar cooperation in interviews. The critical acumen that made her such an excellent editor was equally useful in searching out possible evidential flaws in any spontaneous case. Her case reports are models of their kind.[20]

Survival

Perhaps out of her desire to know whether her lost fiancé had not perished absolutely, survival after death was another of Laura Dale's interests.[21] She had sittings with mediums, her object, always in the tradition of the scientific investigators, to obtain evidential material. She also conducted psychometry sittings.[22] Dorothy Wenberg, a member of the ASPR, who organized and carded its library, knew Laura Dale and wrote me of another attempt she had made to get evidential material from a medium:

> It seems that grieving women often make sort of a shrine by placing a vase of flowers in front of the photograph of a dead loved one. So, even if a medium told them this, it would hardly be evidential. So, what did Laura do? She placed, not flowers, but an apple in this position. No "hits."[23]

Hodgson and Hyslop openly wore survivalist badges on their lapels. Laura Dale gave no clear demonstration of whether she accepted or rejected the survival hypothesis. Mrs. Wenberg is positive that "Laura never allowed herself to believe something because it might be comforting."[24] Indications that she did believe, however, come from Jule Eisenbud to whom she once said that she had evidence in the form of rappings from her dead fiancé[25] and also from her tribute to John F. Thomas who had been killed in an accident.[26] She quoted Aristotle with favor: "In explanation of phenomena—one should always prefer the probable impossible to the improbable possible."[27]

She was impressed by the number of distinguished men and women— Myers, Hodgson, Hyslop, Eleanor Sidgwick, Lodge, Piddington, Alice Johnson, C. Drayton Thomas, and others—who, after extensive sittings with first class mental mediums, were satisfied that the hypothesis of the survival of and communication by a deceased personality was the best explanation for the evidence. For Mrs. Dale, it was another "improbable possible" to scoff at the conclusions of such experienced workers as wishful thinking, stupidity or malobservation.[28] She expressed her "gradually strengthening conviction" for Thomas and perhaps for her dead sweetheart in Thomas Wolfe's words: "To lose the earth you know, for greater knowing; to lose the life you have for greater life; to leave the friends you love for greater loving...."[29]

ASPR Journal

Although Laura Dale will be remembered for her research, it was to the ASPR *Journal* that she was dedicated. In the words of a colleague at the ASPR, it was her "magnificent obsession."[30] The intensity of this obsession can be judged partly from her generally devoting, in addition to her normal 40 hours per week, 20 more hours a week to her job,[31] during all of which she smoked furiously behind her desk, and partly from her telling a close friend in 1975: "I'm at my wits' end with the new printers. Butchers. I just spent two days in Albany with them trying to get things straightened out. Pray for me. Am heartsick."[32]

When Jocelyn Pierson resigned the editorship of JASPR in 1941 to become a member of the Board of Trustees, the Publications Committee took charge of the *Journal*.[33] In 1942 Laura Dale assumed the helm and retained it until 1947 when she gave it up in order to give all her time to research.[34] The *Journal* was then edited by Lydia Allison, chairman of the ASPR Publications

Committee, and thereafter by Rhea A. White. Laura Dale returned to the editorship in 1962. Under her, the number of pages of the *Journal* increased from 208 in 1962, to 316 pages in 1964, to 455 pages 10 years later, to nearly 500 in 1980. Her last year as editor was 1981. Dale also edited many issues of the PASPR.

Laura Dale's JASPR and the stream of ASPR publications which, from 1925 to 1941 followed a populist policy and presented material slanted toward the masses, were poles apart. Mrs. Dale turned her back on the populace and presented material that was of interest to only a learned and scientific nucleus. Her tenure as editor saw the pages of the *Journal*, although they contained some philosophical and theoretical papers, filled mainly with experimental papers. That less than 20 percent of the published papers dealt with survival is puzzling in view of her deep personal and scientific interest in the subject and can perhaps be explained by her desire to heighten the stature of parapsychology and JASPR in the eyes of academic psychologists and physical scientists who do not take the survival issue seriously. Although the JASPR Laura Dale edited was read by fewer, but more select, people and understood by still fewer, it became the permanent and valuable scientific journal she wished it to be.

Laura Dale was painstaking in her detailed examination of authors' citations and quotations. She scanned their manuscripts for typographical, spelling or grammatical errors as well as for factual inaccuracies. In many cases she would retype a manuscript or would suggest changes or corrections. Many authors could say that the clarity and quality of their papers improved markedly in consequence of the revisions produced by Laura Dale's meticulousness and might even confess that, after their contributions had passed through many metamorphoses, they bore little resemblance to the inferior original.

At the same time she was always thoughtful, even under adverse circumstances, in dealing with those who submitted to her material for publication. In my case, for example, in spite of her having broken her arm in an accident which resulted in a heavy cast around it, she typed a letter to me "one-handed" in order not to delay writing to me about my manuscript.[35]

As an editor, Laura Dale was courageous and outspoken. Hyslop had used the *Journal* to unmask prevarication and misrepresentation. When Bertrand Russell criticized the philosophy of Henri Bergson, the foremost French philosopher and president of the SPR, by intimating that Bergson's theories in *Creative Evolution* were based on faulty data, Dale demonstrated that these theories were not so based and let JASPR fly like an arrow even if the target was a member of the House of Lords and the greatest English philosopher of the twentieth century:

> One can only think that Russell deliberately falsified Bergson's thought in order to discredit him and his philosophy. . . . Lord Russell, disdaining intellectual honesty in summarizing Bergson's ideas, leans heavily on faith — the faith of the scientific materialist that determinism has the final word to say about all living things and even about the inner world of consciousness.[36]

In Montague Ullman's words, Laura Dale "was like a tigress protecting her brood when it came to defending the scientific integrity of the *Journal.*"37 To change similes, she had the eye of an eagle for detecting baseless speculations, confused thinking, personal attacks, irrelevancies and non sequiturs, and was as stubborn as a mule in her refusal to publish any material that represented poor research or writing and seemed to her to fall beneath her scientific standards, standards of accuracy and English usage. Her reaction to a work when these standards were violated was unrestrained:

> [It] is a Mishmash of the most awful errors. . . . It really makes me sick to see the glorious E.M.S. [Eleanor Mildred Sidgwick] appear (repeatedly) as Mrs. "Sidgewick"; and it's interesting to learn that Home's middle name was "Douglas" [Daniel Dunglas Home]! And the author's command of English is as poor as his proof-reading ability — how's this for starters? ". . .if psychic surgery is an actual phenomena. . ." Ugh!38

As she could be helpful, kind and thoughtful, so could her editorial axe cut deeply into sensibilities when she rejected material she believed inferior. To one author whose paper was rejected, she wrote that it "is loosely constructed, repetitious, and much too long. It suffers from hasty and inadequately formulated generalizations, and in places the reasoning is vague and unconvincing. Much difficulty was experienced in grasping the main thrust of the paper."39

The charge has been made against Laura Dale that her standards as editor were not always objective. The author who received the rejection letter just quoted complained that his work was not published because of a dispute he had had with Gardner Murphy which "got back to Dale, who was so enraged that she decided that she was going to go to war with me."40 This complaint might be dismissed as an author's natural resentment were it not for the fact that, after the denial of publication in JASPR of six of this author's submissions, he adopted a pseudonym and had three submissions under it accepted immediately for publication. When, from various clues, Dale penetrated this facade, and although his last submission had been recommended for publication by an independent referee, she returned it with the notation: "Papers by non-existent authors are suitable for publication only in non-existent journals."41

Montague Ullman, who considered Laura Dale "an editor's editor"42 and who knew her for nearly 40 years, said that, as ASPR president, he had received "letters from people who fancied themselves of some importance in the field and whose feathers were ruffled by rejection. . .[yet he could] not recall any situation in which Laura's judgment was not vindicated."43 In any case, it was not on Dale's judgment alone that material submitted was rejected. All papers, except for correspondence and book reviews, had to go through a refereeing process, and all recommendations (to accept submissions in their original form, or provisionally if revisions were made, or to reject) regarding material published in JASPR were made by the ASPR Publications Committee.

Interests and Opinions

Laura Dale had three interests apart from parapsychology and JASPR. She wrote about two of them in a letter: "If I could 'live again,' I would like to be (a) a damn good tennis player, (b) a good enough cellist to play Mozart quartets...."[44] Her third interest was dogs. She was an expert. She showed the dogs she owned and was active at dog shows as a licensed judge of the Novice, Open and Utility Obedience classes.

When she lived in New York City, she owned a Boston terrier named "Myra" after a well-known musician. After she moved from New York, she lived with as many as five boxers whom she called the "girls" and to whom she gave musical names such as "Scherzo," "Tina" (short for concertina), and "Mozart." She loved the dogs, although, as Dr. Ehrenwald recalled, they "kept biting her hands and giving her infectious sores on her hands."[45] Her boxers, especially Tina, took ribbons at dog shows and were extolled in dog literature. When Rex Stanford visited her home, Dale "proudly showed me some of the books in which the virtues of her 'Ph.D.' boxers' impeccable performance was highly praised. Clearly, this was not just some personal pride, but pride in her beloved friends.... When she spoke of them, her eyes shone with love and appreciation."[46]

Laura Dale lived simply, her residences unadorned except for photographs of her boxers. Her automobile was a Henry J. When she left her New York City apartment in 1959 and resigned from the ASPR, partly because she "had been overworked and underpaid"[47] and partly to take an editorial post with a publishing house which republished older works in parapsychology, she took up residence first in a modest house in Levittown, Long Island, and then, in 1967, in Centereach, Long Island, "where I have bought a horrible little house with lots of land" because she had "gotten fed up with the 'togetherness' of Levittown, with umpteen million children per square yard...."[48]

In Centereach, she and her dogs would have privacy and freedom on two acres and it was from there that she was able to edit the *Journal* when she went back to its editorship in 1962.

From the time of their initial meeting in 1941, Laura Dale and Dr. Jule Eisenbud became close friends. Fortunately for her biographer, Dr. Eisenbud moved to Denver, Colorado, in 1950 while she remained in New York. This forced an active correspondence between them. Applying Chesterfield's dictum that a letter shows the person by whom it is written, let us, through some of Laura Dale's unpublished letters, see how they reveal to us her wit, her prejudices and critical opinions on many subjects and people, and, above all, show us more of the woman herself.

All the quotations following represent "a sprinkling from about a hundred letters and a few notes that I had from Laura over the years," wrote Dr. Eisenbud when he sent me letters and notes he had selected from this correspondence.

In Relation to J.B. Rhine

The [two parapsychologists] versus Rhine story is a long, complicated,
and decidedly nasty one.... Rhine threw them out on charges of incompetence and says they did practically no work and just sat around
criticizing the Lab.... Well, whatever the rights or wrongs of the
thing, it is a human tragedy.... Oh, damn it anyway! I seem to recall
your saying some three or more years ago something to the effect that
you wouldn't be too surprised if Rhine had a real paranoid break one
day—well, if half of what [the parapsychologists] say is true, he's over
the edge right now.[49]

[T]he Great White Father threw Gaither Pratt out on his ear after 30
years.... As for JBR, he strikes me as being mad, real mad.[50]

In Relation to Gardner Murphy

He has always been a talented fence-sitter, God forgive me for saying
so.[51]

In Relation to the Present Policies and the
Future of Parapsychology

I was more and more uneasy about the "public relations" stance and
the "eagerness to play 'footsie' with the media" type of approach which
seems to be permeating the thinking of PA (and also, alas, of the ASPR
trustees and voting members).... [I]f we make aggressive efforts to
"sell" the media on the "science" of parapsychology (showing them
proudly all our toys and computer games!), we'll continue to find more
castor oil than informed reporting under the [Christmas] tree. On the
other hand, if we wait for the media to take the initiative in approaching us, I'm sure we stand a better chance of getting a fair
shake.[52]

In Relation to Editing Jule Eisenbud's Book
(The World of Ted Serios, 1967)

I'm sure that [the publisher Morrow] would take a dim view of the idea
that I "edit" the job—anyway, this makes little sense to me because,
much as I would adore to make a bit of extra money, either honestly
or even slightly dishonestly, I can't imagine why your MS would need
any editing at all. I can't think of anyone who turns out material so

well written and well organized and in so little need of "editing" — in my experience with your *J.* stuff, for example, I am pleased with my editorial prowess if I find a place where your typewriter has jammed a couple of letters together on the average of once every ten pages. I think I *once* found a misspelled word — this really made me feel as if I were earning my editorial keep![53]

After Eisenbud's book was published:

Found the complimentary copy of your book (for which a thousand thanks) last night when I got home from the ASPR. I sat right down merely intending to glance at it before fixing dinner — and never moved from my chair until many hours later when, tired and hungry, I read the final sentence. . . . In my opinion, this book is by far the most significant and important work to have appeared in our field in the present century. . . .[54]

Yet Laura Dale's editorial axe could fall on Dr. Eisenbud as well as on anyone else whose material was not up to her standards:

Yes, you are right. I do have reservations about the effectiveness of your "Suspicious Behavior" paper and question the wisdom of publishing it. . . . [I]t is cryptic — i.e., that it is vague, and raises many more questions in the reader's mind (at least, in mine) than it answers. . . . Over all, I just can't feel that the paper adds substance to the Serios record, or provides an effective response to Diacones' [sic] insinuations. . . .[55]

In Relation to Other People

When I heard that Mrs. B. was there, I was glad I hadn't been invited. From what I saw of her in Utrecht, she doesn't strike me as being one of our brighter friends, even if she does have a million $$$.[56]

If she can [read Jule Eisenbud's manuscript in an hour], she's a brighter gal than I think she is. (What a cat I am.)[57]

In Relation to the Medium Arthur Ford

About Arthur Ford. First of all, the results of a proxy experiment with him, evaluated by the Pratt-Birge method, were published. . . . Null results. I have no hard-core evidence that Ford cheats, but my strong impression is that he certainly has done so in the past.[58]

In Relation to Unidentified Flying Objects

I must confess that until now discussion of UFOs (even assuming that there might possibly be such things) as having any relevance whatever to psychical research made me feel slightly sick to my stomach (after all, at a minimum one cannot deny that a terrible lot of bilge has been written about this). . . .[59]

In Relation to Tennis

Now I must rush to the TV set to watch the finals at Forest Hills—the brash Jimmy Conners [sic] vs. Manuel Orantes. . . . Hope the latter clobbers the former, whose gross behavior on the court turns me off.[60]

Yes, it was a great match that Orantes played against the Brash One; I enjoyed it to the full. No, alas, I don't play any more (was always the worst kind of Sunday hacker anyway)—too short of breath from years of 2 packs a day.[61]

In Relation to Her Automobile

Driving [to see Dr. Eisenbud in Denver] would be fun, but I don't think Henry-J would make it. It's strictly a piece of junk, and on arrival would probably look more like a hot-rod, stripped for action, than a sedate 2-door sedan. Every time I close a door, something else falls off the car.[62]

In Relation to Dogs

Tina is fine and continuing to win everything but the tents at the shows, in spite of her recent motherhood.[63] I wish I could shove a few things, plus the girls [her dogs], into the Henry J. and get rolling Westward. . . .[64]

In 1953, after attending a conference, Mrs. Dale went to Amsterdam with Dorothy Pope and Betty Humphrey. While they went to the museums, she went with a Dutch friend to visit the Netherlands Kennel Club . . . and then in the afternoon to the Training Center for Guide Dogs for the Blind.[65]

Am judging practically every week-end, and enjoying it.[66]

Although standing all day amid a thousand barking canines while judging at a show doesn't bother me in the least, there is in my books a special place in hell for those thoughtless so-called "neighbors" who let their pets go on and on making nuisances of themselves by barking. To tell you the truth, it drives me just plain crackers.[67]

Death

Karlis Osis described Laura Dale as "a real spark" in the ASPR.[68] And in recognition of her long years of sparkling service an engraved metal plaque was presented to her by the Parapsychological Association at its annual convention in Reykjavik, Iceland, in 1980.[69] But the plaque was presented in absentia, for the spark that was Laura Dale was starting to fade. She retired as editor of JASPR in 1981, and her friends noticed her looking frail and weak a year later during her attendance at meetings of the ASPR Board of Trustees of which she was a member.[70]

Between July 1982 and the beginning of 1983, she spoke several times over the telephone with Jule Eisenbud in Denver. "Although we talked about her worsening cough," he said, "she never let on that it was anything other than her usual smoker's cough."[71]

In one of her letters, Laura Dale said that the *Journal* would never give "the Kiwanis Club treatment" to some subjects "and never will until the day I leave for the Great Tennis Court in the Sky!"[72] When she knew that lung cancer had defeated her on this earthly court, she followed the example of the American Indians she said she admired who go out silently and alone somewhere in nature to die when it is time to die.[73] She said nothing to anyone, not even goodbye, left no notes, drove herself to a hospital and quietly and calmly arranged her affairs and her death. She died in New York on February 2, 1983.

In a research fund that was created from an inheritance of $210,000 the ASPR received from her, Laura Dale lives on to further the work to which she devoted over four decades. She lives on in another way, too. In the language of Dr. Jan Ehrenwald, "Perhaps there will be no bronze plaque or stone memorial erected in her honor, but every page of the *Journal* that she edited will memorialize her spirit."[74]

Bibliography

Besides Mrs. Dale's works cited above, she collaborated with Gardner Murphy in *Challenge of Psychical Research: A Primer of Parapsychology* (1961), was an associate editor for Benjamin B. Wolman's *Handbook of Parapsychology* (1977), and was a coauthor with Rhea A. White of *Parapsychology in Print, 1970* (1970), *Parapsychology in Print, 1971-1972* (1971), and *Parapsychology: Sources of Information* (1973). She also wrote the foreword to G.N.M. Tyrrell's *Science and Psychical Phenomena* when it was republished by University Books (1961).

Louisa E. Rhine: A Cameo

Louisa E. Rhine, an equal collaborator in parapsychology with her husband, as interested, well read and knowledgeable in the field as he, had the qualities to become with him a potent force in American parapsychology. She was, however, a woman with four children and a house to keep. Until the youngest child was in college circumstances did not afford her the same opportunity as Rhine had to work full time at the Duke Laboratory. In spite of these disadvantages, she rose to merit recognition as the doyenne of American parapsychology and to become the third female (after Eleanor Sidgwick and Dame Edith Lyttelton) to hold the post of president of the SPR. But she could never become the dominating personality of the era that her husband was, partly because her prominence came too late in life but mainly because the anecdotal material in which she specialized was not highly esteemed by a parapsychology that was now preoccupied with experimental procedures.

Early Life, Friendship and Education

One of the girls in the photograph Christian Weckesser sent to Sam Ellis Rhine was Louisa Ellen, one of Weckesser's and Ella Long's nine children. Louisa was born in 1891 near Niagara Falls, New York. Her father was a poor truck farmer in whose nursery she transplanted cabbage plants while she received her early schooling. When the family moved to Ohio, she received her teaching credentials and was teaching school in a village when the Rhine family arrived and rented her father's truck farm. She was 20 and four years older than J.B. Rhine but they became immediate friends. Her mind appealed to him and she was attracted to the tall serious boy who read books and was so unlike the neighborhood boys that she knew.

In 1914, she went to Wooster College and later to the University of Chicago where she earned a B.S. degree, entered into graduate studies in the Department of Botany and finally received her Ph.D. in 1923, three years after she and J.B. Rhine were married.

A Family Affair

Pierre and Marie Curie, cowinners in 1903 of the Nobel Prize for physics, were partners in the scientific investigation of radioactivity. It would press the analogy too far to suggest that J.B. and Louisa Rhine will ever receive the world recognition that was accorded the Curies, but in the Rhines we see the same entwining of two loves and lives in scientific exploration.

We glimpse in their own writings the impossibility of separating these Siamese twins of parapsychology, so close were their concerns, interests,

Louisa E. Rhine

careers. As early as high school, Rhine considered this daughter of a truck farmer the most important factor in his life.[75] As young people before and during college days, they shared their religious and philosophical bewilderment and later followed parallel courses by turning toward forestry, becoming graduate biology students and having their imaginations stirred by the possibilities of parapsychology.[76] Significantly, when Louisa Rhine began her last book to tell about her husband's character, personality and purposes, she discovered that she was so much a part of his story that the book could not be his story alone as she had planned, "but rather our story."[77]

Miriam Whaley, Louisa Rhine's sister, made a pertinent observation: "It was Louie-and-Banks then in those early days.... Forever in my mind they are one, two halves of a greater whole, a synergetic unit. They sought together for answers to the large questions of life and they were true partners. Banks could not have done what he did without Louie; she would have been incomplete without him."[78]

That parapsychology at Duke was their joint story is made emphatically clear by those who knew them both at the start and at the end of their careers. First, William McDougall with whom it all began: When he wrote the foreword to J.B. Rhine's *Extra-Sensory Perception,* he took special pains to point out that all his statements regarding Rhine were true also of Louisa Rhine and to recognize as "unique and remarkable" that both had taken parallel

actions in burning their bridges and giving up their careers in order to come
into parapsychology.[79]

K. Ramakrishna Rao knew the Rhines at Duke and later at FRNM and saw
how

> they influenced each other. Often there was mutual reinforcement of
> their basic concern to understand the hidden aspects of human nature.
> As they drove back and forth to work, and during conversations at the
> dinner table and at the side of the fireplace, I am sure they exchanged
> notes constantly. Also, the weekly (and sometimes biweekly) research
> meetings were the occasion for dispassionate and often spirited discus-
> sions. In many ways JBR and LER were alike; yet in other ways they
> were different. Their lives and thinking illustrated nature's principle of
> complementarity at its best.[80]

The book Rao edited as a tribute to Rhine was dedicated "With Much
Love and Admiration to LOUISA E. RHINE Life and Laboratory Partner to J.B.
RHINE for Sixty Years."[81]

An example of this partnership at work in the laboratory? After a
gambler's claim that the fall of dice could be influenced to win on his throws
and to lose for other throwers, serious dice throwing tests began at Duke in
1934 as "a family affair."[82] J.B. and Louisa Rhine, one acting as recorder and
the other acting as subject, threw dice by hand, and, when they collaborated
to write the report of the results of their first experiment, Louisa Rhine was the
senior author.[83]

Their "family affair" in parapsychology lasted six decades and continued
even after Rhine's death when his wife took over as president of the SPR to serve
in place of her husband for the rest of his term of office.

Spontaneous Cases

The importance for the founders of the ASPR of authenticated spontaneous cases was the evidence these cases might provide for psi and survival
after death. Prince's collection of the psychic experiences of "noted witnesses"
was designed to strengthen the case through the testimony of credible
witnesses. Gardner Murphy and Laura Dale spearheaded the resurgence of interest in spontaneous cases partly to use them as evidence and partly because
they thought that these phenomena supply the richest, and what should be
the largest, field studied by parapsychology in order to enlarge psychological
understanding of the fundamental dynamics of the experiences.

Both Rhines also stimulated interest in spontaneous cases, but for reasons
entirely different from those which spurred the ASPR, Prince, Murphy and
Laura Dale. The Rhines did not look on spontaneous psychic experiences as
proof of paranormal phenomena or as strong enough to permit conclusions to
be drawn. For if such experiences constituted proof, further laboratory research
would have been unnecessary. The single usefulness of the spontaneous case

was that it might lead and give direction to new experimental projects by presenting a hypothesis or a question. Dr. Louisa Rhine began in 1948 at the Duke Parapsychology Laboratory to collect spontaneous case reports to discover these insights into paranormal phenomena occurring in a natural setting while, at the same time, psi phenomena were being investigated in the artificial conditions of a laboratory — "almost like an artist watching his scene with intermittent glances, even as he applies the paint to canvas," as Dr. Louisa Rhine said.[84]

Their methods of collection and analysis offer another contrast between Murphy and Laura Dale on the one hand and Louisa Rhine on the other. The former planned carefully every strand in the broad net they threw out in which to catch fresh psychic experiences. They arranged for popular articles on ESP and appeals for cases in Sunday supplements. They organized a staff to gather the expected data. Laura Dale used her skills in follow-up letters to elicit more details. Then three minimum criteria were set up and cases passed through a careful authentication process to be divided into "A" cases of good quality, "B" cases of lesser quality and "C" cases which could not be authenticated.[85]

Louisa Rhine, on the other hand, cast no net. Instead, the spontaneous cases came to her unrequested in the form of thousands of personal experiences reported voluntarily by people who wrote to the Duke Parapsychology Laboratory. Sometimes they wanted to understand what had happened to them; sometimes they wrote because "I hope this will help in your researches."[86] When Louisa Rhine studied the unorganized hodgepodge that had grown over the years to some 15,000 cases, she accepted reports of experiences at face value "with or without supplementary validation if they seemed to be contributed in good faith and by apparently sane individuals."[87] She sent no follow-up letters, made no attempts to authenticate the reports and was satisfied to include them in her collection of cases if they clearly spelled out an incident and circumstances that indicated the possibility either of the acquisition by ESP of information not obtained through sensory channels or of physical happenings caused by psychokinesis.

Although Hornell Hart complained that only the Rhines and those working under them at the Duke Parapsychology Laboratory were permitted access to its collection of spontaneous cases while scholars such as he were denied access,[88] this decision, however annoying to colleagues, was within the province of the Rhines and had nothing to do with the substantiveness of Louisa Rhine's work. Other and more serious charges might be made against her methods. Her acceptance of cases, if ESP was a possibility, is questionable because, in the absence of any attempt to verify through independent testimony the events of experiences reported, no one can be sure that what was reported happened in fact, or, if it did, had a paranormal origin.

Since spontaneous psychic experiences occur outside the controlled conditions of a laboratory, and the evidence arises from the assertions of people, the first duty of an investigator is what Broad called "critical appraisal." The evidence must be tested as it might be tested in a court of law: by cross-examining witnesses, by obtaining corroborative affidavits from independent witnesses, by examining all relevant documents. So legalistic and rigorous should the testing be that Broad and others believe, "The best type of investigator for this purpose would be a person with the training and experience of a judge or a police magistrate."[89] Louisa Rhine had no such training and ignored "critical appraisal," made no effort to cross-examine a single witness or to secure one affidavit from an independent witness in order to insure that the spontaneous cases she studied were veridical and acceptable as reliable evidence of psi from which to draw conclusions. Yet to deprecate her work and to criticize her on this account are to misunderstand her purpose completely.

She did not look upon the 15,000 reports she studied as evidence of psi which needed corroboration and she did not intend to use them to support conclusions. She was searching in them merely to find suggestions for new ideas, questions and insights which might guide future research into ESP and PK. The use of unselected case reports for this limited and nonevidential object seems to justify her failure to subject the cases to "critical appraisal," the more so because the ultimate criterion for any suggestions that might have come out of Louisa Rhine's study was this: "They must be tested, preferably under the controlled conditions of laboratory research before the true and false in them can be conclusively distinguished. That will come at a later stage."[90]

Louisa Rhine recognized the unreliability of human testimony and that some reports in her collection might be suspect. Therefore, she rested her examination on a mass of cases in the belief that "the larger number of cases of a kind, the more likely that they represented a valid process and that individual mistakes of testimony could be considered to be cancelled out."[91] If a suggestion from a spurious report were used as the basis for an experimental test, it would be shown false and nothing would be lost except time. But Louisa Rhine was not interested in single cases and it is doubtful that any experimenter would be. She was looking for trends or patterns suggested by thousands of cases that might lead to experiment. So she made use of a principle akin to the optical illusion of continuous movement when a series of still pictures is projected rapidly on a screen. She wrote:

> By the succession of numbers of closely similar items, meanings stand out which the individual pictures alone do not show. One could proceed here on the assumption that if ESP occurs in nature, it does so more than once. If it is a human ability, even an uncommon one, then by observing carefully the times when with some likelihood it is operating, the true aspect should add up, and the mistakes of individual memory, observation, etc., should, in effect, cancel out. By this method of treatment, a validity based on numbers could be given the material. . . . [T]hrough the patterns of similarities one can glimpse in the background a rationale that could hardly be the result of only a series of mistakes of testimony, over-interpretation, imagination, coincidence and all that.[92]

Her belief that the use of a motion picture principle would allow the glimpsing of lawful patterns is suspect because of the strong possibility that patterns formed included a large number of reports which might have been thrown out after a more meticulous investigation or because, as West expressed the danger, the patterns might not reflect the natural laws of ESP but instead what people like to believe.[93] Nevertheless, since any rationale that might emerge would still need to be tested later in experiments before being considered genuine, the criticism seems irrelevant.

Some Fruits of the Study

Not concerned with evidence establishing psi, Dr. Rhine began her study by classifying and indexing spontaneous cases according to broad types of phenomena indicated by laboratory experiments. Cases that might have involved the influence of mind on matter were categorized as psychokinesis and those involving knowledge not obtained through the senses were categorized in one of the subdivisions of extrasensory perception: telepathy, clairvoyance or precognition. After classification and indexing by types, special problems were studied. Some of the fruits of these studies over so many years came under several rubrics: formulation of forms Louisa Rhine perceived in the ESP category, the nature of psi, the relative importance of agents and percipients in spontaneous telepathic experiences, survival after death and precognitive experiences.

In 1947, G.N.M. Tyrrell distinguished between a process and a product.[94] We are never aware of ESP processes at work in us. We do not say, "I know that I am now receiving a telepathic message from my brother." The process is unconscious. But we are aware of the product of the ESP process when it crosses the threshold of consciousness by means of what Tyrrell called a "mediating vehicle," a subconscious creation of a percipient which conveys knowledge of the paranormal information to consciousness. Louisa Rhine's analysis of 956 cases led her to discover four forms of ESP experiences which may be Tyrrell's "mediating vehicles."[95]

Almost half the cases provided the first form: events pictorially and accurately detailed in realistic dreams (or daydreams). Most of these were precognitive (dealing with future events) while the rest were telepathic or clairvoyant (involving present events). A second form consisted of unrealistic dreams full of drama and fantasy whose symbolism related to some definite event that needed to be interpreted. Two other forms of ESP experiences occurred during waking hours: "psi-hallucinations" in which the person could see or hear the event being experienced as though it were actually occurring,[96] and intuition or "just knowing" about some event through a sudden awareness, impression or emotion that had nothing to do with reasoning. In 1960,[97] as she continued to classify and study spontaneous ESP experiences as a way of discovering new ideas for experiments, Louisa Rhine perceived a fifth special form of ESP experience in which psi might appear: cases of "mind over matter," experiences involving physical and generally inexplicable effects (stopping or starting a clock, falling of pictures, crucifixes or dishes, raps, knocks) supposedly associated with the dead or with crises affecting both healthy and dying people.

The inquiry suggested to Louisa Rhine that a living observer who is emotionally connected with some relative or friend receives information by ESP about that person's death or other crisis situation and then, instead of an ESP dream, hallucination or intuition, uses PK on some object as another form of expressing the message. Is this fascinating theory difficult to accept? In spite of considerable PK experimentation, no clear explanation of this phenomenon has emerged. To attempt as did Louisa Rhine to explain physical effects in crisis cases in terms of PK by the experiencing observer is to explain these occurrences with an unexplainable phenomenon. Yet the theory remains an interesting suggestion to be confirmed or refuted by subsequent research.

One of the urgent needs of Duke research that prompted Louisa Rhine's analysis was to study the nature of psi and its relation to consciousness. In experiments, ESP seemed to operate on the unconscious level with the result that subjects did not know when responses were right. If the ESP process was operative on the unconscious level only, there was little prospect of finding out how to control it, but if it operated on the level of consciousness, perhaps it could be controlled. Louisa Rhine examined waking and dream experiences to see what psychological processes might block the movement of information across the threshold of consciousness. Her inquiry suggested, especially in cases where people are so convinced of the rightness of their ESP-acquired knowledge that they take or refrain from taking some action, that ESP may not remain an unconscious process but that it can emerge into consciousness. Control of ESP under laboratory conditions might therefore be possible.

Louisa Rhine had already ventured into the sensitive area of postmortem survival when her inquiry into spontaneous PK crisis cases suggested that the experiencing observer and not a deceased person was the cause of strange physical effects. As she continued her excursions into this territory, she examined the comparative importance of agents and percipients in cases of telepathy. One of the legacies that had come down to American parapsychology from the founders of the SPR was the notion that, in telepathy, an agent transmits an impression to the percipient. Louisa Rhine's inquiry into 328 cases of telepathy suggested, to the contrary, that the initiative for the telepathic experience rested with the percipient, not the agent.[98] If the source of the telepathic message is indeed the percipient and not a distant agent, the concept that messages in mediumistic sessions come from deceased communicators would be threatened and the reality of mediumistic communications would be undermined totally. Yet Louisa Rhine could not altogether rule out a deceased person as the source of information. In several spontaneous cases, it seemed more probable than not that the initiative for transferring information rested with a dead man, as in the case she reported of a mother who sent Ned, her deceased son, a kiss and asked him to acknowledge her message with a kiss. A few days later her sister called and said that Ned had appeared in her dream and, instead of kissing her, turned his back and kissed the mother.[99]

Still in the field of survival research, Louisa Rhine turned to one of the keystones of survival evidence: apparitions, which Professor Hornell Hart with the cooperation of others, had studied thoroughly. His hypotheses, which explained the available data, were that apparitions of the dead were so similar in fundamental characteristics to conscious apparitions of living and dying persons, and were seen with the same frequency as they were, that apparitions of the dead must be accepted as a fact of reality; and that they were real and etheric counterparts of the physical bodies of the dead. Apparitions were evidence of survival.[100]

Louisa Rhine examined 825 spontaneous cases in one study,[101] 208 cases in another[102] and 567 cases in a third.[103] The cases involved apparitions of living, dying or dead appearers. Her interpretation of the case material was that apparitions of the living or dying were "psi-hallucinations," merely creations and dramatizations by the mind of the living percipient who, through an ESP form of clairvoyance, gained impressions of the appearers and used these impressions in the dramatization. The cases involving dead appearers were not so clear to her but did not seem so markedly different as to warrant any contrary interpretation. Her studies led her to state:

> The indications are . . . that the percipient generates the hallucination, agent and all, and the nature of his projections depends on his knowledge of and expectation of the agent at the time. If influences from the discarnate are to be detected in such experiences, then the suggestion is strong that it would have to be on other grounds than their hallucinatory form.[104]

No needle thrust could have made Hart jump more. He responded vigorously to what he thought were Louisa Rhine's adverse conclusions that apparitions had no bearing on the survival question because they could be explained by the ability of a living percipient to use ESP impressions and to dramatize them. Here is presented a basic dispute between advocates of spontaneous cases, such as Hart, and advocates of quantitative studies, such as the Rhines. The Hart faction considers that authenticated cases of spontaneous psychic experiences, i.e., apparitions, can provide evidence. But the Rhine side believes that such cases never have been and never can be well enough authenticated to be reliable as evidence and are good only to give direction to experimental research.

The Hart-Louisa Rhine disagreement also stresses how slender is the margin between a "conclusion" and a "suggestion" and how fastidious one must be in the use of the language when, like Louisa Rhine, one is not supposed to be drawing conclusions from a study. Hart's rejection of her interpretation stemmed from a possible misinterpretation on his part that she was presenting a conclusion. From Louisa Rhine's careful choice of "indications" and "suggestion" in the above quotation, however, it seems evident that she was trying to steer clear of conclusions and was searching only for insights.

In this case, the result was ironic. The hope that spontaneous cases might play an important part in starting new research had given initial impulse to her study. Here, in the insight that apparitions might not be a way to proceed for survival evidence, the result seems to have had the opposite effect of checking research and lowering interest in apparitions. An examination of the proceedings of the annual conventions of the Parapsychological Association from 1971 to 1986 shows that, of the approximately 450 research papers, symposia, round tables, poster sessions, and invited and presented addresses, there were only nine papers and one symposium on apparitions.

Of all the forms of ESP experiences, precognition has raised the most basic philosophical questions concerning causation, time and free will. As knowledge of an event which has not yet occurred and which could not have been inferred, it seems to imply backward causation in that a future event seems to have caused a person in the present to be aware of it. It also seems to imply that an event is predetermined to occur and that human will or action can do nothing to alter it. Because precognition threatens to reverse fundamental conceptions, some philosophers, and even some parapsychologists,[105] have tried to avoid its implications by showing it to be an impossible phenomenon. But when Louisa Rhine undertook to make her classifications, she found its existence indicated clearly in about 40 percent of the cases.[106]

Except for the placement of an event in the future, Rhine could perceive no special differences between precognitive experiences and telepathic and clairvoyant experiences.[107] Yet she noticed some interesting patterns about the precognitive experiences which seem to set them apart from other ESP experiences. Precognitive experiences made deeper impressions on the subject than did cases of telepathy or clairvoyance; dreams seemed to be more the vehicle for precognitive experiences than waking experiences; and cases of precognition involved the death of a friend or relative as opposed to telepathic or clairvoyance experiences which dealt with their illnesses or accidents. She also examined 433 cases of precognition from the point of view of ascertaining whether percipients had taken steps to try to avoid events that were precognized, such as not taking a train if an accident were foreseen.[108] In most cases no action had been taken, but, in a few narratives, she found that an event precognized did not take place because of intervention.

These case studies raise that interesting question: If precognition is the foreseeing of a future event that has been predetermined to occur, how can any human intervention possibly alter it? So phrased, the question is as baffling for us as it was for Louisa Rhine. But there is no need to frame it in this fatalistic way if we accept the theory of the philosopher Ducasse that not all future events are "fated" to occur regardless of anybody's opposing will or action. A future event is the product of present causes among which are our wills and actions or failures to act which allow an event to happen.[109]

The fruits of Louisa Rhine's studies hang ripe and ready for plucking by researchers in parapsychology. Her research papers are plump with ideas, perceptions, leads, hypotheses, all to be tested.

In her popular books are more fruits to be enjoyed by students and the general public. These books are thorough yet simply written introductions to parapsychology and explanations of psi. And to the worried thousands who have had inexplicable psychic experiences but no answers to their questions of why and how this had happened to them and whether they were mentally disturbed, Louisa Rhine gave peace of mind with the reassurance that thousands had had such experiences and ESP was a normal and healthy process.

Louisa Rhine's Death and Place in History

Louisa Rhine continued to be active into her eighties at the lively research meetings held at FRNM each week. Her mind was still active and critical, her manner still kind and reassuring. After I had described at one of these meetings at which she was present an ESP card-matching experiment I had conducted with five subjects to try to obtain the combination of three pairs of numbers for a lock left by J. Gaither Pratt as a test of his survival, it appeared to me that the experiment had been fantastically successful until an ensuing penetrating discussion at the meeting revealed some flaws I had not considered. As I left somewhat dejected, Louie stopped me. "Good try," she said with a smile. I felt better.

In 1980, following her husband's death, Louisa Rhine began to draw on letters and her old diaries and journals to write a book about J.B. Rhine. She was then 88 years of age. "I have to hurry before my brains run out," she would say frequently in the course of writing her account. They didn't and, in spite of a heart attack in 1982, her book was completed less than two months before she died of another heart attack on March 17, 1983.[110]

By the modern term "parapsychology" as well as the older "psychical research" is meant the systematic study by scientific methods of paranormal phenomena. But is is an amorphous field of study which is immense and comparatively unexplored and extends in more directions than one person can possibly follow. Its branches are so diverse that those who would advance knowledge of the subject must pursue only one avenue and almost disregard the others. Thus they become specialists in one avenue of inquiry or another—as Tyrrell was a specialist in apparitions, Ducasse and Broad in the philosophical aspects of the subject, Hodgson and Hyslop in mediumship and spirit survival, J.B. Rhine in its quantitative side, Gertrude Schmeidler in the analysis of personality in connection with ESP scores, Montague Ullman in the exploration of dreams in relation to ESP, and so on. Although she did PK experiments, and others, Louisa Rhine's specialty was the study of spontaneous psychic experiences. They absorbed her so that she was like a person who lives in a house and never leaves it, intimately familiar with every board, step and corner. It is for this house that Louisa Rhine will be remembered and it is because of this house that Louisa Rhine, who gave years of study to thousands of case reports, is entitled to a niche in the history of parapsychology as the foremost investigator of spontaneous cases in America, if not the world.

Publications

In addition to having been a member of the staff of the Duke Parapsychology Laboratory and the Institute for Parapsychology, Louisa Rhine was coeditor of the *Journal of Parapsychology*. She was the author of many research papers and wrote many books for a wide general audience. These include *Hidden Channels of the Mind* (1961), *ESP in Life and Lab* (1967), *Mind over Matter* (1970), *Psi: What Is It?* (1975), *The Invisible Picture: A Study of Psychic Experiences* (1981) and *Something Hidden* (1983).

Gertrude R. Schmeidler: A Self-Portrait

Editor's Introduction: Just three names are mentioned in the 1958 *Encyclopaedia Britannica*'s discussion of parapsychology: J.B. Rhine, Murphy and Gertrude R. Schmeidler (erroneously referred to as "D.R. Schmeidler" in this article). Both in and out of parapsychology, her name is ranked with the most famous in the field. She is a professor emeritus of the Department of Psychology, City College of the City University of New York. A distinguished experimental psychologist and a veteran parapsychologist for 45 years, she has used psychological discoveries as aids in her quantitative investigations in parapsychology to explore the depth of the human personality. She has produced what Gardner Murphy described as "long and brilliant experimental contributions" which, in 1964, earned her the William McDougall Award for Distinguished Work in Parapsychology established by the Parapsychology Laboratory at Duke University.

She and Murphy corresponded after their meeting in 1942 at the Harvard University Summer Session until she perceived an experimental method of attacking a series of problems. The fall of 1942 found Dr. Schmeidler beginning at Harvard several cycles of ESP card-guessing experiments whose ultimate findings were that "sheep" believing that success was possible in ESP tasks scored higher than "goats" who rejected the possibility of success.

Her studies were presented in *ESP and Personality Patterns* (coauthored with Dr. Robert A. McConnell), a book considered on the highest level of scholarship and one of the best ever written on ESP. Her work produced an important parapsychological discovery.

Although she conceded that Murphy put her on the track of her many valuable experiments, Murphy himself took pains to deny this common misconception. . . . She, from the very beginning was a self-starter, with highly ingenious ideas of her own, and although she welcomed counsel, was in no sense dependent on me for the initiation of research problems, hypotheses, and methods.[111]

Dr. Schmeidler is the former president of the Parapsychological Association and was president of the ASPR from 1981 to 1985. She has written almost 200 articles for parapsychological and psychological publications, edited *Extrasensory Perception* (1969) and *Parapsychology: Its Relation to Physics, Biology, Psychology, and Psychiatry* (1976), and was associate editor of Wolman's *Handbook of Parapsychology* (1977).

Yet who is the real Gertrude Schmeidler? The living woman is concealed behind her impressive titles and mountains of writings. In the witty autobiography that follows, however, she allows us to glimpse dimensions of her professional, personal and family life that, until now, have remained hidden. — A.S.B.

"Work in Progress":
Autobiographical Notes
Gertrude Raffel Schmeidler

This year, 1985, is the fiftieth anniversary of my Ph.D. It is therefore the conventional time to look back; to review the contrasts between then when I was young and in the mainstream of psychology, and now when neither is true. I'm old, and a great many psychologists think that parapsychology has taken me off into an altogether wrong direction.

But the sentence that should come next has unexpectedly become hard to write. Just as soon as I typed the word "contrasts" and tried to think about them, I found myself wondering if the right word would have been "similarities." Similarities are all that come to mind. Maybe it's better not to fight it, and to start with those.

The similarity that especially struck me, in this retrospective mood, is that the doctorate ended my student days. It sent me out from an orderly and stimulating world which had offered time and facilities and encouragement for research on whatever problems interested me. It left me feeling unprepared for anything except carrying on with more of what I had been doing. And the same sort of thing happened just a little while ago when mandatory retirement ended my full-time teaching. That had been orderly and stimulating too; its end also left me with the feeling of being thrust out from the cocoon of familiar activity.

Gertrude R. Schmeidler

Both these times gave me a new title: the doctorate then and now an "emeritus" to be added after professor. And both times I knew what ought to be done next but felt insecure about coping with it. Then it was finding a job, but for months there was only one false lead after another. This year it's something that may be beyond my capacity: writing the book that will not only put my ideas together but will also (and this may be the impossible part) present them more convincingly than I have yet been able to do.

Let's go back and trace what happened in those fifty years. The time to start, because it brought such a rude shock, is the spring of 1935. It was the last semester of my graduate work. Graduate students at Harvard had been led to believe that once they had the doctorate, the department would know of a job, or more probably a choice of jobs, available to them. But 1935 was the depth of the Depression, and our chairman, E.G. Boring, told me that the only job he had available was at the American University in Beirut and it was not suitable for me. What was more, he could not find me any other. The reason was that I was a woman.

He then went on, with impeccable logic, to explain why colleges were unwilling to hire women. A woman, he said, was either married or not. If she was married, the college could expect her, at any inconvenient time, to leave because her husband decided to work somewhere else. This made married women undesirable. Now take a woman who was not married. Either she was celibate or she was not. If she was not celibate there was a risk of a scandal; no college wanted to take that risk. If she was celibate she was probably neurotic, and then a college surely wouldn't want her. He recommended that after the doctorate I study shorthand and become a secretary.

So there I was, adrift. That spring and summer I applied for all sorts of openings, and in late summer one worked out. It was at a little junior college (which I heard of only because it was near my family's summer home). One of Roosevelt's alphabetic agencies had founded it a few years earlier to give rural young people something to do after high school. It had no building; it met in a local high school in the evenings. Salaries were minuscule. It needed someone to teach an introductory psychology class and a strange course called College and Life, but especially to teach a survey course in the physical sciences and another in the biological sciences.

With considerable relief and some misgivings, I began to teach. (My background hadn't prepared me adequately for it, but the Dean reassured me by pointing out that nobody could be adequately prepared.) Once there, I was dismayed, but not too dismayed, to find that my duties included supervising the social dancing and the girls' basketball team, as well as filling in for the sociology instructor when he had appendicitis. It was not what I'd expected after being best of my year at Harvard but it was fun, partly because it's always pleasant to be with eager young people and partly because there was so much more learning to do. Learning how to teach, of course (my training had been only in experimentation and history and theory), but also learning enough of astronomy and meteorology and such, all unfamiliar to me, to keep a jump ahead of the class and even answer a reasonable share of the questions that went beyond our textbooks.

After two years of this, almost as Dr. Boring had foretold, I left the college (at a time that was convenient for them) because my husband and I were about to be married and his work was somewhere else. With that I began to learn to cook and, after a decorous interval, to take care of our babies, and in general to try my best to be a conventional suburban housewife. It was a satisfying life, and it would probably have kept on until our children were grown except for World War II.

Only a few days after Pearl Harbor the army sent my husband overseas. What a change that made! Days were occupied with the three babies, none able to talk or walk yet, but in the evenings there was little to do except write to my husband and worry and brood. Unhealthy. I needed something impersonal to occupy my thoughts, so I wrote up to Harvard and asked if they had a part time job for me. It would have to have flexible hours and pay enough to let me hire household help.

Soon an answer came offering work with Gordon W. Allport. He was coordinating inquiries from civilian psychologists, who wanted to know how best to help the war effort, with what the government wanted done; and he needed someone to assist in the liaison. Though it was far from my specialty in experimentation I gladly accepted. For that war against Hitler and Nazism we all wanted to do what we could.

The work was interesting: not only liaison but also finding ways to scotch the divisive rumors that the Nazis were broadcasting and that their supporters disseminated. The rumors were anti–Semitic, anti–Black, anti–Italian, anti–WAC, and so on. They not only spread distrust or hatred among different groups but also derided and thus lessened the sacrifices needed to conserve for the war. Learning which were the effective and which the ineffective ways to neutralize the rumors led to some theories about the emotional, nonlogical nature of prejudice.

The flexible schedule worked out well for the youngsters. It gave me leeway to be with them if they needed me, or if their nurse was ill, or if there had to be a change of nurses. It even left me with a few free daytime hours when all went serenely. Free hours were a special pleasure at Harvard because so many alluring courses were available to audit. Two that went beyond my graduate training attracted me, that first summer: one in neuropsychology by Lashley, whom we all admired, and a unique, rather bizarre offering by Gardner Murphy, called Psychical Research since William James.

Listening in on both would take too much time. I decided to sit in on one session of psychical research, thinking that the one should be enough to convince me the whole topic was flimsy nonsense, and from then on to audit the Lashley course. But as anyone who knew Gardner Murphy would have predicted, his first session was so sophisticated and so challenging that it demanded another, and then more and more. By the happenstance that his single offering of the course coincided with my being available to hear it, a whole new interest enlarged my life.

In the evenings, that summer, I read the books and articles Dr. Murphy recommended—and wrote my skeptical husband about them. If the data were sound, they implied an amazing new set of theoretical lines to follow. But how sound were the data? To both my husband and myself, with our background in Newtonian physics, it seemed impossible that what was reported could have happened. It conflicted with what we knew of physics. But we realized that we didn't know everything. If there were facts that conflicted with our preconceptions, our preconceptions would have to give way.

When his course ended Murphy—Gardner to me by then—offered me a grant from his Hodgson Fellowship to do an experiment on ESP. I could not refuse. Here was a chance to see for myself if under rigorously controlled conditions ESP actually occurred. My few extra daytime hours were again, after a lapse of years, to be used for experimenting. First, with advice from many in the department, I set up conditions for tight testing: numbered lists of random ESP targets, prepared by an assistant and unseen by me, kept in a locked room; numbered response sheets filled out by subjects under my supervision; careful and independent checks of how the targets matched the responses.

It was easy to find volunteers for the research among the undergraduates or in the department. Results at first, in the pilot study, were tantalizing.

Although most subjects scored a shade better than chance expectation there was no tie-in between the introspections they reported and the scores they obtained. But then, by another happenstance, two subjects in close succession scored far, far below mean chance expectation. Both had expressed strong antagonism to the whole thought of ESP, one saying that even if it was true he wouldn't believe it, the other distressed because I, a fellow-woman who had hitherto been respectable, was now associated with superstitions. Both had agreed to be subjects only because it would help me finish the work that much earlier and thus leave me free to drop the whole project that much sooner.

The coincidence of those two sets of extremely low ESP scores with both subjects' strongly expressed, unequivocal disbelief in ESP made me think that maybe something was going on here. It seemed time to drop the pilot work and test for the pattern that their scores implied. Gardner, who had been keeping in close touch by letters, encouraged me to go ahead.

With his approval, then, I started a formal experiment to test the hypothesis that subjects who were convinced ESP could not occur would have lower ESP scores than the other subjects, who thought ESP would occur or thought it might. (Subjects, of course, were asked their opinion before they saw any of their ESP scores.) But as always happens, a separation of many people into only two groups demanded more than a single, simple criterion. There had to be special rules for special cases. What of subjects who thought ESP very, very unlikely (as I myself did in those days) but not quite impossible? What of subjects who thought that ESP could occur, but that they themselves could not possibly show it? We agreed to class both of these answers in the "might occur" group. And what of subjects who accepted telepathy but not clairvoyance, and thought that ESP was impossible as a response to lists of targets that no one knew? We agreed to class them in the "cannot occur" category, now modified to "cannot occur in the experimental situation."

Results fairly soon showed significantly higher scores for the "might occur" group than for the group of "cannot occur in the experimental situation." This was worth reporting. Gardner recommended that in writing it up for the *Journal of the American Society for Psychical Research*, a society with many lay members, I should use as lively and nontechnical a style as possible. That made sense; I tried to comply. As a result the formal definitions were referred to only briefly, and after the first reference to them I used a metaphor instead of repeating those cumbersome definitions ad nauseam. The metaphor was separating sheep (those who accepted the possibility of ESP in the experiment) from goats (those who did not). The terms caught on better than the formal definitions did; they may have been too lively to hold still for accuracy.

Everyone agrees that one significant finding is not enough for conviction. The next thing for me to do was to run the experiment again and see whether it would stand up to replication or whether that first finding was just a fluke. I did it again, and it replicated. I did it a third time and it replicated again (1943).

When the third series also showed a significant difference, the data obliged me to think that ESP actually did occur. This not only unsettled a lot of my previous fixed ideas, but also raised a host of research questions. How did it occur? Why did some sheep score low? Why did some goats score high? Why did subjects' scores vary so much from one session to the next?

It had grown steadily clearer as I watched and listened to the subjects that the belief-disbelief contrast was only one strand in a pattern of attitudes, more or less emotionally toned, which related to ESP: to hits versus misses and perhaps also to null scores. What were the most relevant parts of the pattern? A few hunches began to emerge from what the subjects said and the way they behaved; and following Gardner's advice I began to explore ways of studying what the important individual differences might be.

By then the civilian war effort had gathered enough momentum that its liaison with the government didn't really need me any more. After a long wrap-up paper with Allport my part time work with him came to an end. In the next few years all my part time work was in ESP research, especially in studying individual differences more intensively. I therefore (through Gardner's mediation) moved the project from Emerson Hall, where Allport's office was, to the charming converted house where Harry A. Murray presided over the Harvard Psychological Clinic. Murray, a brilliant man, had gathered a group with great expertise in psychological testing and personality analysis. There were batteries of psychological tests there, with new ones being invented. Some (especially the Rorschach and Saul Rosenzweig's Picture-Frustration test) began to show clear differences between the sheep who scored high or low and also between the goats who scored low or high.

Then at last the war seemed to be drawing to a close. I could begin to think that when my husband came back he would want to be in New York, not in Cambridge. Gardner was always as concerned with helping his associates' personal lives as with helping their professional work, and to my surprise he arranged an interview for me with the Department of Psychology that he chaired at the City College of New York. The Department hired me to teach for the spring of 1945, and we moved to New York. The children were now old enough to be in nursery school during my teaching hours, and our family stood by to care for them if sickness kept them from attending school.

By the time the war ended my one semester appointment had ended too. Only part time teaching was replacing it when my husband came home. His first desirable job offer came from San Francisco, but Gardner arranged to keep us in New York by offering me the post of research officer at the ASPR. A full time research job was too inviting to say no to; we stayed. After about a year, spent mostly in developing further the Rorschach analyses, a new offer came from City College for full time teaching there. Full time, in those days, meant 16 class hours a week. With our family's stand-by help it was a good schedule for a working mother. It also made research easier because the students in my classes eagerly volunteered to be ESP subjects. I settled in at City College.

Teaching is always a good way to learn and was especially stimulating with the bright students that I had. Even the introductory course kept giving me new information because it changed as psychology grew. Later, preparing for specialized courses was even more instructive. I grew into the habit of offering courses in what interested me and of thus making myself obliged to keep up with what was happening: in perception; in learning, memory, thinking (and after that in creativity as one part of thinking); in personality theory and tests; in altered states of consciousness; and of course in experimental methodology. When the college became part of the City University of New York and my schedule centered chiefly on graduate instruction, keeping up with the cutting edge of psychological research in the areas I taught became that much more of a professional obligation as well as a self-imposed one.

There was only one year's interruption in this teaching: when our fourth child was born. One year of unpaid maternity leave was a college requirement. This gave me time while the baby was sleeping to type a first draft of what later became a book with Robert A. McConnell (1958b). We summarized the sheep-goat work up to then but left the bulk of the related work with the Rorschach to be published by me separately.

All those years I had thought of myself as an experimental psychologist with rather broad interests. It shocked me today, looking over my publication list, to find that from the beginning to the end of my time at City College I published only 18 articles not directed to parapsychology. What was it in parapsychology that so monopolized my research and writing?

In retrospect I can see two different lures. One was a will o' the wisp. It came from data that were significant in supporting some hypothesis or other and thereby seemed to me to show that my thinking was more or less on the right track. But the data were never fully, 100 percent in line with prediction. This surely meant there was more thinking to do and there were further condi- tions to study. Another better experiment was waiting to be done. Such partial success in hypothesis testing always presents an experimentalist with the temp- tation to try one more time along almost the same lines, to stay with familiar methods that are to be modified slightly, to hope that next time will be really right. It was especially tempting to me because it seemed that successive ex- periments did in fact show improvement. (My research has never picked up all the loose ends, but immodestly I think that its use of pretested measures of attitude, personality, and momentary mood to separate subgroups of subjects has at least yielded closer and closer fits between predictions and findings.)

The other lure that kept me in parapsychology was the excitement of testing out theories. Parapsychology opens up a swarm of questions about ourselves and the world we live in. It makes me feel ignorant. At the same time it surely encourages us to try to think up answers, even perhaps radically different answers about ourselves and the world. It's exciting whenever a hunch about one of these fundamental issues comes along. It may be important. The only way to find if the hunch is right is to do research on it. That makes the research exciting too. Here's an example (but you'll find it an example where my hunch was wrong).

One of the questions that troubled me most, in my earliest work at Emerson Hall, was how a sheep could find the target to hit, or a goat find the target to avoid, in that locked room with its stack of numbered targets. How could ESP go down to the umpteenth sheet in a pile of eighty sheets and make a match — or mismatch — with that one? I began to play with the idea that there might be some process like sonar or radar: first a wide scan of possible targets, then with feedback a homing in. Even this wouldn't solve the whole problem, but it seemed plausible as a beginning for it.

Three experiments in 1968 and 1969 tested it out (1969). In each the subject first tried for some part of the target, then was shown what that part was, then tried to call another part of the target. We could see if the partial feedback helped in identifying the rest. The three experiments used widely different methods, and not one of them showed the sonar analogy was on the right track. Naturally I wondered if the null results meant only that experimental conditions were inappropriate, not psi-conducive, but even this last resort could not save the theory. Within each of the three series there was evidence that ESP had occurred; ESP scores varied with session salience, or with mood, or with preference for one type of target over another. The question of how psi finds its target is still a mystery to me — and if I had another hunch about it, I'd be eager to test out the new one.

Here's an example of a hunch that gave good results. It concerned telepathy, a process I'd never studied because working with clairvoyance-type methods is so much easier. They don't need the coordination of a sender's message with a percipient's attempt to respond. Although in the early days of research telepathy had been considered the basic psychical process, the current "party line" at Rhine's laboratory was that there was no good evidence for it. What evidence there was could be explained away as clairvoyance of a sender's brain processes. Telepathy was a nonparsimonious concept and should be disregarded.

Spontaneous cases made telepathy, separable from clairvoyance, seem intuitively reasonable (1956); and I began to think along these lines. Let's grant that no crucial experiment proves the occurrence of telepathy. That doesn't matter. Most of us suspect by now that no experiment in any field will be crucial, and will by itself prove a theory or a theoretical concept, because some other theory can always be modified or a new theory dreamt up to account for that single set of experimental results. Good evidence for a theory comes if many implications of the theory are tested and are supported, and if, though the whole set of results makes sense according to that theory, it needs painfully forced ad hoc explanations without that theory. Well, then, what are the implications of telepathy?

Judging from spontaneous cases, one is that it is most likely to be effective between people who care for each other. Another is that it can send specific messages, and another is that it can send nonspecific or intuitive ones, like mood changes. Folklore suggests that it can send curses as well as blessings; and if we translate this last into experimental terms it implies that telepathy might be able to make a subject either fail or succeed at ESP. I tried to put the four implications together into an experiment, even though it would have to be an elaborate, time-consuming one. In fact, it turned into a series of three experiments, with successively better procedures.

First, how to find if subjects are likely to be in telepathic rapport? I examined various possible tests and finally settled on the one that gives the broadest information about personality and that is the most sensitive of all: the Rorschach. This meant that even if my classes agreed to be subjects and took a group Rorschach together, there would have to be an interview with each of them. (The interview would serve two purposes: an inquiry about any of their written responses that were ambiguous, and the ethical requirement of telling them their test results.) And this meant allowing at least two or three hours per subject for the original tentative scoring, for the interview, and for deciding what the Rorschach of that subject, paired with another, implied about how the two would feel toward each other when one sent messages and the other tried to receive them. It would take a long while, but seemed the best way to go. I decided to class each pair of subjects, before I knew their ESP scores, as likely to be congenial or else likely to be either hostile or reserved.

For specific and general messages, I thought of this: The specific messages could be the usual ESP cards. (I was using colored ESP cards by then, partly because it made the targets more interesting to the subjects and partly because it saved time. With one set of five randomized colors and one set of five randomized ESP symbols, a run of 25 calls would give 50 usable responses.) The nonspecific messages would come from two other runs. On one the sender, without seeing the cards, was to hope the percipient would succeed; and on another, without seeing the cards, the sender was to hope the percipient would fail. Normal expectancy effects would be controlled by keeping the percipient ignorant of the different sending conditions.

If the results showed a difference between success and failure messages, it would imply the nonspecific, mood type of telepathy. If they showed a difference between the sender's seeing and not seeing the targets, it would imply that specific messages are sendable. Further, congenial pairs could be compared with uncongenial pairs. By analogy with sheep-goat findings, we might expect these two groups to have opposite results.

There were three problems in this procedure: two anticipated and one that appeared only while the first series was moving along. The anticipated problems were easy enough to work out. One was how to synchronize timing without imposing too fast or too slow a rate on the percipient. This was handled by having a one-way buzzer that the percipient pushed to show it was time for the next message. One was ethical: How could I keep the percipient ignorant of the different conditions without lying? Here I was able to phrase the instructions so that my conscience was at rest. They were loosely enough worded not to be outright lies; they merely omitted part of the truth.

The unexpected problem was that senders told me they found it unnatural to hope for success when they didn't know what the right answer was and also felt it so unpleasant to send messages for failure that they couldn't bring themselves to do it. Eventually, after trying a good many different ways to make both procedures seem natural, I found instructions that seemed to be persuasive. They started with an analogy to a baseball game, and we agreed that when our team came up to bat, we were likely to think, "Hit that ball!" rather than thinking "Swing low" or "Move your right hand down" or "Move your left foot forward." This general sort of encouragement without specifics was what senders should try to send on the Success run. For the Failure run the baseball analogy was changed to having the other team come to bat, when messages also would be of the general sort, like "Miss that ball!" When all this was described as part of a game, it seemed to take the odium away from sending a failure message.

Of course all the usual procedural precautions were taken. Targets were prepared by someone else from lists of random numbers and were put into opaque envelopes. I was ignorant of the targets until after the subject's calls and therefore could not give inadvertent cues about them. Sender and percipient were in nonadjacent rooms with closed doors, so that only loud sounds could carry; I stayed in the space between rooms and would have heard loud sounds, but there were none. The order of the three types of runs was counterbalanced. All scores were independently checked. However one precaution that would be routine today was not used: I was not blind to the order of the runs, nor to the classification of the pair of subjects.

The first series (1958a) tested 102 pairs of subjects, many of whom were friends. With my first inadequate instructions it gave null results for the two conditions where the sender did not see the cards: the Success and Failure messages. But for runs where the sender saw the targets, scores were significantly above chance for subjects predicted to be congenial and significantly below chance for subjects predicted to be hostile or reserved with each other.

The predictions seemed good, but it was not clear what they meant. They had been made only tentatively after my seeing the Rorschachs and had been firmed up only while the subjects were in their separate rooms for the first ESP run. Quite a few were changed because of my impressions from watching and hearing a pair. I remembered some of the changes I'd made, looked over the data, and decided my impressions from observation were less valid than the first tentative interpretation from the Rorschach.

From then on, I changed the procedure so that the Rorschach interpretation would not be contaminated by other observation. This meant working with pairs that I'd never seen together, and was arranged by asking all my classes if they would like to take a Rorschach, hear an interpretation of it, and act as a subject in an ESP experiment. All agreed enthusiastically. They told me the hours they would be free. Then I paired the free hours of students in different classes (who with few exceptions didn't know each other) and made blind Rorschach interpretations for each pair. Only then did they come for their joint experiment.

The second series tried to study a different question: Whether telepathy would work with someone who did not even know who the other person was. This was tested, with 47 pairs, by scheduling appointments carefully so that the two subjects would not meet until their session ended. The results were null: no evidence at all of ESP. But I do not dare to generalize about telepathy from those null data. It may be that for college students such a secretive, unsociable procedure would be psi-inhibitory because it would make them withdraw, pull into themselves, and while in that mood not try freely to use ESP. If so, it was not a proper test for the limits of telepathy.

The third series, with 50 pairs, gave more satisfying results (1961). Rorschach assignments as either congenial or hostile/reserved were made before I saw the subjects together. When they came for their appointments they were introduced; they heard the instructions together and asked questions if anything was unclear; then the sender went with me into the separated room. This time the Rorschach was vindicated: for runs where the sender saw the targets, scores were significantly higher for subjects predicted to be congenial than for the others. (Scores were somewhat above chance for subjects predicted to be congenial and they were significantly below chance for subjects predicted to be hostile or reserved.)

Further, the data implied very strongly that telepathy had been effective. Analysis of variance showed a significant difference among the senders' three conditions. What was most striking was a reversal of scores between trying to send the targets they saw and the Failure message. When the senders predicted to be hostile or reserved sent messages for Failure, the percipients scored significantly above chance. When senders predicted to be congenial sent messages for Failure, percipients scored below chance. This strongly indicates that even nonspecific telepathic messages can have an impact.

Part of the fun of doing an experiment is that the data are so likely to be surprising at first glance, but after you take a second look they teach you something. Take this last example. From the sheep-goat effect and other similar work we might expect subjects to score below chance when feelings are negative, either because of working with someone who is uncongenial or (if telepathy occurs) because of messages for failure. Each is a negative. But what if there are two different negative conditions at the same time? Shouldn't we expect scores to be even lower? It surprised me when I first saw that these results came out just the opposite way. But then it struck me that the two different negative messages produced a double negative. And with a double negative, what does the second do? It cancels out the meaning of the first one and produces a positive. It's true in conversation; we learned it in algebra; and according to these data it applies to ESP as well. From then on I began to notice the same kind of results in work at other laboratories: a combination of two negative conditions resulted in positive ESP scores or else (in a somewhat more complicated example of the same pattern) a predicted difference between two groups reversed when test conditions changed from being pleasant to unpleasant.

I even speculated about whether this might imply a built-in safeguard against harmful ESP: If an enemy wishes you ill, perhaps it makes you well. But judging from these data, that happy speculation isn't sound. The data imply that if an enemy consciously wishes you well, the effects may be unfavorable.

After all those hundreds of Rorschachs I was more than ready to stop work on telepathy. Besides, there was something else that I wanted to study: precognition. I didn't see how it could happen, in the physical world I knew. Then I began to wonder whether it did happen in the physical world. Maybe not; maybe it happened only in a mental world. Maybe you could precognize events only if later they would be in your mind? Maybe precognition was a present-mind-to-future-mind process? If that was true, the next question would be whether the precognitive knowledge had to be only for events in one's own future or whether it could also be for events that someone else would know, and thus be a telepathic precognition.

These were testable questions in the late 1950s because computers were in use. To translate the questions into a research procedure would require only three sets of random precognitive targets. A computer would select all targets and would also score all responses and print out scores on each run. For one set the computer would print out the targets and then the subjects would see both the targets and their own responses. Success here would mean precognition of something in one's own future. The computer would also print a second set of targets, and I would look closely at them but the subjects would not see them. Success here would be precognition of an event in someone else's future; this could mean there was telepathic precognition. But the third set would be the interesting one. It would be scored by the computer without printing the targets. No one would ever know what the individual targets were. Success here would mean clairvoyant precognition.

If subjects gave only null results on this third set, though they succeeded on the others, it would imply that only what would later be known could be precognized. It would imply a dualistic world where physical events functioned differently from mental ones. (We psychologists have been trained not to like dualism and to feel comfortable when we can think of the world as monistic, but that shouldn't keep a person from trying to find out which is the right kind of theory.)

The next step was to describe the needs of the project to the engineer in charge of the computer room. He told me that studying ESP was silly but the project was doable. He could easily program the computer with a table of random numbers and enter the table at random, then assign targets serially to successive responses. He could also arrange for the scoring and printout that were needed. (Targets would technically be called pseudorandom rather than random because the table of random numbers determined their order, but this did not affect the design.) I went ahead with it.

There were two series here. The first had 50 subjects but there was a partial computer foul-up and proper records could be obtained for only 16 of them. The second series (1964) had 75 subjects and the computer worked well throughout. In both, the order of the three conditions was rotated to compensate for position effects within the session, and the subjects were not aware that their three runs would be treated differently. There was one procedural difference that may have been important: In the first series I knew which set of scores would be treated which way, and that somehow made the procedure more interesting to me. (Maybe, without being aware of it, I even said it was time for the next run with special alertness when the subjects made the calls for clairvoyant precognition.) In the second series I was blind to the condition that would be used for each run.

For the 16 subjects with proper scores in the first series, the clairvoyant precognition runs, where no one ever knew or would know the targets, showed scores significantly higher than chance. (This was a relief to me in one way because I could keep on thinking of the world as monistic, but it was a disappointment in another because it meant I was no nearer understanding precognition than before.) For the 75 subjects of the second series the overall scores were low, but so many significant relationships showed up between ESP and psychological variables, like attitude toward time and creativity and confidence that the data looked as if precognition had been effective for all three sets of targets. In addition, the data showed significant differences between conditions and looked as if scores were quite strongly influenced by whether or not the subjects themselves would see the results of a run rather than having only me see them.

Besides those big projects, there were lots of others in the 1960s and 70s. Most were studies of different personality variables that seemed to offer insights into why ESP failed at some times and succeeded at others. Some of these worked out well, like a series to find what mood was psi-conducive. (Here the results showed that no single mood was always the favorable one. A mood of social affection was appropriate for ESP in a friendly setting; a competitive mood seemed psi-conducive in a competitive group; and the absence of social affection seemed to help ESP scores when a stranger presented the ESP task in a coldly businesslike way.) Other projects were just for fun, like side trips or excursions to look at some problem that happened to show up, after my interest in ESP was known. Here are three that you might find amusing.

The first came in the mid–sixties when a friend told me she thought her house was haunted and asked if I wanted to investigate. Of course I did; who wouldn't? The way we set it up was to learn that the family agreed on two things for this ghost: where in their house they felt its presence, and the kind of ghost it was (a gentle and quiet one). To test location, a draftsman made a plan of the house; I marked it off into units; the family marked the units where the ghost had been felt. To test ghostly personality I used a long, standard checklist of personality traits, and the family encircled the ones they thought true of the ghost and crossed out the ones they thought false, leaving blanks where they had no impression.

Then some people who thought they were psychic were escorted through the house. On copies of the house plan they marked where they had felt the haunting and on copies of the personality checklist they circled and crossed out their descriptions of this ghost's personality. To prevent inadvertent cues the family was absent during the psychics' visits, and psychics were escorted by assistants who knew nothing of what the family had reported. Simple statistics showed more resemblance between the family's descriptions and the psychics' responses than could be accounted for by chance (but of course this might have been due only to the psychics' ESP of the family's reports).

A couple of years later, in California, Thelma Moss was told of a haunting and decided to investigate it with me (1968). This ghost had a physical description, so we made up a physical checklist too; and she improved my method by having a group of people who thought they were not psychic fill out the descriptions to compare with what psychics reported. Again the results came out with a statistically significant resemblance between what witnesses reported and what psychics reported. What seemed especially interesting to me was that the two ghosts appeared so different both to witnesses and to psychics. The first one was described as mild and benevolent, the second as active and aggressive. (Were there ghosts, or did the significant correspondence between witnesses and psychics show only ESP? I don't know; the data don't say.)

Years later Michaeleen Maher learned of an apparent haunting in a New York City apartment and investigated it similarly but with a psychic group and a skeptical control group which tried to outguess the psychics. Again there were significant results from the psychic group. She could find no clues as to what caused the effects, either from history of the location or from the infrared photographs and geiger counter measurements that she arranged.

In short, all that these ghostly studies showed was that something psychic was happening, but we don't know what. It's enough to keep curiosity alive, isn't it?

Another excursion (1970) started when a student I'd never seen before came bursting into my office and said that he knew a swami who wanted to show me ESP. It turned out that the swami wanted a college class to show ESP after he'd talked to them and taken them through some mild exercises. When I mentioned this to my graduate class in experimental psychology (a small class that semester) they volunteered. We agreed that they'd do an ESP run beforehand, then hear the swami, then do another.

Their first ESP scores were near chance. Then the swami spoke to them. They were quiet and polite, but I could feel their skepticism when he launched into a mystical description of how their bodies functioned, a description that was absurd according to what they knew of physiology. He had them meditate briefly and took them through a breathing exercise, then he sat quietly at the side of the room while they wrote their second ESP runs. To their astonishment (and mine) scores on those second runs were significantly high.

Why were the class scores significant, that second time? It may, of course, have been only a statistical fluke. It certainly wasn't positive suggestion: the class attitude was rather a condescending rejection. It wasn't the meditation and breathing: a student of mine later tested meditation with that breathing exercise (and others) for their effect on ESP scores, and none had a consistent effect. I wonder, though, about a fourth possibility. A number of things that I've seen and read seem to imply that someone with strong psychic ability can temporarily transfer that ability to others. If that can happen it certainly ought to be demonstrated by good research and explored. It seems an important possibility. If it can happen, maybe it was what happened here.

The last of these accidental investigations that I'll tell you about was the most interesting of all (1973). It began when an acquaintance invited my husband and me to join a ghost-hunting party. We did, and found it consisted of a fairly large group who had been taking photographs, with a newly available heat sensitive film, in places they thought were haunted. None of the photographs had been developed. We did no hunting; it was only a social evening.

Weeks later a telephone call came to my office from someone we had met in the ghost-hunting group: Ingo Swann. He had hardly said a word all evening but I had noticed that he was much respected by the others. He said he now believed that he could change the temperature of objects, and that he'd like me to set up a well controlled experiment in the college laboratory to find if he really could.

Testing temperature was out of my line. I could do it, but not easily, and I hesitated. In the end, three reasons persuaded me to go ahead with it. One was that it was refreshing to find a person who was considered a psychic and who actually wanted tests of his ability to be well controlled. One was that the others in his own group obviously thought that he was so special. The third, and most persuasive, was what Ingo said had led up to this request.

When the group's photographs were developed, most had shown nothing interesting. But one, taken in a room where Ingo was alone and thinking his own thoughts, showed quite a marked change in the heat-sensitive film, some distance from Ingo. Though the group thought that might be one of the ghosts they'd been hunting, Ingo wondered if he could have produced the heat change. He made a first check by going to a friend's lab; the friend hooked up some temperature measures; Ingo tried to change them and they changed. Now he felt ready to have someone thought by the psychic community to be critical and skeptical check out whether he really could change distant temperatures. This cautious sequence seemed to me to have earned the next step that he was asking for.

An engineer constructed the necessary equipment for temperature measurement. Larry Lewis, a brilliant graduate student, agreed to set up and monitor the equipment. Ingo agreed to my rather tight conditions where order of trying for hotter or colder was counterbalanced and both length and number of trials were preset. He was pleased at each step of increasing rigor: Enclosing the sensor so that it was fully insulated and putting his target 15 feet away. Our series of sessions showed that he could indeed change the temperature recordings, toward either hotter or colder. And of course I was pleased, and rather awed, at working with someone who had such strong ability as he.

A PK effect on temperature hadn't been studied before and therefore was a minor technical advance, but theoretically it posed no new problems. If PK can affect moving dice, it does not take a radical extension to show that it can affect recordings of moving molecules. But two of the things that happened in the experiment and that weren't its main object of study still seem to me to be provocative (as the double negative effect was in the telepathy experiment). It's these odd extra bits of information that come out of research that give icing to the cake for an experimenter: always something new to think about.

One happened the first time that the temperature sensor was enclosed in its insulation. Ingo asked me where within the bundle it was. When I didn't know, he said he'd "probe" for it. The probe, for Ingo, was to use ESP. Both of us sat there quietly. But a moment later Larry Lewis rushed into our room to see if we'd opened the insulation—he had observed a sudden temperature change in the recording. Ever since I've been wondering if ESP involves creating a PK effect upon its target. If we find it does there will be a big step forward in our theoretical understanding [and by now a fair amount of research seems to tell us yes, this happens (1987)].

The other interesting effect came because I'd had the engineer prepare four sensors, though we needed only one for the target. Larry and I set the other three in different places, near the target or farther from it, and attached them to the recording device. When the target's recording showed a change in temperature the other recordings changed, too; and in general the pattern seemed to be that when Ingo made the target hotter, the distant sensors grew colder, and vice versa. It looked as if Maxwell's demon was at work, changing the distribution of the heat. If this really is what happens (and I can't be sure, because it's never been formally tested) then it would modify the question we ask about PK. We'd no longer ask about the source of the extra energy that PK uses to make objects move; we'd ask about how PK changes the energy patterns that it finds.

These have been projects that I did; now I'll mention one of the ones that I was eager to do but couldn't arrange. It's expensive, and though I applied to many sources I couldn't find funding for it. It would have been an investigation of whether personality survives death (which surely is an interesting question, and even has practical applications). The design is worked out in considerable detail, but only on paper, alas (1977). I still think it could give clearer evidence, one way or the other, than anything done yet. Like most of my projects it's designed to give extra information beyond what's needed to check out the major question. If the results are affirmative and seem to give evidence for survival, they will also yield a set of clues as to which aspects of personality change after death and which remain stable. Maybe some day someone will pick it up and do it.

*   *   *

These last pages have been more a history of my ideas than an account of my life. For that matter, even the first page was defective, according to a rule set forth by our younger son. He said, and it sounds reasonable: "An autobiography should begin, 'I was born.'" Here's a fresh start, and it will belatedly begin the right way.

I was born a little late but warmly welcomed, in mid–June of 1912, in New Jersey, half a block from the ocean. (If anyone asks, "Were you born in New York?" I'm likely to say, "No, I was born in the summer." My family used to leave New York for Jersey on the Memorial Day weekend, and go back to the city only at the beginning of October.) It was a stable family. There were six of us: my parents and myself, my mother's parents, and my mother's sister. All loving, all protective, probably all more appreciative than I deserved if anything was done well but quick to point it out when something was done badly. They were sure of the right ways to think and behave, but they could be tolerant of minor deviations: They often told me, for example, that when I was a baby and soup was my favorite part of dinner, they served my soup at the end of the meal so that I'd eat enough of the rest. (That must have been considered more than a minor deviation; a moderately large departure from the way things Ought To Be.) But on some matters they were not tolerant. Grandmother strongly believed that bare legs led to rheumatism, and all through my childhood I wore long stockings while the other children were wearing socks.

The years before school were happy ones, but when I was six there were changes that seem small as I look back at them and still were more than I could manage. We spent that winter and the next in a suburb of New York where I had no ready-made friends. My nurse left; probably up to then I had depended on her for friend-making. I entered school a month late, of course, and felt outside of what everyone else took for granted. The teacher's saying "Fold your hands," for instance, baffled me for a long time because my hands couldn't fold. (Fingers folded, but that was no use; the teacher said hands.) I became painfully shy, and the shyness stayed painful all through adolescence; there are remnants of it still.

School itself went well enough. There was none of today's effort to judge a child's maturity before extra promotions, and I had skipped two years by high school. Missing classes at the beginning and end of the year was no handicap because Mother found what was to be taught in those weeks and coached me. Reading was a pleasure, of course, especially the rhythmic poetry that I could recite to myself when walking alone. At outdoor games I seemed always to be the worst, and wonder now if that could partly be due to a mysterious sickness the summer before the first infantile paralysis epidemic. It was undiagnosed then, but the next year, after I'd recovered, our doctor said that if in the previous year he had been familiar with polio, that's what his diagnosis would have been.

Grandfather died when I was 13, and this was a real grief. He was a gentle, well loved person, kind to others and of course to me, and after he retired we had been together a great deal, walking, talking, even listening together to that new invention, the radio. His death made me start thinking, for the first time, and the thoughts made me become a naive materialist.

Then came a new school, with small classes and interesting teachers: an all girls school to which my parents sent me so that I'd be prepared to enter college at Barnard. I had a few friends there but still felt a social isolate: two years younger than the others, immature even for my age, without the sophistication of my classmates. Soon I began to feel sure I could never do well the social things they did so well and that my family valued. If I couldn't do them, what could I do? Poetry was what I wanted, but even then I suspected that my gift for it was slight.

At high school my academic work had been good enough: many fewer hours at homework then the others and grades that were second-best in the small class. But right after, the roof fell in. Mother wanted me to go to Barnard, probably partly because neither she nor her sister had been allowed to; their parents didn't think college suitable for girls. I applied there and nowhere else. And then I flunked the College Boards in Latin prose. Barnard naturally couldn't accept me, but offered me a second chance if I passed the test in the fall.

That summer I tutored in Latin prose, then took the exam—and made a lower grade than before. Disaster! But the school's headmistress turned to the telephone, and found that Smith would accept me, even so late, because the average of Latin and Latin prose grades brought me up to passing. Mother and I went up to Smith, and soon I was established in a dormitory, with a suitcase and the promise of a trunk to come, with friendly girls around me, and with a stimulating schedule of courses.

It's hard to condense the next four years into a few words. From the career point of view they confirmed my estimate that my poetry wasn't good enough to keep on with. As a second best I thought of science and was first attracted by physics, but the psychology course was an even stronger attraction. It was taught with a lab period each week, and doing the little demonstration experiments, then trying to make sense out of the data, gave the same sort of intellectual pleasure that research has given ever since. Junior year, in the experimental course, an off-the-wall idea was encouraged by J.J. Gibson, our instructor, and turned into a published paper which he and my teammate, Eleanor Jack, used as their wedding announcement (1932). Another experiment, senior year, turned later into another paper with Gibson. My grades were mixed, except in psychology, and my average was a low B; the Phi Beta Kappa in my senior year has never ceased to astonish me. And besides having found a good many friends, both in the dormitory and outside of it, I was part of a lively in-group made up of some of the psychology students and the younger faculty members.

After college a job—of a sort—was waiting. The program in Neuroendocrine Research at Worcester State Hospital hired three of us from Smith to work in statistics with E.M. Jellinek. Pay was room, board, and laundry. At the end of the summer Jellinek offered me full time work, with a pay increase from zero to $30 a month and with enough time off to take courses at Clark. Nothing else was better, that summer of 1932, and off I went to Clark to see about enrolling.

At Clark, there was a perplexing intake interview. Dr. Carl Murchison, the chairman, asked what I had studied. "Perception," I began, but he interrupted: "We don't say perception here." "Sensation?" "We don't say sensation. We say sensory processes." They took me into their M.A. program in spite of my vocabulary problems, and gave a conservative but interesting training in rigid, old line behaviorism—but let me do the thesis research I wanted (1934) under the department's maverick, Ray Willoughby. Midyear they told me that I hadn't qualified for the doctoral program, and this may well have been because of my sometimes using taboo words like "consciousness." At the end of the year they offered me a doctoral fellowship, which I naturally declined without thinking twice.

What next? An interview at Yale suggested some of the same rigidity as at Clark. An interview at Harvard sounded wonderful; I applied there and was accepted. The program was as open as anyone could hope; it even allowed us to audit courses instead of taking them, which left more time free for experimentation.

This had an odd result. After the end of the first year, with the preliminary examination passed, I spoke to a potential thesis advisor about an idea for a doctoral dissertation. He listened to it without any enthusiasm, then asked what I'd done last year. When I told him (work on visual and kinesthetic judgments of length and on the effect of primacy), he said that that was enough for a dissertation, maybe with one short supplementary series. That series went quickly and by midyear I'd completed all requirements for the doctorate. Everyone agreed, though, that there was no point in coming up for the degree before spring because there was nothing else for me to do, so I stayed to audit classes and experiment.

And this is where we came in, but there has to be a supplement. A lot happened professionally that the history of ideas don't describe. I'll run through the highlights.

At City College successive steps were orderly. After the standard minimum number of years came tenure, then promotions up from instructor to assistant and associate and full professor. With mandatory retirement three years ago there was a semester of terminal leave which I spent teaching parapsychology at John F. Kennedy University, near San Francisco, with its fascinating differences in intellectual as well as physical climate. Then I came back to City College and taught the same graduate course in experimental psychology as before. (College regulations allowed it after mandatory retirement so long as my title was changed to adjunct professor emeritus.) That continued for three years, but this year, though flattered to be invited to continue, it seemed to me that it had gone on long enough, and now for the first time in many years, I have no classes.

Within the department at City College my parapsychological interests seemed regarded as a permissible idiosyncrasy rather than a handicap. Other faculty members heard me speak about the topic with courtesy but no interest, and this has never failed to amaze me. (I can understand emotional rejection of ESP and PK, and of course can understand excitement about their implications, but it's beyond me to understand how such intelligent people can listen and then let the topic drop.)

But all was not sweetness and light. When the college became part of City University, psychologists from other colleges at first refused to accept me to the graduate faculty because of my work with ESP. I was shocked, and so were some of the faculty. In a couple of years, happily, the staunch support of our chairman, J.G. Peatman, and a strong letter from Gardner Murphy, then at the Menninger Foundation, persuaded them to change their vote. Once accepted I taught regularly in the doctoral program, both at City and in the Social-Personality program at the university's graduate center, and became active in committee work.

Inconsistent though it seems, from then on the attitude of my colleagues at the other colleges seemed just like the attitude of the ones at City. They occasionally asked me to speak on parapsychology, and they referred graduate students with an interest in ESP to me for courses, tutorials, and even a dissertation.

College work is more than teaching, of course. There was the pleasure of research projects to supervise for undergraduate honors work, masters' theses, doctoral dissertations. About half of each type, more or less, were in parapsychology; fewer at first and more after (through the generosity of Chester Carlson, inventor of the Xerox process) a fund was made available for financial support and also after I gave an occasional course in parapsychology. Committees sometimes meant only hours of talk, but chairing them sometimes demanded hours of labor, especially when I had to coordinate reading lists or examination questions from the different colleges in the university. For a few years I even tried my hand at administration, and headed the M.A. program at City College. This was sometimes rewarding, especially when some student needed a generous rather than a narrow interpretation of the rules and I could present the petition in a persuasive way to a persuadable dean, then watch the student go forward to a successful career; but after enough years so that it was clear I could do it, I dropped it. The rewards from time spent in teaching were more appealing.

Parapsychology also brought committee work and the equivalent of both teaching and research supervision. It is rather like supervising research to referee journal papers or grant proposals or review a book for a journal. All of them need judging the value of the underlying idea but then being as critical as possible about how the idea is carried out, and perhaps making a constructive suggestion or two. And it is obviously similar when, as happens every so often, a research plan or research paper comes from a student somewhere else who has seen my name and asks for my comments.

The equivalent of teaching comes from requests to lecture to some outside group, or to take part in a television or radio program. There have been many of these, the first ones exciting of course, and rather frightening too (though even now I find myself with stage fright at each new appearance before a strange group). Some were flattering, like being asked to talk at the Bell Laboratories or MIT or NASA or the Harvard and Columbia colloquia. Some were especially interesting because the groups were so strange to me, like hypnotists or psychics or devout church members. By and large they turned out to be pleasant after the stage fright had passed but they were disappointing too. Neither the radio and television nor the talks to research-oriented groups led to anything more than expressions of interest.

The committee work has come from three organizations. One is the Parapsychological Association (PA), a brainchild of J.B. Rhine, initiated after he had asked some of us to join in his summer program for teaching parapsychology. (The PA was formally founded in 1957. It is the professional organization for parapsychology and is now an affiliated society of the American Association for the Advancement of Science.) I was its second president and in 1971 was president again (1971) and for years was active on its board or sometimes on program committees for its annual conventions. Next came the ASPR, where my duties as board member were light at first, but then intermittently heavier (1976). After I became president of the ASPR the time needed for administration grew steadily longer; when it began to look as if doing the job properly would demand at least half time work and possibly more, I stepped down. For the Psychical Research Foundation I stayed on the board somewhat longer.

Now we're up to date on my personal doings, but there's been hardly a word about the world they happened in. You don't want me to give you a rundown of global affairs, but maybe I should pick up that unfinished business about how being a woman has affected my career, and should at least mention briefly some of the changes in psychology and parapsychology.

As for being a woman, at City College it seemed no handicap except in small ways like not having access to areas near the men's gym. The psychology department prided itself on lack of prejudice and it deserved to, though as times changed the rest of academia had to catch up with it. Probably an underlying prejudice still favors men for powerful positions, but by now even this isn't the sort of thing that's stated in public. It wouldn't affect me anyhow, because I'm not eager for power.

Even if being a woman didn't handicap me in formal ways like promotions, did it matter in the informal ones? Maybe a little but not much.

Often the others at some meeting or other were men, and it seems to me that my ideas were heard with as much attention as anyone else's. Thinking back, I can remember only one time when there was an explicit remark about it (though not remembering other times may show only my selective forgetting). The anecdote may amuse you; here it is.

It was when the Society for Psychical Research celebrated its centenary at Trinity College, Cambridge. As president of the ASPR, after the banquet I gave a small ceremonial gift from our society to theirs and made the usual complimentary presentation speech. Later a group of us were talking and someone asked if I was the first woman who ever spoke from the high table at Trinity. The question hadn't occurred to me. But it must have been in others' minds because someone else answered quickly, "No, the Queen Mother spoke." Perhaps in England there are more sex distinctions than in the United States? Or perhaps not. Maybe the question and its quick answer showed only that the English are more outspoken about the feelings—and restrictions—that still exist in both countries.

That's been a long comment on gender; now comes a short one on psychology. It's grown tremendously since 1935, with much more clinical and applied work, and more specialization and sophistication in research. It's had an information explosion, and I no longer feel as I did just after the doctorate that I have a good grasp of the field as a whole.

How about parapsychology? It's also grown, but more slowly. And it also became more sophisticated, notably in its journal policies of refereeing articles and of publishing null results as well as significant ones. (On this last issue its policy is ahead of psychology's.) Rigor of research? Parapsychology was the more demanding back in the 1940s when I entered it, but psychology caught up and forged ahead. By now, even though many parapsychological experiments are up to or surpass the standards of contemporary psychology, demands for research rigor seem to be lower in the field as a whole. Even its best journals often publish research reports that do not meet psychology's standards.

What of psychologists' attitudes toward parapsychology? On the whole there may have been some slight warming up but it's nowhere near as much as the large number of fine research reports would have produced if we were living in an ideal world. Maybe what I'm going to say next will sound far-fetched, but here it is anyhow: I think there's a basic resemblance between parapsychology's present unhappy status and the status of women in the old unenlightened days. The theory for my assertion goes like this.

Prejudices are common, and psychologists like other human beings have acquired some, in childhood or later. Prejudices are emotional; they linger even when they conflict with facts or with ideals. Because conflict is uncomfortable, we often hide the conflict from ourselves by resorting to rationalization or some other type of defense mechanism. (OK so far? I could cite reams of researches that support the general ideas.)

Now let's move to specifics. Among established scientists there's long been a prejudice against women and also against parapsychology. These conflict with the noble ideals of equal opportunity and academic freedom, ideals which all decent people avow. But both conflicts can be rationalized. Remember how Dr. Boring took pains to explain to me that only practical reasons kept women from having the same job opportunities as men? And psychologists have similarly found ways to rationalize a prejudice against parapsychology with the ideal, proper thing to say. What they say is that parapsychology should have the same opportunity to prove itself as any other research area. Anyone is free to do research on that or any other topic as long as the research methods are sound and the work is not outright illegal.

And how do they rationalize this ideal of academic freedom with their prejudice? The respectable way is to give specific rather than general reasons for rejecting parapsychology but to slant the argument. You can find examples in the way most introductory psychology texts treat ESP, if they mention it at all. They make their treatment look balanced because it has arguments pro and con, but the evidence in favor of acceptance is either the weaker cases or only a scanty mention of stronger cases. The opposing arguments therefore look correspondingly strong. They look even stronger if they are overloaded, as they often are, with outdated or inappropriate criticisms, or the requirement of higher standards than for the other topics in psychology. (If you feel detached enough, all this is an interesting episode in the history of science, but it sure makes things hard for a young parapsychologist who is looking for a job.)

The general theory fits with my own experience. I've never, in the academic world, heard anyone state a general condemnation of parapsychology. They all know that if it were stated, it would be in trouble. To advocate banning a research area—when a colleague who disagrees can hear you—is not only rude, it also exposes you to seeming mean spirited or ignorant or both. The colleague could put you to shame on the high moral ground of academic freedom or by citing examples from the history of science where areas once banned are now accepted.

And yet the private bias lingers surreptitiously. I've run into it only twice that I know of, once in the doctoral faculty's initial refusal to accept me and once when I asked a division of the American Psychological Association to change my status from member to fellow. They refused and their president told me privately their reason was my ESP research. It made me feel (in Churchill's immortal words) that this was something up with which I would not put. I asked them to reconsider, writing politely, of course; listing again my formal qualifications; and raising the academic freedom question in a tone that was half incredulous, half indignant. After this airing of the issue they made me a fellow. (There may have been other times, as when *Science* rejected a paper, but those two are all I'm sure of.)

What we have is public statements of good faith along with a private bias. Even at City, students have repeatedly told me of particular faculty members who sneer at ESP in teaching their own class. Yet when the same men speak to me about parapsychology, any doubts they raise are only the proper methodological ones. (Did I confront them about it? No, though I've wondered if it was a moral obligation. My reasons were partly selfish, because confrontation could have destroyed the friendly terms of our day to day contacts; partly theoretical, because against emotional bias no logical arguments are effective; and partly practical, because making them angry by putting them in the wrong might make them try to hurt my students whose interest in ESP was known. All went well academically for the students while the men publicly went along with adherence to academic freedom.)

Isn't this similar to what academic reactions to women used to be? No decent, bright man in the 1930s would say that women were inherently incapable of doing academic work, but he'd feel free to use all sorts of weak reasons for denying an academic job to a woman. And a decent, bright psychologist now won't say that parapsychology is inherently unworthy, but yet will find specious reasons for neglecting its findings or refusing to accept them. It looks like the same principle at work in both.

How did all this affect me? Not very much, but more by good luck than good management. Part of the good luck was that at both the college and the university, the other psychologists acted as if neither my sex nor my ESP interests were relevant to my competence. Another part was that running for office in psychological organizations didn't especially interest me. If I had wanted to go in for psychological politics the change of attitudes about women would have raised my status but my shift into parapsychology would have lowered it.

After all these musings and reminiscences, let's go back to the question that perplexed me a few days ago when I began to look backward from 1985 to 1935. Is what stands out the contrast or the similarity between the two periods in my life?

This time I'll start with contrasts. Professionally there's been a whole string of them, of course, like having my status go upward and downward. But if we forget the small ones and turn to the big picture, maybe the biggest are these. After the Harvard doctorate I felt that what there was to know in my field of experimental psychology, I knew. I felt secure intellectually but inadequate in any number of other ways. Almost the opposite is true now. In my newer field of parapsychology, what I feel most sure of is areas of ignorance. And the contrast is just as clear between the professional insecurity of the jobless young woman of 1935 who had done so little except studying and research, and the pensioned professor emeritus in 1985 who's had such a variety of odd jobs from writing encyclopedia articles to chairing committees and even to finding a point that needed changing, here and there, in a proposed legal document.

But are the similarities more important? Maybe in a broad sense they are. Interest in ideas and in doing research to test out the theories has stayed consistent. Another thread that seems to have run through this whole narrative is a self-centered desire to do what I find most stimulating and worthwhile. It may have started in high school, and it surely has been true ever since. Another is a readiness to turn my hand to some or other kind of work, but that's almost a corollary. It follows naturally from wanting to do what is interesting or satisfying.

Socially and in personal life, the superficial differences are clear. In 1935, as the mores prescribed and our sexist vocabulary worded it, I had a good many friendships with girls and dates with men (and felt pleased and surprised about having them, after my shy adolescence). In contrast, because my husband and I find each other interesting and feel content to be together, there are rather few others whom we see socially, far fewer than in the earlier days of our marriage when our energy level was higher. And the children and grandchildren who are such an important part of our lives now were hardly even dreamed of then. Certainly we could never have dreamed of these particular four strong and interesting and so different children nor of the particular [six in 1988] lovable and so different grandchildren whom our children have brought into the world.

Similarities there? Yes, if we make the generalizations broad enough. We have friends now; I had friends then (and some are the same friends). Although only my aunt is still alive from the family I was born into, there is really a very similar family stability. Each of the adults in our family now, I think, feels both love and a responsibility for all of the others. Of course individual relationships change with deaths and births and moving to different locations and the growth of new interests; but when I look back to 1935, my feeling is that the values are the same. I'd have been glad then to look forward to the family and friends we have now.

It's time to stop. There's work to do: a book that's waiting to be written.

References

(1932) with Gibson, J.J., & Jack, E. Bilateral transfer of the conditioned response in the human subject. *J. Experimental Psychology* **15**, 416–421.

(1934) The effect of recall on forgetting. *J. Experimental Psychology* **17**, 828–838.

(1943) Predicting good and bad scores in a clairvoyance experiment: A final report. *JASPR* **37**, 210–221.

(1956) with Frommer, E. Analysis and evaluation of a pair of presumably telepathic dreams. *JASPR* **50**, 74–78.

(1958a) Agent-percipient relationships. *JASPR* **52**, 47–69.

(1958b) with McConnell, R.A. *ESP and Personality Patterns.* New Haven: Yale University Press.

(1964) An experiment on precognitive clairvoyance. Part I. The main results. Part II. The reliability of the scores. *JP* **28**, 1–14; 15–27.

(1968) with Moss, T. Quantitative investigations of a "haunted house" with sensitives and a control group. *JASPR* **62**, 399–410.

(1969) with Lewis, L. A search for feedback in ESP: Part III. The preferential effect and the impatience effect. *JASPR* **63**, 60–68.

(1970) High ESP scores after a swami's brief instruction in meditation and breathing. *JASPR* **64**, 100–103.

(1971) Respice, adspice, prospice. *Proceedings of the Parapsychological Association* **8**, 117–145.
(1973) PK effects upon continuously recorded temperature. *JASPR* **67**, 25–340.
(1976) (Ed.). *Parapsychology: Its Relation to Physics, Biology, Psychology, and Psychiatry*. Metuchen, NJ: Scarecrow Press.
(1977) Looking ahead: A method for research on survival. *Theta* **5**, 2–6.
(1987) Psychokinesis: Recent studies and a possible paradigm shift. In S. Krippner (Ed.). *Advances in Parapsychological Research 5*. Jefferson, N.C.: McFarland.

Montague Ullman: A Self-Portrait

Editor's Introduction: Dreams are such ordinary experiences that for a long time their research potential was ignored by American parapsychologists until Montague Ullman, M.D., a New York psychiatrist and psychoanalyst (his own interest in dream experiences having been aroused in a clinical setting with his patients), stimulated research interest in others. This development is apparent from the frequent references in the dream literature to his dream work at the Dream Laboratory of the Maimonides Medical Center in Brooklyn, which he established in 1962. His work virtually constitutes the one source of experimental evidence that the content of dreams may be affected by telepathy.

The association between dreams and paranormal phenomena has been recorded time and time again. For example, in 1931 the BSPR reported on a questionnaire sent to 10,000 people listed in *Who's Who in America* and noted that 25 percent of the paranormal experiences occurred in dreams. After studying the Parapsychology Laboratory's collection of spontaneous cases, Louisa Rhine found that the great majority of paranormal experiences occurred in the form of dreams. The relationship between dreams and the paranormal persuaded many students of parapsychology that dreams had a great deal to say that was significant about the paranormal. But parapsychologists could only daydream about dreams because it was not possible to make dreams speak experimentally: There was no way of investigating the association between dreams and the paranormal in the absence of any method to determine if a subject was dreaming while sleeping.

Dr. Ullman helped parapsychology make one of its great advances of the past quarter century by utilizing a physiological method for monitoring dreams. He used the EEG to record brain waves and the Rapid-Eye-Movement technique to record eye movements. These techniques permitted Ullman, in his experimental studies, to know when sleeping subjects were dreaming and the length of the dreams. He was then able, during the dreams, to have agents use target pictures in an attempt to influence telepathically the content of the dreams. The subjects, awakened as soon as their dreams ended, tape recorded their dream imagery and their accounts later were blind-matched by judges against the target pictures.

Besides having made possible a nocturnal approach to ESP, Dr. Ullman coedited the *Proceedings of the International Conference on Hypnosis, Drugs, Dreams and Psi* (1968), and was an associate editor of Wolman's *Handbook of Parapsychology* (1977). He has made contributions to the parapsychological and nonparapsychological literature and coauthored with Stanley Krippner *Dream Studies and Telepathy: An Experimental Approach* (1970), with Stanley Krippner and Alan Vaughan *Dream Telepathy* (1973), and with Nan Zimmerman *Working with Dreams* (1979).

A former fellow of the American Association for the Advancement of Science, Dr. Ullman has been president of the Parapsychological Association and the Gardner Murphy Research Institute, was president of the ASPR from 1971 to 1980 and served on its Board of Trustees and Medical Section. He is now clinical professor of psychiatry emeritus at Albert Einstein College of Medicine. — A.S.B.

Autobiographical Notes
Montague Ullman

As everyone who wears glasses knows, as we grow older we have to keep changing lenses to adapt to the changing structure of the eye. If we don't our view of the world loses its clarity and accuracy. The same with memory. If we don't enrich our capacity for reflecting on the past through emotional growth, then those experiences of the past remain impaled on the narrow vision that first greeted them. This is what strikes me as, nearing 72 (I was born in New York City on September 9, 1916), I write about my life with a public in mind. I find it best to begin with the end and use that to point to earlier events in my life.

Family pressures as well as my own aspirations drew me to medicine. An accidental exposure to the world of psychic phenomena while in college oriented me to the mysteries of the unconscious realm of existence, including our dream life. My background in neurology oriented me to the neurophysiology of dreaming; my exposure to psychoanalysis as a student and a practitioner oriented me to the metaphorical structure and healing potential of the dream, and my work in community psychiatry impressed upon me the importance of identifying and sharing the skills necessary to make dreams generally accessible. Hovering in the background throughout all these experiences was my fascination with the paranormal. The latter acted as a kind of Greek chorus, reminding me then and now of how much we still did not know about dreaming and the unconscious dimensions of our existence.

Since I have become more content with and more tolerant of myself I feel better able to dislodge some of the earlier encrusted views of my past. The first

Montague Ullman

such view had to do with the way I felt about my parents as I grew up, best summed up by saying that I felt at odds with them. I grew up rejecting their world of bourgeois, religious, commercial values. Though it might have been less painful otherwise, it was the distance between us that also made it possible for me to follow my own path.

Both my parents were first generation Americans who were born and brought up on the lower east side of New York City. My father's father, Samuel Ullman, came to America at the age of 14 from Hungary. His life was a success story I never got to know or appreciate. By the time I was born he was the head of a successful manufacturing concern along with his oldest son, my father William, who, I was told, was a superb salesman, and with his youngest son, Max. Next in age to my father was Sol, who became a lawyer, and a younger son, Martin, who was a commercial artist. The two youngest children were daughters, Doris and Minnie. I was already launched in the private practice of psychiatry at the time my grandfather died at the age of 81. I recall him as a serious, quiet man toward whom everyone showed the utmost respect. He spoke only when necessary. He was deeply religious and most of the family occasions revolved around the Sabbath and the various Jewish holidays. I was the oldest grandchild and I knew he took great pride in my accomplishments. He was, however, a very distant figure. My feelings toward him were tinged with a sense of guilt as I grew away from the Jewish traditions and began to embrace left wing causes, a far cry from the staunch Republicanism that seemed so much a part of the family tradition.

My father's mother, Katie Grossman, was a different story. A beautiful woman, she was also a "sport." Her place, of course, was relegated to the home and there she was warm, welcoming and nurturing. There was a side of her that managed to escape the "old man's" surveillance. She loved to smoke and play cards and occasionally she would sneak off for holidays to enjoy the baths at Saratoga. I enjoyed her company, her food, her generous spirit.

My mother's parents came from Poland. My grandfather, Herschel Eisler, became a tailor, earned a meager living, lived to a ripe old age and had a wonderful sense of humor. What intrigued me as a child was that he had an artificial leg and, although I knew him into my adult years, I never did discover what caused it. My grandmother died sometime during my adolescence and I have only a hazy recollection of her. The Ullman family, being successful, began to move upward, literally, going first to the Bronx and then to the upper west side of New York along with other prosperous middle class families. My mother's family consisted of an older brother, William, and two younger sisters, Esther and Estelle. They remained on the east side and we began to see less and less of them as my mother became more and more involved with my father's family.

My father was generous to a fault and loved high living. He smoked heavily, drank, overate and, to the despair of my mother, gambled as well. He died in 1935 on his 44th birthday of a coronary. I was then in my second year of medical school. The day he died, synchronistically enough, the lesson in our pathology course was on coronary occlusion. My sister Jean was 16 at the time and my brother, Robert, was 13.

My mother, Nettie, was a very conventional person, eager to be accepted into my father's family. She was a superb cook and baker but given to hysterical anxiety at the slightest provocation. She was irresistibly drawn to babies and small children but didn't do so well when the child's struggles to individuate itself began. My fondest memories of her had to do with the wonderful food she plied us with. Much as I resented her great need to "show off" her children, it also bolstered my ego. My father was the focus of her life and she never quite recovered from the shock of his death. My Uncle Martin took an active interest in the family following my father's death. I felt a special closeness toward him. He inherited my grandmother's capacity to enjoy life.

As far as I can remember I never saw my mother or father ever read a book. But my father's best friend did read and became the first inspirational figure in my life. He was Dr. Irving Krellenstein, our family doctor and a very comforting presence when we were ill. He would overcome our apprehension with the songs he made up as he examined us and the way he made us laugh. He had a high brow which seemed to follow the same shape as the stethoscope he wore. I thought that, in order to be a doctor, you had to have a brow like that. Aside from my grandfather he was the only man I believe my father had a deep respect for. He often came to our house for a Sabbath dinner. He made me feel that being a doctor was special, something apart from and above the world of business.

At the time I started school, the public school system was so overcrowded that a rapid advance system was instituted in order to move students along quickly. This, in addition to the fact that I attended a three year high school (Townsend Harris Hall), resulted in my enrollment in City College just prior to my fifteenth birthday. I was bright enough to handle the work but inside I felt like the immature child I was. I wanted very much to get into medical school and to get the grades necessary for admission. The competition was severe. Classes numbered over a thousand in each year at City College and it seemed to me that most students were taking pre-med courses. My father so wanted me to become a doctor that, despite some resistance and shame on my part, he was not above using influence to ease my admission into medical school at New York University at the end of my third year at college. I had good marks, but so had hundreds of others and I have often wondered whether I would have made it on my own.

The first two years at medical school were difficult. My classmates were older, seemed far more self-possessed and far less fearful of failure than I was. There was, however, a deep satisfaction that came from the fascination of the subject matter and the prestige of being a medical student. At the start of my final year, in the autumn of 1937, I met my future wife, Janet Simon. Courtship was on and off for the next four years, mostly because of my not knowing my own mind. We were married at her home in Brooklyn on January 26, 1941, at the onset of my residency in neurology. Janet, her family and her home provided the warm setting I so badly needed. She taught piano and was the source of our income during my residency years when I earned very little.

At medical school my interest gravitated toward both neurology (I loved watching two masters, E.D. Friedman and Foster Kennedy, do neurological examinations) and psychiatry (where Paul Schilder gave off philosophical as well as psychological sparks in response to any question put to him). With Schilder as our guiding spirit several other students and I managed to get a Medical Psychology Club started. Among those invited to speak were many who later made important contributions to psychiatry, e.g., Joseph Wortis and Nathaniel Ross.

A graduation gift from my grandfather enabled me to spend six weeks in the Soviet Union in the summer of 1938 in the company of two distinguished medical historians — Henry E. Sigerist and Victor Robinson, along with several other doctors, a young lawyer and Sigerist's daughter. Earlier, Sigerist had written a book favorable to the Soviet health system and, as a consequence, we received a warm welcome as we travelled the length and breadth of the land, visiting medical institutions, research centers, collective farms and factories. I was impressed medically with what had been accomplished through public health programs and, politically, with the vision of what seemed to me to be the start of a new and progressive society built on socialist principles. On the way home I spent a day in Berlin where, on a sightseeing trip, in response to a question, the guide denied that Jews were being mistreated in any way. Then followed an exciting week in Paris just before returning home. While there I managed to be in the audience at the Sorbonne when the aging Pierre Janet delivered a lecture.

Upon my return from this trip I kept up a relationship with Victor Robinson who taught medical history at Temple University at the time. He was a prolific writer, turning out very readable and scholarly books on the leading medical figures of the past. These were books that should have but have not found a place in the current medical curricula. A gentle man with a pixieish quality, he plied me with his writings and touched off in me a zeal for writing.

In January 1939, I began four years of hospital training, the first two in a medical internship (Morrisania City Hospital), followed by a year of residency in neurology (Montefiore Hospital), then a year as a psychiatric resident at the New York State Psychiatric Institute. At the end of that year I was called into the Army. I reported for duty as a medical officer in December of 1942 at the Lawson General Hospital in Atlanta. After several months I was transferred to the Kennedy General Hospital in Memphis, where our first child, Susan, was born that June. I remained at Kennedy for a year, serving both as a neurologist and a psychiatrist. Then followed a year and a half abroad in general hospitals, first in England and later in Paris. I returned to the States in December 1945, opened an office, at first for the practice of neurology and psychiatry, then drifting into psychoanalytic practice as I completed training in that subspeciality at the New York Medical College. In 1946 our second child, William, was born.

In 1950 I joined the faculty of the Comprehensive Course in Psychoanalysis at the New York Medical College. The next ten years were devoted to teaching, to practice and to various research endeavors. The latter included a project that explored the relationship of suggestion and the cure of warts, a study undertaken at the invitation of Dr. Marion B. Sulzberger, then head of the Dermatology Department of New York University. Subsequent to that I was a research psychiatrist on a multidisciplinary study of stroke patients at Bellevue Hospital.

I embarked on my psychoanalytic career in 1942 with Bernard Robbins as my analyst. I found him a remarkably sensitive, insightful and supportive therapist and regretted having to interrupt analysis during the three years of army service. Robbins had been analyzed by Harry Stack Sullivan and Karen Horney. Influenced by his ideas I felt more at home with the "culturalists," those who broke from the emphasis on instinct theory to take a closer look at interpersonal and social influences. Robbins was a man of original and progressive views because of which he, along with a number of other analysts, broke with the New York Psychoanalytic Society to develop training centers of their own. Robbins helped found one such center at the New York Medical College, and it was there that I entered into formal psychoanalytic training in 1946, following my return to civilian life. In 1950 I was made a member of the psychoanalytic faculty. I taught there until 1961 when I terminated my private practice to develop a department of psychiatry at what was then known as Maimonides Hospital (later the Maimonides Medical Center). Our last child, Lucy, was born in 1951, shortly after we moved to our present home in Ardsley, New York.

Since the focus of these autobiographical notes is my lifelong interest in psychic phenomena I should like to go back to September 1932, at the start of my sophomore year at the City College of New York. I had just turned 16, knew nothing about psychical research and was studying hard to prepare for admission to medical school. Early in my second year a friend and classmate, Leonard Lauer, confided in me the story of his personal encounter with psychic phenomena. After explaining the term to me he shared the basis for his conviction. He had read the early literature and reeled off strange names to me — Lombroso, Schrenck-Notzing, Flammarion, F.W.H. Myers, Oliver Lodge, T.J. Hudson, William Crookes and, finally, William James. More important, he had been party to and had witnessed some of the extraordinary phenomena he had read about.

I took Leonard Lauer seriously. He was also a science major and fancied himself a hard nosed scientist. At the home of his friend Gilbert Roller, he had witnessed table movement and knockings when he, Gilbert and another friend named Larry (Gilbert Laurence) sat around a small table in the dark in a seance arrangement. They had been sitting for many weeks and were convinced that the effects were not of their own making. Several years earlier poltergeist effects had plagued Gilbert and his family and Gilbert's mother was said to be a medium. The group met every Saturday night and I was invited to join. In addition to my exposure to the literature, what I witnessed was to make me a psychic researcher for the rest of my life. For the next year and a half I, along with the others, devoted Saturday evenings to what rapidly evolved into a very serious project.

At various times I have tried to write an account of these experiences. The first was in the form of an essay for a philosophy course I was taking at the time. What follows are some excerpts from that essay written in 1932:

> The first phenomena we developed goes by the name of telekinesis, or super-normal movement of objects not due to any known force. In these experiments we (four of us) used an ordinary bridge table, keeping contact with the table and with each other by our hands. The room is usually light enough to allow us to see what is taking place. After a few moments the table would start to move and distinct knockings are heard, seemingly coming from

beneath the table. One of the sitters gives commands (it is immaterial who does the talking as long as all the others are thinking along with him) and the response is almost instantaneous. The table moves to the one whose name is mentioned. We then managed to get the table to tilt in whichever direction we asked. After continued experiments of this type we finally decided to get this unknown force to elevate the table. Early attempts in this direction all ended in failure. One night, however, we were thrilled by the sight of the table rising from beneath our hands to the height of two or more feet! We repeated this and were successful at subsequent trials. Once, when the table was elevated we each individually removed our hands from its surface. To our astonishment the table remained suspended in mid-air for about two seconds before collapsing to the ground. Encouraged by this success we kept trying. The height of our accomplishment with telekinesis was an experiment in which we made the table come up to our hands which we held about two feet above it. (We had always found success without contact of the hands rather difficult).

"We gradually became so accustomed to the table motion that it no longer interested us. Our efforts then turned to the field of photography. I should like to note a curious experience we had in this connection. In our first attempt we took a photographic plate and placed it in a tin case (in this position it could not be affected by any physical force). The plate was placed on the table with one of the sitter's hands resting on it. The room was absolutely dark during the entire process and the usual contact was maintained. After several minutes we put the plate aside, thinking it would not be worth developing as we felt it was impossible for the plate to be affected. We then went back to the table and asked the 'force' to give us a message, if there were any, by knocking after the appropriate letter in the alphabet as it was called off by one of the sitters. In this way the word 'P-L-A-T-E' was spelled out. We immediately developed the plate and, sure enough, there was a distinct imprint of the hand. We repeated the procedure and got several other imprints, not only of hands, but of any object we placed on the metal case that held the plate. Thought photographs were the next step. Below is a list of the objects we thought about and the objects received on the plate [numbered as in the original positives]:

Objects thought about	Objects received
5. Page from a book	Column from a newspaper
1. Bottle (large, corkless labelless)	Small, corked iodine bottle with label
6. Message	The letter "C"
4. Picture of a girl's face	Indian idol

"A brief explanation of the above experiments is necessary. In the first we got a picture of an ordinary newspaper column and managed to make out some of the words. In the second the bottle on the plate was entirely different from the one we thought about. We got an iodine bottle that was later found in the medicine chest in the bathroom. In the fourth try we thought about a certain girl, but it seems that during this sitting one of the members could think of nothing but Indians. The only possible object suggested by the image on the plate is an Indian idol. . . . In one of the rooms we later found a small souvenir which was the exact shape of the image on the plate. None of the sitters had been thinking of this idol; only one of them had ever seen it before and that was several years before.

"At the first photographic sitting I accidentally performed an experiment which convinced me that there was no trickery at all in the matter. While one of the sitters had his hands on the case that contained the plate I placed my thumb over his hand and an imprint of my thumb came out on the plate negative. If the plates had been fixed beforehand (they could not have been handled after the sitting because I, myself, developed them), this would not have happened."

There were many more remarkable events which followed the writing of the above account. These included a series of written messages purporting to come from someone identifying himself as Dr. Bindelof, a physician who had died in 1919 but who made known his continuing desire to be of help to us in both a fatherly and a healing way. These writings were obtained without anyone touching the pencil. Sitting about a night table with our hands in contact above we had placed a pencil and paper on the lower shelf. Soon after the lights were turned off the pencil would start writing at a furious rate. At the completion of the message it would be slammed down and the paper crumpled.

In the full flush of these exciting results Leonard and I took our case to the ASPR, then located in the Hyslop House at 23 Street and Lexington Avenue in New York City. There we related our experiences to Frederick Bligh Bond, then editor of the *Journal*. He listened with polite interest. In the 1933 account I wrote I seemed to have felt somewhat positive about the visit. When, much later, I checked with Leonard, his recollection was that he came away feeling disappointed at what he felt was a cool reception.

Sittings continued with other friends, including girl friends, joining us from time to time until the spring of 1934 when the group finally disbanded. Until then the group sat regularly, usually at weekly intervals, over the course of a year and a half. In summary, we experienced a gradual and climactic unfolding of almost the full gamut of psychical phenomena as such phenomena were known and defined by writers on the subject in the 19th and early 20th century. The developmental sequence led to such startling phenomena as levitation of a table, messages purportedly written by someone who had died and photographs taken without exposure of the plates. Heady stuff for a group of 16 and 17 year olds! Either that or mere foolishness and nonsense.

In the spring of 1966 I succeeded in bringing together five of the original group that had participated in the seances in the thirties. The purpose was to compare our recollection of these sittings, to assist each other in filling the gaps in our memories, to establish areas of consensual agreement as to what had actually taken place, and to define those aspects of the experience where the passage of time made any semblance of accurate reconstruction impossible. The events in question were extraordinary both at the time they occurred and in their lasting impact over the years. The meeting took place that summer on a Saturday. It was a day devoted to the boisterous recapturing of what was the strangest and most powerful experience of our youth. The phenomena struck us back then and also subsequently as inexplicable, as truly paranormal. Any differences among us concerned interpretations of the nature of the paranormal event and not about the fact that it *was* paranormal. Because we could neither explain it away nor seriously consider a 33-year sustained fraud, joke or deception by any member of the group or any combination thereof, we accepted it collectively as a compelling and powerful aspect of our respective lives. We subsequently had several reunions of this sort in the hope that some day a full account would emerge.

It is not an unusual psychological event for middle-aged men to seize on any pretext to regress to an adolescence they never completely outgrew. It happens at football games and at college reunions. Perhaps these dynamics played a role in what happened on that Saturday in 1966 or on the other occasions when, after many years of separation, we came together to reexamine the events that had welded us into a group in the first place. Within a few moments of being together we again began to re-experience passionately and intensely the harrowing and exciting times we had had earlier. It wasn't simply reliving the experiences of our lost youth. It was a good deal more than that. It was re-encounter with an aspect of our existence that, while still mysterious and inexplicable, was enduringly real for each of us.

What was undeniable was the deep and lasting impact these experiences had on the direction my life took. Despite periods when they were in cold storage (when I tried to learn how to view the world scientifically during my medical training and during service in World War II) they were never completely submerged. It would only take the sympathetic interest of another person to open the locked closet. Even while in the army and stationed at a hospital outside of Paris I managed to get three fellow medical officers interested in conducting a number of seances, unfortunately with no results.

The most sympathetic ear I ever encountered in connection with my early psychic experiences was that of Gardner Murphy. One of the first things I did in December of 1945, while on terminal leave, was to visit the ASPR whose headquarters were then at 34th Street. I happened to pick a day when there was an elevator strike and had to climb eleven stories to the offices. It was well worth it. Murphy was there, made himself available and quietly listened as I poured out the entire story of my earlier encounter with psychic phenomena. It was the start of what proved to be a deep and lasting relationship.

Soon after I opened my office we began to collaborate in informal weekly sessions on Saturdays that aimed at exploring ESP under conditions of light trance and hypnosis. Our subjects were students from Gardner's courses at City College. We took turns as experimenters. Gardner and I would meet for lunch beforehand and I used those occasions to share with him the paranormal dreams I had encountered with my patients the preceding week. These lunches were memorable. Gardner listened with rapt attention to these accounts. He was supportive, never challenging and, at times, would call attention to historical parallels. He was always in pursuit of some objectifiable evidence of psi but it never dampened his enthusiasm for its spontaneous manifestations. I know he was concerned with some way of objectifying the data we were getting in the exploratory studies we were doing with the students. I'm afraid his gentle exhortation fell on deaf ears. Quantitative methods were not my dish of tea.

Lois Murphy often joined us at these Saturday sessions and she soon began to participate on a regular basis. She had a flair for it. Her ability to zero in on the target while, at the same time, to observe and articulate what she was going through was most impressive. It sparked my hope for a developmental approach for cultivating ESP. The work with Lois went on from the end of 1947 to the beginning of 1949. The work with the students went on for a year or so but with no spectacular successes.

With Lois, however, something of interest did happen, something that shed light on her inner mental processes as she sought to respond to the target picture. She identified two distinct stages. The first was a passive one that she referred to as free wheeling. She would let images come and go, trying to keep any voluntary control or interfering thoughts at a minimum. She would draw one image after another while keeping up a running commentary. Sometimes there was a clustering of images with obvious similarities; sometimes there were no obvious connections. Where the impressions took a distinct form she would name the object that seemed to be forming in her mind. This brought her to the second stage where, because of the perseveration of certain forms and impressions, she would come to a felt impression of what she thought the target was. She referred to this as focussing. Not infrequently her conceptualization of the image was wrong but the forms she drew came closer and closer to the forms suggested by the target as she went on with them. The trick was to keep her ego out of it—to push aside such thoughts as, "Oh, it couldn't be this; we had that target last week."

Another rather definite and striking finding was that Lois was sensitive to the "soft" or "hard" quality of the target picture. She shied away from pictures that suggested aggression, violence, hardness, etc., doing better with pictures drawn from nature, babies, food, etc. She did better with "soft" targets than with "neutral" targets (bicycle, boat, etc.). Also worth noting was the importance of her antecedent mood prior to the experimental session. She was always given the opportunity before we started to talk freely about this.

This was my introduction to experimental parapsychology. The work was informal, exploratory and relatively loose but it was congenial to Gardner, Lois and myself in our pursuit of both objective and subjective factors related to ESP. We worked largely with free hand drawings with the subject, whether Lois or one of Gardner's students, lying on the couch in varying stages of relaxation and trance. The most interesting results occurred with Lois and not, as might have been expected, with students even when deeply hypnotized. The Murphys' move to Topeka terminated these meetings but the cross fertilization continued. When, in 1961, I gave up private practice to become director of the department of psychiatry at the Maimonides Hospital, it was Gardner who obtained the grant that initiated our explorations into dreams and telepathy.

Gardner had a way with young people. True to his given name he offered the right combination of support and stimulation needed to fertilize the germinal ideas of others. Many people are well read, but Gardner seemed to have read everything and to have everything he read immediately available when relevant to the question at hand. His way of roaming freely over his past reading recovered for others much of value and helped to fit things into broad overarching theoretical structures. More personally he fullfilled my need for a respected and respectful mentor. He shared his books and writings with me and from that came a deep appreciation for the range of his knowledge, the humility with which it was set forth and his genuine openness and responsiveness to all that was human. He was the most selfless person I had ever known.

My contacts at the ASPR soon led me to a growing friendship with Laura Dale. Laura was deeply devoted to Gardner, to the ASPR and to the field of psychical research in general. There were many troubled sides to Laura's makeup but she managed to rise above them as she set about singlemindedly to make the *Journal* of the ASPR the repository of the finest theoretical and experimental contributions to parapsychology. In this she succeeded admirably. Knowing the field as she did and being a meticulous worker she was about as perfect an editor as one could be. Our friendship grew both through our mutual interest in the ASPR and through the secretarial work she did for me in the late fifties. She was an expert stenotypist which made dictating easy. I have never known anyone else who could turn out manuscripts as rapidly and as perfectly. Later Laura did most of the editorial work for the *Handbook of Parapsychology.*

Laura, Gardner and I went together on one rather fanciful adventure in Maine to see if dowsers could do better than the Maine state geologist in finding underground water. They didn't but they did give us insights into unusual and colorful personalities.

In the early fifties all we knew about the physiology of dreams was that they occurred from time to time during the night. With the idea of a dream-telepathy experiment in mind in this pre-REM era I enlisted Laura's cooperation in planning a series of exploratory experiments, using a gadget known as a dormiphone. It could be set to awaken the sleeper at various intervals throughout the night and deliver a recorded message. Laura and I then set about recording our dreams, she most often acting as the recipient and I as the sender. We experimented with different stimuli on the tape from nonsense syllables to meaningful names and phrases, hoping that they would stimulate a dream. We also kept diary notes oriented to recording any emotionally charged events in our lives. We met weekly at my home, Laura driving up with her prize-winning dogs. There was much excitement as we compared dreams and diary notes. The results were encouraging enough for us to stay with it for several years. They also paved the way for the more formal dream-telepathy studies I undertook at Maimonides.

We never did succeed in quantifying the mass of data we accumulated although Laura Dale made a valiant attempt. It wasn't in my nature to do it nor do I think we would have captured what was the essence of the experience, namely, the subtle and subjective factors at play.

At Murphy's invitation I joined the Board of the ASPR in 1948 and remained a trustee until 1986. At the time I joined, George H. Hyslop was president, later succeeded by Murphy. The situation in psychical research has changed considerably since those early days. In the forties the ASPR was the only agency oriented to both research and to the maintenance of the scientific image of psychic research in the minds of the public. It flourished under Murphy's leadership. In the late forties he encouraged Laura and me to set up a Medical Section of the Society so that those psychiatrists who were gathering examples of paranormal dreams could meet to share their experiences. The participants in this endeavor, which lasted until 1953, included, in addition to Laura and myself, Jan Ehrenwald, Jule Eisenbud, Robert Laidlaw, Geraldine Pedersen-Krag, Gotthard Booth, Adelaide Smith and, from time to time, invited guests. Among the latter were Fritz Wittels and Hyman Spotnitz.

The decade from 1950 to 1960 was one in which I was involved with the three major interests in my life — the exciting new approaches to psychoanalytic thinking and practice, a growing interest in dreams, and my efforts to bring my interest in the paranormal into the mainstream of my life. By day I was busy with my practice and research projects at Bellevue Hospital with stroke patients (a study of symbolic and behavioral changes in patients with strokes), and later at the old Skin and Cancer Unit of Bellevue with a study of suggestion and warts. In the latter half of the decade I began what turned out to be a ten year federally funded project at the Skidmore College of Nursing with the goal of integrating psychiatry into a collegiate nursing program.

In 1953 Aserinsky and Kleitman monitored sleeping subjects in a sleep laboratory electroencephically and electrooculographically. They discovered what we now know as the REM stage of sleep associated with the dreaming cycle. A young graduate student, William Dement, participated in the work. Several years later he came to New York to intern at the Mount Sinai Hospital. About that time I conceived of the idea of using this monitoring technique to collect the dreams of sleeping subjects in a controlled dream telepathy experiment. Could a sleeping subject produce telepathic dreams relating to target material being "sent" by an experimenter under circumstances where we could now collect all the dreams of a given night and compare them to the targets which were either free hand drawings or striking photographs?

With Dr. Dement on the scene I arranged for a meeting with Eileen Garrett sometime in 1959. Robert Laidlaw had introduced me to Eileen some years before and I had had several experimental sessions with her at my office where, in her self-induced trance state, one or the other of her controls would speak. On the occasion referred to in 1959 Dement outlined the sleep monitoring procedure and I presented the design of an experiment for exploring ESP in dreams. Eileen responded favorably. She placed two rooms of the Parapsychology Foundation at the disposal of Karlis Osis, Douglas Dean and myself and provided the necessary funds to buy an electroencephalograph and hire a technician to run it through the night. Douglas arranged the intercom system so that we could awaken the subject (generally a friend, student or colleague I could dragoon into cooperating) at the time of dreaming.

Our plan was to awaken the subject after each dreaming episode as noted on the electroencephalogram and then ask for a report on any dreams. These were recorded on tape and later transcribed. We were guided by our subjective impressions as to whether any interesting correspondences had occurred between what we had chosen as target material and the dreams. Eileen Garrett was our first subject and she produced a spectacular hit as well as an unusual electroencephalogram, the latter never dipping much below the level of the Stage I REM dreaming phase of the sleep cycle. Later, Gardner also volunteered as a subject. The repeated awakenings made return to sleep difficult for him and nothing noteworthy occurred. I was generally the sender during these sessions and initially I preferred working with free hand drawings made in the course of the night. Later, prepared targets of photographs were used and chosen randomly. We were impressed with the number of striking correspondences that were obtained over the two year period we worked together.

The early exploratory work with Laura Dale, followed by the efforts of Karlis Osis, Douglas Dean and myself to use the REM monitoring technique as a way of capturing a good yield of the night's dreaming, thus facilitating an investigation into dream telepathy, played an important role in my decision to give up private practice in favor of a full time position in a hospital and the opportunity to shape a research program devoted solely to the pursuit of that elusive quarry, the paranormal dream. I remain grateful to Eileen Garrett and the Parapsychology Foundation for setting me on that course.

Within the first year of that transition in 1961 Gardner arranged a grant from the Scaife and Ittelson Foundations, administered through the good graces of the Menninger Foundation, which enabled me to set up the beginnings of a laboratory. We didn't really get moving along the lines of a systematic approach until Stanley Krippner joined our staff the next year with the responsibility to develop the research methodology. Stan had been at Kent State University and was ready to make a move. Gardner got wind of this and, knowing that I was looking for someone to head up the laboratory, sent him east to Brooklyn and the beginning of a productive collaboration. At a later point Charles Honorton joined our staff and took over from Stan when he left to join what is now the Saybrook Institute.

Stan was instrumental in working out what we felt was a foolproof design for the experimental approach we had in mind (a design which has withstood the test of time) to bring telepathic and precognitive dreaming into the laboratory. The results have been dealt with extensively elsewhere. They are admirably summarized along with the subsequent replication studies and a critique of the critics in a recent article by Irvin Child ("Psychology and Anomalous Observations," *American Psychologist,* **40**, 11 [Nov. 1985], 1219–1230). All in all we felt we had made a successful start in subjecting the paranormal dream to laboratory investigation. The positive statistical studies we obtained in 9 of the 12 formal studies we conducted supported the hypothesis that altered states of consciousness, such as dreaming and hypnosis, can be associated with telepathic and precognitive effects. Subsequent to Stan's departure Charles Honorton went on, through his Ganzfeld studies, to further explore the relationship of altered states and psi.

In 1970 I had six months off on a sabbatical leave from my duties at the hospital and medical school (the Downstate Medical Center). Janet and I had planned a trip that was to include visits to the socialist countries for the purpose of exploring their version of psi research. I was to go on to lecture and teach in Israel, India, Japan and Hawaii. Unfortunately, two months into the trip, Janet became ill and we had to return home. I nevertheless did see what I wanted to in the Soviet Union, Czechoslovakia and Bulgaria. In Moscow Edward Naumov gave me an overview of what was going on there and arranged a lecture for me. I also spent time with Dr. Raikov and was impressed with his way of using hypnosis to facilitate the emergence of musical and artistic talent in young people. The most exciting feature of the visit to the Soviet Union was the week we spent in Leningrad where, through the help of Dr. Sergeyev, I met Nina Kulagina and witnessed several striking psychokinetic efforts performed by her in my hotel room.

Zdenek Rejdak was our host in Czechoslovakia. One evening, while in Prague, we witnessed, along with another parapsychologist from the States, Thelma Moss, some of the experiments of a Czech engineer named Pavlita, who purported to show it was possible to store psychic energy in special metal configurations he had designed and then later, to release that energy to produce telekinetic effects. We were shown how a small wooden object, a match stick, for example, could be affected by one of these metal objects and made to move. Being there as visitors we could not validate the effect for ourselves. The entire encounter was shrouded in secrecy and no details or explanations were forthcoming. This encounter was quite different from my meetings with Sergeyev and Kulagina. Sergeyev responded openly to my questions, shared the data he had and told us about the many interesting results he had had with Kulagina.

In Sofia, Bulgaria, I managed a number of visits at Dr. Lozanov's rapid learning institute and there, too, I was impressed with his ability to use relaxation techniques to expedite learning languages and school projects with greater speed and less stress than might be expected.

In addition to my interest in the work of the Dream Laboratory at Maimonides and the task of securing the funds necessary to keep it operative, my main professional duties related to the Department of Psychiatry and the development and operation of a community mental health center. The latter came into being in 1967 and was noteworthy for the many innovative community programs it launched in its approach to the challenge of preventive psychiatry. As these undertakings grew I found myself involved in administrative responsibilities that made it more and more difficult to pursue my interest in research and teaching, both of which I found more to my liking.

In 1974 the opportunity I had been waiting for to return to teaching arrived. It was an invitation to me and another psychoanalyst from New York, the late Adolfo Caccheiro, to train Swedish psychology students and other professionals in psychodynamically oriented psychotherapy. The students had taken their basic courses at the Psychological Institute of the University of Gothenburg and had now organized their own institute for training and clinical experience. I was more than ready for the change and responded eagerly to the invitation. I stayed in Sweden for a year and a half, feeling drawn to the country and to the students I worked with. In the course of teaching about dreams my present way of working with dreams in groups evolved. This was based upon an experiential approach that brought home to the students in a direct and personal way the creativity of the dream, the information embedded in the imagery, and the healing potential of dream work.

Ever since my return to the States in 1976 I have continued to visit Sweden in the fall and spring for about two months at a time to teach and supervise students. Gradually more of my time there was devoted to group dream work at various hospitals and psychotherapy training centers. The demand for this type of training developed far beyond my expectations. I soon began to train Swedish professionals as well as nonprofessionals in the technique of leading a dream group. There are now many who are well-trained and are leading groups in almost all the major Swedish cities. Over the past three years the work has spread to Norway and Denmark.

My travels in Scandinavia afforded me an opportunity to meet those who were engaged in psychical research there. Rolf Ejvegard has made valiant efforts to keep serious interest in parapsychological research alive in Sweden. He was and is still instrumental in maintaining a scientific point of view in his tenure as president of the Swedish Society for Psychical Research.

Another after-effect of my experience in Sweden was my enthusiasm for group dream work. The process I had developed there I found suitable, not only as a training instrument for professional therapists, but also as a way of making dream work accessible to the interested layman. On my return I joined two faculties, the Albert Einstein College of Medicine and the Westchester Center for the Study of Psychoanalysis and Psychotherapy, for the purpose of teaching therapists in training about dreams experientially in a group setting. In addition I developed private groups and leadership training groups open to anyone interested in this approach. The work in this country thus paralleled my work abroad.

As this work developed I became more and more convinced that serious and effective dream work could extend beyond the consulting room and into the community. Since dreaming is a universal and natural event, access to the resulting dreams should be universal. For this to occur it takes a proper naturalistic setting where the skills involved can be identified and shared and where metapsychological concepts are jettisoned in favor of an understanding of the basic phenomenologic features of the dream.

I succeeded Gardner Murphy as president of the ASPR in 1971. I sought to keep the Society on the same course that he had embarked upon. Difficult financial years followed so that increasing deficit spending made it hard to maintain all the programs we had started. In addition, many of the differences among members of the Board around the aims and goals of the Society, differences that had simmered under the surface during Murphy's term of office, were more out in the open and not always easy to contain. Laura Dale continued to do an excellent job as editor of the *Journal*. Karlis Osis managed to pursue his studies of apparitions, out-of-body experiences and spontaneous cases despite the dwindling financial support, and Marian Nester succeeded in developing a range of services offered by the Education Department, including the very well received ASPR *Newsletter*. The management of the administrative affairs of the Society were in the competent hands of Fanny Knipe.

In the early seventies the outlook for research in parapsychology was a most precarious one. The various young parapsychologists scattered around the country were having a difficult financial struggle to maintain their full time commitment to parapsychology. They had the hope that, by coming together, they might have a catalytic effect on each other and also work out the strategies necessary to solve the problems they were facing. I was asked to head the newly formed organization which was named the Gardner Murphy Research Institute. We met yearly with Gardner in attendance until the onset of his illness. Although these meetings deepened personal and professional ties and, in some instances, fostered conjoint studies, it never got much beyond that and was finally dissolved.

In 1980 I resigned as president of the ASPR and from the Board in 1986. The late Arthur Twitchell succeeded me as president, followed by Gertrude Schmeidler, whose deep and longstanding commitment to parapsychology served the Society well. She was succeeded in turn by Howard Zimmerman, an able administrator and someone dedicated to the exploration of the full range of implications of psychical research. Earlier, Howard's wife, Nan, had collaborated with me on our book, *Working with Dreams*.

As I look back it seems to me that I have had the good fortune to have had three very different kinds of encounters with psi phenomena. As an adolescent I was exposed to the range of seance room phenomena that characterized an earlier epoch of psychic research. As a psychoanalyst my interest was rekindled as patients related dreams that struck me as telepathic. This was the direct precursor to my efforts to approach the problem of the paranormal dream experimentally.

In more recent years I have in some ways combined what I learned from these three levels of experience in exploratory studies conducted at the ASPR, making use of a group approach to dream sharing which involved going beyond surface correspondences to get at underlying motivational dynamics and, through the pursuit of psi events over a long period of time, allow for incipient psi abilities to develop.

Murphy believed in casting a wide net in our search for understanding psi. He embraced the old literature as well as the new, the qualitative as well as the quantitative. It has always seemed to me that, because of our ignorance, we had much more to learn about the natural outcropping of psi before we could (if ever) capture its essence in the laboratory. We have to avoid letting our ignorance constrain our efforts at exploration. In the recent group experiment referred to above we sought to learn more about the natural human predicaments that bring about a psi event and how such an event registered in a dream.

I end with the hope that future researchers will move into the future not only with computers and other sophisticated technologies but also with the breadth of vision of such pioneers as Myers, James and Murphy.

Major Works by Ullman

Ullman, M. An Experimental Approach to Dreams and Telepathy, Methodology and Preliminary Findings. *Archives of General Psychiatry,* June, 1966, pp. 35–62.

Ullman, M. A Nocturnal Approach to Psi. *Proceedings of the Parapsychological Association,* No 3, Durham, N.C.: Parapsychological Association, 1966; pp. 35–62.

Ullman, M. Bio-Communication in Dreams. *Journal of the American Academy of Psychoanalysis* 1,4 (1973), pp. 429–446.

Ullman, M., and Krippner, S., with Vaughan, A. *Dream Studies and Telepathy: An Experimental Odyssey.* New York: Macmillan; London: Turnstone Press, 1973.

Ullman, M. Parapsychology and Psychiatry. In A. Freedman, H. Kaplan and B. Saddock (Eds.), *Comprehensive Textbook of Psychiatry, 2nd Edition.* Baltimore: Williams and Wilkins, 1974; Vol. 2, pp. 2552–2561.

Ullman, M., and Zimmerman, N. *Working with Dreams.* Los Angeles: J.P. Tarcher, 1979.

Ullman, M. Psi Communication Through Dream Sharing. In B. Shapin & L. Coly (Eds.), *Communication and Parapsychology.* New York: Parapsychology Foundation, 1980; pp. 202–220.

Wolman, B., and Ullman, M. Access to Dreams. In B. Wolman and M. Ullman (Eds.), *Handbook of States of Consciousness.* New York: Van Nostrand Reinhold, 1986.

Ullman, M., and Limmer, C. (Eds.). *The Variety of Dream Experience.* New York: Continuum, 1987.

6
Brief Portraits of
Contemporary Parapsychologists

Stephen E. Braude

Associate Professor of Philosophy, University of Maryland

(Mailing address: Department of Philosophy, University of Maryland, Baltimore County, Catonsville MD 21228)
Born April 17, 1945, in Las Vegas, Nevada. Divorced, no children. Ph.D.
A professional musician since 1961, Dr. Braude earned his doctorate at the University of Massachusetts in 1972 after being graduated magna cum laude from Oberlin College in 1967 and receiving his M.A. in 1970 from the University of Massachusetts. Currently at the University of Maryland, he also taught philosophy at the University of Massachusetts.
A few distinguished philosophers have recognized the relevance of parapsychology to their own field. Among them have been C.D. Broad, C.J. Ducasse and H.H. Price. Dr. Braude follows in their tradition. "My main interests in parapsychology, recently," he writes, "have been in turn-of-the-century evidence for physical mediumship." But previously in 33 articles published in scholarly and parapsychological journals and in two books, including *ESP and Psychokinesis: A Philosophical Examination* (1979), his interest also has been in the analysis of the complex philosophical and theoretical issues raised by parapsychology. In the cited book, he not only took up the experimental evidence to discuss the conceptual foundations as well as the philosophical implications of parapsychology, but he also endeavored to formulate, as Broad and Ducasse had done, a definition of the paranormal. Dr. Braude's latest book is *The Limits of Influence: Psychokinesis and the Philosophy of Science* (1986).
Dr. Braude has been the recipient of several research grants for the continued pursuit of the queer but elusive facts of parapsychology which give rise to interesting philosophical problems.

Richard S. Broughton

Director of Research,
Institute for Parapsychology, Durham, North Carolina

(Mailing address: Institute for Parapsychology, P.O. Box 6847, Durham NC 27708)

Born October 27, 1946, in Brooklyn, New York. Married, two children. Ph.D.

Dr. Broughton's main interest is in computerized psi research. His interest in parapsychology was sparked by one of Lawrence LeShan's writings.

He joined the Institute for Parapsychology in 1981 where he became senior research associate. On the departure of K. Ramakrishna Rao for India in 1984, Dr. Broughton was appointed acting director of research and subsequently director of research. His duties included management of the research and support team, assisting with the *Journal of Parapsychology* and supervising visiting scholars.

He received his B.A. degree from Seton Hall University in 1968 and was awarded a Ph.D. in 1978 from the University of Edinburgh, Scotland, for his thesis, "Brain Hemisphere Differences in Paranormal Abilities with Special Reference to Experimenter Expectancies."

He worked at the Parapsychology Laboratory, Department of Psychology, State University of Utrecht, The Netherlands, until 1979 and became a research associate at the Department of Behavioral Sciences, State College of Optometry, State University of New York, until 1981.

Dr. Broughton's other research interests have included studies of animal psi, experiments with so-called "observational theories" and investigations of the relationship between ESP and the two hemispheres of the brain.

He was president of the Parapsychological Association in 1986. His several publications include "The Use of Computers in Psychical Research," which appears as Chapter 19 in I. Grattan-Guinness (ed.) *Psychical Research: A Guide to Its History, Principles and Practices* (1982).

Irvin L. Child

Professor Emeritus, Department of Psychology, Yale University

(Mailing address: Department of Psychology, P.O. Box 11A Yale Station, New Haven CT 06520)

Born March 11, 1915, in Deming, New Mexico. Married, one son and one daughter. Ph.D.

He was educated at the University of California at Los Angeles, where he received his B.A. degree in 1935, and was awarded a Ph.D. in psychology by Yale University in 1939.

Some humanistic psychologists, such as William James and Gardner Murphy, were drawn to parapsychology and the possibility of ESP because of their openness to new ideas, to the experiences of others and to systematic research. As a humanistic psychologist Dr. Child's interest in parapsychology began at an early age when his maternal grandfather related some puzzling experiences and continued in his teens when Upton Sinclair's *Mental Radio* made a deep impression on him. An instructor at Harvard University and later professor of psychology at Yale University, Dr. Child, attracted to parapsychology because he perceived a definite overlapping between humanistic psychology and the question of extrasensory perception, taught an undergraduate course in parapsychology at Yale and engaged in research in parapsychology at the Psychology Department at Yale and as a visitor at the Institute for Parapsychology in Durham where he conferred with J.B. Rhine.

His research activities have embraced the study of data to determine the relationship between errors made by an outstanding ESP subject in standard ESP tasks and his errors in visual tasks and the effect on ESP performance of unbalanced target decks of cards. Dr. Child also has written analyses and reviews of parapsychological experimentation and of its critics.

He served in 1981 as president of the Parapsychological Association and is the author of about 25 articles dealing with parapsychology. His extensive publications include "Psychology and Anomalous Observations" published in *American Psychologist* and *Humanistic Psychology and the Research Tradition* (1973), in which Chapter 8 is devoted to ESP.

William Edward Cox

Staff Member, Institute for Parapsychology, Durham, North Carolina

(Mailing Address: 20 Southbrook Drive, Rolla MO 65401)
Born September 12, 1915, in Wilmington, North Carolina. Married.

Mr. Cox studied at Louisburg College in North Carolina, Antioch College in Ohio, and at the University of the South in Tennessee. After serving in the Armed Forces during World War II, he was employed in radio production and management until 1950 and in newspaper feature and advertising until 1956.

His interest in magic, in 1932, led him to parapsychology. Mr. Cox writes that "Rhine's works, from ESP-60 onwards, were my mainstay." In 1957, he began to devote the greater part of his time to parapsychology and joined the staff at the Parapsychology Laboratory at Duke University.

From that time to the present, at the Parapsychology Laboratory, the Institute for Parapsychology and in Rolla, Missouri, his research activities have been concerned mainly with psychokinesis. Mr. Cox has been called by the

European Journal of Parapsychology "the most creative and ambitious worker in that field of research." He introduced "PK placement" in 1951, a method now widely employed, and adapted the "majority vote technique" to PK tests.

Mr. Cox has invented numerous PK testing devices to replace the conventional dice throwing procedures, among them sophisticated electromechanical devices which use the "placement" techniques for releasing target objects on special surfaces (such as a checkerboard). His present research includes studies of qualitative, as well as quantitative, physical phenomena.

A founding member of the Parapsychological Association, he served on the Board of Directors at FRNM and at the first Indian Centre for Parapsychology at Andhra University. Mr. Cox has published over 50 articles. His "The Influence of 'Applied Psi' Upon the Sex of Offspring" (1957) was awarded a prize by the SPR for the best and most original essay on parapsychology, and his "Physical Phenomena and Survival Evidence" (1958) was awarded a prize by the College of Psychic Science.

Hoyt L. Edge

Professor of Philosophy, Rollins College

(Mailing Address: Department of Philosophy and Religion, Rollins College, Winter Park FL 32789)

Born February 23, 1944, in Louisville, Kentucky. Married, one daughter. Ph.D.

Dr. Edge earned a bachelor's degree (magna cum laude) from Stetson University in 1966 and a master's degree and a doctorate in philosophy in 1968 and 1970, respectively, from Vanderbilt University. Prior to becoming professor of philosophy at Rollins College, he held teaching positions at the Pädagogische Hochschule in Freiburg, West Germany, and in the Parapsychology Laboratory of Royal University of Utrecht, Holland. In 1973 and in 1982, he received awards for outstanding teaching.

Dr. Edge is one of the rare breed of contemporary philosophers who recognizes the philosophical implications of parapsychology. One such implication gave rise to his interest in the field. "I am interested in what it means to be a person," he said. "Insofar as the data of parapsychology point to aspects of the person which are not fully explainable at this time by our traditional world view, it tells us something about what can be a new vision of what it means to be human." But he has not confined himself merely to an armchair philosophical interest in parapsychology. He has conducted experiments in paranormal healing, the use of psychokinesis on plants and the importance of feedback in parapsychological experiments, and has gained insights into the nature of science and the scientific process beyond any that a purely philosophical interest would have provided.

He has made many contributions to parapsychology through experiments, 26 articles and 13 reviews published in the parapsychological literature, and two books, including *Foundations of Parapsychology* (coauthored with Robert Morris, Joseph Rush and John Palmer) and *The Philosophical Dimensions of Parapsychology* (coedited with James M.O. Wheatley).

Dr. Edge is a member of the American Philosophical Association and of the Board of Trustees of the ASPR.

Jan Ehrenwald

Consulting Psychiatrist

(Mailing Address: 265C Heritage Hills, Somers NY 10589)
Born March 13, 1900. Married, one daughter. M.D.

After receiving his M.D. at the University of Prague and his psychoanalytic and neuropsychiatric training at the University of Vienna, he emigrated from Europe to England in 1939. From there he came to the United States to begin a private practice and to become consulting psychiatrist at the Roosevelt Hospital in New York.

A diplomate of the American Psychiatric Association, Dr. Ehrenwald also is a fellow of the New York Academy of Medicine and former president of the Schilder Society of Psychotherapy and Psychopathology.

As a student of both parapsychology and psychoanalysis, Dr. Ehrenwald, in *Telepathy and Medical Psychology* (1948), outlined a theory of telepathy based on compensation for an existing minus function or neuropsychological deficit, and in *New Dimensions of Deep Analysis: A Study of Telepathy in Interpersonal Relationships* (1954), argued that psi impressions emerge from the unconscious, from the Freudian id or from Myers' subliminal domain. More recently, Dr. Ehrenwald has also been concerned with various agent-percipient relationships in which psi seems to be emancipated from left hemisphere restraints, e.g., in the child-parent symbiosis and in the doctor-patient relationships. In a celebrated article published as "Telepathy in Macbeth?" in JSPR in 1941, Dr. Ehrenwald indicated that Macbeth's ambitious desires to become Thane of Glamis and Thane of Cawdor actually had been conveyed by telepathy to the witches who then prophesied that he would be king. The prophecy pushed him on to his bloody deed.

In pursuit of a psychoanalytical approach to parapsychology, Dr. Ehrenwald became a member of the ASPR Medical Section in 1948 and wrote several books which, besides those already cited, include *The ESP Experience: A Psychiatric Validation* (1978) and *Anatomy of Genius, Split Brains and Global Minds* (1984).

Jule Eisenbud

Psychiatrist

(Mailing Address: 4634 East 6th Avenue, Denver CO 80220)

Born November 20, 1908, in New York City. Married, three children, four grandchildren. M.D.

Prior to 1950 when he assumed the posts of associate clinical professor of psychiatry at the University of Colorado School of Medicine and attending psychiatrist at the United States Veterans Hospital in Denver, he received his M.D. and a doctor of medical science degree from Columbia College of Physicians and Surgeons in 1934 and 1939 respectively.

Dr. Eisenbud writes, "My interest [in parapsychology] basically began with my psychiatric and psychoanalytic practice. For some reason I saw a lot of telepathic dreams and other material provided by my patients...."

He was one of many distinguished psychiatrists, including Montague Ullman and Jan Ehrenwald, who became active in the Medical Section the ASPR established in 1948. In a number of articles published in psychoanalytic and psychiatric journals from 1946 on, and in *Psi and Psychoanalysis* (1970), Dr. Eisenbud demonstrated his interest in the significance of telepathic dreams and other psi phenomena for psychiatry and psychoanalysis.

In *The World of Ted Serios* (1967; second edition, 1989), an extraordinary and erudite book, Dr. Eisenbud reported his intensive investigations of a subject who appears to have been able to imprint pictures on film just by staring into the lens of a (Polaroid Land) camera. The book stimulated parapsychologists to search out the causes of mental images thus imprinted, and to try to determine if they were normal or paranormal.

In *Paranormal Foreknowledge: Problems and Perplexities* (1982), Dr. Eisenbud discussed clinical cases from his psychiatric and psychoanalytic practice which suggested precognition. Disdaining the hypothesis of backward causation, he explored the explanatory value of the various combinations of PK, ESP and telepathic influence. The book broke new ground theoretically in regard to the possible range of influence of these factors under proper psychodynamic conditions.

Dr. Eisenbud is a life member of the American Psychiatric Association and the American Psychoanalytic Association.

Edward F. Kelly

Founder and President of Spring Creek Institute

(Mailing Address: Spring Creek Institute, 3500 Westgate Drive, Suite 704, Durham NC 27707)

Born June 12, 1940, in Mt. Kisco, New York. Married, one child. Ph.D.

Before earning his doctorate at Harvard University in 1970 in psycholinguistics and cognitive science, he obtained his B.A. in 1962 from Yale University, where he was a member of Phi Beta Kappa and was graduated magna cum laude. He thereafter held several postdoctoral fellowships in computational linguistics. He also was consultant to the Laboratory of Social Relations at Harvard University and directed an effort to improve computer-aided content analysis by endowing Harvard's "General Inquirer" system with the capacity to resolve the lexical ambiguity of 2000 high-frequency English words.

With an interest in parapsychology developed after personal experiences involving his sister, and after corresponding and conferring with J.B. Rhine, Dr. Kelly entered the field in 1972 as postdoctoral research fellow at the Institute for Parapsychology. He also worked from 1973 to 1983 as research associate and visiting scholar in the Department of Electrical Engineering at Duke University where, in the Experiential Learning Laboratory, hardware and software resources were developed for the psychophysiological investigation of psi. These efforts were summarized in "A Computer-Based Laboratory Facility for the Psychophysiological Study of Psi" (1980) which Dr. Kelly coauthored (with James E. Lentz and John L. Artley).

Dr. Kelly also has published a chapter in Wolman's *Handbook of Parapsychology* (1977) on statistical methods in parapsychological research as well as approximately 30 scientific articles and 15 research papers presented at conventions. In *Altered States of Consciousness and Psi: an Historical Survey and Research Prospectus,* a monograph Dr. Kelly coauthored (with Ralph G. Locke) which was published by the Parapsychology Foundation, he strongly advocated tying the study of psi to more general investigations of altered states of consciousness.

Stanley Krippner

Director of the Center for Consciousness Studies, Saybrook Institute

(Mailing Address: Saybrook Institute, Graduate School and Research Center, 1772 Vallejo Street, San Francisco CA 94123)

Born October 4, 1932, in Edgerton, Wisconsin. Married, two stepchildren. Ph.D.

In his autobiography, *Song of the Siren: A Parapsychological Odyssey* (1975), Dr. Krippner relates that his career in parapsychology started when, as a 14 year old boy in Wisconsin, he was startled by the thought that his Uncle Max was dead. A moment later, the telephone rang and his mother was told that Max had died suddenly and without warning. Later, during his student days at the University of Wisconsin, he invited Rhine to speak there and, after graduation in 1954, visited Duke University and the Rhines and talked with the staff at the Parapsychology Laboratory.

After he earned his doctorate in education at Northwestern University in 1961, he was appointed director of the Child Study Center at Kent State University, where he conducted his first experiment in parapsychology. He went on to become director of the Dream Laboratory at Maimonides Medical Center in Brooklyn, New York, to collaborate with Montague Ullman in the pioneering explorations of telepathic dreaming, and to coauthor with Ullman two books, *Telepathy and Dreams* (1970) and (with Alan Vaughan) *Dream Telepathy* (1973; second edition, 1989).

Besides having authored or coauthored numerous other writings and ten books and having edited or coedited nine others, he is the editor-in-chief of *Advances in Parapsychological Research: A Biennial Review*. Dr. Krippner's main interests, after psi and altered states of consciousness, psi and personality and anomalous healing, include forging international links in consciousness research, primarily in Europe, Asia and Latin America. In 1971 he gave the first lecture in the Soviet Union on parapsychology ever presented at the USSR Academy of Pedagogical Sciences in Moscow, and in 1981 he presented another paper on parapsychology at the Chinese Academy of Sciences in Beijing. In 1980 he received the Marius Volkoff Award for notable contributions in parapsychology and became president of the Parapsychological Association in 1982.

Lawrence LeShan

Director, Research Project on Development of a Scientific Model for Paranormal Phenomena, Psychophysical Research Laboratories

(Mailing Address: 263 West End Avenue, New York NY 10023)

Born September 8, 1920, in New York. Married, one daughter, one granddaughter. Ph.D.

He received a B.S. degree from the College of William and Mary in 1942 and an M.S. in psychology in 1943 from the University of Nebraska. From 1943 to 1946 and again from 1949 to 1951, he served as clinical psychologist for the United States Army. In 1954, he was awarded a doctorate in human development by the University of Chicago. Prior to holding his current post, Dr. LeShan taught at Roosevelt University, Pace College, Union Theological Seminary and the New School for Social Research, and was director of a 12-year research project on the psychosomatic aspects of neoplastic disease.

Dr. LeShan describes his major interest in parapsychology as the "theoretical and scientific models of psi." In the development of these models, he worked closely for five years with Eileen Garrett, the famous medium, collaborated with Gertrude R. Schmeidler in the study of data from ESP tests, investigated the relationship between consciousness and reality and the place of parapsychology in this scheme, and called attention to the striking similarity in the views of the universe between those pictured by the modern theoretical physicist and those perceived by the psychic and mystic.

His celebrated *The Medium, the Mystic and the Physicist* (1975) was the first major work to develop this idea, although later Dr. LeShan retracted much of this view and stated that the similarities were more apparent than real. His book, however, remained a particularly valuable insight into the structure of unorthodox or psychic healing, which he separated into two types: Type 1, in which the healer and healee merge into one entity, and Type 2, in which the healer's hands are the perceived means of curative powers. It was in what he called the "clairvoyant reality" perceived by sensitives and mystics that the merger in Type 1 was hypothesized as taking place. Dr. LeShan's healing theory and technique attracted many adherents.

Dr. LeShan is the author of about 75 papers published in the professional literature. In addition to the cited book, his other books include *The Mechanic and the Gardener: Understanding the Wholistic Revolution in Medicine* (1984).

Robert A. McConnell

Research Professor Emeritus of Biological Sciences, University of Pittsburgh

(Mailing Address: Department of Biological Sciences, University of Pittsburgh, Pittsburgh PA 15260)
Born 1914 in Pennsylvania. Married, one son. Ph.D.

Although he took his B.S. in physics in 1935 from Carnegie Mellon University, conducted the dynamic testing of aircraft at the United States Naval Aircraft Factory from 1939 to 1941, helped develop the Doppler radar design during World War II at the M.I.T. Radiation Laboratory, holds many radar patents, was awarded his Ph.D. in physics in 1947 by the University of Pittsburgh and, from 1947 on, was assistant professor of physics and then research professor of biophysics at the University of Pittsburgh, Dr. McConnell is also a university scientist with a broad interest in parapsychology.

He was its first president when the Parapsychological Foundation was founded in 1957. As a coauthor with Gertrude R. Schmeidler of *ESP and Personality Patterns* (1958), which presented her data from well-known tests she conducted on sheep-goat attitudes, Dr. McConnell provided the statistical analysis to give the studies a solid base. In addition to studies of PK data and the conduct of PK tests, Dr. McConnell devised and improved conditions for such tests including the motion picture recording of dice during their fall.

His interests in the field have veered as well toward education. His *ESP Curriculum Guide* (1970) was written for the secondary school and college teachers wishing to teach ESP or to recommend library materials for ESP student projects. His latest effort has been the worldwide free distribution to scientists and teaching libraries of 4800 copies of the following books written primarily to correct the indifference or hostility which mark the attitudes of conventional scientists toward parapsychology: *Encounters with Parapsychology* (1982), *Parapsychology and Self-Deception in Science* (1983) and *An Introduction to Parapsychology in the Context of Science* (1984). Dr. McConnell's most recent book, *Parapsychology in Retrospect: Light and Shadow* (1987) summarizes what he has learned about people and parapsychology in the 40 years he has devoted to this field.

Robert Lyle Morris

Koestler Professor of Parapsychology, University of Edinburgh

(Mailing Address: Department of Psychology, University of Edinburgh, 7 George Square, Edinburgh EH8 9JZ, Scotland)

Born in Canonsburg, Pennsylvania, July 9, 1942. Married and has twin daughters. Ph.D.

He is the first holder of the Chair of Parapsychology established in the United Kingdom under the will of Arthur Koestler.

Early interested in aspects of human experience that seemed to be ignored by the scientific community, he took his parapsychological training and research at the Institute for Parapsychology in 1969, the year in which he received his Ph.D. degree from Duke University with a study of avian social behavior. He had earned a B.S. degree in 1963 from the University of Pittsburgh. On the completion of postdoctoral research at Duke in avian social behavior, he became a research associate at the Psychical Research Foundation in Durham where he conducted experimental studies of out-of-body experiences and restricted-choice ESP experiments.

After that, he taught parapsychology and psychology courses at the University of California at Santa Barbara and at Irvine where his interest was focused on research into purported techniques for improving psychic performance. He continued this research at the School of Computer and Information Science at Syracuse University where he was senior research scientist.

He was on the Council of the American Association for the Advancement of Science from 1971 to 1973, was twice president of the Parapsychological Association (in 1974 and again in 1985) and has published widely.

Carroll Blue Nash

Emeritus Professor of Biology, St. Joseph's College, Philadelphia

(Mailing Address: 16493 Horado Court, San Diego CA 92128)

Born on January 29, 1914, in Louisville, Kentucky. Married, no children. Ph.D.

Dr. Nash received his B.S. in 1934 from George Washington University, his M.S. in 1937 and, in 1939, his Ph.D. in biology from the University of Maryland. He has been a member of the biology departments at the University of Arizona, Widener University, American University, Washington College and St. Joseph's College.

Before J.B. and Louisa E. Rhine published their dice-influencing experiments, Dr. Nash used the dice method in 1940 to test for PK at the University of Arizona. In 1947, in an experiment to test the effect of distance on psychokinesis, the extra-chance scores he obtained were no lower at the greatest distance (30 feet) at which significant results have been obtained in psychokinesis than at three feet. These results were obtained without there being a human psi-source between the ostensible PK agent and the target dice.

Dr. Nash was the first: to conduct ESP tests on television, to provide experimental evidence that subjects may use ESP unconsciously to fulfill a need or desire, to teach a parapsychology course for college credit and to receive from the Duke Parapsychology Laboratory the William McDougall Award for Distinguished Work in Parapsychology.

In 1956 Dr. Nash founded and became the director of the Parapsychology Laboratory at St. Joseph's College and continued in that capacity until his retirement. He coined the terms "holistic shift," "psiology" and "psi masking." His theories have guided research in psychokinesis, precognition and other areas.

Dr. Nash has been president of the Parapsychological Association and initiated its membership application to the American Association for the Advancement of Science.

He is the author of 122 psi publications, 12 of which he coauthored with his wife, Catherine S. Nash. He has published important articles in JASPR, JP and JSPR. His books include *Parapsychology: The Science of Psiology* (1986).

Karlis Osis

Chester F. Carlson Research Fellow Emeritus,
American Society for Psychical Research

(Mailing Address: Douglas Road, Glen Ridge NJ 07028)

Born 1917 in Riga, Latvia. Married, two children and four grandchildren. Ph.D.

After earning a Ph.D. in psychology in 1950 at the University of Munich, he immigrated to America where Rhine invited him to become a member of the staff of the Parapsychology Laboratory at Duke University. From 1957 to 1962, he held the post of director of research for the Parapsychology Foundation's Division of Research. In 1962, he became director of research at the

ASPR and subsequently was appointed Chester F. Carlson Research Fellow (now Emeritus).

Dr. Osis has studied the problem of whether there is in us some duplicate self that can leave the body and has designed a series of brilliant tests to determine if there are physical indices that something has separated from the body. In 1961, he did a pioneer survey of the deathbed observations of physicians and nurses in India and America and, with Erlendur Haraldsson, conducted a further survey of the observations of the experiences of dying persons which resulted in the best-selling *At the Hour of Death* (1977). In addition to experiments with mediums, Dr. Osis has investigated apparitions and poltergeist cases, has used animals in ESP experiments, has explored relations between ESP and creative processes, has conducted ESP experiments over distances of thousands of miles, and has studied the effect of relaxation and meditation on ESP scores. Over a period of more than 30 years as an investigator, Dr. Osis has earned a reputation both in and out of parapsychology, according to Gardner Murphy, as "one of the most mature and competent investigators in the world of parapsychology today."

Dr. Osis, the author of approximately 70 scientific articles, is a past president of the Parapsychological Association, a fellow of the Society for the Scientific Study of Religion, and a member of the American Psychological Association and of the ASPR.

John Albert Palmer

Senior Research Associate, Institute for Parapsychology

(Mailing Address: Institute for Parapsychology, P.O. Box 6847, Durham NC 27708)

Born October 30, 1944, in Philadelphia, Pennsylvania. Unmarried. Ph.D.

He received his B.A. in 1966 from Duke University where he was a member of Phi Beta Kappa and received the Karl E. Zener Award as the most outstanding undergraduate psychology major. Following the receipt of his doctoral degree from the University of Texas at Austin in 1969, he received faculty appointments at McGill University and John F. Kennedy University and was research associate at the University of Virginia Medical School and the University of Utrecht.

Dr. Palmer, who worked under Rhine at the Parapsychology Laboratory at Duke University, received grants from the Parapsychology Foundation and the James S. McDonnell Foundation for research in parapsychology and from the European Research Office of the United States Army for a critical review of parapsychology. He has presented 23 research papers, published 27 articles in publications such as JASPR, JSPR, the *European Journal of Parapsychology* and *Parapsychology Review,* contributed five book chapters, including one for Wolman's *Handbook of Parapsychology* (1977) and another for Krippner's

Advances in Parapsychological Research (1982), and coauthored (with Hoyt L. Edge, Robert L. Morris and Joseph H. Rush) *Foundations of Parapsychology: Exploring the Boundaries of Human Capability* (1986).

His work, which has included a survey of the published experimental evidence of the relationship between attitudes toward ESP and ESP performance and studies of spontaneous psychic experiences and out-of-body experiences, has made some of the most positive theoretical and experimental contributions to parapsychology.

Dr. Palmer was president of the Parapsychological Association in 1979, has been editorial consultant for JASPR and the *Journal of Parapsychology* and is a member of the American Psychological Association.

Dorothy H. Pope

Consulting Editor, Journal of Parapsychology

(Mailing Address: Foundation for Research on the Nature of Man, *Journal of Parapsychology*, P.O. Box 6847, Durham NC 27708)

Born December 28, 1905, in Providence, Rhode Island. Married, twin daughters.

In 1927 she received her B.A. degree cum laude from Brown University where she majored in English literature and was a member of Phi Beta Kappa. Mrs. Pope did graduate work in education, was a teaching assistant in psychology courses in the Extension Division of Brown University, and, in 1938, began her work as a member of the staff at the Parapsychology Laboratory at Duke University.

Louisa Rhine described her as a highly competent person who soon became interested in the *Journal of Parapsychology*, a connection which has lasted five decades. She was the managing editor of the *Journal* from 1942 to 1963, coeditor from 1964 to 1976 (with Louisa E. Rhine) and from 1977 to 1982 (with K. Ramakrishna Rao). She has been consulting editor since. Like Laura Dale, who edited JASPR, Mrs. Pope has maintained the strictest standards for the articles published and helped make the *Journal of Parapsychology* one of the most prestigious and also one of the most technical of all parapsychological publications.

In addition to her work on the JP, Mrs. Pope coauthored (with J. Gaither Pratt) two articles which appeared in JP (1942) and researched and wrote the material for the *Parapsychology Bulletin* from 1946 to 1965. The *Bulletin*, a companion piece to the JP, published, among other items, accounts of research not suited to formal presentation as well as news of professional interest.

As a member of the Parapsychology Laboratory, Mrs. Pope was one of the group whose discussions with J.B. Rhine led to the formation of the Parapsychological Association. When this organization was founded in 1957, she was a member of the committee appointed to draw up its constitution. Mrs. Pope is listed in *Who's Who of American Women.*

K. Ramakrishna Rao

Vice Chancellor of Andhra University, India, and Director of the Institute for Parapsychology

(Mailing Address: Institute for Parapsychology, P.O. Box 6847, Durham NC 27708)

Born in Andhra Pradesh, India, on October 4, 1932. Married, three children. Ph.D. (Although not an American parapsychologist, Dr. Rao is included in these miniatures because he has been on the American scene a long time and has been one of the leaders of parapsychology in this country.)

His interest in parapsychology began, he wrote, when, as "a graduate student, I was unable to reconcile the traditional conception of man contained in Indian Philosophy and Western Psychology." His interests have included both the nature of consciousness and the experimental study of ESP. In the course of this study, he conducted a valuable series of experiments to explore the relationship between ESP and personality traits and devised a series of experiments with targets in English and Telugu in order to see if ESP could be used to break the language barrier. Dr. Rao has also made significant contributions toward theoretical understanding of psi in its various aspects.

To take up his post as vice chancellor of Andhra University, Dr. Rao in 1984 took extended leave from the Institute for Parapsychology in Durham, where he had studied and worked with J.B. and Louisa E. Rhine and where he had been director since 1977. Prior to that date he had been a research fellow at the University of Chicago from 1950 to 1960, research associate at the Parapsychology Laboratory from 1961 to 1965 and professor of psychology at Andhra University from 1969 to 1976. After his return in 1984 to Andhra University, he founded the Institute for the Study of Yoga and Consciousness, an interdisciplinary center for the study of psychic phenomena, and secured for it a government endowment of two and a half million rupees. After three years in India, he returned to resume his role as director of the Institute for Parapsychology.

Dr. Rao has been editor of the *Journal of Parapsychology* and the *Journal of Indian Psychology* and, besides holding memberships in various professional and international organizations, was president of the Parapsychological Association in 1965 and 1978. His scientific publications include *Experimental Parapsychology* (1966). He edited *J.B. Rhine: On the Frontiers of Science* (1982) and *Basic Experiments in Parapsychology* (1984) and has authored a large number of research papers.

D. Scott Rogo

Lecturer in parapsychology, John F. Kennedy University

(Mailing address: 18132 Schoenborn Street, Northridge CA 91324)
Born on February 1, 1950. Unmarried.
After taking his B.A. degree at California State University in North-ridge in 1972, he did graduate work in the psychology of music until he elected to focus his interest primarily on parapsychology. Since then he has taught a course on parapsychology at the University of California, has conducted seminars at Whitman College, has presented papers at international conferences sponsored by the Parapsychology Foundation and has been a researcher and writer. He has also worked with the Psychical Research Foundation, the (former) Maimonides Medical Center's Division of Parapsychology and the Southern California Society for Psychical Research.

Mr. Rogo has devoted his attention to half a dozen aspects of this field. He has studied the out-of-body experience by conducting experiments and making and analyzing case collections. He has been concerned with the investigation of cases of poltergeists and hauntings, has made experimental studies of ESP and its relation to altered states of consciousness, including sensory deprivation, and has surveyed psychokinesis extensively in his writings.

Another area of interest consists of bizarre forms of phenomena such as religious miracles. A final area entered by Mr. Rogo has been education. He published *Methods and Models for Education in Parapsychology* (1973), and, in his attempt to educate the general public about parapsychology, has written 27 books on parapsychology including *The Welcoming Silence* (1973), *Parapsychology: A Century of Inquiry* (1975) and *Minds and Motion* (1978). He is also the author of over 75 articles contained in other books and periodicals.

William George Roll

Professor of Psychology and Psychical Research, William James Laboratory for Psychical Research, West Georgia College

(Mailing Address: Department of Psychology, West Georgia College, Carrolltown GA 30118)
Born of American parents July 3, 1926, in Bremen, Germany. Divorced, one daughter, two sons, two grandchildren. M. Litt.
After receiving his B.A. degree in 1949 from the University of California at Berkeley, he pursued research in parapsychology at Oxford University,

England, under Professor H.H. Price. In 1960, Professor Roll earned his B. Litt. and in 1961 his M. Litt. from Oxford.

At the invitation of J.B. Rhine, Professor Roll came to Duke University in 1957. Beginning in 1958, he worked as research associate at Rhine's Parapsychology Laboratory. In 1960, under a grant to Duke University from Charles E. Ozanne, he conducted research into the question of the survival of the human personality after death. That same year Ozanne created the Psychical Research Foundation to advance scientific study of the question of human survival. Professor Roll became its project director, a position he continues to hold.

He has studied out-of-body experiences, mediumship, psychometry and haunting phenomena and is a leader in studies of poltergeist phenomena. His contributions to the theoretical aspects of parapsychology include the psi system theory according to which psychic interactions occur on a level of the organismic system that encompasses individuals and their environment.

Among the more than 100 papers he has authored and the 13 books he has written or edited are *The Poltergeist* and 11 volumes of the PA's official proceedings, *Research in Parapsychology*. He also has served in editorial posts for the *Journal of Parapsychology* and *Theta*. Professor Roll was one of the founders of the Parapsychological Association and has been its president.

Joseph H. Rush

Retired Physicist

(Mailing Address: 1765 Sunset Boulevard, Boulder CO 80302)

Born April 17, 1911, in Mt. Calm, Hill County, Texas. Married, three children. Ph.D.

Prior to obtaining his doctorate in physics in 1950 from Duke University, he became seriously interested in parapsychology about 1937 when he discovered some of the literature of parapsychology in the Dallas City Library. This interest has developed over the years and has been second only to his professional work in physics because of his conviction, he says, that parapsychology has "implications for science and philosophy. Persistent, intractable data imply that something is missing in our conventional world view."

This interest in parapsychology grew partly during experiments he conducted as a coexperimenter with Ann Jensen to explore whether distant, as well as near, objects could be targets of psi. Significant results were reported in the *Journal of Parapsychology* (1949) in his experiments with drawings when the agent and subject were separated by 200 to 500 miles. But primarily Dr. Rush has been an author who has surveyed the problems, experiments and findings in parapsychology, especially in PK. He contributed "Problems and Methods in Psychokinesis Research" to Stanley Krippner's *Advances in Parapsychological Research 1* (1977) and *3* (1982), and "Physical Aspects of Psi Phenomena" to Gertrude R. Schmeidler's *Parapsychology: Its Relation to Physics, Biology, Psychology and Psychiatry* (1976), and is a coauthor (with Hoyt L. Edge, Robert L. Morris and John Palmer) of *Foundations of Parapsychology: Exploring the Boundaries of Human Capability* (1986).

Dr. Rush is a member of Phi Beta Kappa and Sigma Xi, the American Association for the Advancement of Science and the Optical Society of America.

Helmut H.W. Schmidt

Research Associate, Mind Science Foundation

(Mailing Address: Mind Science Foundation, 8301 Broadway, Suite 100, San Antonio TX 78209)

Born February 21, 1928, in Danzig, Germany. Married, three children. Ph.D.

After earning a doctorate in physics in 1954 from the University of Cologne in Germany, he was, from 1955 to 1957, research fellow at the National Academy of Sciences at the University of Michigan in Ann Arbor and the University of California at Berkeley. He served as assistant professor and docent at the Institute for Theoretical Physics at the University of Cologne and senior research scientist at the Boeing Scientific Research Laboratories in Seattle, Washington, from 1965 to 1969.

He then served as director of the Institute for Parapsychology in Durham until 1972. "My interest in psi arose out of my study of theoretical physics," Dr. Schmidt explained. "With the role of the human observer in quantum theory rather obscure and controversial, and with psi effects indicating some experimental limits to the validity of quantum theory, I see this borderline between physics and psi as a most interesting intellectual challenge."

His practical contributions to parapsychology include the invention of automated ESP and PK test machines and the use of sophisticated mechanical devices in place of the conventional methods of testing ESP and PK with card guessing and dice throwing.

On the theoretical side, he has integrated parapsychology with physics by conducting experiments to explore the apparent violation of causality by psi and a theory based on quantum mechanics that a subsequent observer can have a retroactive PK effect on an event.

Dr. Schmidt is a member of the American Association for the Advancement of Science and the American Physical Society. His scientific publications include "Quantum Processes Predicted?" (1969) and "PK Effect on Pre-Recorded Targets" (1976).

Rex G. Stanford

Professor of Psychology, St. John's University

(Mailing Address: Psychology Laboratory, SB-15, Marillac Hall, St. John's University, Jamaica NY 11439)
Born June 21, 1938, in Robstown, Texas. Married, no children. Ph.D.
After being graduated with high honors in 1963 from the University of Texas in Austin as a member of Phi Beta Kappa, and after earning a Ph.D. there in 1967 in personality-social psychology, he joined the faculty of West Carolina University, became research associate in the Division of Parapsychology of the Department of Psychiatry at the University of Virginia Medical School and, later, director of the Center for Parapsychological Research at Austin. He was associate professor of psychology at St. John's University from 1973 to 1976 and again from 1980 to 1983. Since 1983 he has held his present post.

In 1967 after summer research fellowships at the Parapsychology Laboratory at Duke University, he became a staff member of the Institute for Parapsychology. Dr. Stanford says that "J.B. Rhine played a major role in my training" and that parapsychology "seemed to hold promise of major advances in understanding our world."

This appeal, his own reading and experimentation and the opportunity to observe what might have been ESP experiences in his family shaped his interest in the field which has focused on systematic, process-oriented experimental work with the potential of laying the groundwork for understandng anomalies of organism-environment interaction. Dr. Stanford's research activities, which include studies of the psychology of the Ganzfeld as an ESP-favorable setting, are considered among the most highly perceptive and respected in the field.

Dr. Stanford has published 62 articles in parapsychological journals and 16 chapters in books. He has published articles which are the only general, systematic guides to career development and training in parapsychology.

Dr. Stanford was president of the Parapsychological Association in 1973, is an editorial consultant for JASPR and the *Journal of Parapsychology* and is a member of the American Association for the Advancement of Science and the American Psychological Association, including Division 8, Society for Personality and Social Psychology.

Ian Stevenson

Carlson Professor of Psychiatry, University of Virginia Medical School

(Mailing Address: Department of Behavioral Medicine and Psychiatry, Box 152, Medical Center, University of Virginia, Charlottesville VA 22908)

Born October 31, 1918, in Montreal, Canada. M.D.
Educated at the University of St. Andrews in Scotland and McGill University in Montreal, in 1943 he received his doctor of medicine degree from the School of Medicine at McGill University.

He trained in psychosomatic medicine at Cornell University Medical College and at New York Hospital, and, in psychoanalysis, at the New Orleans and Washington Psychoanalytic Institutes. From 1949 to 1957 he was assistant, then associate, professor of psychiatry at Louisiana State University School of Medicine, and, from 1957 to 1967, professor and chairman of the Department of Psychiatry at the University of Virginia Medical School. In 1967 he became Carlson Professor of Psychiatry there.

Dr. Stevenson writes, "My main interest in parapsychology is in the evidence of life after death, with special emphasis on the evidence provided by young children who claim to remember past lives," in researching which he has found instances which seem to him to give suggestive evidence. His books, including *Twenty Cases Suggestive of Reincarnation* (1974) and four volumes of a series called *Cases of the Reincarnation Type* (1975, 1977, 1980, 1983), have become standard reference works. In 1960, the ASPR awarded him the William James Prize for his essay on reincarnation.

Dr. Stevenson has also said, "I have a wide interest in all types of spontaneous cases, including near-death experiences, and also in paranormal healing." He has evaluated poltergeist cases, has studied spontaneous cases of xenoglossy and precognition and has evaluated telepathic impressions. He believes that ESP experiences occur and may affect our feelings and conduct.

Dr. Stevenson's publications include eight books on parapsychology and 136 articles dealing with psychosomatic medicine, the psychological effect of drugs and psychotherapy and over 70 articles in the field of parapsychology. Besides having been president in 1968 and 1980 of the Parapsychological Association (from which he resigned in 1986), he belongs to many other professional societies, including the American Association for the Advancement of Science, the American Psychiatric Association and the American Medical Association.

Russell Targ

President of Bay Research Institute and Senior Staff
Scientist at Lockheed Research and Development

(Mailing Address: 3251 Hanover St., Department 9701, Palo Alto CA 94304)
Born April 11, 1934, in Chicago, Illinois. Married, three children.
After receiving a B.S. in physics from Queens College, New York, in 1954, and doing graduate work in physics at Columbia University, Targ

performed experimental microwave work at Sperry Gyroscope Company and laser research at GTE Sylvania.

In 1972, he became senior research physicist at Stanford Research Institute (SRI International) where, in a program cofounded with Harold Puthoff, he did research and applications in remote viewing for the United States government.

In *Mind-Reach: Scientists Look at Psychic Ability* (coauthored with Harold Puthoff; 1977), Mr. Targ described experiments conducted over a period of three years with more than 20 subjects at the Electronics and Bioengineering Laboratory of Stanford Research Institute to investigate the abilities of individuals to detect distant targets without the aid of the sensory channels. The experimenters, who were not parapsychologists per se, attempted to use rigorous laboratory procedures to collect a solid data base in order to demonstrate the existence of paranormal ability and to give that ability scientific credibility and a technique that could be replicated. Indeed, the "remote viewing" protocol has been replicated widely by FRNM, the Mind Science Foundation and by Mundelein College.

In 1983, Mr. Targ was invited to address the Soviet Academy of Sciences on "remote viewing" research.

Mr. Targ has also coauthored (with Keith Harary) *The Mind Race: Understanding and Using Psychic Abilities* (1984) and coedited (with C. Tart and H. Puthoff) *Mind at Large: IEEE Symposium on the Nature of Extrasensory Perception* (1979).

Charles T. Tart

Professor of Psychology, University of California at Davis

(Mailing Address: Department of Psychology, University of California, Davis CA 95616)

Born April 29, 1937, in Morrisville, Pennsylvania. Married, two children. Ph.D.

Charles T. Tart studied electrical engineering at the Massachusetts Institute of Technology until he decided that his real interest lay in understanding the human mind. This interest led him to Duke University and then to the University of North Carolina at Chapel Hill, where he completed his B.A. and M.A. degrees and earned his doctorate in 1963. The next two years he conducted hypnosis research and lectured in psychology at Stanford University and, from 1965 to 1966, was on the faculty of the Department of Psychiatry of the School of Medicine, University of Virginia, Charlottesville. While at Duke University he frequented the Parapsychology Laboratory and developed guidelines for the investigations of hauntings, poltergeists, and psychometry and for the use of hypnosis in psi research.

His contributions toward an understanding of the human mind have included research in hypnosis, dreams, altered states of consciousness, psychophysiology, the human aura, meditation, transpersonal psychology, and marijuana intoxication. He also devised ESP training machines.

He served as a consultant at Stanford Research Institute (now known as SRI International) in remote viewing projects and conducted oft cited research into the out-of-body experience and into the "decline effect" in parapsychology.

Dr. Tart was president of the Parapsychological Association in 1977 and is a member of the American Association for the Advancement of Science and a fellow of the American Society for Clinical Hypnosis. He is a diplomate in experimental hypnosis and is listed in *American Men and Women of Science.* He is a frequent contributor to JASPR, has published articles and chapters in a variety of nonparapsychological works and is the coauthor of two books and editor or author of eight more, including *Altered States of Consciousness* (1969), which became a text for the study of such states. He is also the publisher of a quarterly, *The Open Mind.*

Debra H. Weiner

Research Consultant, Institute for Parapsychology

(Mailing Address: Institute for Parapsychology, P.O. Box 6847, Durham NC 27708)

Born on March 10, 1952, in Wausau, Wisconsin. Unmarried.

Debra H. Weiner did undergraduate work at the University of California at Santa Barbara and Berkeley as well as at Sonoma State University in California where she majored in psychology and took her B.A. in 1977. She did graduate study in climatology at the University of North Carolina at Chapel Hill in 1983–1984.

"I cannot recall a time when I was not interested in parapsychology," wrote Ms. Weiner who started her career in the field in 1974 when, at Sonoma State University, she began doing psi experiments as part of courses on research design and statistics and taught an undergraduate course for credit on parapsychology. In 1976 she attended the Summer Study Program at the Institute for Parapsychology and returned after graduation to join the staff as a research fellow.

Although Louisa E. Rhine's investigations of spontaneous cases attracted Ms. Weiner sufficiently for her to coauthor for the JP "Charting Hidden Channels: A Review of Louisa E. Rhine's Case Collection" (1983), other interests have played an important role in her career in parapsychology. Some of these comprised laboratory experimentation, particularly micro-PK, and empirical tests of observational theories which formed the basis for "The Checker Effect Revisited" (1986), which she coauthored for the JP (with Nancy L. Zingrone). Ms. Weiner also has examined parapsychologists' concepts and assumptions, about which she wrote in a chapter contained in *Current Trends in Psi Research* (B. Shapin and L. Coly, eds., 1986).

Besides being senior editor of *Research in Parapsychology* in 1985 and 1986, Ms. Weiner has presented a large number of research papers at Parapsychological Association Conventions, was secretary of the Parapsychological Association from 1983 to 1985, and in 1986 became its president.

Rhea A. White

Editor of JASPR and Founder of the Parapsychology Sources of Information Center

(Mailing Address: 2 Plane Tree Lane, Dix Hills NY 11746)
Born May 6, 1931, in Utica, New York. Unmarried. M.L.S.

Following her receipt of a B.A. degree from Pennsylvania State University in 1953, Rhea White worked as a research fellow at the Parapsychology Laboratory at Duke University and, later, as research associate of the ASPR and the Menninger Foundation. Thereafter, she was awarded an M.L.S. by the Pratt Library School and held several posts as librarian.

Ms. White has written over 70 experimental and theoretical papers and has authored or coauthored several books, including *Parapsychology: Sources of Information* (with Laura A. Dale) (1973) and *The Psychic Side of Sports* (with Michael Murphy) (1978).

As an editor, she has held numerous posts. As an investigator she has conducted numerous ESP tests and, with Gardner Murphy and Laura Dale, has studied cases of spontaneous psychic experiences.

As an educator, with Frederick C. Dommeyer she made a comprehensive historical study of the relationship between universities and parapsychology in America and abroad. In addition, she contributed an article to JASPR (1965) and a chapter to *Education in Parapsychology* (B. Shapin and L. Coly, eds., 1976) on how to use the library to find information on parapsychology. She has also provided valuable bibliographies of books on parapsychology and, in running annotated bibliographies in Stanley Krippner's *Advances in Parapsychological Research,* has surveyed over 300 titles under various subject headings. Ms. White is continuing to educate people through *Parapsychology Abstracts International* which she founded in 1983, the Parapsychology Sources of Information Center founded by her in New York in 1981 and the Psi Line Database System she created as the first computerized database of the parapsychological literature.

Ms. White was on the Founding Council of the Parapsychological Association and was its president in 1984. She is also a member of the American Association of University Women and was a member of the Board of Trustees of the Academy of Religion and Psychical Research.

Respice, Adspice, Prospice

The great seal of the City College of the City University of New York, where Gardner Murphy was head of the Department of Psychology from 1940 to 1952, bears the words "Respice, Adspice, Prospice" and three faces, one looking back, one looking about and one looking forward.

This book, in keeping with two faces of the seal, has explored the past 100 years of American parapsychology and has given us a look at the contemporary scene. It has not, however, looked forward with the third face to the next century of American parapsychology. Yet who is not interested in the future even though we will never live to see it? It is impossible to think that American parapsychology will not have a future because, of all the sciences, it is the only discipline attempting to part the curtain of mystery drawn over human nature and to defy the materialist thesis that mental events are merely epiphenomena of brain processes. If for no other reason, parapsychology can lay claim to its right to continue as an important enterprise on the ground that it alone searches among the "unclassified residuum" for empirical data to throw light on the question of whether a mind may be independent of the brain and may survive the death of the body.

But the foothold parapsychology has achieved thus far has become, in recent years, increasingly slippery because of growing attacks. These assaults are not made only by hostile external critics, including academic psychologists, science writers, such as Martin Gardner, concerned skeptics who belong to the Committee for the Scientific Investigation of Claims of the Paranormal, and physicists, such as John Wheeler who, in 1979, asked the American Association for the Advancement of Science to force parapsychology out of the workshop of science. Assaults are launched also by parapsychologists inside the field itself who challenge the best ESP experiments and deny the very existence of psi phenomena. As we peer into the future, a more secure footing for parapsychology can be glimpsed in the coming new century if certain conditions are met.

Even educated people must stop equating it with Spiritualism.

Parapsychologists must stop exacerbating feelings and fears by referring to themselves, as did Pratt, as "revolutionists," and hostile critics must stop describing parapsychology as a "pseudoscience." Parapsychology may offend many personal belief systems and some scientific assumptions about the world and the human being, but it is a "thorn in the flesh" which may ultimately force modifications of these systems and assumptions. It is neither "revolutionary" nor a "pseudoscience" when it applies scientific methods and, although its hypotheses may seem fantastic, it plays by the rules of the scientific game.

Parapsychologists must recognize fair and valid criticisms and establish a constructive dialogue with informed external as well as internal skeptics and critics in order to disclose mistakes in assumptions or procedures or to bring out alternative interpretations of data.

Parapsychologists must make no claims and draw no conclusions beyond those warranted by the data and must acknowledge that these data remain ambiguous and still carry no scientific conviction. Yet they must also continue to insist that the subject matter they study, although ignored by other branches of science, warrants continued and intensified scientific investigation.

Parapsychologists must stop assuming that their experimental research is free from flaws, must apply higher standards of research to avoid tainting their work with methodological and statistical errors and, as illustrated by the case of the "Amazing Randi," must tighten controls against trickery.

There must be a continuing infusion into the field of creative young people who see its subject matter as important. While neither a doctorate in parapsychology nor any other area is a prerequisite, newcomers must have high intellectual and critical gifts and a healthy respect for scientific methods and findings.

Great gaps remain, including funding, replicable experiments and any broad theory which will assimilate and accommodate the phenomena and guide future research.

Murphy, however, although aware of these and other problems, looked forward, like the third face on the City College seal, into a future beyond his life and was still able to make this optimistic prophecy for American parapsychology:

"I believe that . . . the house founded by J.H. Hyslop will stand and do solid work in the nurture, encouragement, and training of research scientists in the prosecution of research, and in the establishment of an intelligent public attitude toward psychical research in this generation and those that are to come."[112]

References

The following abbreviations are used: JASPR for the *Journal of the American Society for Psychical Research;* PASPR for the *Proceedings of the American Society for Psychical Research;* JSPR for the *Journal of the Society for Psychical Research;* PSPR for the *Proceedings of the Society for Psychical Research;* JP for the *Journal of Parapsychology.*

Introduction

1. C.D. Broad. (1962). *Lectures on Psychical Research.* New York: Humanities Press.

2. R.H. Thouless and B.P. Wiesner. (1947). "The Psi Processes in Normal and 'Paranormal' Psychology." PSPR, 48, 177–196.

3. C.J. Ducasse. (1976). "The Philosophical Importance of 'Psychic Phenomena'." In J.M.O. Wheatley and H.L. Edge (Eds.), *Philosophical Dimensions of Parapsychology* (pp.30–45). Springfield, Ill.: Charles C. Thomas. Original work published in 1954 in the *Journal of Philosophy.*

4. H.H. Price. (1967). "Psychical Research and Human Personality." In J.R. Smythies (Ed.), *Science and ESP* (p. 38). New York: Humanities Press; London: Routledge & Kegan Paul.

5. W. James. (1956). "What Psychical Research Has Accomplished." In W. James, *The Will to Believe and Other Essays and Human Immortality* (pp. 299–300). New York: Dover Publications. Original essay published 1897 in *The Will to Believe and Other Essays.*

1. Independence Gained and Lost (1851–1905)

1. A. Gauld. (1968). *The Founders of Psychical Research.* New York: Schocken Books, p. 29.

2. E.W. Capron. (1855). *Modern Spiritualism.* Boston: Bela Marsh.

3. F.W.H. Myers. (1900). "In Memory of Henry Sidgwick." PSPR, 15, 452–462.

4. W.H. Salter. (1970). *The Society for Psychical Research: An Outline of Its History.* London: Society for Psychical Research, p. 6.

5. E.M. Sidgwick. (1932). "The Society for Psychical Research: A Short Account of Its History and Work on the Occasion of the Society's Jubilee." PSPR, 41, 1, fn. 3.

6. E.M. Sidgwick. (1925). "In Memory of Sir William Fletcher Barrett, F.R.S." PSPR, 35, 413–418. See also Renée Haynes. (1982). *The Society for Psychical Research 1882–1982: A History* (p. 5), London & Sydney: MacDonald & Co.

7. "Objects of the Society." (1882). PSPR, 1, 3–6.

8. H. Sidgwick [President's Address]. (1882). PSPR, 1, 8.

9. Circular No. 1. (1885). PSPR, 1, 3–4.

10. In *Aristocracy of the Dead* (Jefferson, N.C.: McFarland, 1987), I referred to this medium as "Leonore Piper" and so followed in the steps of many other writers who have done the same. Other authors, however, have called her "Leonora Piper" and still others have preferred to take no stand and have referred to her only as "L.E. Piper," "Mrs. Piper" or, as William James and Richard Hogson often did, just plain "Mrs. P." I now believe that her correct given name was "Leonora," which is the name I have used in this book.

11. S. Newcomb. "Address of the President." (1886). PASPR, 1, 84.

12. H. Sidgwick. (1889). "Opening Address at the Thirtieth General Meeting" [President's Address]. PSPR, 5, 399–402.

13. W.D. Bayley. (1920). "Entrance Upon Psychical Research, and Characteristics." JASPR, 14, 435.

14. "Report of the Committee on Thought-Transference." (1885). PASPR, 1, 6–49.

15. W. James and G.M. Carnochan. (1886). "Report of the Committee on Hypnotism." PASPR, 1, 95–102.

16. W. James. (1886). "Report of the Committee on Mediumistic Phenomena." PASPR, 1, 102–106.

17. W.H. Pickering. (1886). "A Research on the Reality of Reichenbach's Flames." PASPR, 1, 127.

18. Committee on Apparitions and Haunted Houses. (1886). "Circular No. 6." PASPR, 1, 129–131.

19. G. Murphy and R.O. Ballou (Eds.). (1961). *William James on Psychical Research*. London: Chatto and Windus.

20. W.D. Bayley. (1920). Op. cit., p. 435.

21. A. Gauld. (1968). *Founders of Psychical Research*. Op. cit., pp. 145–146, 258.

22. Annual Business Meeting. (1895). JASPR, 7, 18.

23. A. Gauld. (1968). Op. cit., p. 148.

24. W. James. (1956). "What Psychical Research Has Accomplished." Op. cit., pp. 299–327.

25. A.J. Baird. (1949). *The Life of Richard Hodgson: The Story of a Psychical Researcher and His Times*. London: Psychic Press.

26. E. Sidgwick. (1907). "Richard Hodgson: In Memoriam." PSPR, 19, 356–361.

27. G. Murphy and R.O. Ballou (Eds.). (1961). *William James on Psychical Research*. Op. cit., p. 64.

28. Ibid.

29. R. Hodgson. (1878, March 18). Letter to J.T. Hackett. ASPR Archives.

30. Ibid.   31. Ibid.

32. R. Hodgson. (1877, May 13). Letter to J.T. Hackett. ASPR Archives.

33. R. Hodgson. (1892). "A Record of Observations of Certain Phenomena of Trance." PSPR, 8, 65.

34. R. Hodgson. (1882, March 12). Letter to J.T. Hackett. ASPR Archives.

35. H. James, Jr. (1949). Quoted in A.T. Baird, Op. cit. (pp. 282–283).

36. A.S. Pier. (1949). Quoted in A.T. Baird, op. cit. (p. 286).

37. PSPR. (1907). 19, page opposite p. 355.

38. R. Hodgson. (1879, March 8). Letter to J.T. Hackett. ASPR Archives.

39. A.T. Baird, Op. cit., pp. 254–255.

40. M.A. de Wolf Howe. (1907). "Richard Hodgson: In Memoriam." PSPR, 19, 370–371.

41. W. James. (1909). "Report on Mrs. Piper's Hodgson-Control." PSPR, 23, 30.

42. Ibid., p. 6.

43. E.M. Sidgwick. (1907). Op. cit., pp. 358–359.

44. G. Murphy and R.O. Ballou (Eds.). (1961). *William James on Psychical Research*, op. cit., p. 32.

45. E.M. Sidgwick. (1907). Op. cit., p. 357.
46. A.S. Pier. (1949). Quoted in A.T. Baird, Op. cit., p. 286.
47. Ibid., p. 3.
48. R. Hodgson. (1900, March 21). Letter to C.J. Capron. ASPR Archives.
49. R. Hodgson. (1900, September 6). Letter to W. James. ASPR Archives.
50. Ibid.
51. H. Carrington. (1931). *The Story of Psychic Science.* New York: Ives Washburn. As quoted in A.T. Baird (1949). Op. cit., p. 66.
52. R. Hodgson. (1900, September). Letter to W. James. Houghton Library Archives, Harvard University.
53. Ibid.
54. J.G. Piddington. (1907). "Richard Hodgson: In Memoriam." PSPR, 19, 363.
55. A.T. Baird. (1949). Op. cit., p. 27.
56. R. Hodgson. (1879, March 8). Letter to J.T. Hackett. ASPR Archives.
57. Ibid.
58. R. Hodgson. (1878, March 18). Letter to J.T. Hackett, ASPR Archives.
59. A.T. Baird. (1949). Op. cit., p. 3.
60. R. Hodgson. (1892). "A Record of Observations of Certain Phenomena of Trance." PSPR, 8, 60.
61. Ibid.
62. R. Hodgson. (1877, April 22). Letter to J.T. Hackett. ASPR Archives.
63. R. Hodgson. (1894, October 25). Letter to J.T. Hackett. ASPR Archives.
64. A.S. Pier. (1949). Quoted in A.T. Baird, Op. cit., p. 287.
65. R. Hodgson. (1878, March 18). Letter to J.T. Hackett. ASPR Archives.
66. R. Hodgson. (1879, February 12). Letter to J.T. Hackett. ASPR Archives.
67. R. Hodgson. (1881, July 24). Letter to J.T. Hackett. ASPR Archives.
68. R. Hodgson. (1880, August 27). Letter to J.T. Hackett. ASPR Archives.
69. E.M. Sidgwick. (1907). Op. cit., p. 357.
70. R. Hodgson. (1879, March 30). Letter to J.T. Hackett. ASPR Archives.
71. R. Hodgson. (1879, May). Letter to J.T. Hackett. ASPR Archives.
72. "Members, Associates, Honorary and Corresponding Members" (1883). PSPR, 1, 323.
73. R. Hodgson. (1884, June 5). Letter to J.T. Hackett. ASPR Archives.
74. R. Hodgson. (1885). "Account of Personal Investigations in India, and Discussion of the Authorship of the 'Koot Hoomi' Letters." PSPR, 3, 210.
75. R. Hodgson. (1886, January 1). Letter to J.T. Hackett. ASPR Archives.
76. C.D. Broad. (1938). "Henry Sidgwick and Psychical Research." PSPR, 45, 140.
77. "Report of the Committee Appointed to Investigate Phenomena Connected with the Theosophical Society." (1885). PSPR, 3, 205.
78. Ibid., p. 207.
79. R. Hodgson. (1893). "The Defence of the Theosophists." PSPR, 9, 129–159.
80. A.S. Berger. (1985). "The Mighty Stranger: An Example of Interaction Between the Transcendental and the Psychical" (1985 prize paper, Robert M. Ashby Memorial Award competition, Academy of Religion and Psychical Research). In "Explorations in Psycho-Spiritual Transformations." *Proceedings of the Academy of Religion and Psychical Research,* 79–87.
81. R.H. Thouless. (1968). "Review of Obituary—The 'Hodgson Report' on Madame Blavatsky by Adlai E. Waterman." JSPR, 44, 344.
82. R. Hodgson. (1885). "Account of Personal Investigations in India, and Discussion of the Authorship of the 'Koot Hoomi' Letters." Op. cit., pp. 314–317.
83. Ibid., p. 208.
84. V. Harrison. (1986). "J'Accuse: An Examination of the Hodgson Report." JSPR, 53, 286–310; B. Inglis. (1986). "Correspondence." JSPR, 53, 478.

85. G. Murphy and R.O. Ballou (Eds.). (1961). *William James on Psychical Research*, Op. cit., p. 64.

86. R. Hodgson. (1886, September 3). Letter to J.T. Hackett. ASPR Archives.

87. R. Hodgson and S.J. Davey. (1887). "The Possibilities of Malobservation and Lapse of Memory From a Practical Point of View." PSPR, 4, 381–404.

88. R. Hodgson. (1892). "Mr. Davey's Imitations by Conjuring of Phenomena Sometimes Attributed to Spirit Agency." PSPR, 8, 279.

89. W.H. Salter. (1950). "History of the Society for Psychical Research." JASPR, 44, 138–147.

90. W.H. Salter. (1970). *The Society for Psychical Research: An Outline of Its History* (p. 22), London: Society for Psychical Research.

91. G. Murphy and R.O. Ballou (Eds.). (1961). *William James on Psychical Research*, Op. cit., pp. 36–37.

92. R. Hodgson. (1881, November 14). Letter to J.T. Hackett. ASPR Archives.

93. Ibid.   94. Ibid.

95. R. Hodgson. (1888, December 23). Letter to J.T. Hackett. ASPR Archives.

96. R. Hodgson. (1888, January 29). Letter to J.T. Hackett. ASPR Archives.

97. J.W. Warren. (1889). "Report of the Committee on Mediumistic Phenomena." PASPR, 1, 320.

98. J.F. Brown and (Mrs.) J.F. Brown. (1889). "Some Experiments in Thought-Transference." PASPR, 1, 322–349.

99. C.S. Minot. (1889). "Second Report on Experimental Psychology upon the Diagram Tests." PASPR, 1, 302–317.

100. Ibid.

101. R. Hodgson. (1888, March 11). Letter to J.T. Hackett. ASPR Archives.

102. G. Murphy and R.O. Ballou (Eds.). (1961). *William James on Psychical Research*, Op. cit., p. 31.

103. R. Hodgson. (1889, May 12). Letter to J.T. Hackett. ASPR Archives.

104. R. Hodgson. (1890, November 23). Letter to J.T. Hackett. ASPR Archives.

105. R. Hodgson. (1897). "Editorial." JSPR, 8, 117–120.

106. "Society for Psychical Research, Officers and Council for 1899." (1899). PSPR, 14, Part XXXV (July 1899), cover.

107. "Meeting of the Council." (1899). JSPR, 9, 98.

108. E.M. Sidgwick. (1907). Op. cit., p. 360.

109. L. Edmund (1907, June 17). Letter to J.H. Hyslop. ASPR Archives.

110. W. James. (1886). "Report of the Committee on Mediumistic Phenomena." PASPR, 1, 102–106.

111. R. Hodgson. (1888, January 29). Letter to J.T. Hackett. ASPR Archives.

112. J.H. Hyslop. (1901). "A Further Record of Observations of Certain Trance Phenomena." PSPR, 16, 10–11.

113. R. Hodgson. (1892). "A Record of Observations of Certain Phenomena of Trance." PSPR, 8, 57.

114. Ibid., p. 58.

115. R. Hodgson. (1898). "A Further Record of Observations of Certain Phenomena of Trance." PSPR, 13, 335, 471–472.

116. Ibid., pp. 336–337, 481–482.   117. Ibid., pp. 337, 449–452.

118. Ibid., p. 290.   119. Ibid., p. 328.

120. Ibid., pp. 96, 405–406.

121. R. Hodgson. (1904, September 26). Letter to J.T. Hackett. ASPR Archives.

122. Ibid.

123. R. Hodgson. (1892). "A Record of Observations of Certain Phenomena of Trance." Op. cit., pp. 1–67.

124. R. Hodgson. (1898). "A Further Record of Observations of Certain Phenomena of Trance." Op. cit., pp. 413–441.

125. Ibid., pp. 442–478. 126. Ibid., pp. 479–535.

127. Ibid., pp. 536–582.

128. H. de G. Verrall. (1910). "Report on the Junot Sittings with Mrs. Piper." PSPR, 24, 351–664.

129. W. James. (1909). "Report on Mrs. Piper's Hodgson-Control." PSPR, 23, 6.

130. Ibid. 131. Ibid.

132. Ibid.

133. R. Hodgson. (1900, March 6). Letter to J.H. Hyslop. ASPR Archives.

134. R. Hodgson. (1900, February 23). Letter to J.T. Hackett. ASPR Archives.

135. F.W.H. Myers (1890). "A Record of Observations of Certain Phenomena of Trance. Introduction." PSPR, 6, 436–442.

136. O.J. Lodge. (1890). "A Record of Observations of Certain Phenomena of Trance. Part I." PSPR, 6, 443–557.

137. W. Leaf. (1890). "A Record of Observations of Certain Phenomena of Trance. Part II." PSPR, 6, 558–646.

138. O.J. Lodge. (1909). *The Survival of Man*. New York: George H. Doran.

139. E.W. Stevens. (1887). *The Watseka Wonder*. Chicago: Religio-Philosophical Publishing House.

140. As quoted in F.W.H. Myers. (1903). *Human Personality and Its Survival of Bodily Death*. London: Longmans, Green. 2 vols. Vol. 1, p. 308.

141. R. Hodgson. (1891). "A Case of Double Consciousness." PSPR, 7, 221–257.

142. W. James. (1901). *Principles of Psychology*. London: Macmillan. 2 vols. Orig. pub. 1890.

143. Ibid., p. 392.

144. F.W.H.Myers. (1892). "On Indications of Continued Terrene Knowledge." PSPR, 8, 200–205.

145. Ibid., pp. 180–193.

146. C. Richet. (1893). "Experiences de Milan." *Annales des Sciences Psychiques,* 3, 1–31.

147. F. Podmore. (1893). "Notices of Books." PSPR, 9, 218–225.

148. O.J. Lodge. (1894). "Experience of Unusual Physical Phenomena Occurring in the Presence of an Entranced Person (Eusapia Paladino)." JSPR, 6, 307–308.

149. R. Hodgson. (1895). "The Value of the Evidence for Supernormal Phenomena in the Case of Eusapia Paladino." JSPR, 7, 36–55.

150. W. James. (1903, December 11). Letter to R. Hodgson. Houghton Library Archives, Harvard University.

151. F.W.H. Myers. (1895). "Reply to Dr. Hodgson." JSPR, 7, 55–64.

152. O.J. Lodge. (1895). "Additional Remarks by Professor Lodge." JSPR, 7, 64–67.

153. C. Richet. (1895). "A Propos des Experiences Faites avec Eusapia Paladino." JSPR, 7, 67–75.

154. J. Ochorowitz. (1895). "Réponse à M. Hodgson." JSPR, 7, 75–79.

155. H. Sidgwick. (1895). "Eusapia Paladino." JSPR, 7, 159.

156. B. Inglis. (1986). "Correspondence." JSPR, 53, 478–479.

157. M. Cassirer. (1983). "Palladino at Cambridge." JSPR, 52, 52.

158. E. Sidgwick. (1909). "Reviews. Psicologia e 'Spiritismo': Impressioni e note critiche sui fenomeni medianici di Eusapia Paladino, by E. Morselli." PSPR, 21, 516–525.

159. G. Murphy and R.O. Ballou (Eds.). (1961). *William James on Psychical Research,* Op. cit., p. 312.

160. F.W.H. Myers. (1899). "The Society for Psychical Research and Eusapia Paladino." JSPR, 9, 35.

161. F.W.H. Myers. (1902). "On the Trance Phenomena of Mrs. Thompson." PSPR, 17, 73.

162. R. Hodgson. (1900). "General Meeting." JSPR, 9, 294.

163. R. Hodgson. (1902). "Report on Six Sittings with Mrs. Thompson." PSPR, 17, 138.

164. Ibid., pp. 142–143.

165. F.W.H. Myers. (1903). *Human Personality and Its Survival of Bodily Death.* Vol. 1, Op. cit., Ed. Note, p. x.

166. W. James. (1903, July 28). Letter to T. Flournoy. In R.C. LeClair (Ed.). (1966). *The Letters of William James and Théodore Flournoy* (p. 146). Madison and London: University of Wisconsin Press.

167. O.J. Lodge. (1909). *The Survival of Man,* Op. cit., p. 349.

168. As quoted in A.T. Baird. (1949). Op. cit., p. 286.

169. E. Bennett. (1949). Foreword to A.T. Baird, ibid., p. xviii.

170. As quoted in A.T. Baird, ibid., p. 286.

171. W. James. (1909). "Report on Mrs. Piper's Hodgson-Control." PSPR, 23, 2.

172. R. Hodgson. (1905, May 13). Letter to J.T. Hackett. ASPR Archives.

173. As quoted in A.T. Baird. (1949). Op. cit., p. 286.

174. G. Murphy and R.O. Ballou (Eds.). (1961). *William James on Psychical Research,* Op. cit., p. 111.

175. R. Hodgson. (1898). "A Further Record of Observations of Certain Phenomena of Trance." Op. cit., p. 406.

176. E.M. Sidgwick. (1900). "Discussion of the Trance Phenomena of Mrs. Piper." PSPR, 15, 16–38.

177. R. Hodgson. (1900, March 6). Letter to J.H. Hyslop. ASPR Archives.

178. E.M. Sidgwick. (1915). "A Contribution to the Psychology of Mrs. Piper's Trance Phenomena." PSPR, 28, 2.

179. R. Hodgson. (1905, May 13). Letter to J.T. Hackett. ASPR Archives.

180. W. James. (1909). "Report on Mrs. Piper's Hodgson-Control." Op. cit., p. 5.

181. G. Murphy and R.O. Ballou (Eds.). (1961). *William James on Psychical Research,* Op. cit., p. 268.

182. F.W.H. Myers. (1890). Op. cit., p. 439.

183. E.M. Sidgwick. (1917). "On the Development of Different Types of Evidence for Survival in the Work of the Society." PSPR, 29, 253.

184. E.M. Sidgwick. (1932). "The Society for Psychical Research: A Short Account of Its History on the Occasion of the Society's Jubilee." Op. cit., p. 26.

185. G. Murphy and R.O. Ballou (Eds.). (1961). *William James on Psychical Research,* Op. cit., p. 32.

186. W. James. (1909). "Report on Mrs. Piper's Hodgson-Control." Op. cit., p. 121.

187. F. Podmore. (1911). *The Newer Spiritualism.* New York: Henry Holt, p. 314.

188. G. Murphy and R.O. Ballou (Eds.). (1961). *William James on Psychical Research,* Op. cit., p. 268.

2. Out of the Ashes (1906–1920)

1. W. James. (1909). "Report on Mrs. Piper's Hodgson-Control." PSPR, 23, 30.

2. G. Murphy and R.O. Ballou (Eds.). (1961). *William James on Psychical Research.* London: Chatto and Windus, p. 111.

3. W. James. (1909). Op. cit., p. 31.

4. "Report of the Council for the year 1906." (1907). JSPR, 13, 23.

5. "Dissolution of the American Branch." (1907). JASPR, 1, 1.

6. W.D. Bayley. (1920). "Entrance Upon Psychical Research, and Characteristics." JASPR, 14, 436.

7. W.D. Bayley. (1929). Preface to G. Tubby, *James H. Hyslop — X His Book: A Cross Reference Record.* York, Pa.: York Printing Co., p. 17.

8. J.H. Hyslop. (1904, March 6). "Autobiography." ASPR Archives. This document will be called "Autobiography" hereafter.

9. Autobiography, p. 8.   10. Ibid., p. 6

11. J.H. Hyslop. (1901). "A Further Record of Observations of Certain Trance Phenomena." PSPR, 16, 27.

12. Autobiography, p. 3.   13. Ibid., p. 6.
14. Ibid.   15. Ibid., p. 12.
16. Ibid., pp. 10–11.   17. Ibid., p. 12.

18. J.H. Hyslop. (1901). "A Further Record of Observations of Certain Trance Phenomena." Op. cit., p. 307.

19. Autobiography, p. 12.   20. Ibid., p. 13.
21. Ibid., p. 14.   22. Ibid., p. 13.
23. Ibid.   24. Ibid.
25. Ibid., pp. 13–14.   26. Ibid., p. 10.
27. Ibid.   28. Ibid., pp. 7–8.
29. Ibid., p. 8.   30. Ibid., p. 15.
31. Ibid.   32. Ibid., p. 17.
33. Ibid.

34. J.H. Hyslop. (1901). "A Further Record of Observations of Certain Trance Phenomena." Op. cit., p. 28.

35. Autobiography, p. 18.   36. Ibid., p. 27.
37. Ibid.   38. Ibid., p. 31.
39. Ibid., p. 32.   40. Ibid., p. 33.
41. Ibid.   42. Ibid., p. 34.
43. Ibid., p. 37.   44. Ibid., p. 38.
45. Ibid., pp. 39–40.   46. Ibid., p. 40.
47. Ibid.   48. Ibid., p. 41.

49. J.H. Hyslop. (1901). "Further Record of Observations of Certain Trance Phenomena." Op. cit., p. 28.

50. Autobiography, p. 41.   51. Ibid., p. 42.
52. Ibid., p. 43.   53. Ibid., p. 42.
54. Ibid.   55. Ibid., p. 44.
56. Ibid., p. 55.   57. Ibid., p. 56.
58. Ibid., p. 55.   59. Ibid., p. 56.
60. Ibid.   61. Ibid.

62. J.H. Hyslop. (1901). "A Further Record of Observations of Certain Trance Phenomena of Trance." Op. cit., p. 297.

63. Ibid., pp. 1–649.

64. J.H. Hyslop. (1898). "The Consciousness of Dying." JSPR, 8, 250–255.

65. "Meeting of the Council." (1900). JSPR, 9, 162.

66. R. Hodgson. (1900, January 5). Letter to J.H. Hyslop. ASPR Archives.

67. Autobiography, p. 51.

68. R.C. Le Clair (Ed.). (1966). *The Letters of William James and Théodore Flournoy.* Madison and London: University of Wisconsin Press, p. 114.

69. J.H. Hyslop. (1901). "A Further Record of Observations of Certain Trance Phenomena." Op. cit., p. 4 fn.

70. "Professor Hyslop on Mrs. Piper." (1899). JSPR, 9, 132.

71. J.H. Hyslop. (1900, February 27). Letter to W.D. Bayley. ASPR Archives.
72. R. Hodgson. (1900, March 1). Letter to J.H. Hyslop. ASPR Archives.
73. R. Hodgson. (1900, February 23). Letter to J.H. Hyslop. ASPR Archives.
74. Autobiography, p. 50.
75. W.R. Newbold. (1920). "An Estimate." JASPR, 14, 493.
76. N.M. Butler. (1914, May 25). Letter to J.H. Hyslop. ASPR Archives.
77. W.R. Newbold. (1920). "An Estimate," Op. cit., 493–494.
78. Autobiography, p. 51.   79. Ibid., p. 52.
80. J.H. Hyslop. (1907). "History of the American Institute for Scientific Research." PASPR, 1, 1–2.
81. W. James. (1902, August 18). Letter to R. Hodgson. Houghton Library Archives, Harvard University.
82. "Letters of Indorsement." (1907). PASPR, 1, 33–34.
83. Pierre Janet. (1907). "Letter of Dr. Pierre Janet." JASPR 1, 73–93.
84. "Letters of Indorsement." (1907). Op. cit., 44–45.
85. Ibid., pp. 32–33.   86. Ibid., p. 40.
87. I.K. Funk. (1906, May 8). Letter to J.H. Hyslop. ASPR Archives.
88. W.D. Bayley. (1920). "Entrance Upon Psychical Research, and Characteristics." Op cit., pp. 435–436.
89. W. James. (1904, October 11). Letter to T. Flournoy. In Robert C. Le Clair (Ed.) (1966). *The Letters of William James and Théodore Flournoy,* Op. cit., p. 161.
90. J.H. Hyslop. (1906, February 12). Letter to W.D. Bayley. ASPR Archives.
91. Ibid.
92. J.H. Hyslop. (1906, March 17). Letter to W.D. Bayley. ASPR Archives.
93. Ibid.   94. Ibid.
95. W.D. Bayley. (1920). "Entrance Upon Psychical Research, and Characteristics." Op. cit., p. 436.
96. J.H. Hyslop. (1907). "Editorial." JASPR, 1, 38.
97. "Objects of the Institute." (1907). JASPR, 1, 22.
98. "The American Society for Psychical Research." (1948). JASPR, 42, 117.
99. As quoted in G.H. Hyslop. (1950). "James H. Hyslop: His Contribution to Psychical Research." JASPR, 44, 137.
100. Ibid., p. 132.   101. Ibid.
102. L. Edmunds. (1907, June 18). Letter to J.H. Hyslop. ASPR Archives.
103. Ibid.
104. "Editorial." (1907). JASPR, 1, 35.
105. "Needs of the Institute." (1907). JASPR, 1, 28.
106. J.H. Hyslop. (1909, October 6). Letter to W.D. Bayley. ASPR Archives.
107. "Needs of the Institute." (1907). Op. cit., pp. 28–32.
108. "Editorial." (1914). JASPR, 8, 20, 22.
109. J.H. Hyslop. (1906, May 25). Letter to W.D. Bayley. ASPR Archives.
110. I.K. Funk. (1906, June 2). Letter to J.H. Hyslop. ASPR Archives.
111. J.H. Hyslop. (1906, June 20). Letter to W.D. Bayley. ASPR Archives.
112. "Additional Members." (1907). JASPR, 1, 546.
113. "Treasurer's Report." (1907). Ibid.
114. J.H. Hyslop. (1906, September 3). Letter to W.D. Bayley. ASPR Archives.
115. "Local Societies." (1907). JASPR, 1, 111–112.
116. I.K. Funk. (1906, June 2). Letter to J.H. Hyslop. ASPR Archives.
117. Ibid.
118. "Editorial." (1907). JASPR, 1, 37.
119. "Editorial." (1907). Ibid., p. 108.

120. J.H. Hyslop. (1906, June 20). Letter to W.D. Bayley. ASPR Archives.
121. G.B. Dorr. (1906, May 24). Letter to J.H. Hyslop. ASPR Archives.
122. "Editorial." (1907). Op. cit., p. 38.
123. I.K. Funk. (1906, June 2). Letter to J.H. Hyslop. ASPR Archives.
124. W. James. (1904, October 11). Letter to T. Flournoy. In R.C. Le Clair (Ed.) (1966). *The Letters of William James and Théodore Flournoy,* Op. cit., p. 161; and W. James (1902, August 18). Letter to R. Hodgson. Houghton Library Archives, Harvard University.
125. "Editorial." (1907). Op. cit., p. 37.
126. J.H. Hyslop. (1909). "The Problems of Psychic Research." JASPR, 3, 199.
127. Ibid., p. 200.   128. Ibid., p. 203.
129. Ibid., p. 208.
130. "Prospectus." (1907). JASPR, 1, 32–35.
131. J.H. Hyslop. (1908). "Professor Muensterberg and Dr. Hodgson." JASPR, 2, 23.
132. "Editorial." (1909). JASPR, 3, 249.
133. J.H. Hyslop. (1908, December 8). Letter to W.D. Bayley. ASPR Archives.
134. "Professor Jastrow and Science." (1908). JASPR, 2, 141–171.
135. "Editorial." (1908). JASPR, 2, 409–415.
136. J.H. Hyslop. (1908). "Professor Muensterberg and Dr. Hodgson," Op. cit., p. 23.
137. A.E. Tanner. (1910). *Studies in Spiritism.* New York: D. Appleton.
138. J.H. Hyslop. (1911). "President G. Stanley Hall's and Dr. Amy E. Tanner's Studies in Spiritism." JASPR, 5, 1–98.
139. O.J. Lodge. (1894). "Experiences of Unusual Physical Phenomena Occurring in the Presence of an Entranced Person." JSPR, 6, 306–336.
140. H. Sidgwick. (1895). "Eusapia Paladino." JSPR, 7, 148–159.
141. "Editorial." (1907). JASPR, 1, 108–114.
142. "Editorial." (1908). Op. cit.
143. Ibid., p. 467.
144. H. Carrington. (1920). *The Physical Phenomena of Spiritualism: Fraudulent and Genuine* (3rd ed.). New York: American Publishing Co. Orig. pub. 1907.
145. H. Carrington. (1909). "Report of a Two-Weeks' Investigation into Alleged Spiritualistic Phenomena, Witnessed at Lily Dale, New York." PASPR, 2, 7–117.
146. E. Feilding, W.W. Baggally and H. Carrington. (1909). "Report on a Series of Sittings with Eusapia Palladino." PSPR, 23, 309–569.
147. Ibid., p. 555.
148. H. Carrington. (1909). "Personal Experiments with Eusapia Palladino." JASPR, 3, 592.
149. J.H. Hyslop. (1910). "Eusapia Palladino." JASPR 4, 169–185.
150. H. Carrington. (1954). *The American Seances with Eusapia Palladino.* New York: Garrett Publications.
151. J.H. Hyslop. (1910). "Eusapia Palladino," Op. cit., p. 170.
152. "Editorial." (1914). JASPR, 8, 18.
153. W.H. Hamilton, J.S. Smyth and J.H. Hyslop. (1911). "A Case of Hysteria." PASPR, 5, 26.
154. H. Carrington. (1911). "Eusapia Palladino and the Burton Case." JASPR, 5, 487.
155. "Editor's Reply." (1911). JASPR, 5, 488.
156. Ibid., p. 489.
157. H. Carrington. (1911). "Eusapia Palladino and the Burton Case," Op. cit., p. 487.
158. "Editor's Reply" (1911), Op. cit., p. 491.
159. G.O. Tubby. (1920). "Testimony of a Co-Worker." JASPR, 14, 483.
160. G.H. Hyslop. (1950). "James H. Hyslop: His Contribution to Psychical Research." JASPR, 44, 134.
161. T. Pope. (1915, April 22). Letter to W.C. Peyton. ASPR Archives.
162. E.W. French. (1915, April 23). Letter to J.H. Hyslop. ASPR Archives.

163. Autobiography, p. 54.

164. W.R. Newbold. (1920). "An Estimate," Op. cit., p. 493.

165. W.D. Bayley. (1929). Preface to G.O. Tubby, *James H. Hyslop – X His Book*, Op. cit., p. 16.

166. J.H. Hyslop. (1901). "A Further Record of Observations of Certain Trance Phenomena." Op. cit., pp. 1–649.

167. Ibid., pp. 290–291.

168. J.H. Hyslop. (1907). "Preliminary Report on the Trance Phenomena of Mrs. Smead." PASPR, 1, 525–722.

169. J.H. Hyslop. (1909). "A Case of Veridical Hallucinations." PASPR, 3, 1–469.

170. J.H. Hyslop. (1909). "Observations on the Mediumistic Records in the Thompson Case." PASPR, 3, 593–613.

171. J.H. Hyslop. (1908). "Clairvoyant Diagnosis and Other Experiments." PASPR, 2, 139–206.

172. J.H. Hyslop. (1910). "A Record and Discussion of Mediumistic Experiments." PASPR, 4, 467–501.

173. Ibid., pp. 388–467.

174. W.H. Hamilton, J.S. Smyth and J.H. Hyslop. (1911). "A Case of Hysteria." Op. cit., pp. 1–672.

175. J.H. Hyslop. (1912). "A Record of Experiments." PASPR, 6, 1–939.

176. J.H. Hyslop. (1913). "The Subconscious and Its Functions." PASPR, 7, 5–192.

177. G.H. Hyslop. (1950). "James H. Hyslop: His Contribution to Psychical Research." Op. cit., p. 135.

178. J.H. Hyslop. (1913). "A Case of Musical Control." PASPR, 7, 429–569.

179. J.H. Hyslop. (1913). "Report by James H. Hyslop." PASPR, 7, 703–745.

180. J.H. Hyslop. (1914). "Some Unusual Phenomena in Photography." PASPR, 8, 395–464.

181. J.H. Hyslop. (1914). "Experiments in Non-Evidential Phenomena." PASPR, 8, 486–777.

182. J.H. Hyslop. (1917). "The Doris Case of Multiple Personality." PASPR, 11, 5–866.

183. J.H. Hyslop. (1919). "A Case of Pictographic Phenomena." PASPR, 13, 131–204; also see J.H. Hyslop. (1919). *Contact with the Other World*. New York: Century Co., p. 111.

184. W.F. Prince. (1923). "The Mother of Doris." PASPR, 17, vii.

185. J.H. Hyslop. (1919). *Contact with the Other World*, Op. cit., p. 480.

186. L.P. Jacks. (1918). "On the Evidence for Survival." JSPR, 18, 122.

187. R.L. Moore. (1977). *In Search of White Crows: Spiritualism, Parapsychology and American Culture*. New York: Oxford University Press, p. 163.

188. J.H. Hyslop. (1911, July 13). Letter to W.D. Bayley. ASPR Archives.

189. J.H. Hyslop. (1919). *Contact with the Other World*, Op. cit., p. 40.

190. H.N. Gardiner. (1920). "Reminiscences." JASPR, 14, 471.

191. W.R. Newbold. (1920). "An Estimate." JASPR, 14, 493.

192. Autobiography, pp. 57–58.

193. R. Hodgson. (1898). "A Further Record of Observations of Certain Phenomena of Trance." PSPR, 13, 284–582.

194. Autobiography, p. 58.

195. Miles M. Dawson. (1920). "Professor Hyslop's Engrossing Interest in Psychical Research." JASPR, 14, 454.

196. W.D. Bayley. (1920). "Entrance Upon Psychical Research, and Characteristics." Op. cit., p. 435.

197. J.H. Hyslop. (1919). *Contact with the Other World*, Op. cit., p. 425.

198. J.H. Hyslop. (1906). *Borderland of Psychical Research*. Boston: Small, Maynard Co., p. 417.

199. Autobiography, p. 15.

200. J.H. Hyslop. (1918). *Life After Death: Problems of the Future Life and Its Nature.* New York: E.P. Dutton, pp. 322–333.

201. Ibid., p. 332.   202. Ibid., p. 322.

203. Ibid., p. 321.

204. W.D. Bayley. (1929). Preface to G.O. Tubby, *James H. Hyslop — X His Book,* Op. cit., p. 17.

205. H. de G. Verrall. (1910). "Report on the Junot Sittings with Mrs. Piper." PSPR, 24, 351–664.

206. F. Nicol. (1972). "The Founders of the S.P.R." PSPR, 55, 363.

207. J.H. Hyslop. (1909). "Report of Sir Oliver Lodge." JASPR, 3, 665.

208. I. Stevenson. (1969). "Some Implications of Parapsychological Research on Survival After Death." PASPR, 28, 19–20.

209. R.L. Moore. (1977). *In Search of White Crows,* Op. cit., p. 161.

210. I.K. Funk. (1906, June 2). Letter to J.H. Hyslop. ASPR Archives.

211. F.C.S. Schiller. (1919). "Review of *Life After Death, Problems of the Future Life and Its Nature* by James H. Hyslop." JSPR 19, 130–132.

212. W. James. (1902, August 18). Letter to R. Hodgson. Houghton Library Archives, Harvard University; and W. James. (1901, December 26). Letter to T. Flournoy. In R.C. Le Clair (Ed.) (1966). *The Letters of William James and Théodore Flournoy,* Op. cit., p. 114.

213. O.J. Lodge. (1920). "In Memoriam: James Hervey Hyslop." JSPR, 19, 240.

214. W.F. Barrett. (1920). "In Memory of Dr. Hyslop." JASPR, 14, 441–442.

215. H.N. Gardiner. (1920). "Reminiscences." Op. cit., p. 470.

216. W.F. Barrett. (1920). "In Memory of Dr. Hyslop." Op. cit., p. 441.

217. G.O. Tubby. (1956). "My Relation to James H. Hyslop as His Secretary." JASPR, 50, 141.

218. G.W. Douglas. (1920). "A Secular Saint." JASPR, 14, 456.

219. G.O. Tubby. (1920). "Testimony of a Co-Worker." JASPR, 14, 484.

220. W.F. Prince. (1920). "James Hervey Hyslop: Biographical Sketch and Impressions." JASPR, 14, 431–432.

221. G.H. Hyslop. (1920). "My Father." JASPR 14, 481.

222. W.F. Barrett. (1920). "In Memory of Dr. Hyslop." Op. cit., p. 444.

223. R.L. Moore. (1977). *In Search of White Crows,* Op. cit., p. 170.

224. G.H. Hyslop. (1920). "My Father," Op. cit., p. 481.

225. G.O. Tubby. (1929). *James H. Hyslop — X His Book,* Op. cit., p. 40.

3. The Blue-Eyed Woman (1921–1938)

1. T.R. Tietze. (1973). *Margery.* New York: Harper & Row, p. xx.

2. "Survey and Comment." (1921). JASPR, 15, 318.

3. "Announcement and Comment." (1922). JASPR, 16, 289.

4. C. Murchison (Ed.). (1927). *The Case for and against Psychical Belief.* Worcester, Mass.: Clark University, p. 94.

5. "Private Meeting." (1928). JASPR, 24, 186.

6. C. Murchison (Ed.). (1927). *The Case for and against,* Op. cit., p. 212.

7. E.J. Dingwall. (1925). "The 'Margery' Mediumship." JSPR, 22, 61.

8. J.M. Bird (Ed.). (1926–1927). "The Margery Mediumship." PASPR, 20–21, 365.

9. C. Murchison. (1927). *The Case for and against,* Op. cit., p. 83.

10. J.M. Bird. (1925). "The Latest Margery 'Exposure'." JASPR, 19, 717.

11. L.R.G. Crandon, M.W. Richardson, C.S. Hill, A.W. Martin, S.R. Harlow, and J. DeWyckoff. (1925). *Margery-Harvard-Veritas: A Study in Psychics.* Privately printed by Crandon and others.

12. C. Murchison. (1927). *The Case for and against,* Op. cit., p. 213.

13. "Editorial Notes." (1930). *Psychic Research*, 24, 3.

14. J.M. Bird (Ed.). (1929). "A Series of Psychical Experiments." *Psychic Research*, 23, 209–232.

15. I. Stevenson. (1974). *Twenty Cases Suggestive of Reincarnation* (2nd rev. ed.). Charlottesville: University Press of Virginia. Orig. pub. 1966 in PASPR, 26, p. 318.

16. "New York Sectional Activities." (1930). *Psychic Research*, 24, 532; T.R. Tietze, *Margery*. Op. cit., pp. 137–139.

17. G.H. Hyslop. (1930). "Certain Problems of Psychic Research." *Psychic Research*, 24, 358.

18. J.B. Rhine and J.G. Pratt. (1954). "A Review of the Pearce-Pratt Distance Series of ESP Tests." JP, 18, 165–177.

19. "The Margery Mediumship: An Interesting Development in the Fingerprint Series. Statement on Behalf of the Research Committee." (1932). JASPR, 26, 266–268.

20. Ibid., p. 267.

21. "The Margery Mediumship." (1932). JASPR, 26, 405.

22. "Concerning the 'Margery' Case: Editorial Note." (1927). JSPR, 24, 25.

23. "Notes on Periodicals." (1933). JASPR, 28, 16.

24. W.H. Button. (1934). "Mr. Thorogood's Report on Fingerprint Phenomena in the Margery Mediumship." JASPR, 28, 9–13.

25. "Statement to Members. Exhibit 1." (1935). JASPR, 29, Supplemental Number, 155.

26. Ibid., p. 156.

27. H. Cummins. (1935). "Notes on 'Walter' Thumbprints of the 'Margery' Seances." PSPR, 43, 15–23.

28. "Editorial Notes." (1935). JASPR, 29, 130–134.

29. "Statement to Members." (1935). JASPR, 29, Supplemental Number, 153–154.

30. W.H. Button. (1936). "To the Voting Members of the A.S.P.R. President's Report at the Annual Meeting, January, 1936." JASPR, 30, 54.

31. W.H. Button. (1935). "The Margery Mediumship: Cross-Correspondences." JASPR, 29, 293–309.

32. J. Pierson. (1936). "Psychical Research in Recent Periodicals." JASPR, 30, 365–374.

33. W.H. Button. (1936). "To the Voting Members of the A.S.P.R. President's Report at the Annual Meeting, January, 1936." Op. cit., p. 52.

34. J.B. Rhine. (1976). "A Review of Current Needs and Expectations." In B. Shapin and L. Coly (Eds.), *Education in Parapsychology, Proceedings of an International Conference Held in San Francisco, California, August 14–16, 1975*. New York: Parapsychology Foundation, p. 2.

35. W.F. Prince. (1915). "The Doris Case of Multiple Personality." PASPR, 9, 172.

36. *Walter Franklin Prince: A Tribute to His Memory*. (1935). Boston: Boston Society for Psychic Research, p. 14. This work will be referred to hereafter as Tributes.

37. Tributes, p. 15.   38. Ibid., p. 16.

39. Ibid., p. 56.   40. Ibid., p. 59.

41. Ibid., p. 61.   42. Ibid., p. 89.

43. Ibid., p. 13.   44. Ibid.

45. W.F. Prince. "The Doris Case of Multiple Personality." Op. cit., p. 157.

46. Ibid., pp. 152–153.   47. Ibid., p. 172.

48. Ibid., p. 256.   49. Ibid., p. 264.

50. Ibid., p. 265.   51. Ibid., p. 286.

52. Ibid., p. 290.   53. Ibid., p. 307.

54. Ibid., p. 308.   55. Ibid., pp. 308–309.

56. W.F. Prince. (1916). "The Doris Case of Multiple Personality." PASPR, 16, 864.

57. W.F. Prince. (1915). "The Doris Case of Multiple Personality," Op. cit., p. 251.

58. Ibid., pp. 32–33.   59. Ibid., p. 32.

60. Tributes, pp. 70–71.   61. Ibid., p. 57.

62. Ibid., p. 72.

63. W.F. Prince. (1915 and 1916). "The Doris Case of Multiple Personality." PASPR, 9, 1–700 and PASPR, 10, 701–1332.

64. Tributes, p. 81.

65. W.F. Prince. (1930). "Presidential Address." PSPR, 39, 273.

66. W.F. Prince. (1930). "James Hervey Hyslop. Biographical Sketch and Impressions." JASPR, 14, 431.

67. W.F. Prince. (1930). "Presidential Address," 276.

68. W.F. Prince. (1916). "The Doris Case of Multiple Personality." Op. cit., p. 767.

69. Ibid., p. 768, fn. 427.   70. Ibid., pp. 1060–1061.

71. Ibid., p. 1264.   72. Tributes, p. 79.

73. W.F. Prince. (1926). *The Psychic in the House*. Boston: Boston Society for Psychic Research, p. 26.

74. Tributes, p. 12.

75. Ibid.

76. W.F. Prince. (1920). "James Hervey Hyslop. Biographical Sketch and Impressions." Op. cit., p. 431.

77. Ibid.

78. W.F. Prince. (1912). "Christian Believers and Psychic Research." JASPR, 6, 577–608, 637–679.

79. W.F. Prince. (1930). "Presidential Address." Op. cit., p. 276.

80. W.F. Prince. (1923). "The Mother of Doris." PASPR, 17, 1.

81. G.H. Hyslop. (1920). "My Father." JASPR, 14, 481.

82. W.F. Prince. (1920). "James Hervey Hyslop. Biographical Sketch and Impressions." Op. cit., p. 431.

83. Tributes, p. 21.

84. C. Murchison (Ed.). (1927). *The Case for and against*, Op. cit., p. 188.

85. Tributes, p. 53.   86. Ibid., p. 33.

87. W.F. Prince. (1921). "A Survey of American Slate-Writing Mediumship." PASPR, 15, 315–603.

88. Ibid., p. 316.   89. Tributes, p. 10.

90. W.F. Prince. (1922). "The Survival of Dogmatism: A Reply to Dr. Farrar's 'The Revival of Spiritism'." JASPR, 16, 533–552.

91. J.H. Hyslop. (1912). "A Record of Experiments." PASPR, 6, 837.

92. C.T.K. Chari. (1962). "Paranormal Cognition, Survival and Reincarnation." JASPR, 56, 158–163.

93. E. Osty. (1923). *Supernormal Faculties in Man*. London: Methuen.

94. R.C. Johnson. (1953). *The Imprisoned Splendour*. Wheaton, Ill.: Theosophical Publishing House, pp. 176–180.

95. F.C.S. Schiller. (1924). "Review of Supernormal Faculties in Man by E. Osty." PSPR, 34, 333–335.

96. W.F. Prince. (1924). "Studies in Psychometry." PASPR, 18, 204–218.

97. W.F. Prince. (Ed.). (1920). "A Notable Psychometric Test. Reported by G. Pagenstecher, M.D." JASPR, 14, 401.

98. Ibid., pp. 386–417.

99. W.F. Prince. (1921). "Psychometric Experiments with Señora María Reyes de Z." PASPR, 15, 191.

100. Ibid., p. 192.   101. Ibid., p. 193.

102. Ibid., p. 227.   103. Ibid., p. 200.

104. Ibid., p. 196.   105. Tributes, p. 35.

106. R.C. Johnson. (1953). *The Imprisoned Splendour*, Op. cit., p. 176.

107. W.G. Roll. (1957–1964). "The Psi Field." *Proceedings of the Parapsychological Association,* 1, 1–32.
108. W.F. Prince. (1921). "Psychometric Experiments with Señora María Reyes de Z." Op. cit., p. 314.
109. "Announcement and Comment." (1923). JASPR, 17, 114.
110. "Conversazione." (1927). JSPR, 24, 131.
111. "The Paris Congress for Psychical Research." (1927). JSPR, 24, 134.
112. "State and Local Councils." (1923). JASPR, 17, 321.
113. A.S. Berger. (1987). *Aristocracy of the Dead.* Jefferson, N.C., and London: McFarland. In this book, I called for democratizing survival research because parapsychological societies and the great majority of their members are not carrying it on.
114. G.H. Hyslop. (1930). "Certain Problems of Psychic Research." *Psychic Research,* 24, 358.
115. This information has been taken from an unpublished memorandum in the ASPR Archives. Dated January 8, 1925, it bears neither title nor the name of any author. It purports to be a memorandum addressed to the ASPR Board of Trustees who were elected in January 1925. It is in the first person and apparently was prepared by a Trustee for the benefit of the others on the Board. References are made to Frederick Edwards, Waldemar Kaempffert, Miles M. Dawson, Titus Bull, Weston D. Bayley, Lawson Purdy. The remaining trustees were John I.D. Bristol and George H. Hyslop. It is probable that the author of the anonymous piece was Hyslop.
116. Tributes, p. 55.
117. G. Murchison (Ed.). (1927). *The Case for and against,* Op. cit., pp. 201–202.
118. Ibid., p. 205.
119. L.E. Rhine. (1983). *Something Hidden.* Jefferson, N.C., and London: McFarland, p. 100.
120. R.L. Moore. (1977). *In Search of White Crows: Spiritualism, Parapsychology and American Culture.* New York: Oxford University Press, p. 176.
121. J.M. Bird (Ed.). (1926–1927). "The Margery Mediumship." PASPR, 20–21, p. 143.
122. W.F. Prince. (1927). "Specimens from the Telepathic Mine." *Scientific American,* September 1927, pp. 210–213.
123. E. Worcester. (1928). "Presidential Address Given Before the Boston Society for Psychic Research at Its Annual Meeting of May 14, 1928." Papers from the Rev. Elwood Worcester Collection, Episcopal Diocese of Massachussetts, Boston.
124. Ibid.
125. Ibid.
126. L.E. Rhine, *Something Hidden,* Op. cit., p. 104.
127. W.F. Prince. (1934). Introduction to J.B. Rhine, *Extra-Sensory Perception.* Boston: Boston Society for Psychic Research, p. xix. Republished in 1964 by Bruce Humphries.
128. Quoted in D. Brian. (1982). *The Enchanted Voyager: The Life of J.B. Rhine.* Englewood Cliffs, N.J.: Prentice-Hall, p. 56.
129. Ibid., p. 62.
130. G.H. Estabrooks. (1927). "A Contribution to Experimental Telepathy." *Bulletin of the Boston Society for Psychic Research,* 5, 1–30.
131. J.B. Rhine. (1934). *Extra-Sensory Perception.* Op. cit.
132. S.H. Mauskopf and M.R. McVaugh. (1980). *The Elusive Science: Origins of Experimental Psychical Research.* Baltimore and London: Johns Hopkins University Press, p. 241.
133. E. Worcester. (1928). "Presidential Address Given Before the Boston Society for Psychic Research, May 14, 1928, by Elwood Worcester."
134. I. Jephson. (1928). "Evidence for Clairvoyance in Card-Guessing: A Report on Some Recent Experiments." PSPR, 38, 223–271.
135. E. Worcester. (1928). "Papers on Psychical Research Read to the Clericus Club

March 4, 1928." Papers from the Rev. Elwood Worcester Collection, Episcopal Diocese of Massachussetts, Boston.

136. Tributes, p. 53.

137. *Bulletin of the Boston Society for Psychic Research*, 1, March, 1925.

138. W.F. Prince. (1926). "Carbon Monoxide or Carbon Monoxide Plus: a Critical Study of 'Haunting' Phenomena in a Boston Residence." *Bulletin of the Boston Society for Psychic Research*, 2.

139. "The Psychical Congress in Paris: A Report of the Meeting of the Third International Congress of Psychical Research Held in Paris, Sept. 26th to Oct. 2nd, 1927." (1927). *Bulletin of the Boston Society for Psychic Research*, 6.

140. "Experiments with Physical Mediums in Europe: A Detailed Study in the Interpretation of Indicia." (1928). *Bulletin of the Boston Society for Psychic Research*, 7.

141. W.F. Prince. (1928). Foreword to S. Keene, "Evidence of Things Not Seen: An Account of Psychical Experiences." *Bulletin of the Boston Society for Psychic Research*, 8.

142. "Incidents and Discussions: An Account of Several Spontaneous and Experimental Psychical Experiences." (1929). *Bulletin of the Boston Society for Psychic Research*, 10.

143. "Two Old Cases Reviewed: The Cases of C.B. Sanders and Millie Fancher." (1929). *Bulletin of the Boston Society for Psychic Research*, 11.

144. "Human Experiences: A Report on the Results of a Questionnaire Sent to 10,000 Persons Listed in Who's Who in America." (1930). *Bulletin of the Boston Society for Psychic Research*, 13.

145. "The Sinclair Experiments Demonstrating Telepathy." (1932). *Bulletin of the Boston Society for Psychic Research*, 16.

146. "Mainly on Physical Phenomena." (1933). *Bulletin of the Boston Society for Psychic Research*, 19.

147. "A Certain Type of Psychic Research and Other Reviews." (1933). *Bulletin of the Boston Society for Psychic Research*, 21.

148. "The 'Walter'-'Kerwin' Thumb Prints." (1934). *Bulletin of the Boston Society for Psychic Research*, 22.

149. Tributes, p. 44.

150. W.F. Prince. (1915). "The Doris Case of Multiple Personality." Op. cit., p. 57.

151. W.F. Prince. (1923). "Is the Possession of 'Psychical' Faculty Pathological?" JASPR, 17, 478.

152. W.F. Prince. (1926). *The Psychic in the House*, Op. cit., pp. 33–36.

153. E.M. Sidgwick. (1900). "Discussion of the Trance Phenomena of Mrs. Piper." PSPR, 15, 37.

154. W.F. Prince. (1926). *The Psychic in the House*, Op. cit., p. 2.

155. Ibid., p. 35.

156. W.F. Prince. (1923). "Is the Possession of 'Psychical' Faculty Pathological?" Op. cit., p. 479.

157. W.F. Prince. (1926). *The Psychic in the House*, Op. cit., p. 2.

158. D.J. West and G.W. Fisk. (1953). "Dual Experiment with Clock Cards." JSPR, 37, 188.

159. W.F. Prince. (1926). *The Psychic in the House*, Op. cit., p. 3.

160. W.F. Prince. (1927). *The Case of Patience Worth*. Boston: Boston Society for Psychic Research. Republished 1934, University Books, pp. 18–19.

161. Ibid., p. 20.   162. Ibid., p. 487.

163. As quoted Ibid., p. 56.   164. As quoted Ibid., pp. 59–60.

165. Both newspapers as quoted in Ibid., p. 77.

166. J.H. Hyslop. (1919). "The Sorry Tale. By Patience Worth. Communicated through Mrs. John H. Curran." JASPR, 13, 194.

167. W.F. Prince. (1927, 1934). *The Case of Patience Worth,* Op. cit., p. 428.
168. R.L. Moore. (1977). *In Search of White Crows,* Op. cit., p. 181.
169. R.H. Thouless. (1959). "The Sixth Sense: An Enquiry into Extra-Sensory Perception." JSPR, 40, 142.
170. W.F. Prince. (1927, 1934). *The Case of Patience Worth,* Op. cit., p. 509.
171. "Circular No. 1." (1885). PASPR, 1, 3.
172. "Report of the Committee on Thought-Transference." (1885). PASPR, 1, 6.
173. "Circular No. 6 Committee on Apparitions and Haunted Houses." (1886). PASPR, 1, 129–131.
174. W.F. Prince. (1928). *Noted Witnesses for Psychic Occurrences.* (1963). Boston: Boston Society for Psychic Research. Republished 1963, University Books, p. 5.
175. G. Murphy. (1928). Introduction to W.F. Prince, *Ibid.,* p. vi.
176. W.F. Prince. (1928). *Noted Witnesses for Psychic Occurrences,* Op. cit., p. 8.
177. W.F. Prince. (1923). "Incidents. Four Peculiarly Characterized Dreams." JASPR, 17, 89–101.
178. W.F. Prince. (1928). *Noted Witnesses for Psychic Occurrences,* Op. cit., p. 8.
179. H. Sidgwick. (1882). [President's Address]. PSPR, 1, 8.
180. W.F. Prince. (1930). *The Enchanted Boundary.* Boston: Boston Society for Psychic Research, p. 19.
181. Ibid., Preface, p. ix.
182. "Annual Report of the Council for the Year 1930." (1931). JSPR, 27, 23.
183. W.F. Prince. (1930). "Presidential Address." PSPR, 39, 279.
184. Ibid., pp. 287–289.
185. W.F. Prince. (1921). "Psychometric Experiments with Señora María Reyes de Z." Op. cit., p. 314.
186. W.F. Prince. (1927). "Is Psychical Research Worth While?" In C. Murchison (Ed.), *The Case for and against,* Op. cit., p. 193.
187. E. Worcester. (1928). "Presidential Address Given Before the Boston Society for Psychical Research at Its Annual Meeting of May 14, 1928."
188. G. Murphy. (1928). Introduction to W.F. Prince, *Noted Witnesses for Psychic Occurrences,* Op. cit., p. v.
189. W.F. Prince. (1927). "Is Psychical Research Worth While?" Op. cit., p. 188.
190. W.F. Prince. (1922). "An Investigation of Poltergeist and Other Phenomena Near Antigonish." JASPR, 16, 441.
191. W.F. Prince. (1930). "Presidential Address." Op., cit., p. 277.
192. Tributes, p. 58.
193. J.B. Rhine. (1934). *Extra-Sensory Perception,* Op. cit., Preface, p. xxvi.
194. Tributes.
195. Ibid., p. 83.
196. Ibid., p. 12.
197. Ibid., p. 57.
198. Ibid.
199. Ibid., p. 83.
200. Ibid., p. 82.
201. D.S. Rogo. (1982). "ESP and Schizoprenia: An Analysis from Two Perspectives." JSPR, 51, 329–342. In this article Mr. Rogo stated: "It is not generally known that Doris broke completely and died insane after Prince's death" (p. 339). Mr. Rogo explained in a letter to me that he obtained his information from T. R. Tietze. (1974). "Who Was the 'Real Doris'?" In M. Ebon (Ed.), *Exorcism: Fact Not Fiction.* New York: New American Library, pp. 177–185; see also T.R. Tietze. (1976). "Ursa Major: An Impressionist Appreciation of Walter Franklin Prince." JASPR, 70, 1–34. Mr. Rogo answered my further inquiry concerning where Tietze obtained his information that Doris died insane by stating that Tietze learned of Doris' insanity from Laura Dale who, in turn, had been given the information by Lydia Allison. Evidence of Doris' insanity, therefore, is based on hearsay—on what Lydia Allison said to Laura Dale and then on what Laura Dale said

to Mr. Tietze—and readers will be within their rights if they decide to disregard my statement about Doris' insanity. But even in the law there are recognized exceptions to the hearsay rule. I have made an exception out of a high regard for both women who had no motive for distorting the truth and who would not have accepted or repeated the information if they did not have reason to believe in its truth.

202. As quoted in C.R. Burt. (1968). *Psychology and Psychical Research.* London: Society for Psychical Research, p. 8.

203. C. Murchison. (Ed.). (1927). *The Case for and against,* Op. cit., p. 311.

204. W. McDougall. (1961). "William McDougall." In C. Murchison (Ed.), *A History of Psychology in Autobiography, Vol. 1.* New York: Russell and Russell, p. 192. Orig. pub. 1930 by Clark University. "Autobiography" will be used in subsequent references to this writing from which biographical data have been drawn.

205. Ibid., pp. 209, 215, 218.   206. Ibid., p. 223.

207. W. McDougall. (1923). "The Need for Psychical Research." JASPR, 17, 5–6.

208. W. McDougall. (1920). "Presidential Address." PSPR, 31, 107.

209. Ibid., pp. 108–109.   210. Ibid.

211. Ibid., p. 109.   212. Ibid.

213. G.N.M. Tyrrell. (1945). "Presidential Address." PSPR, 47, 301.

214. Autobiography, p. 191.   215. Ibid.

216. Ibid., p. 192.   217. Ibid.

218. Ibid., p. 203.   219. Ibid., p. 192.

220. Ibid.   221. Ibid., p. 193.

222. Ibid.   223. Ibid., p. 194.

224. Ibid., p. 195.   225. Ibid., p. 194.

226. Ibid., p. 195.   227. Ibid., p. 196.

228. Ibid., p. 197.   229. Ibid., p. 199.

230. Ibid., pp. 202–203.   231. Ibid., p. 203.

232. Ibid.   233. Ibid., p. 204.

234. Ibid., p. 207.

235. E.R. Dodds. (1962). "Experimental Research at the Universities and in the Society." PSPR, 53, 248.

236. Autobiography, p. 208.

237. J. Beloff. (1968). "Explorer of the Mind. William McDougall. Studies in Psychical Research." JSPR, 44, 415.

238. As quoted in K. Richmond. (1939). "William McDougall. 1871–1938." PSPR, 45, 192.

239. Autobiography, p. 211.   240. Ibid., p. 212.

241. E. Worcester. (1937). *Life's Adventure: The Story of a Varied Career.* New York: Scribner's, p. 325.

242. Autobiography, p. 203.   243. Ibid., p. 205.

244. Ibid., p. 219.

245. W. McDougall. (1927). "Psychical Research as a University Study." In C. Murchison (Ed.). *The Case for and against,* Op. cit., pp. 156, 157.

246. Autobiography, p. 208.

247. W. McDougall. (1906). "Exposures of Mr. Craddock." JSPR, 12, 275–276.

248. W.W. Baggally. (1910). "Some Sittings with Carancini." JSPR, 14, 195, 211.

249. "Meeting of the Council." (1913). JSPR, 16, 50.

250. "Meetings of the Council." (1920). JSPR, 19, 152.

251. "Meetings of the Council." (1921). JSPR, 20, 32.

252. Autobiography, p. 212.   253. Ibid.

254. J.E. Coover. (1927). "Metaphysics and the Incredulity of Psychologists." In C. Murchison (Ed.). *The Case for and against,* Op. cit., p. 237.

255. L.T. Troland. (ca. 1917). *A Technique for the Experimental Study of Telepathy and Other Alleged Clairvoyant Processes.* Albany, n.d., no publisher. Reprinted in 1976 in JP, 40, 194–216.

256. L.E. Rhine. (1983). *Something Hidden,* Op. cit., pp. 93–94.

257. Autobiography, p. 213.

258. L.E. Rhine. (1983). *Something Hidden,* Op. cit., p. 141.

259. Autobiography, p. 213.

260. L.E. Rhine. (1983). *Something Hidden,* Op. cit., p. 141.

261. Ibid.

262. "Mr. E.J. Dingwall's Study of 'Margery'." (1925). JASPR, 19, 124.

263. J.M. Bird. (1925). "Dr. McDougall and the Margery Mediumship." JASPR, 19.

264. W. McDougall. (1925). "Further Observations on the 'Margery' Case." JASPR, 19, 299, fn. 1.

265. Ibid., p. 297.   266. Ibid., pp. 305–306.

267. Ibid., p. 307.

268. C. Murchison. (Ed.). (1927). *The Case for and against Psychical Belief,* Op. cit., p. 206.

269. W. McDougall. (1925). "Further Observations on the 'Margery' Case." Op. cit., pp. 301, 304–305.

270. E.J. Dingwall. (1925). "Professor McDougall, 'Margery' and Mr. Bird." JASPR, 19, 455.

271. W. McDougall. (1925). "Further Observations on the 'Margery' Case." Op. cit., 303.

272. E.J. Dingwall. (1928). "A Report on a Series of Sittings with the Medium Margery." PSPR, 36, 79–155.

273. L.R.G. Crandon. (1928). "Appendix. Note by Dr. L.R.G. Crandon." PSPR, 36, 156.

274. L.R.G. Crandon. (1925). "Dr. McDougall and the Margery Mediumship." JASPR, 19, 361.

275. Ibid., p. 365.

276. "Mr. E.J. Dingwall's Study of 'Margery'." (1925), Op. cit., p. 124.

277. E.M. Sidgwick. (1925). "In Memory of Sir William Fletcher Barrett, F.R.S." PSPR, 35, 413.

278. R. Haynes. (1982). *The Society for Psychical Research 1882–1982: A History.* London: MacDonald, p. 5.

279. F. Nicol. (1972). "The Founders of the S.P.R." PSPR, 55, 343.

280. W. McDougall. (1923). "The Need for Psychical Research." Op. cit., p. 11.

281. Ibid.

282. "A Letter from Sir Arthur Conan Doyle." (1923). JASPR, 17, 265–266.

283. W. McDougall. (1923). "The Need for Psychical Research." Op. cit., pp. 11–12.

284. W.F. Prince. (1921, May 24). Letter to W. McDougall. ASPR Archives.

285. W. McDougall. (1921, May 22). Letter to W.F. Prince. ASPR Archives.

286 S.H. Mauskopf aand M.McVaugh. (1980). *The Elusive Science: Origins of Experimental Psychical Research.* Op. cit., p. 19.

287. Ibid., p. 20.

288. "The Annual Meeting." (1923). JASPR, 17, 232.

289. "A Letter from Sir Arthur Conan Doyle." (1923). Op. cit., 265.

290. F. Edwards. (1923). "Sir Arthur Conan Doyle." JASPR, 17, 272, 273.

291. F. Edwards. (1923). "Leakage." JASPR, 17, 267.

292. E. Worcester. (1937). *Life's Adventure: The Story of a Varied Career,* Op. cit., p. 331.

293. E. Worcester. (1928). "Paper on Psychical Research Read to the Clericus Club March 4, 1928." Op. cit.

294. E. Worcester. (1937). *Life's Adventure: The Story of a Varied Career,* Op. cit., p. 332.

295. Autobiography, p. 220.

296. In C. Murchison (Ed.). *The Case for and against,* Op. cit., Preface.
297. W. McDougall. (1927). In C. Murchison (Ed.). *The Case for and against,* Op. cit., pp. 152–153.
298. Ibid., pp. 154–155. 299. Ibid., p. 157
300. Ibid., p. 160.
301. J.G. Pratt. (1970). "William McDougall and Present-Day Psychical Research." JASPR, 64, 387.
302. Ibid., p. 388.
303. S.H. Mauskopf and M. McVaugh. (1980). *The Elusive Science,* Op. cit., p. 69.
304. W. McDougall. (1934). Foreword to J.B. Rhine, *Extra-Sensory Perception,* Op. cit., p. xv.
305. Ibid.
306. J.F. Thomas. (1937). *Beyond Normal Cognition.* Boston: Boston Society for Psychic Research.
307. L.E. Rhine. (1983). *Something Hidden,* Op. cit., p. 115.
308. J.B. Rhine. (1937). *New Frontieers of the Mind.* New York: Farrar and Rinehart, p. 42.
309. W. McDougall. (1934). Foreword to J.B. Rhine, *Extra-Sensory Perception,* Op. cit., p. xvii.
310. J.B. Rhine. (1937). *New Frontiers of the Mind,* Op. cit., pp. 43–44.
311. See G. Murphy. (1950). "Psychical Research and Personality." JASPR, 44, 4.
312. W. McDougall. (1920). "Presidential Address." Op. cit., p. 110.
313. Ibid., p. 112.
314. B. Russell. (1945). *A History of Western Philosophy.* New York: Simon and Schuster, p. 584.
315. W. McDougall. (1920). "Presidential Address." Op. cit., p. 114.
316. E.M. Sidgwick. (1922). "An Examination and Analysis of Cases of Telepathy Between Living Persons Printed in the 'Journal' of the Society for Psychical Research Since the Publication of the Book 'Phantasms of the Living' by Gurney, Myers, and Podmore, in 1886." PSPR, 33, 419.
317. W. McDougall. (1920). "Presidential Address." Op. cit., p. 112.
318. Ibid., 120.
319. K. Zener. (1939). "Obituary." *Science,* 89, No. 2305, March 3, 1939, pp. 191–192.
320. L.E. Rhine. (1983). *Something Hidden,* Op. cit., p. 189.
321. Autobiography, p. 223.
322. K. Richmond. (1939). "William McDougall, 1871–1938." Op. cit., p. 191.
323. J. Beloff. (1968). "Explorer of the Mind. William McDougall. Studies in Psychical Research." Op. cit., p. 415.
324. Ibid.
325. "Professor William McDougall." (1938). JSPR, 30, 294.
326. J.B. Rhine. (1980). "My Partner, Gardner Murphy." JASPR, 74, 62.
327. As quoted in D. Brian. (1982). *The Enchanted Voyager: the Life of J.B. Rhine.* Op. cit., p. 62.
328. J.G. Pratt. (1970). "William McDougall and Present-Day Psychical Research." Op. cit., p. 386.
329. I. Stevenson. (1980). "Gaither Pratt: An Appreciation." JASPR, 74, 278.
330. J.G. Pratt. (1970). "William McDougall and Present-Day Psychical Research." Op. cit., p. 388.
331. Ibid., p. 387.
332. L.E. Rhine. (1983). *Something Hidden,* Op. cit., p. 189.

4. Storms and Reorientation (1939–1980)

1. T.R. Tietze. (1973). *Margery*. New York: Harper and Row, pp. 184–185.

2. S.E. Morison and H.S. Commager. (1937). *The Growth of the American Republic*. New York: Oxford University Press, p. 184.

3. G. Murphy. (1957). "Notes for a Parapsychological Autobiography." JP, 21, 173. "Parapsychological Autobiography" will be used from now on to refer to this writing.

4. L.W. Allison. (1958). "The American Society for Psychical Research." JASPR, 52, 42; also S.H. Mauskopf and M. McVaugh (1980). *The Elusive Science: Origin of Experimental Psychical Research*. Baltimore and London: Johns Hopkins University Press, p. 298.

5. See, for example, "Survey and Comment." (1939). JASPR, 33, 314–315; "Survey and Comment" (1940). JASPR, 34, 91; J. Pierson. (1940). "A Partial Review of the Evidence for Telepathy." JASPR 34, 159, 168, 171; "Notice to Members." (1940). JASPR 34, 205.

6. "Editorial Notes." (1939). JASPR, 33, 321–324.

7. "Notice to Members." (1941). JASPR, 35, 29–30; "Notice to Members." (1941). JASPR 35, 85–86.

8. Ibid.

9. "The American S.P.R." (1941). JSPR, 32, 70.

10. Boston Society for Psychic Research (1941, March 27). Letter to Lydia Allison. ASPR Archives. The signature of the author of the letter on the letterhead of the Boston Society for Psychic Research is not clear. It is either "Carrie" or "Connie" (for Constance Worcester, daughter of Elwood Worcester?).

11. "The American S.P.R." (1941). Op. cit., p. 69; also "Reorganization of the American S.P.R." (1941). Ibid., p. 24.

12. G.H. Hyslop. (1941). "Statement by the President of the Society." JASPR, 35, 113–114.

13. G. Murphy. (1945). "An Outline of Survival Evidence." JASPR, 39, 2–34; G. Murphy. (1945). "Difficulties Confronting the Survival Hypothesis." JASPR, 39, 67–94; G. Murphy. (1945). "Field Theory and Survival." JASPR, 39, 181–209.

14. "Our New President." (1949). JSPR, 35, 29.

15. G. Murphy. (1953). "The Importance of Spontaneous Cases." JASPR, 47, 89–103.

16. "Presidential Remarks by Dr. Gardner Murphy." (1962). JASPR, 56, 202.

17. G.R. Schmeidler. (1969). "Introduction." In "Lecture Forum Honoring the Memory of Chester F. Carlson." PASPR, 28, 3.

18. J.G. Pratt. (1973). "A Record of Research with a Selected Subject: An Overview and Reappraisal of the Work with Pavel Stepanek." PASPR, 30, 1–78.

19. G. Murphy. (1967). "Gardner Murphy." In E.G. Boring and G. Lindzey (Eds.), *A History of Psychology in Autobiography, Vol. V*, New York: Appleton-Century-Crofts, p. 256. ("Murphy Autobiography" will be used to designate subsequent references to this autobiography and to distinguish it from the "Parapsychological Autobiography.")

20. Unpublished interview of Gardner Murphy by Montague Ullman, M.D. on May 17, 1966, hereafter called "Interview."

21. Murphy Autobiography, p. 256.   22. Ibid.

23. Interview.   24. Murphy Autobiography, p. 255.

25. Interview.   26. Murphy Autobiography, p. 255.

27. M. Ullman. (1980). "Letter to a Late Friend—Gardner Murphy." JASPR 74, 23.

28. S.A. Mednick. (1980). "Additional Tributes to Gardner Murphy from Colleagues and Friends." JASPR 74, 132.

29. E. Hartley. (1960). "Profile of a Professor." In J.G. Peatman and E.L. Hartley (Eds.), *Festschrift for Gardner Murphy*. New York: Harper and Bros., pp. 6–7.

30. Murphy Autobiography, p. 276.   31. Interview.

32. G. Murphy. (1966). Foreword to R.C. Le Clair (Ed.), *The Letters of William James and Théodore Flournoy*. Madison: University of Wisconsin Press, pp. v–vii.

33. G. Murphy. (1949). *Historical Introduction to Modern Psychology*, rev. ed. New York: Harcourt, Brace and World.

34. G. Murphy. (1947). *Personality: A Biosocial Approach to Origins and Structure*. New York: Harper and Row.

35. G. Murphy. (1949). *William James and Psychical Research*. JASPR, 48, 85–93.

36. G. Murphy. (1958). "Our Pioneers III: William James." JSPR, 39, 309–314.

37. G. Murphy and R.O. Ballou (Eds.). (1961). *William James on Psychical Research*. London: Chatto and Windus.

38. Murphy Autobiography, p. 276.

39. Parapsychological Autobiography, p. 165.

40. S. David Kahn. (1980). "Ave Atque Vale: Gardner Murphy." JASPR 74, 45.

41. G.R. Schmeidler. (1979). "Gardner Murphy and His Thinking: A Retrospect and a Prospect." JP, 43, 86–87.

42. Murphy Autobiography, p. 274.   43. Ibid., p. 261.

44. L. Dale. (1952, October 3). Letter to Jule Eisenbud.

45. Murphy Autobiography, pp. 278–280.

46. G. Murphy and L. Murphy. (1969). *Western Psychology*. New York: Basic Books.

47. Murphy Autobiography, p. 260.   48. Interview.

49. Ibid.   50. Murphy Autobiography, p. 256.

51. Parapsychological Autobiography, p. 166.

52. Murphy Autobiography, p. 256.   53. Interview.

54. Murphy Autobiography, p. 257.

55. Parapsychological Autobiography, p. 166.

56. Ibid.   57. Interview.

58. Parapsychological Autobiography, p. 166.

59. Ibid.   60. Murphy Autobiography, p. 257.

61. Ibid.   62. Interview.

63. Parapsychological Autobiography, p. 167.

64. Interview.   65. Murphy Autobiography, p. 259.

66. Ibid., p. 276.

67. Parapsychological Autobiography, p. 170.

68. Murphy Autobiography, p. 259.

69. Ibid., p. 261.   70. Ibid., p. 276.

71. Ibid., p. 264.   72. Ibid.

73. L. Murphy. (1985, October 8). Letter to the author.

74. Murphy Autobiography, p. 276.   75. Ibid., p. 274.

76. J.G. Peatman and E.L. Hartley (Eds.). (1960). *Festschrift for Gardner Murphy*, Op. cit., p. 2.

77. Ibid., p. 12.   78. Ibid., p. iii.

79. Murphy Autobiography, p. 274.

80. G. Murphy and R.O. Ballou (Eds.). (1961). *William James on Psychical Research*, Op. cit., p. 327.

81. L. Murphy. (1985, October 8). Letter to author.

82. Murphy Autobiography, p. 271.

83. Parapsychological Autobiography, p. 169; also see L.B. Murphy. (1987). "The Evolution of a Parapsychologist: the Life and Thinking of Gardner Murphy." ASPR *Newsletter*, 13, 21.

84. As quoted in M. Ullman. (1980). "Letter to a Late Friend—Gardner Murphy," Op. cit., p. 25.

85. Ibid; also see L.B. Murphy cited supra in note 83.

86. Murphy Autobiography, p. 259.
87. L. Murphy. (1985, October 30). Letter to author.
88. Ibid.
89. Parapsychological Autobiography, pp. 165–166.
90. Ibid.   91. Ibid., p. 166.
92. Murphy Autobiography, p. 257.
93. Parapsychological Autobiography, p. 167.
94. Ibid., pp. 167–168.   95. Ibid., p. 168.
96. Ibid., p. 169.   97. Ibid.
98. Ibid., p. 170.
99. C. Murchison (Ed.). (1927). *The Case for and against Psychical Belief.* Worcester, Mass.: Clark University, pp. 265–278.
100. Murphy Autobiography, p. 260.
101. Parapsychological Autobiography, p. 170.
102. A.S. Berger. (1984). "Foreword—A Tribute to Robert H. Thouless." In S. Krippner (Ed.), *Advances in Parapsychological Research 4.* Jefferson, N.C., and London: McFarland, pp. 1–8.
103. J.G. Pratt. (1980). "Gardner Murphy: Teacher, Mentor, Co-Worker, Friend." JASPR, 74, 69–70.
104. Parapsychological Autobiography, p. 171.
105. J.B. Rhine. (1980). "My Partner, Gardner Murphy." JASPR, 74, 62.
106. J.G. Pratt. (1980). "Gardner Murphy: Teacher, Mentor, Co-Worker, Friend." Op. cit., p. 72.
107. J.B. Rhine. (1980). "My Partner, Gardner Murphy." Op. cit., p. 62.
108. M. Ullman. (1980). "Letter to a Late Friend—Gardner Murphy." Op. cit., p. 23.
109. Murphy Autobiography, p. 271.
110. J.B. Rhine. (1980). "My Partner, Gardner Murphy." Op. cit., p. 64.
111. L. Murphy. (1985, October 8). Letter to author.
112. J.B. Rhine. (1980). "My Partner, Gardner Murphy." Op. cit., p. 64.
113. Ibid., p. 63.
114. Parapsychological Autobiography, p. 173.
115. G.R. Schmeidler and R.A. McConnell. (1958). *ESP and Personality Patterns.* New Haven and London: Yale University Press, p. ix.
116. Murphy Autobiography, p. 271.
117. L.W. Allison. (1958). "The American Society for Psychical Research." Op. cit., p. 42; S.H. Mauskopf and M. McVaugh. (1980). *The Elusive Science,* Op. cit., p. 298.
118. "Editorial Notes." (1939). JASPR, 33, 321–324.
119. W.H. Button and J.J. O'Neill. (1940). "Editorial Comment." PASPR, 23, ii–iii.
120. G. Murphy. (1966). "George H. Hyslop and the American Society for Psychical Research." JASPR, 60, 3.
121. L. Murphy. (1985, October 8). Letter to author.
122. G. Murphy and R.O. Ballou (Eds.). (1961). *William James on Psychical Research,* Op. cit., p. 18.
123. Parapsychological Autobiography, p. 173.
124. Ibid.
125. G.R. Schmeidler. (1980). "Gardner Murphy: A Short Biography." JASPR, 74, 10.
126. Murphy Autobiography, p. 271.
127. L. Murphy. (1985, October 30). Letter to author.
128. Murphy Autobiography, p. 271.
129. Parapsychological Autobiography, p. 174.

130. G.R. Schmeidler. (1980). "Gardner Murphy: A Short Biography." Op. cit., p. 10.
131. E.P. Gibson. (1944). "An Examination of Motivation as Found in Selected Cases From Phantasms of the Living."JASPR, 38, 83–105.
132. G.R. Schmeidler. (1980). "Gardner Murphy: A Short Biography." Op. cit., p. 1.
133. K. Osis. (1985). "The American Society for Psychical Research 1941–1985: A Personal View." JASPR, 79, 504.
134. Ibid.
135. Parapsychology Autobiography, p. 173.
136. G.R. Schmeidler. (1980). "Gardner Murphy: A Short Biography." Op. cit., p. 13.
137. K. Osis. (1985). "The American Society for Psychical Research 1941–1985: A Personal View." Op. cit., p. 522.
138. Murphy Autobiography, p. 276.
139. G. Murphy and R.O. Ballou (Eds.). (1961). *William James on Psychical Research,* Op. cit., p. 331.
140. A bibliography of Murphy's writings on parapsychology, writings in nonparapsychological publications, contributions to books and reference works and selected nonparapsychological publications can be found in "Tributes Honoring the Memory of Gardner Murphy." (1980). JASPR, 74, 139–146.
141. G. Murphy and L. Dale. (1941). "Some Present Day Trends in Psychical Research." JASPR, 35, 118–132.
142. G. Murphy and E. Taves. (1942). "Current Plans for Investigations in Psychical Research." JASPR, 36, 15–28.
143. G. Murphy and L. Dale. (1943). "Concentration Versus Relaxation in Relation to Telepathy." JASPR, 37, 2–15.
144. G. Murphy. (1943). "Psychical Phenomena and Human Needs." JASPR, 37, 163–191.
145. G. Murphy. (1944). "Removal of Impediments to the Paranormal." JASPR, 38, 2–23.
146. G. Murphy, E.H. Taves and L. Dale. (1945). "American Experiments on the Paranormal Cognition of Drawings." JASPR, 39, 144–150.
147. G. Murphy. (1946). "Psychical Research and the Mind-Body Relation." JASPR, 40, 189–207.
148. G. Murphy. (1947). "Personality Appraisal and the Paranormal." JASPR, 41, 3–11.
149. G. Murphy. (1948). "An Approach to Precognition." JASPR, 42, 3–14.
150. G. Murphy. (1948). "Needed: Instruments for Differentiating Between Telepathy and Clairvoyance." JASPR, 42, 47–49.
151. G. Murphy, L. Dale et al. (1951). "Dowsing: A Field Experiment in Water Divining." JASPR, 45, 3–16.
152. G. Murphy, A.O. Ross and G.R. Schmeidler. (1952). "The Spontaneity Factor in Extrasensory Perception." JASPR 46, 14–16.
153. G. Murphy. (1952). "Current Developments in Psychical Research." ibid., pp. 47–61.
154. G. Murphy. (1952). "The Natural, the Mystical and the Paranormal." ibid., pp. 125–142.
155. G. Murphy. (1959). "A Comparison of India and the West in Viewpoints Regarding Psychical Phenomena." JASPR, 53, 43–49.
156. G. Murphy. (1962). "A Qualitative Study of Telepathic Phenomena."JASPR, 56, 63–79.
157. G. Murphy. (1963). "Creativity and Its Relation to Extrasensory Perception."JASPR, 57, 203–214.
158. G. Murphy. (1964). "Lawfulness Versus Caprice: Is There a 'Law of Psychic Phenomena'?" JASPR, 58, 238–249.
159. G. Murphy. (1966). "Research in Creativeness: What Can It Tell Us about Extrasensory Perception?" JASPR, 60, 8–22.
160. G. Murphy. (1967). "Direct Contact with Past and Future: Retrocognition and Precognition." JASPR, 61, 3–23.

352   Portraits of Contemporary Parapsychologists

161. G. Murphy. (1969). "The Discovery of Gifted Sensitives." JASPR, 63, 3–20.

162. G. Murphy. (1970). "Are There Any Solid Facts in Psychical Research?" JASPR, 64, 3–17.

163. G. Murphy. (1971). "The Problem of Repeatability in Psychical Research." JASPR, 65, 3–16.

164. W. James. (1886). "Report of the Committee on Mediumistic Phenomena." PASPR, 1, 102–106.

165. A.S. Berger. (1987). *Aristocracy of the Dead.* Jefferson, N.C., and London: McFarland.

166. G. Murphy. (1969). "Scientific Approaches to the Study of Survival." In A.H. Kutscher (Ed.), *Death and Bereavement,* Springfield, Ill.: Charles C. Thomas, pp. 139, 145.

167. Matthew 25: 31–46.

168. C.D. Broad. (1962). *Lectures on Psychical Research.* New York: Humanities Press, p. 430.

169. G. Murphy. (1945). "Difficulties Confronting the Survival Hypothesis." Op. cit., p. 94.

170. G. Murphy and L. Dale. (1961). *Challenge of Psychical Research: A Primer of Parapsychology.* New York and London: Harper and Row.

171. Ibid., p. 273.

172. W. James. (1909). "Report on Mrs. Piper's Hodgson-Control." PSPR, 23, 121.

173. G. Murphy and R.O. Ballou (Eds.). (1961). *William James on Psychical Research,* Op. cit., p. 310.

174. G. Murphy. (1945). "Difficulties Confronting the Survival Hypothesis." Op. cit., p. 93.

175. G. Murphy and L. Dale. (1961). *Challenge of Psychical Research,* Op. cit., pp. 271–272.

176. G. Murphy. (1945). "Difficulties Confronting the Survival Hypothesis." Op. cit., pp. 67–70.

177. Ibid., pp. 70–71.   178. Ibid., pp. 71–72.

179. Ibid., pp. 74–82.

180. F.W.H. Myers. (1903). *Human Personality and Its Survival of Bodily Death.* London: Longmans, Green, 2 vols.

181. J.H. Hyslop. (1919). *Contact with the Other World.* New York: Century Co.

182. H. Hart. (1959). *The Enigma of Survival: The Case for and against an Afterlife.* Springfield, Ill.: Charles C. Thomas.

183. W.H. Salter. (1961). *Zoar or the Evidence of Psychical Research Concerning Survival.* London: Sidgwick and Jackson.

184. C.J. Ducasse. (1961). *A Critical Examination of the Belief in a Life After Death.* Springfield, Ill.: Charles C. Thomas.

185. G. Murphy. (1945). "An Outline of Survival Evidence." JASPR, 3, 2–34.

186. G. Murphy. (1961). "Hornell Hart's Analysis of the Evidence for Survival." JASPR, 55, 17.

187. G. Murphy and L. Dale. (1961). *Challenge of Psychical Research,* Op. cit., p. 273.

188. W. James. (1909). "Report on Mrs. Piper's Hodgson-Control." PSPR, 23, 121.

189. G. Murphy and R.O. Ballou (Eds.). (1961). *William James on Psychical Research,* Op. cit., p. 323.

190. A.S. Berger. (Unpublished manuscript). "An Investigation Into the Veridicality of the Apparitional Experiences of Dying or Nearly Dying Patients."

191. G. Murphy. (1973). "A Carington Approach to Ian Stevenson's Twenty Cases Suggestive of Reincarnation." JASPR, 67, 117–129.

192. In G.R. Schmeidler's approach ([1977]. "Looking Ahead: A Method for Research on Survival." *Theta,* 5, 2–6), volunteer subjects are given personality tests by clinical technicians and are interviewed about how they would try to communicate posthumously. Based on such tests and interviews, psychologists will predict differences in communications following the deaths of the interviewees. Predicitons will be evaluated statistically. R.H. Thouless ([1948]. "A Test for

Survival." PSPR, 48, 253–263), I. Stevenson ([1968] "The Combination Lock Test for Survival." JASPR, 62, 246–254), and I (Berger. *Aristocracy of the Dead,* Op. cit.) have devised tests for survival based on antemortem plans made by subjects who intend to communicate after death a secret and unwritten key which will decipher a message in cipher or open a combination lock. A positive posthumous result following unsuccessful attempts by sensitives to obtain the key by ESP during the lifetime of a subject would be new and strong evidence of postmortem survival and communication. Also, I (Berger [1987], ibid.) have described some new perspectives on the survival question and constructed a profile of the "ideal" mediumistic communicator which, if used as a guide by future researchers, may provide better survival evidence.

193. G. Murphy. (1945). "Field Theory and Survival." JASPR, 39, 206.

194. "Case of the Will of James L. Chaffin." (1928). PSPR, 36, 517–524.

195. G.W. Balfour. (1917). "The Ear of Dionysius: Further Scripts Affording Evidence of Personal Survival." PSPR, 29, 197–243.

196. G. Murphy and L. Dale. (1961). *Challenge of Psychical Research,* Op. cit., p. 252.

197. G. Murphy. (1945). "Field Theory and Survival." Op. cit., p. 208.

198. G. Murphy. (1957). "Triumphs and Defeats in the Study of Mediumship." JASPR, 51, 132.

199. G. Murphy. (1945). "Field Theory and Survival." Op. cit., pp. 210–211.

200. Ibid., p. 208.

201. J.G. Pratt. (1974). "Some Notes for a Future Einstein for Parapsychology." JASPR, 68, 134.

202. Murphy Autobiography, p. 272.

203. G. Murphy. (1945). "Difficulties Confronting the Survival Hypothesis." Op. cit., p. 71.

204. H.H. Price. (1939). "Haunting and the 'Psychic Ether' Hypothesis; With Some Preliminary Reflections on the Present Condition and Possible Future of Psychical Research." PSPR, 45, 307–343.

205. W. Carington. (1944). "Experiments on the Paranormal Cognition of Drawings, IV." PSPR, 47, 155–228.

206. G.D. Wassermann. (1956). *Ciba Foundation Symposium on Extrasensory Perception.* Boston: Little, Brown, p. 240.

207. W.G. Roll. (1957–1964). "The Psi Field." *Proceedings of the Parapsychological Association,* 1–32.

208. S.D. Kahn. (1980). "Ave Atque Vale: Gardner Murphy." Op. cit., p. 47.

209. G. Murphy. (1945). "Field Theory and Survival." Op. cit., pp. 186, 198.

210. G. Murphy and R.O. Ballou (Eds.). (1961). *William James on Psychical Research,* Op. cit., p. 324.

211. G. Murphy. (1945). "Field Theory and Survival." Op. cit., p. 203.

212. Ibid., pp. 185–194.

213. G. Murphy. (1949). "Psychical Research and Personality." PSPR, 49, 11–12.

214. G. Murphy. (1945). "Field Theory and Survival." Op. cit., p. 197.

215. Ibid., p. 192.   216. Ibid., p. 190.

217. G. Murphy and L. Dale. (1943). "Concentration Versus Relaxation in Relation to Telepathy." JASPR, 37, 2–15.

218. G. Murphy. (1945). "Field Theory and Survival." Op. cit., pp. 201–202.

219. Ibid., p. 200.   220. Ibid., pp. 205–206.

221. Ibid., p. 203.   222. Ibid.

223. Ibid., p. 204.   224. Ibid., p. 192.

225. G. Murphy. (1949). "Psychical Research and Personality." Op. cit., p. 11.

226. R.B. Perry. (1935). "William James and Psychical Research." JASPR, 29, 276.

227. G. Murphy and R.O. Ballou (Eds.). (1961). *William James on Psychical Research,* Op. cit., p. 18.

228. G. Murphy. "Psychical Research and Personality." Op. cit., pp. 1–15.

229. Ibid., p. 15.

230. G. Murphy. (1955). "Plans for Research on Spontaneous Cases." JASPR, 49, 96.

231. G. Murphy. "Psychical Research and Personality." Op. cit., p. 15.

232. G. Murphy. (1953). "The Importance of Spontaneous Cases." JASPR, 47, 89–103.

233. G. Murphy. (1957). "Triumphs and Defeats in the Study of Mediumship." Op. cit., pp. 134–135.

234. G. Murphy. "The Importance of Spontaneous Cases." Op. cit., p. 102.

235. G. Murphy. (1953). "Psychology and Psychical Research." PSPR, 50, 37.

236. "Editorial Notes." (1930). JASPR, 24, 3.

237. W.H. Button. (1939, January 3). "President's Report." Bulletin to the Voting Members of the American Society for Psychical Research. ASPR Archives.

238. G. Murphy. (1953). "Psychology and Psychical Research." Op. cit., pp. 26–28.

239. G. Murphy. (1949). "Psychical Research and Personality." Op. cit., p. 14.

240. G. Murphy. (1953). "Psychology and Psychical Research." Op. cit., p. 31.

241. G. Murphy. (1963). "Parapsychology." In N. Faberow (Ed.), *Taboo Topics.* New York: Atherton Press, pp. 56–63.

242. G. Murphy and L. Dale. (1961). *Challenge of Psychical Research,* Op. cit.

243. R.W. Emerson. (1933). "Self-Reliance." In T. McDowell (Ed.), *Romantic Triumph from 1830–1860.* New York: Macmillan, p. 181.

244. G. Murphy and L. Dale. (1961). *Challenge of Psychical Research,* Op. cit., pp. 5, 6.

245. B. Markwick. (1978). "The Soal-Goldney Experiments with Basil Shackleton; New Evidence of Data Manipulation." PSPR, 56, 250–277.

246. G. Murphy and L. Dale. (1961). *Challenge of Psychical Research,* Op. cit., p. 285.

247. Ibid., p. 291.

248. G. Murphy and R.O. Ballou (Eds.). (1961). *William James on Psychical Research,* Op. cit., p. 14.

249. G. Murphy. (1955). "Plans for Spontaneous Cases." Op. cit., p. 89.

250. Ibid., pp. 96–97.

251. L.A. Dale, R. White, G. Murphy. (1962). "A Selection of Cases from a Recent Survey of Spontaneous ESP Phenomena." JASPR, 56, 3–47.

252. G. Murphy. (1955). "Plans for Research on Spontaneous Cases." Op. cit. p. 96.

253. G. Murphy. (1953). "The Importance of Spontaneous Cases." Op. cit., p. 101.

254. J.G. Pratt. (1973). *ESP Research Today: A Study of Developments in Parapsychology Since 1960.* Metuchen, N.J.: Scarecrow Press, p. 28.

255. S.H. Mauskopf and M.R. McVaugh. (1980). *The Elusive Science,* Op. cit., p. 217.

256. K. Osis. (1985). "The American Society for Psychical Research 1941–1985: A Personal View." Op. cit., p. 505.

257. S.D. Kahn. (1980). "Ave Atque Vale: Gardner Murphy." Op. cit., p. 51.

258. E.L. Hartley. (1960). "Profile of a Professor." Op. cit., p. 1.

259. G.R. Schmeidler. (1980). "Gardner Murphy: A Short Biography." Op. cit., p. 8.

260. E. Hartley. (1960). "Profile of a Professor." Op. cit., p. 2.

261. G.R. Schmeidler. (1979). "Gardner Murphy and His Thinking: A Retrospect and a Prospect," Op. cit., p. 87.

262. Ibid.

263. J.G. Pratt. (1977). *Parapsychology: An Insider's View of ESP.* Metuchen, N.J.: Scarecrow Press, p. 11. This book contains Pratt's autobiographical account from which I have drawn material for this cameo.

264. S. Krippner. (1975). *Song of the Siren: A Parapsychological Odyssey*. New York: Harper and Row, p. 11.

265. L.E. Rhine. (1983). *Something Hidden*. Jefferson, N.C., and London: McFarland, p. 259.

266. I. Stevenson. (1980). "Gaither Pratt—An Appreciation." JASPR, 74, 279.

267. L. Dale. (1963, October 18). Letter to J. Eisenbud.

268. J.B. Rhine. (1937). "Some Selected Experiments in Extra-Sensory Perception." JP, 1, 70–80.

269. J.B. Rhine et al. (1965). *Parapsychology from Duke to FRNM*. Durham, N.C.: Parapsychology Press, p. 10.

270. J.G. Pratt and J.L. Woodruff. (1939). "Size of Stimulus Symbols in Extrasensory Perception." JP, 3, 121–158.

271. J.G. Pratt. (1936). "Towards a Method of Evaluating Mediumistic Material." *Bulletin of the Boston Society for Psychic Research*, 23. Republished in 1969 as *On the Evaluation of Verbal Material in Parapsychology* (Parapsychological Monograph No. 10). New York: Parapsychology Foundation.

272. J.G. Pratt. (1977). *Parapsychology: An Insider's View*, Op. cit., pp. 237–271.

273. W.E. Cox. (1986, January 16). Letter to the author.

274. J.G. Pratt. (1977). *Parapsychology: An Insider's View*, Op. cit., pp. 99–147.

275. J.G. Pratt. (1973). *ESP Research Today*, Op. cit., p. 118.

276. J.G. Pratt. (1977). *Parapsychology: An Insider's View*, Op. cit., p. 146.

277. J.G. Pratt. (1973). "A Decade of Research with a Selected ESP Subject: An Overview and Reappraisal of the Work with Pavel Stepanek." Op. cit., pp. 1–78.

278. J.G. Pratt. (1973). *ESP Research Today*, Op. cit., p. 57.

279. Ibid., p. 61.   280. Ibid., p. 77.

281. Ibid.

282. H.H.J. Keil, M. Ullman, B.N. Herbert and J.G. Pratt. (1976). "Directly Observable Voluntary PK Effects: A Survey and Tentative Interpretation of Available Findings from Nina Kulagina and Other Known Related Cases of Recent Date." PSPR, 56, 197–235.

283. G.R. Schmeidler. (1985, October 18). Letter to the author.

284. W.E. Cox. (1986, January 16). Letter to the author.

285. I. Stevenson. (1980). "Gaither Pratt—An Appreciation." Op. cit., p. 287.

286. P. Stepanek (1980). "Correspondence. A Tribute to Gaither Pratt from Pavel Stepanek." JASPR, 74, 377.

287. Ibid., p. 378.

288. L. Dale. (1979, November 6). Letter to W.E. Cox.

289. Except where otherwise indicated, the facts given here about J.B. Rhine's early life were taken from an autobiographical sketch written by him when he was in college and presented in L.E. Rhine (1983). *Something Hidden*, Op. cit.

290. D. Brian. (1982). *The Enchanted Voyager: The Life of J.B. Rhine*. Englewood Cliffs, N.J.: Prentice-Hall, p. 10.

291. Ibid.

292. J.B. Rhine. (1937). *New Frontiers of the Mind*. New York: Farrar and Rinehart, p. 52.

293. D. Brian. (1982). *The Enchanted Voyager*, Op. cit., p. 12.

294. Ibid., p. 13.

295. L.E. Rhine. (1983). *Something Hidden*, Op. cit., p. 19.

296. D. Brian. (1982). *The Enchanted Voyager*, Op. cit., p. 15.

297. J.B. Rhine. (1937). *New Frontiers*, Op. cit., p. 53.

298. L.E. Rhine. (1983). *Something Hidden*, Op. cit., p. 84.

299. J.B. Rhine. (1937). *New Frontiers*, Op. cit., p. 53.

300. Ibid., p. 10.

301. D. Brian. (1982). *The Enchanted Voyager,* Op. cit., p. 11.
302. J.B. Rhine. (1937). *New Frontiers,* Op. cit., p. 10.
303. L.E. Rhine. (1983). *Something Hidden,* Op. cit., p. 89.
304. J.B. Rhine. (1937). *New Frontiers,* Op. cit., pp. 10–12.
305. Ibid., pp. 19–20.   306. Ibid., p. 54.
307. Ibid., p. 51.
308. D. Brian. (1982). *The Enchanted Voyager,* Op. cit., p. 22.
309. J.B. Rhine. (1937). *New Frontiers,* Op. cit., p. 53.
310. J.B. Rhine. (1980). "My Partner, Gardner Murphy." Op. cit., p. 62.
311. Ibid.
312. J.B. Rhine and L.E. Rhine. (1927). "One Evening's Observations on the Margery Mediumship." *Journal of Abnormal and Social Psychology,* 21, 401–421.
313. L.E. Rhine. (1983). *Something Hidden.* Op. cit., p. 102.
314. D. Brian. (1982). *The Enchanted Voyager,* Op. cit., pp. 39–40.
315. Ibid., p. 42.
316. L.E. Rhine. (1983). *Something Hidden,* Op. cit., p. 99.
317. J.B. Rhine. (1937). *New Frontiers,* Op. cit., p. 42.
318. Ibid., p. 50.
319. L.E. Rhine. (1983). *Something Hidden,* Op. cit., p. 115.
320. As quoted in M. Ullman. (1980). "Letter to a Late Friend—Gardner Murphy," Op. cit., p. 25.
321. N.A. Hintze and J.G. Pratt. (1975). *The Psychic Realm: What Can You Believe?* New York: Random House, p. 76.
322. L.E. Rhine. (1983). *Something Hidden,* Op. cit., p. 139.
323. Ibid., p. 183.
324. D.H. Rawcliffe. (1959). *Illusions and Delusions of the Supernatural and Occult (The Psychology of the Occult).* New York: Dover Publications, p. 9.
325. J.B. Rhine. (1937). *New Frontiers of the Mind,* Op. cit., p. 40.
326. C. Murchison (Ed.). (1927). *The Case for and against Psychical Belief.* Worcester, Mass.: Clark University, p. 160.
327. W. McDougall. (1934). Foreword to J.B. Rhine, *Extra-Sensory Perception.* Boston: Boston Society for Psychic Research, p. xiii. Republished 1964, by Bruce Humphries.
328. Ibid., p. xvi.
329. C. Richet. (1884). "La Suggestion de Probabilités." *Revue Philosophique,* December, 1884.
330. J.B. Rhine. (1937). *New Frontiers of the Mind,* Op. cit., p. 60.
331. Ibid., pp. 59–60.   332. Ibid., p. 60.
333. Ibid., p. 74.   334. Ibid., pp. 77–78.
335. Ibid., pp. 94–95.   336. Ibid., p. 96.
337. Ibid., pp. 99–100.
338. J.H. Hyslop. (1918). "Leland Stanford University in Psychic Research." JASPR, 12, 543.
339. J.B. Rhine. (1964). *Extra-Sensory Perception,* Op. cit., Preface, p. xxx.
340. Ibid., "About This Book," p. xxxvi.
341. Ibid., p. xxxiii.
342. R.A. McConnell. (1970). *ESP Curriculum Guide.* New York: Simon and Schuster, p. 23.
343. J.B. Rhine. (1964). *Extra-Sensory Perception,* Op. cit., Preface, p. xxvii.
344. J.B. Rhine. (1971). "Psi and Psychology: Conflict and Solution." In J.B. Rhine (Ed.), *Progress in Parapsychology.* Durham, N.C.: Parapsychology Press, p. 243.
345. L.E. Rhine. (1983). *Something Hidden,* Op. cit., p. 208.

346. W. Kaempffert. (1934). "This Week in Science." *New York Times,* May 20, 1934, viii, p. 6, col. 1.
347. L. Welch. (1935). "Some Research in Telepathy." *New York Times,* December 15, 1935, vi, p. 27, col. 1.
348. A. Carrel. (1935). *Man the Unknown.* New York: Harper and Bros., pp. 124–125.
349. *Literary Digest,* February 15, 1936.
350. *New York Times,* October 28, 1936, p. 24.
351. E.H. Wright. (1936). "The Case for Telepathy. A Record of Some Remarkable Experiments." *Harper's Monthly Magazine,* Nov. 1936, pp. 575–586.
352. D. Brian. (1982). *The Enchanted Voyager,* Op. cit., p. 102.
353. Ibid., p. 103.
354. J.B. Rhine. (1937). *New Frontiers of the Mind,* Op. cit.
355. Ibid., p. 8.
356. J.B. Rhine. (1971). "Eileen Garrett As I Knew Her." JSPR, 46, 59.
357. J.B. Rhine. (1937). *New Frontiers,* Op. cit., pp. 223–224.
358. J.B. Rhine. (1971). "Eileen Garrett As I Knew Her," Op. cit., p. 60.
359. D. Brian. (1982). *The Enchanted Voyager,* Op. cit., pp. 113–114.
360. L.E. Rhine. (1983). *Something Hidden,* Op. cit., p. 201.
361. J.B. Rhine et al. (1965). *Parapsychology from Duke to FRNM,* Op. cit., p. 17.
362. J.B. Rhine. (1964). *Extra-Sensory Perception,* Op. cit., Preface, p. xxvii.
363. J.B. Rhine. (1937). *New Frontiers,* Op. cit., p. 121.
364. J.G. Pratt, J.B. Rhine, B.M. Smith, C.E. Stuart. (1940). *Extra-Sensory Perception After Sixty Years.* Boston: Bruce Humphries, p. 191.
365. J.B. Rhine. (1937). *New Frontiers,* Op. cit., pp. 120–121.
366. W. McDougall. (1964). Foreword to J.B. Rhine, *Extra-Sensory Perception,* Op. cit., pp. xvi–xvii.
367. R.R. Willoughby. (1935). "A Critique of Rhine's Extra-Sensory Perception." *Journal of Abnormal and Social Psychology,* 30, 199–207.
368. C. Kellog. (1937). "New Evidence (?) for Extra-Sensory Perception." *Scientific Monthly,* 45, October, 1937, 331–341.
369. E.J. Dingwall. (1937). "'Extra-Sensory Perception' in the United States." JSPR, 30, 140–1.
370. R.H. Thouless. (1935). "Review of Dr. Rhine's Recent Experiments on Telepathy and Clairvoyance and a Reconsideration of J.E. Coover's Conclusions on Telepathy." PSPR, 43, 34.
371. C.V.C. Herbert. (1938). "Experiment in Extra-Sensory Perception." JSPR, 30, 216.
372. J.B. Rhine. (1937). *New Frontiers,* Op. cit., p. 49.
373. J.B. Rhine. (1938). "Experiment in Extra-Sensory Perception." JSPR, 30, 257.
374. L.E. Rhine. (1983). *Something Hidden,* Op. cit., p. 221.
375. Ibid., p. 225.
376. J.B. Rhine et al. (1965). *Parapsychology from Duke to FRNM,* Op. cit., p. 27.
377. J.B. Rhine. (1964). "About This Book." In his *Extra-Sensory Perception,* Op. cit., p. xxxvi.
378. Ibid., p. xxxv.
379. J.B. Rhine. (1980). "My Partner, Gardner Murphy." Op. cit., p. 63.
380. L.E. Rhine. (1983). *Something Hidden,* Op. cit., p. 232.
381. J.B. Rhine. (1947). *The Reach of the Mind.* New York: William Sloane Assoc., p. 67.
382. J.B. Rhine. (1938). "Experiments Bearing on the Precognition Hypothesis." JP, 2, 38–54.
383. J.G. Pratt, J.B. Rhine, B.M. Smith, C.E. Stuart. (1940). *Extra-Sensory Perception after Sixty Years,* Op. cit.
384. L.E. Rhine and J.B. Rhine. (1943). "The Psychokinetic Effect: I. The First Experiment." JP, 7, 20–43.

385. J.B. Rhine. (1947). *The Reach of the Mind,* Op. cit., p. 104.
386. L.E. Rhine. (1983). *Something Hidden,* Op. cit., p. 220.
387. J.B. Rhine. (1947). *The Reach of the Mind,* Op. cit.
388. Ibid., p. 3.   389. Ibid., pp. 154–155.
390. S. Krippner. (1975). *Song of the Siren: A Parapsychological Odyssey,* Op. cit., pp. 9–10.
391. L.E. Rhine. (1983). *Something Hidden,* Op. cit., p. 261.
392. (1953). New York: William Sloane Assoc.
393. J.B. Rhine. (1947). *The Reach of the Mind,* Op. cit., p. 209.
394. G.R. Price. (1955). "Science and the Supernatural." *Science,* 122, 359–367.
395. J.B. Rhine. (1956). "Comments on Science and the Supernatural." *Science,* 123, 11–14.
396. G.R. Price. (1972). "Apology to Rhine and Soal." *Science,* 122, 359–367.
397. (1957). Springfield, Ill.: Charles C. Thomas.
398. Ibid., p. 6.   399. Ibid., p. 11.
400. G.R. Schmeidler. (1983). "Psychical Research in 1957 and in 1982." In W.G. Roll, J. Beloff and R.A. White (Eds.), *Research in Parapsychology, 1982.* Metuchen, N.J.: Scarecrow Press, p. 4.
401. L.E. Rhine. (1983). *Something Hidden,* Op. cit., p. 259.
402. Ibid.
403. J.B. Rhine et al. (1965). *Parapsychology from Duke to FRNM,* Op. cit., p. 10.
404. Ibid.
405. (1968). New York: Citadel Press.
406. (1971). Durham, N.C.: Parapsychology Press.
407. L.E. Rhine. (1983). *Something Hidden,* Op. cit., p. 279.
408. Ibid., p. 280.
409. J.B. Rhine. (1975). "Comments. Second Report on a Case of Experimenter Fraud." JP, 39, 306–325.
410. "General Report." (1980). JSPR, 50, 333.
411. S.R. Feather. (1982). "J.B. as a Family Man." In K.R. Rao (Ed.), *J.B. Rhine: On the Frontiers of Science.* Jefferson, N.C., and London: McFarland, p. 9.
412. E.A. McMahan. (1982). "Joseph Banks Rhine: Teacher and Friend." Ibid., pp. 14–15.
413. J. Kapchan. (1986, October 11). Personal interview with author.
414. D. Brian. (1982). *The Enchanted Voyager,* Op. cit., p. 277.
415. J.B. Rhine. (1947). *New Frontiers of the Mind,* Op. cit., p. 52.
416. D.J. West. (1982). "J.B. Rhine and European Parapsychology." In K.R. Rao (Ed.), *J.B. Rhine: On the Frontiers of Science,* Op. cit., p. 167.
417. R.G. Stanford. (1986, January 26). Letter to author.
418. J.G. Pratt. (1970). "William McDougall and Present-Day Psychical Research." JASPR, 64, 388.
419. K.R. Rao. (1981). "A Tribute to J.B. Rhine." *Journal of Indian Psychology,* 3, 1.
420. K.R. Rao. (1966). *Experimental Parapsychology.* Springfield, Ill.: Charles C. Thomas, pp. 3–4, 23.
421. R.H. Thouless. (1942). "The Present Position of Experimental Research into Telepathy and Related Phenomena." PSPR, 47, 13.
422. J. Beloff. (1983). "Presidential Address." In W.G. Roll, J. Beloff and R.A. White (Eds.), *Research in Parapsychology 1982.* Op. cit., pp. 318, 319.
423. R.A. McConnell. (1970). *ESP Curriculum Guide,* Op. cit., p. 24.
424. J.B. Rhine. (1964). "About This Book." In his *Extra-Sensory Perception,* Op. cit., pp. xxxiii–xxxiv, xxxvi.
425. Ibid., Preface, p. xxviii.
426. J.B. Rhine. (1947). *The Reach of the Mind,* Op. cit., p. 206.

427. Ibid., p. 207.
428. A.S. Berger. (1987). *Aristocracy of the Dead*, Op. cit.
429. J.B. Rhine. (1947). *The Reach of the Mind*, Op. cit., p. 212.
430. J.B. Rhine. (1949). "The Question of Spirit Survival." JASPR, 43, 51.
431. J.B. Rhine. (1947). *The Reach of the Mind*, Op. cit., pp. 213–214.
432. S.H. Mauskopf and M.R. McVaugh. (1980). *The Elusive Science*, Op. cit.
433. D. Brian. (1982). *The Enchanted Voyager*, Op. cit.
434. L.E. Rhine. (1983). *Something Hidden*, Op. cit.
435. K.R. Rao. (1982). *J.B. Rhine: On the Frontiers of Science*, Op. cit.
436. L.E. Rhine. (1983). *Something Hidden*, Op. cit. p. 281.

5. Contemporary Parapsychology (1981–1987)

1. C. Akers. (1984). "Methodological Criticisms of Parapsychology." In S. Krippner (Ed.), *Advances in Parapsychological Research 4*. Jefferson, N.C.: McFarland, pp. 112–164.
2. I.L. Child. (1985). "Psychology and Anomalous Observations." *American Psychologist*, 40:1219.
3. R. Hyman. (1986). "Parapsychological Research: A Tutorial Review and Critical Appraisal." *Proceedings of the IEEE*, 74:823.
4. S. Blackmore. (1986). *The Adventures of a Parapsychologist*. Buffalo, N.Y.: Prometheus Books.
5. D. Wenberg. (1985, November 1). Letter to the author.
6. G. Murphy. (1957). "Notes for a Parapsychological Autobiography." JP, 21, 173.
7. L.A. Dale. (1946). "The Psychokinetic Effect: the First A.S.P.R. Experiment." JASPR, 40, 123–151.
8. J.L. Woodruff and L.A. Dale. (1952). "ESP Function and the Psychogalvanic Response." JASPR, 46, 62–65.
9. G. Murphy and L.A. Dale. (1943). "Concentration Versus Relaxation." JASPR, 37, 2–15.
10. J.L. Woodruff and L.A. Dale. (1950). "Subject and Experimenter Attitudes in Relation to ESP Scores." JASPR, 44, 87–112.
11. L.A. Dale. (1951). "Dowsing: A Field Experiment in Water Divining." JASPR, 45, 3–16.
12. G. Murphy and L.A. Dale. (1941). "Some Present-Day Trends in Psychical Research." JASPR, 35, 118–132.
13. M. Ullman and S. Krippner. (1970). *Dream Studies and Telepathy: An Experimental Approach* (Parapsychological Monograph No. 12). New York: Parapsychology Foundation.
14. E. Taves and L.A. Dale. (1943). "The Midas Touch in Psychical Research." JASPR, 37, 57.
15. E. Taves, L.A. Dale and G. Murphy. (1944). "A Further Report on the Midas Touch." JASPR, 38, 160–170.
16. L.A. Dale. (1946). "Spontaneous Experiences Reported by a Group of Experimental Subjects." JASPR, 40, 55–93.
17. L.A. Dale. (1951). "A Series of Spontaneous Cases in the Tradition of Phantasms of the Living." JASPR, 45, 85–101.
18. L.A. Dale. (1952). "Spontaneous Cases." JASPR, 46, 31–35; L.A. Dale. (1952). "Spontaneous Cases." JASPR, 46, 154–158; L.A. Dale. (1953). "Unusual Experiences." JASPR, 47, 84–88.
19. L.A. Dale, R.A. White and G. Murphy. (1962). "A Selection of Cases from a Recent Survey of Spontaneous ESP Phenomena." JASPR, 56, 3–47.
20. G. Schmeidler. (1983). "Memories of Laura Dale." JASPR, 77, 275.
21. L.A. Dale. (1944). "An Informal Experiment with Mrs. Chester Grady." JASPR, 38, 202–221.

22. Ibid.
23. D. Wenberg. (1985, November 1). Letter to the author.
24. Ibid.
25. J. Eisenbud. (1985, August 12). Personal interview with the author.
26. L.A. Dale. (1941). "Dr. John F. Thomas (In Memoriam)." JASPR, 35, 1–8.
27. Ibid., p. 1.   28. Ibid., p. 7.
29. Ibid., p. 8.
30. K. Osis. (1985). "The American Society for Psychical Research 1941–1985: A Personal View." JASPR, 79, 520.
31. Ibid.
32. L.A. Dale. (1975, March 21). Letter to J. Eisenbud.
33. "Notice to Members." (1941). JASPR, 35, 85–86.
34. "Notice to Members." (1947). JASPR, 41, 184.
35. L.A. Dale. (1980, December 8). Letter to the author.
36. L.A. Dale. (1941). "Henri Bergson, Realist." JASPR, 35, 62–63.
37. M. Ullman. (1984). "A Tribute to Laura Dale." JASPR, 76, 251.
38. L.A. Dale. (1975, December 4). Letter to J. Eisenbud.
39. L.A. Dale. (1974, January 12). Letter to D.S. Rogo.
40. D.S. Rogo. (1985, September 3). Letter to the author.
41. L.A. Dale. (1981, May 20). Letter to D.S. Rogo.
42. M. Ullman. (1982). "A Tribute to Laura Dale." Op. cit., p. 252.
43. Ibid., p. 251.
44. L.A. Dale. (1975, August 18). Letter to J. Eisenbud.
45. J. Ehrenwald. (1985, September 6). Letter to the author.
46. R.G. Stanford. (1983). "A Tribute to Laura Dale." JASPR, 77, 285.
47. K. Osis. (1985). "The American Society for Psychical Research 1941–1985." Op. cit., p. 510.
48. L.A. Dale. (1967, September 29). Letter to J. Eisenbud.
49. L.A. Dale. (1952, October 24). Letter to J. Eisenbud.
50. L.A. Dale. (1963, October 18). Letter to J. Eisenbud.
51. L.A. Dale. (1952, October 24). Letter to J. Eisenbud.
52. L.A. Dale. (1979, December 24). Letter to J. Eisenbud.
53. L.A. Dale. (1964, February 5). Letter to J. Eisenbud.
54. L.A. Dale. (1967, March 9). Letter to J. Eisenbud.
55. L.A. Dale. (1978, November 8). Letter to J. Eisenbud.
56. L.A. Dale. (1953, December 16). Letter to J. Eisenbud.
57. L.A. Dale. (1953, February 2). Letter to J. Eisenbud.
58. L.A. Dale. (1969, June 17). Letter to J. Eisenbud.
59. L.A. Dale. (1974, May 21). Letter to J. Eisenbud.
60. L.A. Dale. (1975, September 7). Letter to J. Eisenbud.
61. L.A. Dale. (1975, September 17). Letter to J. Eisenbud.
62. L.A. Dale. (1953, February 18). Letter to J. Eisenbud.
63. L.A. Dale. (1950, October 4). Letter to J. Eisenbud.
64. L.A. Dale. (1953, February 18). Letter to J. Eisenbud.
65. L.A. Dale. (1953, November 2). Letter to J. Eisenbud.
66. L.A. Dale. (1955, October 7). Letter to J. Eisenbud.
67. L.A. Dale. (1976, January 29). Letter to J. Eisenbud.
68. K. Osis. (1985). "The American Society for Psychical Research 1941–1985: A Personal View." Op. cit., p. 506.
69. J. Beloff. (1981). "Preface: The Twenty-Third Annual Convention." In W.G. Roll and J. Beloff (Eds.), Research in Parapsychology 1980. Metuchen, N.J.: Scarecrow Press, p. vi.

70. M. Ullman. (1983). "Loyal Friend, Respected Colleague, Dedicated Worker." JASPR, 77, 279.

71. J. Eisenbud. (1985, September 1). Letter to the author.

72. L.A. Dale. (1979, July 8). Letter to J. Eisenbud.

73. C.A. Werner. (1984). "In Memory of Laura Dale." JSPR, 52, 342.

74. J. Ehrenwald. (1983). "Gentle Guide." JASPR, 77, 282.

75. L.E. Rhine. (1983). *Something Hidden*. Jefferson, N.C., and London: McFarland, p. 10.

76. J.B. Rhine. (1937). *New Frontiers of the Mind.* New York: Farrar and Rinehart, p. 53.

77. L.E. Rhine. (1983). *Something Hidden,* Op. cit., pp. xi–xii.

78. As quoted in S.R. Feather. (1983). "Something Different: A Biographical Sketch of Louisa Rhine." JP, 47, 301.

79. W. McDougall. (1934). Foreword to J.B. Rhine, *Extra-Sensory Perception.* Boston: Boston Society for Psychic Research. Republished, 1964, Boston: Bruce Humphries, p. xiv.

80. K.R. Rao. (1983). "L.E. Rhine on Psi and Its Place." JP, 47, 347.

81. K.R. Rao. (Ed.). (1982). *J.B. Rhine: On the Frontiers of Science.* Jefferson, N.C., and London: McFarland, dedication.

82. J.B. Rhine. (1947). *The Reach of the Mind.* New York: William Sloane Assoc., p. 97.

83. L.E. Rhine and J.B. Rhine. (1943). "The Psychokinetic Effect: I. The First Experiment." JP, 7, 20–43.

84. L.E. Rhine. (1961). *Hidden Channels of the Mind.* New York: William Sloane Assoc., p. 8.

85. L.A. Dale, R.A. White and G. Murphy. (1962). "A Selection of Cases from a Recent Survey of Spontaneous ESP Phenomena." JASPR, 56, 3–47.

86. L.E. Rhine. (1961). *Hidden Channels of the Mind,* Op. cit., p. 9.

87. L.E. Rhine. (1951). "Conviction and Associated Conditions in Spontaneous Cases." JP, 15, 165–166.

88. H. Hart. (1965). *Towards a New Philosophical Basis for Parapsychological Phenomena* (Parapsychological Monograph No. 6.). New York: Parapsychology Foundation.

89. C.D. Broad. (1962). *Lectures on Psychical Research.* New York: Humanities Press, p. 9.

90. L.E. Rhine. (1961). *Hidden Channels of the Mind,* Op. cit., p. 12.

91. L.E. Rhine. (1970). "Dr. L.E. Rhine's Reply to Dr. Stevenson." JP, 34, 149–163.

92. L.E. Rhine. (1961). *Hidden Channels of the Mind,* Op. cit., pp. 10–11.

93. D.J. West. (1970). "ESP in Life and Lab. by Louisa E. Rhine." JSPR, 45, 308.

94. G.N.M. Tyrrell. (1947). "The 'Modus Operandi' of Paranormal Cognition." PSPR, 48, 65–120.

95. L.E. Rhine. (1952). "Subjective Forms of Spontaneous Psi Experiences." JP, 17, 77–114.

96. L.E. Rhine. (1956). "Hallucinatory Psi Experiences: I. An Introductory Survey." JP, 20, 233–257.

97. L.E. Rhine. (1960). "The Evaluation of Non-Recurrent Psi Experiences on Post-Mortem Survival." JP, 24, 8–25.

98. L.E. Rhine. (1956). "The Relationship of Agent and Percipient in Spontaneous Telepathy." JP, 20, 1–33.

99. L.E. Rhine. (1961). *Hidden Channels of the Mind,* Op. cit., pp. 278–279.

100. H. Hart et al. (1956). "Six Theories About Apparitions." PSPR, 50, 153–239.

101. L.E. Rhine. (1956). "Hallucinatory Psi Experiences: I. An Introductory Survey." Op. cit.

102. L.E. Rhine. (1957). "Hallucinatory Psi Experiences: II. The Initiative of the Percipient in Hallucinations of the Living, the Dying, and the Dead." JP, 21, 13–47.

103. L.E. Rhine. (1957). "Hallucinatory Psi Experiences: III. The Intention of the Agent and the Dramatizing Tendency of the Percipient." JP, 21, 186–227.

104. Ibid., p. 224.

105. W.G. Roll. (1961). "The Problem of Precognition." JSPR, 41, 115–128.
106. L.E. Rhine. (1954). "Frequency of Types of Experience in Spontaneous Precognition." JP, 18, 93–123.
107. Ibid.
108. L.E. Rhine. (1955). "Precognition and Intervention." JP, 19, 1–34.
109. C.J. Ducasse. (1976). "Knowing the Future." In J.M.O. Wheatley and H.L. Edge (Eds.), Philosophical Dimensions of Parapsychology. Springfield, Ill.: Charles C. Thomas, pp. 193–197. Orig. pub. 1955 in Tomorrow, Garrett Publications.
110. S.R. Feather. Foreword to L.E. Rhine. (1983). Something Hidden, Op. cit., pp. ix–x.
111. G. Murphy. (1947). "Notes for a Parapsychological Autobiography." JP, 21, 173.
112. "Presidential Remarks by Dr. Gardner Murphy." (1962). JASPR, 56, 204.

Index

363

Annales des Sciences Psychiques 28
Antioch College 307
Apollo 14, 145
Apparitions 5, 6, 9, 16, 27, 42, 96, 102,
   103, 133, 147, 166, 168, 170, 171, 182,
   258–259, 260, 274–275, 276, 303, 316
Aristotle 114, 243
Arizona, University of 315
Articles of Confederation 136
Artley, J.L. 311
Aserinsky, E. 299
ASPR *Newsletter* 303
Associate Presbyterians 336
Associated Press 42
Astral forms 16, 17
Astrology 232
At the Hour of Death (Osis and
   Haraldsson) 316
Atlantic Monthly 69
Aura, human 181, 325
Autobiography (Hyslop) 36, 45, 46

B., Mrs. 248 Balfour, A. 7, 103, 105
Bancroft Hotel 125
Barclay, L. *see* Murphy, L. B.
Barker, Mrs. 29
Barnard College 279
Barrett, W.F. viii, 7, 8, 25, 62, 63, 102,
   105, 121, 133, 158
Barrows Neurological Institute 145
Basic Experiments in Parapsychology
   (Rao) 318
Bateman, F. 165
Bay Research Institute 323
Bayley, W.D. viii, ix, 44, 47, 48, 50, 51,
   52, 60
Beauchamp, S. 82, 83, 128
"Bede, Dr." 94
Beecher, H.W. 239
Bell Telephone Laboratories 282
Bellevue Hospital 292, 299
Beloff, J. viii, 114, 131, 132, 228
Ben Hur (Wallace) 99
Benedict, R. 154, 155
Benson, E.W. 6
Berger, A.S. viii
Berger, J. vii
Bergson, H. 105, 244
Besant, A. 18, 19
Besterman, T. 94, 208
Bindelof, Dr. 295
Biofeedback 166, 181
Bird, J.M. ix, 67–70, 90, 91–92, 133;
   McDougall and 119, 201; Prince and 92,
   201; J.B. Rhine and 200–201, 202, 203

Birge, W.R. 248
Blackmore, S. 232, 238
Blavatsky, H.P. 7, 16–20, 21, 23, 28, 225
Body and Mind (McDougall) 114, 126, 204
Body, Mind and Spirit (Worcester) 78
Boeing Scientific Research Laboratories 321
Bolton, F.P. 214, 215, 230
Bond, F.B. 70, 73, 74, 138, 295
Book of Martyrs (Foxe) 37, 38
Booth, G. 299
Borderland of Psychical Research (Hyslop) 58
Boring, E.G. 138, 154, 163, 263, 264, 284
Boston Medical Library 137
Boston Society for Psychic Research 68, 69,
   71, 72, 74, 75, 93–95, 107, 124, 135, 137,
   160, 162–163, 185, 191, 212, 287; *Pro-*
   ceedings 68, 95
Boston University 93
Bourne, A. 27, 43, 83
Bowditch, H. 8, 117
Boyce Thompson Institute for Plant
   Research 200
"Brain Hemisphere Differences in Para-
   normal Abilities with Special Reference to
   Experimenter Expectancies" (Broughton)
   306
Braude, S.E. 305
Brian, D. 231
Briefer General Psychology (Murphy) 154
Brier, R. 225
Bristol, J.I.D. 65, 69, 71
Bristol, University of 238
British Association 7
British Journal of Psychology 114
British Museum 19, 20
Broad, C.D. 1, 17, 168, 254–255, 260, 305
Broughton, R.S. 236, 238, 306
Brown, A.J. 27
Brown University 218, 317
Browning, R. 13, 103
Brugmans, H.J.F.W. 89
Bucknell University 42
Buddhism 175
Bulgaria 301
Bulletins of the Boston Society for Psychic
   Research 68, 95
Burbank, L. 103
Bureau of Naval Personnel 188
Burton, A. 58
Butler, N.M. 42, 45–46
Button, W.H. ix, 71, 73, 74, 137, 138,
   163–164, 179

Caccheiro, A. 302
Caldwell, F. 71, 73

"Wundt's Theory of Psychic Systhesis"
(Hyslop) 42

"X, Mr." 71, 72, 73
Xenoglossy 323

Yale and New Englander Review 57
Yale Mobile Hospital Unit 153
Yale University 77, 152, 153, 154, 158, 159,
280, 307, 311
Yerkes, R.M. 153
Yost, C.S. 99

Zener, K.E. 71, 130, 207–208, 215–216,
219; Karl E. Zener Award 316
Zenith Broadcasting Company 213
Zetetic 146, 234, 235
Zeus 109
Ziehen, T. 113
Zierold, M.R. de 87ff., 97, 101, 107
Zimmerman, H.M. 237, 303
Zimmerman, N. 303, 304
Zingrone, N.L. 325
Zola, E. 19